Big Law in Latin America and Spain

Manuel Gómez • Rogelio Pérez-Perdomo
Editors

Big Law in Latin America and Spain

Globalization and Adjustments in the Provision of High-End Legal Services

palgrave
macmillan

Editors
Manuel Gómez
Florida International University
Miami, Florida, USA

Rogelio Pérez-Perdomo
Universidad Metropolitana
Caracas, Venezuela

ISBN 978-3-319-65402-7 ISBN 978-3-319-65403-4 (eBook)
https://doi.org/10.1007/978-3-319-65403-4

Library of Congress Control Number: 2017958611

Cover illustration: Rafael Pasquini / EyeEm

Printed on acid-free paper

This Palgrave Macmillan imprint is published by Springer Nature
The registered company is Springer International Publishing AG
The registered company address is: Gewerbestrasse 11, 6330 Cham, Switzerland

Acknowledgments

The research that forms the basis of this book could not have been conducted without the cooperation of the many lawyers and other legal professionals, business people, corporate officers, government officials, scholars, and other individuals interviewed for the different the chapters. In order to encourage candor and respect the professional careers of those involved and their organizations, we agreed to keep the identity of our interviewees confidential, except when they agreed to be identified. We gratefully acknowledge their willingness to give of their time and to share their knowledge, experience, and perspectives.

The collaborative effort that produced this book was initiated by an international conference sponsored by Stanford Law School in 2014 through its Center for the Legal Profession, and a generous gift from Sidley Austin LLP. We gratefully acknowledge the support of all those who contributed to the discussion, and those who provided feedback and valuable comments during presentations at the Annual meetings of the Law and Society Association in Minneapolis (2014), Seattle (2015), New Orleans (2016), and Mexico City (2017). We especially thank Deborah R. Hensler for her invitation to participate in the Stanford Project on the Future of the Legal Profession, and for her continued support. All of the authors gratefully acknowledge the support of their home institutions for their research and writing and for enabling the group to convene in various parts of the world to share their findings. The co-editors would like also to thank Marisol Floren-Romero at Florida International University College of Law for her valuable research assistance throughout the project, and to Marcus Nielsen for his help during the final stages of the editorial process.

Contents

List of Figures

List of Tables

PART I

Introduction

CHAPTER 1

Corporate Lawyers and Multinational Corporations in Latin America and Spain: 1990–2015

Manuel Gómez and Rogelio Pérez-Perdomo

This book explains the changes that have occurred in the provision of high-end corporate legal services in 15 Latin American countries and Spain between 1990 and 2015. We use the term high end to denote sophisticated, complex, and generally costly legal work demanded by multinationals, large domestic corporations, and other business clients. This type of work is usually performed by teams of prestigious lawyers and other professionals through large or mid-sized multiservice or highly specialized firms with more than one office and an internal organizational hierarchy. Other lawyers offer their professional services through small and highly specialized (boutique) law firms. These lawyers and the law firms to which they belong are the main providers of legal services in the corporate world and are precisely the focus of this collective work.

The modern infrastructure, visibility and corporate image, organizational arrangement, and client management strategies employed by these

M. Gómez (✉)
Florida International University College of Law, Miami, FL, USA

R. Pérez-Perdomo
Universidad Metropolitana, Caracas, Venezuela

M. Gómez, R. Pérez-Perdomo (eds.), *Big Law in Latin America and Spain*, https://doi.org/10.1007/978-3-319-65403-4_1

Latin American law firms resemble the so-called "Big Law" of the United States. As a result, this book uses the term "Big Law" to also refer to the Latin American firms that share those same features. The chapters that comprise this volume address the evolution and recent changes affecting the corporate legal sector providers in the selected countries, taking into account their specific social, political, and economic context.

The research presented here is drawn from a combination of interview and quantitative data, historical records, and other sources, which enabled the authors to paint a dense and contextualized sketch of the corporate legal services sector, and more generally about the legal profession of each country. This book covers the majority of countries in Latin America. It includes studies about countries ranging from the main economies like Brazil and Mexico to smaller ones like Nicaragua. This book also includes a chapter on Spain, given the strong historical, economic and political ties between Latin America and Spain, and the recent expansion of Spanish law firms into Latin America. This book pays special attention to the heightened interaction between Spanish and Latin American enterprises and their lawyers during recent times.

The time span covered in this book (1990–2015) has been a period of intensification of cross-border trade, migratory movements, the rise of different forms of communication, and other technological advancements. These are also times of important social, political, and cultural transformations, not only in the Americas and Spain but also globally. On the other hand, during these years, the world has faced unique challenges regarding threats to the protection of human rights, the legitimacy of democratic institutions, the preservation of the environment, and the attainment of equality, peace, and security.

Concern for these issues is not confined to the geographical boundaries of a single country, but has rather crossed over to the regional and global arenas. The term globalization is generally used to convey this phenomenon. Globalization means diffusion, influence, and movement, but not always in the physical sense. The dissemination and movement can also be of ideas, images, thought processes, and patterns of behavior. In this sense, globalization is undoubtedly a cultural phenomenon (Friedman 2001; Giddens 1999).

Whether directly or indirectly, globalization has had an impact on the role of lawyers in society, and more generally on the function of law. Some areas such as international trade and business law are more susceptible to be affected by globalization than, say, tenant-landlord regulations. The same occurs to the lawyers and other legal professionals who practice or specialize in those areas. Legal professionals who handle cross-border transactions or working for multinational corporate clients tend to be more familiar with foreign and international laws, practices, and global trends, than those representing juvenile offenders in local courts. However, the world is not neatly divided between globalized and non-globalized law, or between fully globalized and fully domestic lawyers. What occurs in reality is that both the international/globalized and the domestic/local dimensions of the law are generally intertwined, or, at the very least, exist and operate in parallel. Friedman (2001) has used the term "legal diglossia" to identify this phenomenon, which seems to be common in the high-end corporate legal sector of most Latin American countries and Spain, and demands practitioners with both local and international competence.

The bulk of the official law enacted by the national legislatures has remained domestic both in content and scope, and legal education continues to primarily train students to practice law in their own countries. Notwithstanding, the law firms that provide services to multinational corporate clients—which is the subset that occupies our attention—appear to have become "boundaryless" regarding their organizational structures, their relationship with their clients, and the type of services they offer. Many of the law firms whose members were interviewed for this book exemplify this trend.

The globalization of Latin American and Spanish business lawyers should come as no surprise if one takes into account the fact that their clientele is comprised mainly of large corporations, national, foreign, or multinational. The way in which these lawyers organize their practices, carry out their activities, and business relationships is consistent with a rapidly expanding transnational reality. As a result, the lawyers that serve such clients are obviously pressured to meet the increasingly complex demands of the market, and to align or synchronize their structure with that of their clients. At the same time, those lawyers are expected to stay attuned to their domestic legal landscape and the changes affecting their own legal system.

The corporate legal sector of the United States is the most common and certainly the best- documented reference of this phenomenon. After all, it is where many of the multi-service, multi-office law firms originated, developed, and continue to exist. The fact that the United States is the benchmark should come as no surprise because many of the important players in the business world, who demand the services of the aforementioned lawyers, are also American corporations with a worldwide presence.

As mentioned earlier, the term *Big Law* was precisely coined to identify the American firms that fit this bill, and more generally the stratum where they operate. Needless to say, *Big Law* does not mean that the type of law practiced by their members is bigger or more important than the law handled by solo practitioners that represent the rest of us mortals. In this sense, there is no substantive difference between small law and Big Law. There are instead different work styles, client management strategies, organizational arrangements, and levels of expertise and experience needed from the lawyers and other professionals, depending on the complexity of the relevant legal issues, the parties involved, and the financial stake.

More than 30 years ago, Galanter (1983) aptly called *mega-lawyering* the occupation of the legal professionals operating in complex, transnational, and high-stake environments. What appears to have occurred since then, though, is that mega-lawyering is not confined anymore to large high-end corporate law firms, but has also permeated—to varying degrees—the realm of NGOs, in-house legal departments, and other organizations. For this book, we undertook the task to investigate the lawyers whose services are demanded by large and mid-size corporate clients in the selected countries or transnationally. We were particularly interested in learning how those lawyers are organized, and how the development of the business sector, and, more broadly, how the social, economic, and political conditions of each country has influenced them.

One cannot accurately ascertain the role of *Big Law* in Latin America and Spain without looking at the legal profession as a whole and the changes that have resulted from globalization. In the remainder of this introductory chapter, as a way to prepare the context for the rest of the book, we briefly discuss the growth and transformation of the legal profession in Latin America and Spain. We then turn to analyze the rise and transformation of the corporate law firms in the region, and finally, we discuss the internationalization—or globalization—of business lawyering as a roadmap for the rest of the book.

Legal Profession: Growth and Diversification

One of the main difficulties posed to anyone undertaking a comparative study of the legal profession is to ascertain the criteria used by each country to determine who is a lawyer and who is not. Clarifying this concept is crucial for understanding the landscape of the legal profession, its structure, internal dynamics, the different occupations of legal professionals, and the role of lawyers in society. Fortunately, in the countries represented in this book, the meaning of "lawyer" is basically the same: a person authorized to give consultations and appear in court (i.e. practice law) upon the award of a professional degree by an academic institution.

Whether that person actually practices law or not is a different question, and it does not affect their lawyer title. In all the countries represented in this study, the conferral of a law degree is the result of the successful culmination of several years of formal studies at the undergraduate level in a law school. Most law schools are integrated into universities, which subjects them to many rules and standards usually set by the Ministry of Education or an equivalent government agency.

In most Latin American countries and Spain, the completion of a standard law school curriculum is sufficient to graduate and obtain the qualification to practice law. The two notable exceptions are Brazil and Spain. In the case of Brazil, aspiring lawyers are required to take a special qualification exam administered by the Order of Attorneys (*Ordem dos Advogados*) as a prerequisite to obtain the license to practice law. In Spain, special legislation that entered into force in 2011 requires law graduates to take additional professional skills courses, do practical training, and pass a written examination supervised by the Ministry of Justice. The purpose of these additional requirements, some of which are common in many European countries and the United States, is to ensure that those entering the legal profession meet some minimum standards of quality and experience.

Despite the formal entry barriers to the legal profession, one clear trend in Latin America and Spain has been the accelerated growth in the number of lawyers, at a much higher rate than in the rest of Europe and the United States, although the baseline considered by scholars in determining the latter was higher (Galanter 2011). It is important to note that in Latin America and Spain, the number of lawyers refers to people authorized to practice law, and not necessarily to those actually practicing it. The hypothesis is that the latter number is much smaller given that legal studies are usually offered at the undergraduate level, and their content is general enough which many law graduates regard as a basic foundation for several professional occupations, careers, or employment, not necessarily directly related to the practice of law.

Table 1.1 contains the most recently available data regarding the number of lawyers in five Latin America and Spain between 1990 and 2014, with some important caveats. The first one has to do with the lack of uniformity

Table 1.1 Number of lawyers (estimate) in five Latin American countries and Spain (1990–2015)

Country	*1990*	*2000*	*2014–2015*
Brazil	148,875	N/A	839,758
Chile	9308	11,400	40,000
Colombia	N/A	112,000	225,000
Spain	55,076	98,922	249,694
Mexico	141,538	200,000	321,000
Venezuela	31,350	66,383	181,367

Sources: Data for 1990 and 2000: Pérez-Perdomo (2006: 110, 2006b: 14). Data for 2003–2004: CEJA (2005). Brasil 2014: Gómez and Conti, this volume. Spain 1990: Toharia (2003); Spain 2000 and 2014: Méndez, this volume. México 2014: Meneses and Caballero, this volume. Colombia 2013: Bosqué: "Colombie/Un barreau en devenir". *La semaine juridique* 39, 2013. Venezuela 2015: Gómez and Pérez Perdomo, this volume

in the data collection procedures across countries and institutions. There are no uniform or official criteria regarding the collection of information about lawyers. In each country, the source may be different whereas in some countries, the data comes from a government agency in charge of compiling statistics or official census data; in others, the data might be collected by a university, bar association, or the welfare organization in charge of administering the insurance that lawyers are required to take.

Such disparity may obviously hinder the possibility of doing a proper comparison, which makes intra-country comparisons much easier to do given that national data often follows the same criteria, methodology, and are collected by the same institution. As a result, Table 1.1 might be more useful to observe the changes that occurred within a particular country than across several of them. We included countries for which two or more numbers were available regarding our period of study.

Alongside a significant increase in the number of lawyers in the region, the number of law schools also experienced an exponential growth during the last decades. Unsurprisingly, the number of students enrolled in their academic programs rose as well. Two dramatic examples of the growth in the number of law schools are Brazil and Mexico, each with more than 1000 law schools at the time of writing. The curricula, teaching methods, educational materials, faculty, infrastructure, and overall quality of the law schools within each country also vary greatly, which in turn contributes to their placement in the—mostly unofficial—rankings and reputation.

Historically, legal education across Latin America and Spain was very similar. The curricula, which usually required around five years of formal enrolment in a law school, contained the same list of courses—all mandatory—designed to provide a broad and general intellectual platform to the future lawyers. History, philosophy, and political economy were usually offered along with more traditional legal courses like criminal law, civil law, and constitutional law. Courses on alternative dispute resolution and human rights were nonexistent, partly because these fields had not fully developed yet. Unlike in the United States where law students are taught through the discussion of court cases, legal reasoning, and other lawyering skills deemed necessary for their trade, the future lawyers of the Latin countries were exposed to a general education and a systematic vision of law.

To this end, the main course materials used in law school were handbooks and commentaries written by the professors largely inspired by classical treatises of prominent French, Italian, German, and Spanish scholars of the nineteenth century. Some courses incorporated more recent handbooks authored by national authors—mostly the drafters of the relevant legislation—whereby they analyzed the pertinent legal provisions or underlying theories connected to the subject matter, but always keeping their European forbearers present. Given the historical connection between Latin America and Latin Europe, it was common for the law curricula of the former to devote attention to the study of European legislation such as the Code Napoléon of 1804, the Franco-Italian Draft Code of Obligations, or the Spanish Penal Code of 1870. The use of cases was limited, and the main pedagogical tool was the lecture (*clase magistral*, in Spanish) by the professor and the memorization of concepts by the students.

The recent years have witnessed important changes in the legal education of Latin America and Spain. The convergence of several factors, including an upsurge in the number of law schools, changes in the legal market, and the influence of globalization have motivated their leadership to innovate. The leading law schools in most countries have undertaken important changes in their curricula. Courses on international trade, corporate finance, human rights, environmental law, arbitration, mediation, and negotiation have populated the offerings. Clinical legal education, moot court competitions, exchange programs with foreign universities, and other opportunities to foster oral advocacy skills, practical experience, and international and comparative law concepts have also been added to the academic offerings. Furthermore, some law schools have added courses taught in foreign languages to their programs and increasingly encourage their students to become multidisciplinary by exposing them to other fields that might overlap with law, mostly in the realm of science and technology (Gómez 2014).

There has also been a change in the intellectual production of legal scholars. Academic law journals and other scientific publications have proliferated throughout the region, and the production of academic work has increased as well (Pérez Perdomo 2014a, 2015). The type of research being disseminated nowadays is not limited anymore to the interpretation of legal texts and court cases, but also empirical research addressing the relationship between law, culture and society, economics, and politics. These changes are also a response to the competition that exists between law schools and the job market for lawyers and the stratification of the legal profession. The incredible variations that exist among law programs in the region—and even within countries—rule out the idea that there is just one type of legal education being offered in Latin America. The landscape is vast and very diverse.

Another important development of the last two decades has been the flow of Latin American and Spanish lawyers toward foreign countries—primarily the United States—to pursue postgraduate degrees in law in order to acquire knowledge and sometimes even practical experience in transnational legal fields. Some foreign lawyers go beyond obtaining an academic degree and seek to become licensed to practice law in states like New York, California, and Texas, whose rules allow foreign lawyers to join the local legal profession. Conversely, United States' law schools have expanded their academic offerings to respond to the foreign demand, which has also impacted the legal profession in the United States (Vides et al. 2011).

The government and the corporate sector are currently the main employers of lawyers in Latin America. This should come as no surprise given that their activities generate all sorts of complex and mundane legal work. In this sense, most public and private institutions are, according to Galanter (1974), *repeat players*. Their frequent use of the legal system and interaction with lawyers puts them in a different category from, say ordinary citizens, who tend to use lawyers much less frequently if at all. For the most part, the average person retains a lawyer only when there is an important legal conflict in their lives that requires the intervention of an expert, like in the case of a divorce, a criminal prosecution, or a civil lawsuit. These events are exceptional occurrences, so is their interaction with lawyers. Galanter (1974) used the term *one shooter* to refer to the occasional users of the formal legal system.

The bigger an organization is, and the more resources it mobilizes, the greater the likelihood that it will require the services of a lawyer. The size and economic capacity of the client and the complexity of its activities also determines the frequency with which lawyers are employed and the qualifications and skills demanded from those lawyers. In addition to being repeat players, large multinational companies or government entities tend to also have the financial capacity to assemble large legal teams and hire specialized lawyers, sometimes in different parts of the world, depending on their needs. In addition to being *repeat players,* Galanter (1974) would also call them *haves.*

Lawyers have responded to the demand of these *haves* by creating multinational law firms and other similar arrangements, and by honing their skills in areas of practice that match the activities of their clients. Law firms, however, are not the only organizational forms through which lawyers serve the business sector or the government. Another traditional structure frequent in medium-sized to large companies, state agencies, and other organizations is the legal department or in-house counsel. It consists of a lawyer or a team of lawyers, and perhaps other professionals, whose main activity is to advise and represent an organization in all of its routine legal affairs. In-house counsel might frequently coordinate the work of external lawyers, including setting their fees. They also serve as information brokers between the company management and the outside world.

As the name suggests, the in-house counsel is a unit within the company, in other words, a single-client lawyer (Van Houtte 1999; Liggio 1997). The size of the legal department varies depending on the need of the organization they serve and other factors, and it may range from one or a few members to hundreds of lawyers spread across multiple locations. For example, when Pérez Perdomo (2001) studied the legal department of Venezuela's state-owned oil company PDVSA, it was the largest legal service provider in the country, with more than 140 lawyers. At that time, the largest law firm in the country, Baker & McKenzie did not even reach the 100-lawyer mark.

If we look outward, in addition to large multiservice law firms, business clients may also retain the services of much smaller but highly specialized law firms, which professionals are highly regarded because of their reputation in that particular niche. These types of law firms are known as *boutiques* to signify the exclusivity of their services, their ability to offer personalized attention to their clients, and the commensurate high price charged by their professionals. Boutique law firms have become important players in the legal sectors of Latin America and Spain, and many of them have resulted from the spinoff of a practice group or specialized department at large multi-service law firms.

On the other end of the spectrum, we find the *grand advocates* (Galanter and Robinson 2013), that is, influential and prestigious lawyers who are highly regarded in a particular area of law. These grand advocates tend to work independently with a small support team, their portfolio of clients is very exclusive, and the matters they handle are usually of high importance. These grand advocates are well regarded not only because of their technical expertise but also because of their ability to navigate the legal system, and more importantly because of their influence and political connections.

Criminal defense lawyers are perhaps the most common type of grand advocates found in Latin America. More recently, the upsurge of constitutional and human rights-related litigation has also seen the emergence of grand advocates in those areas. Most corporate clients do not generate sufficient criminal or constitutional matters that merit the hiring of a criminal defense or a constitutional law specialist to join their legal department. Even if they did, most grand advocates value their independence and social and political capital and therefore have no incentive in being absorbed by a large organization. This may help explain why multiservice law firms do not have grand advocates among their members.

Despite the important contribution of the grand advocates, in-house counsel, and boutique law firms to the development of the high-end corporate legal sector in Latin America and Spain, the most visible players are still the multiservice firms. We now turn our attention to these players, which have gained visibility in handling significant commercial transactions or complex legal matters usually on behalf of multinational corporations, government entities, and other similar clients.

The Growth of Multiservice Business Law Firms

Interestingly, most of the law firms that handle the bulk of foreign investment legal work and other important business matters are themselves multinational enterprises. The largest firms have thousands of lawyers and offices in many parts of the world. As of now, Dentons is the largest law firm globally in terms of size, with more than 7,300 lawyers. This astronomical figure resulted from a recent merger involving a Singaporean firm (Rodyk) and an Australian firm (Gadens). The second largest law firm in the world is Baker & McKenzie with 4,245 lawyers, and the third place goes for DLA Piper, which has 3,700 lawyers. Other forms of measuring the size of these law firms are revenue and number of offices in different countries (global expansion). Of the three law firms mentioned above, Baker & McKenzie is the one with the largest presence in Latin America: 850 lawyers, 15 offices, and 7 countries. As we will see in this book, Baker & McKenzie was also the first American law firm to establish an outpost south of the border by opening an office in Caracas more than 60 years ago (Gómez and Pérez Perdomo, in this volume; Bauman 1999).

The current Latin American landscape of foreign law firms has changed dramatically during the last decades. Aside from United States-based firms like White & Case, Skadden Arps, Jones Day, and Hughes Hubbard, Latin America has seen the arrival of European firms like Spain's Garrigues and Uría Mendéndez, as well as Great Britain's Clyde & Co. Although many international or foreign firms are still identified by the country where they were first established, or where their management is located, some of the largest ones cannot be tied to a particular country anymore. The structure adopted by these "global" firms often comprises complex layers of partnerships and other arrangements, under a decentralized leadership operating on behalf of a voluntary association such as a Swiss *verein*. Dentons, Baker & McKenzie, DLA Piper, Hogan Lovells, Norton Rose Fulbright, and Squire Patton Boggs, all with presence in Latin America, are some of the most visible examples.

Because of local regulatory restrictions or other factors, some foreign law firms do not have their own offices in Latin America, but rather a local representative, "best friend" alliance, or mutual referral arrangement with local lawyers. Others—usually the smaller foreign firms—are tied to their Latin American and Spanish counterparts through professional networks like Lex Mundi and Affinitas, or Latin America's Bomchil Group.

Latin American lawyers have not taken the back seat in this situation. On the contrary, the regional law firm market has also grown exponentially, although in a different scale compared to the United States. Some countries have witnessed the rise and consolidation of local law firms and their expansion from small family-owned practices to large and strong organizations with multiple offices, hundreds of lawyers, and the capacity to compete with the largest global players in their own turf. Pinheiro Neto and Mattos Filho from Brazil, Allende & Brea from Argentina, Ferrere from Uruguay, Brigard & Urrutia and Posse Herrera Ruiz from Colombia, and D'Empaire Reyna & Bermúdez from Venezuela are some examples.

In this book, we are both interested in the local actors and their foreign counterparts. The central focus of our query are the mid-sized and large Latin American and Spanish law firms and also the international firms with a presence in Latin America and Spain. Our original intention was to separately study the international firms established in Latin America and Spain and the local firms. Notwithstanding, as soon as we began our research, we realized that such distinction was not meaningful—the vast majority of lawyers and other professionals employed by international firms are local. Conversely, many of the domestic firms that exist throughout Latin America and Spain have developed such strong international connections that make them look like international firms. The initial revelation was that most business law firms—regardless of their country of origin—are always international. They maintain strong ties with lawyers from around the world, much of their work is conducted in English and other languages, their client management strategies and billing criteria are the same with local adaptations, and their professionals have both training and knowledge in the legal systems and cultures of countries different from their own.

The size of the law firms is relative to the time and place. In the United States, during the 1960s, a firm with 100 lawyers was considered large (Smigel 1964; Galanter 1983). Currently, a large firm in the United States has to have more than 1,000 lawyers, and a firm with 100 members is regarded as medium-sized or small. There is also a correlation between the size of a law firm, the degree of specialization of its members, and the range of services offered to its clients. The larger firms count on multiple specialists, who are often divided into departments or practice groups across different locations. As a result, those law firms are able to offer multinational clients a panoply of services suited to their industry or specific activity. They are, in other words, a one-stop shop when it comes to corporate legal services.

The reality of the Latin American legal market is different from that of the United States in some ways. The average size of a business law firm is much smaller in Latin America, but their infrastructure, client management strategies, and overall organization are often very similar to their US counterparts. In most Latin American countries, a law firm of 100 lawyers is considered large in terms of size. Moreover, some countries do not even have law firms that reach that number, but the multinational clients still deal with them as if they were Big Law. Table 1.2 shows the evolution—in terms of size—of business law firms in seven Latin American countries between 1999 and 2015.

As we can see, the number of law firms with more than 100 lawyers has grown, although at a different pace across countries. The most dramatic changes have occurred in Brazil and Venezuela. Whereas the former has experienced the biggest growth, the number of firms in Venezuela has increased only slightly. Another important change shown in Table 1.3 is the growth in the average number of lawyers at the ten largest firms of the same seven countries.

Whereas the data shows a general growth in the number of lawyers and the size of business law firms, not all the changes occur for the same reasons. A decrease in the number of firms, for example, may have resulted from the fact that some law firms absorbed smaller ones or merged with

Table 1.2 Business law firms in seven Latin American countries by size (1999–2015)

Country	*Number of lawyers*	*1999*	*2009*	*2015*
Argentina	100+	2	3	5
	50–99	7	10	7
	20–49	10	6	8
Brazil	100+	4	15	20
	50–99	4	11	23
	20–49	10	9	15
Chile	100+	0	1	2
	50–99	1	4	7
	20–49	7	7	9
Colombia	100+	0	0	3
	50–99	0	4	2
	20–49	8	5	7
Mexico	100+	1	2	3
	50–99	2	10	9
	20–49	7	14	18
Peru	100+	0	1	4
	50–99	1	4	8
	20–49	4	10	6
Venezuela	100+	0	0	0
	50–99	1	1	2
	20–49	11	13	7

Source: Pérez Perdomo (2014b), Latin Lawyer 250 (2015)

Table 1.3 Ten largest business law firms in seven Latin American countries by size

Country	*1999*	*2015*	*Growth*
Argentina	85.4	114.6	134%
Brazil	87.3	372.8	427%
Chile	29.5	87.9	298%
Colombia	25.4	67.5	266%
Mexico	56.1	97.7	174%
Peru	26.2	98.6	376%
Venezuela	41.5	40.4	−1%

Source: Latin Lawyer 250 (1999, 2015)

their competitors. Conversely, an increase in the number of lawyers at a firm or in the number of firms may be the consequence of individual lawyers or entire departments moving from one firm to another, or becoming independent and establishing their own firm.

There also appears to be a correlation between law firm growth and the economic performance of a country. Variations in the rate of investments are a useful example. If we look at Argentina, for instance, one of the most important economies of the region, we can see that by 1999 its business law firms rivaled their Brazilian counterparts in terms of average size. In 2009, Argentina felt slightly far behind Brazil, but by 2015, the gap between the two was much wider. This latter period coincided with a decrease in the Argentine economy and an expansion of the Brazilian economy (Bergoglio on Argentina and Craveiro and Gómez on Brazil, in this volume). In México the size of the ten largest law firms almost doubled between 1999 and 2015 (Meneses and Caballero, in this volume). Chile and Colombia, where the average size of business law firms almost tripled between 1999 and 2015, also had a period of economic expansion (De la Maza et al. on Chile, and Lamprea and Díaz Chalela on Colombia, in this volume). In the case of Peru, the growth during the same period is 376 per cent (Gonzáles Mantilla, in this volume). Conversely, Venezuela has experienced stagnation with just a slight negative variation, which should come as no surprise given the deep crisis that has affected the country during the entire period (Gómez and Pérez Perdomo, in this volume).

Central America is the least explored sub-region. Upon gaining independence from Spain, the territories of present-day Nicaragua, Costa Rica, El Salvador, Honduras, and Guatemala formed a federation called

United Provinces of Central America, and later on the Federal Republic of Central America. The five republics that exist today were formed upon the federation's dissolution in 1824. Their combined population is of approximately 44 million inhabitants, and their territory occupies 522,760 km^2 of land.

Since becoming independent, these countries have developed their own legal and political systems, and their societies have taken their own path. Notwithstanding, there have also been important efforts toward the formation of a common economic market. The establishment of regional law firms with presence in the capital of the different countries of the region is a testament of it. Latin Lawyer 250 (2009) reported the formation and rapid expansion of some of these firms, in part because of the upsurge of regional transactions between Central America and the rest of the world (Taboada and Gómez, in this volume).

The absence of ethical rules that require Central American law firms to carry the last name of their partners has allowed them to adopt evocative names such as Consortium, BLP or Lexincorp. In terms of size, Central American law firms are no different from their counterparts in the rest of the region. For example, Consortium Legal has 143 lawyers, while Lexincorp has 80 lawyers. There are also regional law firms that originated in one country and then expanded to other countries while keeping the original names of their founders. Some examples are Aguilar Castillo Love, Arias & Muñoz (112 lawyers), and Pacheco Coto (38).

Compared to the rest of the region, the economies of Central American countries are small, but their integration efforts and their opening to foreign investment have created an incentive for a robust corporate legal sector to emerge. The success of some of the recently formed regional law firms lies in their capacity to operate across national borders, which brings our attention to the more general theme of internationalization of business lawyering.

Internationalization of Business Lawyering in Latin America and Beyond

In 2015, the legal industry guide, Latin Lawyer 250, published a list of 48 international firms with a presence in Latin America. Six years earlier, the same publication did not contain such a list. This does not mean that in 1999 there were no international firms in the region, but their presence might not have been as noticeable as it is currently. Table 1.4 contains a

Table 1.4 International law firms with most presence in six Latin American countries (1999–2015)

		1999		*2015*	
Country	*Law firm*	*# Lawyers*	*Position*	*# Lawyers*	*Position*
Argentina	Baker & McKenzie	55	9	54	11
Chile	Baker & McKenzie	0	0	42	10
Colombia	Baker & McKenzie	0	0	69	5
Colombia	Holland & Knight	0	0	31	8
Colombia	Norton Rose Fulbright	0	0	22	12
Mexico	Baker & McKenzie	105	1	215	1
Mexico	White & Case	32	9	64	10
Mexico	Curtis Mallet Prevost	22	14	0	0
Mexico	Hogan Lovells	0	0	77	7
Peru	Baker & McKenzie	0	0	101	4
Venezuela	Baker & McKenzie	76	1	60	1
Venezuela	Steel Hector & Davis	22	13	0	0
Venezuela	Norton Rose Fulbright	15	14	41	5

Source: Latin Lawyer 250 (1999–2015)

list of international law firms with most presence in the region between 1999 and 2015.

Despite the fact that the list of international firms with presence in Latin America is close to 50, only few of them have the largest offices in each country. Baker & McKenzie is at the top of that list with the largest law offices in Venezuela and Mexico. Baker's other Latin American outposts include Chile, Colombia, Argentina, Peru, and Brazil. The case of Brazil is particularly interesting when it comes to the penetration of foreign firms. Notwithstanding the enormous size of the Brazilian economy and its regional and global importance, its national legal sector is strongly protected. The local bar associations have imposed severe restrictions that prevent foreign lawyers from entering and international law firms from mingling with their Brazilian counterparts. Foreign firms can only set up small shops to advise their clients on foreign law matters, and nothing else. Brazilian firms that have also built strong alliances overseas with the key players in the global arena do the bulk of the corporate legal work. Even then, there are about 25 international law firms with presence in Brazil (Conti Craveiro and Gómez, in this volume).

The case of Venezuela and Mexico is very different. These two countries opened their doors to foreign lawyers many decades ago. In the

1950s, Baker & McKenzie chose Caracas, Venezuela, to open its first office outside of Chicago. The main incentive behind such a move was to provide on-site legal advice to one of its international clients that had established a subsidiary in the South American country. "Following the client" became the main expansion strategy of US law firms in the years that followed.

The Caracas office of Baker & McKenzie was opened in cooperation with Ramón Díaz, a prominent local lawyer who soon thereafter became the firm's first international partner. Other local lawyers joined the effort, and Baker & McKenzie soon became the largest law firm in Venezuela, a position that it still holds to this day. Despite the openness of the local market to foreign lawyers, and the presence of prominent practitioners from the United States, Italy, Spain, and Mexico, the arrival of other international firms in Venezuela did not occur until the 1990s with the opening of the hydrocarbons industry to multinational companies and the influx of foreign capital. The chapter on Venezuela included in this book explains that episode in great detail. The political orientation and the hostility to foreign and national business corporations have reduced the size of some firms, but new foreign firms have entered into this market in search of new opportunities (Gómez and Pérez Perdomo, in this volume).

Baker & McKenzie was also the first foreign law firm to arrive in Mexico with an opening of an office in 1961. Over the years, it grew exponentially and spread throughout the country with offices in five cities. In the early nineties, the Mexican government further liberalized the market, which incentivized other international law firms such as White & Case, Curtis, Mallet-Prevost, and Haynes & Boone to establish a presence in the North American country. More recently, Chadbourne & Parke, Jones Days, DLA Piper, Greenberg Traurig, Holland & Knight, and Spain's Garrigues also opened offices in Mexico. In 2014, the global firm Hogan Lovells entered the local market through the acquisition of Barrera, Siqueiros & Torres Landa, one of the largest Mexican firms, and became one of the strongest players in the country. It is also important to note the overseas expansion of Mexican firms toward Europe. The two most salient examples are Nader, Hayaux & Goebel, which has an office in London; and Goodrich, Riquelme & Asociados, which has an office in Paris since 1971 (Meneses and Caballero, in this volume).

Argentina also experienced an early arrival of Baker & McKenzie, more than 35 years ago. In 2009, Cleary Gottlieb opened an office in Buenos

Aires, and more recently, Curtis, Mallet-Prevost, also established a small office there. Argentine law firms have grown exponentially and expanded their presence beyond their national borders. Some examples are Cabanellas Etchebarne Kelly, Marval O'Farrel Mairal, which have offices in New York, and Brons & Salas, which has an office in Montevideo, Uruguay (Latin Lawyer 250, 215:19; Bergoglio, in this volume).

Until 1999, international law firms had no meaningful presence in Peru, but the recent years have witnessed an important influx of them. In 2012, the ubiquitous Baker & McKenzie established an office in the country after acquiring Estudio Echecopar. The firm currently has 94 lawyers and 29 partners, and it is among the largest in the country. More recently, the Ibero-American firm Philippi Pietrocarrizosa & Uría—which in turn resulted from a merger between a Colombian, a Chilean and a Spanish firm—has made its way into the Peruvian market with a merger including the local firms Ferrero and Delmar Ugarte. The resulting law firm adopted the name Philippi Pietrocarrizosa Ferrero DU & Uría. In 2014, the Spanish law firm Garrigues also opened an office in Lima. Regarding the internationalization of Peruvian firms, we can mention the expansion of Muñiz Ramirez Perez-Tayman & Olaya toward Ecuador, and the opening of a Chilean branch by Rebaza Alcázar & De Las Casas, which also has an affiliation with Squire Sanders (Gonzáles Mantilla, in this volume).

In the case of Chile, its corporate legal market is still dominated by local firms such as Carey (176 lawyers and 25 partners) and Claro & Cía (87 lawyers and 19 partners). In terms of foreign firms, Baker & McKenzie (41 lawyers and 13 partners) is the only player, unless we also count the newly formed Philippi Pietrocarrizosa Ferrero DU & Uría (112 lawyers and 17 partners). In this sense, the Chilean landscape is *sui generis.* The corresponding chapter will delve into explaining the factors that have affected its development.

Colombia's favorable investment flow has had a direct impact on the recent expansion of the corporate legal sector. Like in other countries of the region, Baker & McKenzie has longstanding ties and a large office in Bogotá (80 lawyers and 11 partners). Colombia is also one of the main locations of the Colombo-Peruvian-Chilean-Spanish firm Pietrocarrizosa Ferrero DU & Uría (104 lawyers, 14 partners), and one of the few Latin American countries where Spain's Garrigues has established an outpost (35 lawyers). The recent years have also seen the arrival of other foreign firms such as Holland & Knight (36 lawyers, 6 partners), Norton Rose

Fulbright (22 lawyers), DLA Piper (18 lawyers), and Dentons (Latin Lawyer 250, 2016: 345).

The establishment of foreign law firms is an important sign of the internationalization of business lawyers in Latin America, but certainly not the only one. Another important indicator of internationalization is the growing interest of Latin American lawyers in pursuing graduate studies in the United States and Europe, as a way to become versed in the legal system of another country and perfect their knowledge of a foreign language. The most preferred path followed by foreign lawyers is the year-long Master in Laws (LL.M.) offered by many law schools in the United States and other countries. The United States is also the main destination for Latin American lawyers. Upon graduation, many foreign lawyers opt for doing an internship in an American law firm or legal department.

As we said earlier about globalization, even today's most seemingly domestic legal matter may have a transnational element in it. Any important business enterprise or company, regardless of the country where it is located or the industry to which it belongs, is normally associated to the import and/or export of capital and technology. Joint ventures, partnerships, alliances, and other similar arrangements involving persons and entities located in different countries are also fairly common. The lawyers that represent those business clients are obviously compelled to become globalized as well.

Most countries tend to be supportive of globalization, especially when it refers to the exchange of goods and commercial activity. The flow of people is also accepted when the foreigners visit a country as tourists, students, or to invest in the local economy. Other types of immigrants are less welcomed. In fact, one of the biggest challenges of globalization is the flow of illegal immigrants from countries facing economic or political instability to more peaceful and prosperous countries. The lawyers from Latin America and Spain are not the exception, although their migration tends to be legal. Venezuela and Argentina may be the two countries that have witnessed the most significant migration of lawyers and other professionals to other countries. More than a decade ago, the same was for Chile, Peru, and Colombia. The patterns of professional migration have followed the political, economic, and social situation of the countries involved. It is a situation in permanent flux, and this book hopes to contribute to its understanding.

References

Bauman, Jon R. 1999. *Pioneering a Global Vision: The Story of Baker & McKenzie.* Chicago: Hartcourt Professional Education Group.

Bosqué, Manuel. 2013. Colombie/Un barreau en devenir. *La semaine juridique* 39.

CEJA. 2005. *Sistemas judiciales* 9 *(Abogacía y educación legal).*

Conti Craveiro, Mariana, and Manuel A. Gómez. *Big Law in Brazil: Rise and Current Challenges*, Chapter 3, in this book.

Friedman, Lawrence M. 2001. Erewhon: The Coming Global Legal Order. *37 Stanford Journal of International Law* 347.

Galanter, Marc. 1974. Why the Haves Come out Ahead: Speculations on the Limits of Legal Change. *Law and Society Review* 9: 95–160.

———. 1983. Mega-law and Mega-lawyering in Contemporary United States. In *The Sociology of the Professionals: Lawyers, Doctors, and Others*, ed. R. Dingwood and P. Lewis. London: Macmillan.

———. 2011. More Lawyers than People/the Global Multiplication of Legal Professionals. In *The Paradox of Professionalism. Lawyers and the Possibility of Justice*, ed. S. Cummings. Ann Arbor: Michigan University Press.

Galanter, Marc, and N. Robinson. 2013. India's Grand Advocates: A Legal Elite Flourishing in the Era of Globalization. *International Journal of the Legal Profession* 20: 241–265.

Giddens, Anthony. 1999. *Runaway World: How Globalization is Reshaping Our Lives.* New York: Routledge.

Gómez, Manuel A. 2014. *Innovaciones en la educación jurídica latinoamericana y políticas públicas en materia de globalización.* Manuscrito no publicado.

Gómez, Manuel A., and Rogelio Pérez-Perdomo. *Big Law in Venezuela: From Globalization to Revolution*, Chapter 10, in this book.

Lamprea, Everaldo, and Mariana Díaz Chalela. *The Rise of Big Law in Colombia*, Chapter 6, in this book.

Latin Lawyer 250. 2015. Latin America's Leading Business Law Firms.

Latin Lawyer. (1999). *Latin Lawyer: A Who's Who of Latin American Law Firms.* 1st ed.

———. 2009. Latin America's Leading Business Law Firms.

———. (2015). *Latin Lawyer: Latin America Leading Law Firms.* 17th ed.

Liggio, Carl D. 1997. The Changing Role of Corporate Counsel. *Emory Law Journal* 46 (3): 1201–1222.

Meneses, Rodrigo, and José Antonio Caballero. *Global and Traditional: A Profile of Corporate Lawyers in Mexico*, Chapter 7, in this book.

Pérez-Perdomo, Rogelio. 2006. *La formación jurídica en América Latina. Tensiones e innovaciones en tiempos de globalización.* Bogotá: Universidad Externado de Colombia.

———. 2001. Oil Lawyers and the Globalization of the Venezuelan Oil Industry. In *Rules and Networks: The Legal Culture of Global Legal Transactions*, ed. Richard Appelbaum, W. Felstiner, and V. Gessner. Oxford: Hart.

———. 2014a. *Los juristas académicos de Venezuela. Historia institucional y biografía colectiva*. Caracas: Universidad Metropolitana.

———. 2014b. Advogados e a educação jurídica na América Latina. Algumas tendências, conjecturas e questões. *Cadernos FGV Direito Rio* 10: 39–58.

———. 2015. Las revistas jurídicas venezolanas en tiempo de revolución. *Boletín Mexicano de Derecho Comparado* 142: 223–274.

Smigel, Erwin O. 1964. *The Wall Street Lawyer: Profesional Organization Man?* New York: Free Press of Glencoe.

Toharia. 2003. The Organization, Functioning, and Evaluation of the Spanish Judicial System. In *Legal Culture in the Age of Globalization. Latin America and Latin Europe*, ed. L. Friedman and R. Pérez-Perdomo. Stanford: Stanford University Press.

Van Houtte, Jean. 1999. Law in the World of Business: Lawyers in Large Industrial Enterprises. *International Journal of the Legal Profession* 6 (1): 7–25.

Vides, Marta, Manuel A. Gómez, and Luis F. Pérez-Hurtado. 2011. The American Way: Los Abogados Latinoamericanos como Estudiantes de Maestría en los Estados Unidos de América, 130 Boletín Mexicano de Derecho Comparado, p. 351.

Manuel Gómez is an Associate Professor of Law and Associate Dean of International and Graduate Studies at Florida International University College of Law (USA). Professor Gomez's research and teaching focuses on comparative civil procedure, dispute resolution, globalization of the legal profession and legal education, and private systems of governance.

Rogelio Pérez-Perdomo is a Professor of Law, and Dean Emeritus of the Universidad Metropolitana Law School (Caracas, Venezuela), frequent Visiting Professor at Stanford Law School, former Scientific Director of the Institute for the Sociology of Law (Oñati), and Member of the National Academy of History in Venezuela. Professor Perez-Perdomo's research and teaching focuses on the legal profession, law and society, and legal history.

PART II

Big Law in Latin America and Spain

CHAPTER 2

Law Firms in Argentina: Challenges and Responses to a Crisis

Maria Inés Bergoglio

Introduction

In recent decades, Argentina has undergone numerous changes. In the nineties, the political agenda was driven by neoliberal policies that promoted the liberalization and internationalization of the economy, but the 2001 crisis prompted an abrupt shift in policy. Immediately following the debt crisis, with a nation gripped by rising unemployment and poverty, economic policy shifted inwards. The economic model was then refocused on domestic consumption and the restriction of foreign relations.

Although, unlike previous events, this crisis did not lead to the breakdown of democracy, sudden changes have impacted the level of legitimacy of institutions. According to public opinion data, the vast majority of Argentines believe in democracy, but trust in institutions is quite low,[1] while perception of corruption reaches significant levels.[2]

The legal profession has also experienced, as in most Latin American countries, a rapid process of change since the return of democracy. The expansion of higher education associated with democratization has contributed to an increase in the number of lawyers and has diversified the

M.I. Bergoglio (✉)
Universidad Nacional de Córdoba, Córdoba, Argentina

M. Gómez, R. Pérez-Perdomo (eds.), *Big Law in Latin America and Spain*, https://doi.org/10.1007/978-3-319-65403-4_2

social composition of this professional group in terms of gender, class, and geographic origin.

The plethora of law graduates has encouraged competition within the profession; the consequences of economic change have led to the emergence of new forms of organizations within the legal field (Bergoglio 2009; Pérez Perdomo 2010).

This chapter presents an overview of these changes, focusing especially on the situation of an important segment of the profession: large law firms, oriented toward the corporate sector. The first part of this chapter outlines the political and economic changes the country has experienced since 1990.

The presentation of trends in the legal profession starts by analyzing the expansion of large firms in the nineties and continues by describing large law firms' responses to the 2001 crisis. It concludes by showing their efforts to adapt to a context of recurrent economic crises and marked changes in foreign relations.

Decades of Change in Argentina

The Nineties: Democratic Consolidation and Economic Openness

The nineties witnessed two main processes: the consolidation of democracy, with the arrival of a second civilian president to the government, and the implementation of a neoliberal economic model. In 1994, the main political parties agreed to reform the 1853 constitution.

This change of rules, together with economic success, allowed President Menem to run for a second term, 1995–1999. The stability of a ten-year-long administration offered a vivid contrast to the sharp political oscillations of the seventies.

Controlling inflation was a priority for the second civilian government. After 1991, the Convertibility Plan[3] halted inflation and opened up the economy. Structural reforms—the privatization of public enterprises, refinancing of external debt, and the consolidation of regional integration—led to economic growth. For the first time in many years, the gross domestic product (GDP) expanded for a sustained period.

The economic policy aimed to control inflation and attract foreign investment. As part of this strategy to attract international capital, Argentina signed 55 bilateral investment treaties; most of them stipulated that the country was subject to the jurisdiction of the International

Centre for Settlement of Investment Disputes (ICSID).[4] Large companies that could internationalize their operations were the main beneficiaries of this model. Some of the largest Argentine companies began their expansion into other countries in Latin America and became multinationals (ECLAC 2014).

However, the limitations of the open economic model soon became visible. The disappearance of medium and small industrial enterprises, the loss of jobs, and the reduced social spending worsened the economic situation for large segments of the population. The achieved economic growth was not matched by a recovery in wages: the industrial real wage of 1995 represented less than half that recorded in 1971. The levels of income inequality in Argentina in 1995 were higher than those reported 40 years earlier (Altimir 1997).[5]

As seen in other Latin American countries, the economic structural adjustments of the nineties resulted in the accentuation of income distribution inequality. Poverty levels stabilized in unknown figures for the country. According to official data, at the end of the decade, 32% of Argentines were living in poverty.[6]

The 2001 Crisis

At the beginning of the new century, the country suffered a severe crisis with major political and economic consequences. Over the previous decade, the unrestricted opening of the economy had caused the external debt to grow excessively. The exhaustion of reserves brought currency convertibility to a halt, which further destabilized the financial system. Measures restricting cash withdrawals, known as financial *Corralito*,[7] caused a regressive redistribution of income and generated intense discontent among those with limited savings. Later that year, the country was declared to be in default; external debt, which consisted, in part, of bonds under legislation of eight different jurisdictions, exceeded US $ 130 billion (Minaverry 2013).

The crisis led to the resignation of President Fernando de la Rua on December 20, 2001. Social protests, which began that December, continued for several months: most of the participants in these protests were self-summoned and did not belong to political parties or specific social movements. Their motto "Out with them all!" reflected the decline of institutional legitimacy that accompanied the economic crisis.

During the first few days of January 2002, three successors of De la Rúa (Ramón Puerta, the Chairman of the Senate; Adolfo Rodriguez Saa, elected by the Legislative Assembly; and Eduardo Camaño, the President of the Chamber of Deputies) each took office and subsequently resigned from the presidency, and Eduardo Duhalde was appointed with the mission to call elections.

The deep recession and falling employment drove poverty levels up, reaching 57% of the population by October 2002.[8] This abrupt change in economic conditions also frustrated foreign investors who had arrived during the convertibility regime: many began to raise their differences with Argentina before the ICSID. In this context, congress passed an emergency law to expand the powers of the executive branch on issues, which included food and public services pricing and management of the exchange rate.

The presidential elections were held in a context of crisis of bipartisanship and political fragmentation. In May 2003, Néstor Kirchner, a little-known politician coming from the Peronist Party, took office. He came to power with only 22% of the vote.

The Kirchner Administrations

The Kirchner administration raised the exchange rate and adopted an import substitution industrialization strategy as a method to lower unemployment levels and develop an internal market. Following Peronist traditions, social expenditures grew. As general conditions improved, poverty levels began to fall, returning to pre-crisis levels by mid-2006.[9]

In a favorable international context, marked by increased demand for agricultural exports, Argentina's economy turned around and by 2003 began to grow. The role of the state in the economy expanded, and several of the privatized companies in the previous decade were renationalized.[10] The abandonment of the neoliberal model also meant a significant increase in the regulation of the economy, multiplying the regulations that companies were required to conform to.

The expansion of social spending, through initiatives like the Universal Child Allowance (AUH), a conditional cash transfer program targeted at the children and young adults, was effective in reducing poverty. However, its implementation also fueled the electoral clientelism, chronic in Argentina, to even higher levels (Szwarcberg 2011). The Kirchner administration managed to expand its constituencies, and in 2007, Cristina

Fernandez de Kirchner, wife of Nestor Kirchner, assumed the presidency with 46% of the vote. In the presidential election of 2011, which occurred shortly after the sudden death of her husband, she was reelected by an even wider margin, receiving 54% of the vote.

The large parliamentary majority allowed the Kirchner administrations to tackle large legislative projects, including the Media Law and the new Civil and Commercial Code. It also made it possible for congress to renew the authorization for the executive to decide on issues such as public services and food pricing, despite the changing social conditions. Twelve years after this delegation of powers was enacted, despite official rhetoric emphasizing progress made during this decade, the Emergency Law remained in force.

Following in the footsteps of previous Peronist administrations, personality-driven leadership spread. Reviewing the performance of the executive on the 30th anniversary of democracy, Pérez Liñán summarized the role played by the presidents in the first decade of this century: "Today, the presidential figure continues to dominate the political scene, just as it did in late 1983. The Executive Power initiates public policies, largely controls the allocation of budgetary resources, sets the media agenda and defines the tempo of national policy" (Pérez-Liñán 2013, p. 389).[11]

The negotiations to restructure the defaulted debt, initiated in 2005, were ongoing throughout the decade and strained relations with creditors' home countries. In December 2005, Kirchner chose to liquidate the Argentine debt to the International Monetary Fund (IMF) in a single payment, without refinancing, for a total of US $ 9.8 billion; the decision was framed in a nationalist rhetoric. The change in the orientation of foreign policy was remarkable, and relationships with other Latin American countries were also strengthened—especially after the creation of the Union of South American Nations (UNASUR) in 2008. Ties with China grew during this time period as well.

The concentration of political power achieved through a congressional majority in the House and Senate, along with the continuity of three consecutive Kirchner administrations, created favorable conditions for the growth of corruption, a phenomenon deeply rooted in Argentine politics. The multiplication of allegations and scandals highlighted the limited capacity of the judiciary to deal with this kind of economic crime.[12] From an institutional point of view, one of the most serious events was the Ciccone case (June 2014), where the vice president Amado Boudou was charged with bribery and improper negotiations using the public office.

In this context, the efforts of the administration to control judicial appointments were continuous. The clashes between the executive and the judiciary worsened, especially after some key political projects, such as the Media Law, were delayed by judicial intervention. One such initiative to limit judicial independence, called The Plan for the Democratization of Justice, was enacted in 2013 and generated intense resistance.

After the economic crisis of 2009, the international stage ceased to be favorable for Argentina, and the weaknesses of the Cristina Fernandez de Kirchner administration became evident. The high social expenditure and losses from renationalized companies deepened the imbalance of the federal reserves. Inflation became worrying again and real wages started to deteriorate.

During the first decade of the century, other Latin American countries, such as Brazil, Chile, and Colombia, were able to take advantage of the favorable international cycle to boost growth, since they received considerable flows of foreign investment and expanded in the regional market. However, a restrictive trade policy drove Argentina into economic stagnation and increasing financial difficulties.[13] Towards the end of the third Kirchner presidency, Argentina had a stagnant economy where inflation, poverty, and debt were ongoing problems. Democratic institutions have been weakened due to the concentration of power in the executive branch, allegations of corruption, and the tension between the executive and the judiciary.

In January 2015, federal prosecutor Alberto Nisman, who was investigating the 1994 bombing of a Jewish cultural center where 85 people died, accused the president of plotting to cover up Iran's alleged role in the bombing. His death, which came just hours before he was due to give details of his findings to a congressional committee, highlighted how intertwined the judiciary and politics have become in Argentina, triggering serious concerns about the judicial independence and institutional stability.

Large Law Firms in the Nineties

Traditionally, Latin American lawyers worked on their own, whether at an individual office or sharing it with a small group of professionals tied by close personal bonds. Such associations were not generally true partnerships, since they only shared expenses, not profit.[14] These forms of legal practices were suitable for societies where ties between the client and his/

her lawyer were based upon personal relationships, and where networking was one of the central pillars that guaranteed professional success.

The expansion of higher education, connected to democratization, has contributed to an increase in the number of lawyers and has diversified the social composition of this professional group in terms of gender, class, and ethnicity. This process, which involves democratizing access to education, has been visible in the massive incorporation of women into law school (Bergoglio 2010a).

Over the last few decades, the plethora of law graduates has encouraged competition within the profession, and lawyers developed different strategies to position themselves in the legal services market. Growing specialization, as well as a tendency to associate with other professionals, has been one of the most utilized mechanisms. These have resulted in an increase in law firm size, as De la Maza (2001) thoroughly described with regards to Chile.

In Argentina, a limited number of traditional firms got established in the nineteenth century and had a long history in serving international clients. O'Farrell, founded in 1883, has been acting on behalf of Ford in Argentina since 1913. Similarly, Beccar Varela, founded in 1897, has represented Citibank in the country since 1914. This early development of local firms oriented towards the legal needs of the foreign investors helps explain the limited presence of multinational law firms in Argentina. During the last two decades of the twentieth century, when Anglo-American law firms were increasing their global expansion to follow the activities of their customers (Silver 2001), Buenos Aires was not an attractive place for expansion, since local firms were already quite active in that field. The only foreign firm to open an office in Argentina was Baker & McKenzie in 1981, when it had 59 attorneys.

The economic opening of the nineties generated many opportunities for these firms. The privatization of public services and the arrival of foreign investments to various economic areas generated a demand for specialized legal services, causing large law firms to grow in size. At the same time, new technology, such as word processing, customer communications, and technical information search (legislative and jurisprudential databases) stimulated this trend; however, only large firms could finance the high cost of computer equipment at that time.

Older firms, with experience advising foreign clients and offering bilingual services, along with newer firms,[15] expanded their number of professionals and began to organize using the American model. Frequently, they grew by merging with other corporate offices, similar to their clients. As shown in Table 2.1, by the end of the decade, Argentina had the largest number of big law firms (over fifty lawyers) in Latin America.

Providing legal counsel to transnational clients required extensive linguistic and communicational competence, as well as the capacity to operate in various locations. Unlike Brazil, opening branches in cities outside of the capital was not part of their strategy (Bergoglio 2010a). These firms generally operate within the country through networks of correspondents, formed through personal contacts with lawyers from the provinces, usually former classmates.

In the field of foreign relations, building networks of correspondents was also the overall strategy of the firms with headquarters in Buenos Aires; most of these firms managed to structure correspondent agreements with organizations in different countries, while maintaining their operational independence.[16] In contrast, only three firms opened branches abroad, in the United States (New York) and Europe (Madrid).[17]

Specialization Fields and Internal Organization

Professional practices of these law firms include all aspects of business law. They offer advice on labor, tax, administrative, and regulatory matters related to financial services, capital markets, and mergers and acquisitions.

In these law firms, the division of work is pronounced: lawyers specialize in areas that are increasingly narrow. Frequently, fields of specialization are more related to clients' activities than to academic classifications. It is usual that these law enterprises include specialized departments to deal with issues like energy, infrastructure projects, automotive sector, mining industry, telecommunications, television and media, tourism, or health.

Table 2.1 Large law firms in Latin America

Country	*1999*[a]
Argentina	9
Brazil	8
Chile	1
Mexico	5
Venezuela	2

Source: Pérez Perdomo and Friedman (2003)

[a]This includes firms with 50 lawyers or more

Law practices oriented towards the solution of individual problems are not frequent. However, it is common to offer advice in immigration law, a service particularly relevant to foreign companies that transfer technical and managerial staff from their home countries.

Another prominent feature of these firms has been their rapid adhesion to alternative dispute resolution mechanisms, whose diffusion in Argentina was promoted by the Libra Foundation using US funds. In 1997, after the National Mediation Act, the 18 largest corporate firms came together to create the Business Mediation and Arbitration Center, a space for resolving business disputes in a private setting. The list of mediators and arbitrators offered included managing partners and consultants of leading companies.

The growth of firms also entailed changes in their internal organization. In large law firms, the informality of the organization was lost and the internal organization became more hierarchical, marking the differences between partners, associates, and employees. Many of these firms, which grew out of family practices, attempted to build a rational and open organization, inspired by the Anglo-American model of law firms, where the achievements, rather than personal relationships, are the central criterion for allocating rewards. In practice, this process was streamlined in newer firms and quite slower in offices with a long-established model of family organization.[18]

In an expansive business climate, optimistic for young people,[19] the contrast between the two types of firms was clearly visible in recruitment methods. Still influenced by the image of the lawyer as a gentleman, whose extensive networks of social relationships and fine manners allowed him to conduct himself properly in complex conflict situations,[20] offices founded before World War II tended to choose their professionals among members of the elites—educated in certain schools, or members of some distinguished sport clubs. Newer firms adapted more rapidly to criteria based on academic excellence and began, in imitation of large US firms, to offer career plans for their members, encouraging internships abroad and specialized training.

The Impact on the Profession in General

New forms of work impacted the temporal organization of professional activities. The preventive dimension of legal assistance, the search for technical support in structuring business and work rhythms typical of other cultures combined to make this pressure particularly significant on firms with international clients[21]:

> The business rhythms and the rhythms of the economy are different than what was traditional among lawyers. Corporations need a lawyer much more expeditious and much faster when advising and when it is time to say what to do. And yes, you work under pressure and you spend long hours working. I don't believe we have reached the level current in the US, but, offices working with clients who have international issues for example, have a much faster pace than other smaller or calmer ones. (Case 4, Associate Attorney, Buenos Aires)

Trends in the business organization within the profession were not limited to large firms, but tended to spread to medium-sized firms. As the neoliberal model in the economy took hold, it stimulated new work styles, inspired by the search for efficiency and speed of service.

The impact of these transformations on the social organization of the profession was remarkable. When law firms began to organize as corporations, lawyers increasingly found themselves working not as solo practitioners but as employees of bureaucratically organized law firms or in government agencies. A study based on census and household survey data showed that the percentage of law graduates practicing independently went from 51% in 1995 to 33% in 2003 (Bergoglio and Carballo 2005).[22]

Differences in types of work and income levels accentuated the fragmentation of the profession, highlighting the gaps between different types of lawyers. Towards the end of the decade, the contrast between the two hemispheres of the profession—described by Heinz, Nelson and Laumann (2001) in Chicago—could be clearly seen. On the one hand, we found those lawyers who worked following the classical models, who dealt with different conflicts of individuals and small companies, and got incomes similar to those of their clients. On the other hand, lawyers who practiced in large law firms that rendered highly specialized services to large companies benefited from an economic model that emphasized the concentration of income (Bergoglio 2007a).

Facing the Crisis

The crisis of 2001 caused an abrupt change in the political and economic climate, thus altering the workload at large law firms. For business lawyers, the first reaction, like many Argentines, was fear and disorientation. Juan

Cambiaso, managing partner of Marval, O'Farrell and Mairal, commented that he called US firms for advice, asking old partners to tell him how they had handled the great depression in 1930.[23] After the initial shock, firms were overwhelmed with cases, as the massive destruction of contracts generated a lot of work. All offices were expanding and hiring people to cope with the volume of cases triggered by the emergency regulations.

During the nineties, the exchange rate was fixed at one Argentine peso per US dollar; after the end of the convertibility, three Argentine pesos were needed to purchase one dollar. The Emergency Law demanded a restructuring of public and private contracts that had been agreed to in a foreign currency under Argentina law. It was also established that the prices and tariffs resulting from such contracts would be set in the local currency.

Faced with these conditions, many foreign companies that had invested in the country raised their differences with Argentina before the ICSID. Therefore, the country accumulated almost 50 cases with requests for financial compensation for more than 50 billion (Minaverry 2013). Most of these claims were brought by Argentine law firms, together with firms from the investor's country of origin. This occurred in 18 of the 26 cases that were closed, as the ICSID case information website reports.[24]

In contrast to what happened in some conflicts that had been brought before the same international body in the last few years of the previous decade, the government did not seek the assistance of private firms, which had seasoned lawyers in international disputes. Within the scope of the Procuración Nacional del Tesoro (National Treasury Attorney), a special unit was created to organize presentations in court and to defend the provinces, as the national state was also a guarantor of their obligations. This office was provided with the latest technological advances, and professors at public universities were called as experts. A university professor who participated in these cases described her experience in these terms:

> We have come to process more than seven million pages in less than two months, which would have been impossible without technology. Of course it is impossible to eliminate individual intellectual work but let us say that the management of information has changed radically. Then, we have current information online in real time from the United States, France. (Case 14, senior lawyer)

The processing of these cases lasted a long time, and its results were less adverse to the country than expected, as many companies—particularly from European origin—preferred to renegotiate contracts where possible (Rodríguez Jiménez 2010).

As often happens in cases submitted to arbitration, the achieved outcomes were mixed. A recent study indicates that Argentina currently has nine cases closed with final awards issued and sixteen cases closed with signed agreements. It also has eight cases suspended waiting for the parties to reach an agreement and finally, seventeen cases are pending for a final award or annulment decision (Minaverry 2013).

Argentine law firms gained significant experience in the field of international arbitration, and subsequently advised the Attorney General of the Republic of Venezuela,[25] taking advantage of the political rapport between the two countries under the Kirchner administrations.

Law Firms Under the Kirchner Administrations

With the consolidation of the Kirchner administration, the restrictive trade policy extended beyond the emergency. After the fever of restructuring contracts ebbed, the workflow at large law firms declined, and business lawyers needed to rethink their work strategies. This section discusses these changes, with particular emphasis on the 2006–2014 period. We present a detailed analysis of the organization of the thirteen largest law firms and the general characteristics of the lawyers who work there, based on the information posted on their websites.[26] This research project also included personal interviews and a review of the information concerning these firms published in specialized press.

Structure of the Firms

There were thirteen law firms with more than fifty attorneys in Argentina in 2006, four more than in 1999. Twelve of them were headquartered in Buenos Aires; only one was part of a legal multinational headquartered abroad.

Eight years later, the number of large firms was identical, although the list of names had some modifications. Cárdenas Di-Cio closed, and other firms, such as Nicholson and Cano and Bruchou-Fernandez Madero, absorbed several of its departments. A new firm, Mitrani-Ojam Caballero, was also founded. Overall, 1,382 lawyers are working in this sector in 2017, while in 2006, the large law firms comprised of 1,152 professionals (Table 2.7, Appendix).

This picture of relative stagnation contrasts with the continued growth in other Latin American countries, such as Chile. De la Maza Gazmuri, Mery Nieto, and Vargas Viancos (Forthcoming) report that in Santiago there were nine firms with more than fifty lawyers in 2014, while there was only one in 1999, according to Pérez Perdomo and Friedman (2003).

The services offered are concentrated in the legal field. The incorporation of professionals from other fields is rare in large firms, most of which have at least 50 years of existence. However, there are some economics graduates, primarily concerned with firm administration, and one or two science graduates, acting as support in the departments of intellectual property and patenting.

The effects of workflow stagnation can also be seen in the firm structure. No branches in the other provinces have been opened, even as the national economic policy fosters the growth of domestic consumption. Instead, the network of correspondents in the provinces has extended slightly. The number of branches abroad remains stable, and correspondents abroad have decreased slightly (Table 2.2).

The changes in the orientation of relations to foreign countries are perceptible. As in national foreign policy, relations within Latin America have become more important, and there are several firms that accompany their clients in these markets. It is worth noting that two firms also have a special section dedicated to relations with China, though they do not offer services in that language.

Large firms pay attention to their visibility for international customers and enroll in directories such as Chambers Latin America or Latin Lawyer. Many of them display awards received from various international organizations on their websites. Some of their members regularly participate in general professional associations such as the International Bar Association or specialized by topic, such as the International Fiscal Association. However, only three law firms are involved in international associations of firms such as Lex Mundi.

Table 2.2 Firms' structure in 2006 and 2014

Structure of the firms	*2006*	*2014*
With branches abroad	3	3
With correspondents abroad	8	6
With branches in the country	3	2
With correspondents in the country	6	8

Note: Data for 12 firms with headquarters in Buenos Aires

Specialization Fields

In a context of declining investments, where new projects are not abundant, mergers and acquisitions departments are less active. A firm manager commented:

> We can't deny that, in recent years in Argentina, in the world of business lawyers, activity has been very different from other countries in the region. What has happened in these years is a kind of lethargy and boredom in some tasks.[27]

The firm activity is concentrated in the departments oriented toward regulatory fields. In an economy where the level of state economic intervention is increasing, companies are more and more concerned about the overall compliance to the rules governing each activity as they risk facing penalties, delay, or inconvenience in their production processes. "This trend is even clearer in consumer companies, where the risk is increasing," says the head of a compliance department.[28]

The managing partner at the biggest Argentina firm declared, "[t]here is a profound change in our activities: work in labor, tax, regulatory and litigation areas has grown. The advances of the state generate many conflicts."[29] The weight of the contentious issues within the activities of the firms has grown. One firm states that litigation management absorbs 60% of its resources. They handle a portfolio of 30,000 cases, using

> A customized and computerized proprietary management system, which allows us to optimize resources assigned to this activity and manage large volumes of evidence and documentation, which is supplemented by our correspondent network in all jurisdictions in Argentina. Our system enables remote connection with our clients and attorneys from any place in the world, in order to be informed on the status of a court proceeding.[30]

Restrictions on movements in foreign currency and tax regulations are a source of numerous conflicts since their breach generates strong state responses. A recent case illustrates the importance of these issues. In early November 2014, the Federal Administration of Public Revenue suspended the enrollment of the multinational Procter & Gamble on the registered list of importers and exporters, for alleged overbilling imports by $138 million. The federal agency warned that their operations could be considered not only as tax evasion but also as aggravated smuggling; it asked the judiciary to issue a travel ban for the company's executives who were based in Argentina.

In this context, it is not surprising that 46% of large firms have recently built specialized corporate criminal law departments, while in 2006, only one firm included this area in its practice.

The collective dimension of labor law has also acquired new importance. Inflation, chronic in the country, has increased labor unrest. One firm reports its longstanding relationships with trade unions and their experience in joint negotiations representing employers in these terms:

> Our performance in collective labor law is linked more to the management of collective enterprise disputes, anticipating the risk of strikes, providing solutions and representing the company in the relationship with the enforcement authority, negotiating collective agreements, either by enterprise groups or by activity groups, and the formulation of the general labor strategy of business entities or individual companies ... Our cordial relations and constant communication with the labor associations in almost all productive activities in our country have fostered a positive environment for trade union debates and collective bargaining. All our customers appreciate these facilities as an added value in defining conflicts or their frameworks, giving our firm a position of preeminence over other actors of the stage.[31]

To cope with the drop in workflow, several large firms have also incorporated departments oriented to address individual problems on issues such as immigration, wills and estates, or even family, practices infrequent in 2006. Given the high rate of motor vehicle accidents in Argentina, one firm has opened the Prompt Response Department, which provides 24-hour legal assistance and handles cases of liability losses in automotive accidents.

Professionals in Business Firms

Traditionally, lawyers came mostly from the upper classes and were trained in law schools of large national universities like Córdoba, Buenos Aires, and La Plata. After the University Reform of 1918, the role of education as a channel for social mobility (Agulla 1968) strengthened, and thus the social origin of lawyers slowly began to diversify, in terms of both age and gender (Bergoglio 2007a).

The lawyers who started the first business firms—those founded before 1960—were usually members of the upper strata or had strong ties with them. As the political elite, they had been educated in Argentine public universities. Their work involved contact with members of the large exporting companies and foreign investors, who began to arrive in the country beginning in the late nineteenth century. Their task was easier because it was a common practice in aristocratic families to hire foreign governesses to ensure that their children learned other languages.

As indicated in section "Large Law Firms in the Nineties," the first business law firms were mainly family firms that brought together professionals linked by personal ties. For example, Horacio Beccar, whose family had been prominent in the political sphere during different points of the nineteenth century, studied law at the National University of Buenos Aires. Along with his fellow students, Emilio Jimenez Zapiola, Romulo Naon, and Manuel Maria de Iriondo, he founded one of the first business firms in 1897.

Large public universities have remained the dominant centers of training for business lawyers, even after the creation of private universities in 1960. However, along with the greater availability of public education after the return of democracy in 1983, private universities have gradually gained ground. As seen in the table, until 1975 only a quarter of business lawyers had graduated in a private university. For lawyers who obtained their degree after 2010, this proportion now exceeds 50% (Table 2.3).[32]

This increasing dominance of private universities as training centers for business lawyers suggests that despite the diversification of social origins

Table 2.3 Types of university in different periods

	University		
Graduated in	*Public*	*Private*	*Total*
Up to 1975	74.2%	25.8%	100.0%
1976–1989	64.8%	35.2%	100.0%
1990–1999	58.7%	41.3%	100.0%
2000–2009	62.5%	37.5%	100.0%
2010 onwards	48.7%	51.3%	100.0%
Total	62.1%	37.9%	100.0%

N = 956 business lawyers

that can be found today in the legal profession as a whole, the presence of members of the upper and upper-middle class among business lawyers remains significant; these are the only groups that can afford the high cost of tuition. The universities that currently play a central role in the formation of the business elite are San Andrés, Di Tella, and Austral universities. These private institutions emphasize proficiency in foreign languages, an issue that receives little or no attention in public universities. They also have agreements with large firms to offer internships to their students, which in turn favors future hiring decisions for alumni.

The legal work in large business firms involves a high degree of specialization, causing many of these professionals to undertake graduate studies, although this is not a condition of engagement. As shown in Table 2.4, 80% of associates have no postgraduate education. However, the promotion to partner usually requires postgraduate education. Several law firms report on their websites that they offer financial assistance for graduate studies. The figures shown in the table indicate that two-thirds of large firms' partners have completed graduate studies; most of them (43%) have attended foreign universities, usually in the United States.

The information in the table differentiated by graduation year and hierarchy also shows that postgraduate training is becoming more prevalent. While half of the partners who graduated before 1975 had completed graduate school, now two-thirds of the members of this group hold

Table 2.4 Postgraduate studies by position in the firm and period

		Postgraduate studies				
Position	*Graduated in*	*No*	*National*	*Abroad*	*Both*	*Total*
Associates	Up to 1975	66.7%	3.3%			100.0%
	1976–1989	50.0%	31.3%	18.8%		100.0%
	1990–1999	51.5%	31.3%	13.1%	4.0%	100.0%
	2000–2009	85.3%	9.2%	4.7%	0.9%	100.0%
	2010 onwards	100.0%				100.0%
	Total	79.9%	12.8%	6.1%	1.3%	100.0%
Partners	Up to 1975	50.0%	3.3%	36.7%	10.0%	100.0%
	1976–1989	42.6%	16.0%	36.2%	5.3%	100.0%
	1990–1999	28.1%	28.1%	34.2%	9.6%	100.0%
	2000–2009	33.3%	16.7%	50.0%		100.0%
	Total	36.5%	20.1%	35.7%	7.8%	100.0%

N = 756 business lawyers

graduate-level degrees. The number of professionals who have completed graduate studies abroad has increased, as has attendance in local graduate programs.

The story of the founders of Allende and Brea summarizes these trends. Juan Martin Allende, descendant of an aristocratic Córdoba family, where colonial officers and soldiers of the Independence war were born, graduated as a lawyer from the National University of Cordoba. He also completed graduate studies at the Latin American Law Institute, New York University, in 1948 and went on to practice at an American firm, Breed, Abbott & Morgan. Back in Buenos Aires, he met Teodosio Brea, who had followed a similar career path: graduating from an Argentine public university, he had pursued further study at New York University and had worked in the same New York firm.[33]

The firm they created together in 1957 grew rapidly. Two years later, it had 30 lawyers and was drafting the concession agreements for the new automobile manufacturers in the country.

Today the grandson of one of the founders is working there. Young Juan Martin Allende began working at the firm as a student at a private university, Austral. He received his law degree in 2002, after spending a semester at Duke University and completing graduate studies at the Academy of American and International Law, Southwestern Legal Foundation in Dallas. Later he worked abroad in the firms Tozzini Freire Advogados (Sao Paulo) and Kraft & Frey Niederer (Zurich). Back in Argentina, he returned to the family office, where he was promoted as a partner in 2013.

Relations with the State

In an economy where government intervention is increasingly prominent and where the national economic policy is deeply critical of corporations,[34] business firms must treat federal agencies with care.

The first observation is that business law firms' staff have less work experience in organizations of various branches of the government. Senior consultants and partners report on their resumes that they have worked in courts or certain administrative agencies. In the past, it was frequent for young lawyers to start out their careers by working in the courts, where they could learn the everyday judicial practices from the inside. Now it is common for recent graduates to begin their careers working in the private sector.

Moreover, the high degree of state intervention in the economy makes administrative procedures in state agencies more complex. A partner reported:

> There are merger and acquisition cases, rapidly resolved before, that now have become tortuous. The National Commission for Protection of Competition, for example, has become an instrument that the administration uses to discriminate and issue arbitrary decisions.[35]

In this context of strong state intervention, the role of lawyers as mediators between private companies and state agencies has acquired new importance. This is not a new trend: observers have previously emphasized the importance of this role. A sociological study of Argentine elites conducted in 1964 observed:

> If there is trouble with the authorities, or it is necessary to articulate an interest in state agencies, Central Bank, official banks, ministries, provincial administrations for tax purposes, communal authorities for fees and charges, these all are tasks for the Argentinian lawyer. This attorney, whose name is in the board of different companies, who has friends, who keeps his networks from college and faculty and uses them for his benefit, who knows ministers, knows how to deal with state agencies principals and how to stimulate the interest of a bank manager, is indispensable. (De Imaz 1965, p. 146)[36]

Analyzing the situation in Argentina, Dezalay and Garth (2002) indicated that this role of lawyers has been strengthened because of the risks involved in governmental activities. Currently, in a context of growing tension between the business world and government economic teams, the role of the lawyer as mediator becomes more important to unlock the complexity of various operations, especially those involving foreign relations.

Compensation and Fees

Worldwide, the crisis unleashed after the collapse of Lehman Brothers disrupted the financial services sector, affecting the progress of law firms. The research literature has reported that in the central countries, the effects of the crisis are observable among the companies demanding legal services. These corporations have progressively abandoned the practice of entrusting all their affairs to one firm; instead, they select different providers for different services, forcing offices to compete with each other to get the customer. The encouragement of competition among lawyers that this practice involves has been recorded in different segments of practice, including solo practitioners (Henderson and Zahorsky 2011; Flood 2013).

Locally, companies also seek to cut their legal costs. In-house lawyers prefer to outsource fewer issues. In the listings of Latin Lawyer it is possible to observe large corporations working simultaneously with several firms, since the habit of asking two or three estimates before starting a project has spread, increasing competition among law firms.[37]

Boutique offices—smaller firms highly specialized in topics such as tax law, environmental law, or intellectual property—are the main beneficiaries of this shift. Encouraged by the continued expansion of legal studies at the graduate level (González 2012), these legal consultancies—having improved their visibility through international directories—compete with large firms. Their smaller size allows them to adapt, with more flexibility, to times of crisis and to offer lower rates.

The habitual practices of negotiating fees end up affecting the attorney–client relationship: the economic aspect is emphasized and the bond becomes more impersonal.

"For better or worse, firms work hard in times of expansion, but also in times of conflict. This is a time of conflict, with the main focus on the state. Our activity will not decrease, but another thing is the collection,"[38] said the managing partner of the Buenos Aires office of a multinational legal services firm. The main invoicing arrangements used today in Argentina in the business field are monthly payments, contingency fees, and hourly rates. Different schemes can be combined considering the case and its importance for both the firm and the client.

As in other places in the world, the valuation of work based on the hourly rate is strongly questioned. Inflated workloads and the inability to quantify final costs have increased the number of clients who prefer fixed payments or contingency fees in lawsuits and administrative issues. "Today the hourly rate is mostly a pattern of reference for measuring productivity. In many cases you have to accept a fixed fee which is more the rule than the exception, and that is set according to the reality of each market."[39]

The search for reduced costs, a typical feature in times of crisis, present in many countries and worsened in Argentina by the stagnation of the country, has led to a relative decline in professional fees. "Statistically, Argentine rates are the lowest in the region. Brazil rates are double those of Argentine, in Chile, fees are 50–100% more expensive and even in

Colombia and Uruguay rates are more expensive"[40] observed a managing partner.

The low rate of professional fees in Argentina, compared with other countries in the region, is probably one of the reasons for the limited presence of international law firms in the country. The managing partner of the local office of Baker and McKenzie said,

Interviewer: Why are you the only international law firm in Argentina?[41]

AR: My explanation, which is one of the possible ones, is that we are the sole [international] firm here because, when Baker was established in Argentina, first more informally and then more formally, the barriers to entry were very low. There wasn't, dare I say, even a mature market in the country. Business opportunities at that time were many and the competition was not so intense. Today all that has changed. I mean the last 20 years. Today there is a lot more competition in a market that has at least slowed down, with a context in which large international law firms do not consider Argentina as a priority in the region. Today, when they look over here, they think Brazil, Brazil and Brazil. There is no other. In Latin America, large international firms who have entered in recent years have established mainly in that country. And it's curious because Brazil, precisely, has significant legal obstacles in the regulation of the profession, but they have worked them out. (p. 29)[42]

Internal Organization

As shown by the comparative analysis of large Argentine, Mexican, and Brazilian law firms (Bergoglio 2010a), the influence of the Anglo-American organizational model can clearly be perceived. The business lawyers embraced the model of law firm enthusiastically.[43] However, many of these firms had built their reputation by highlighting their long trajectories, shown in their elegant offices, decorated with antique furniture and fine art. It was not easy to abandon the family model and adopt a more rational criterion of organization in these firms. But the intensification of competition between large law firms and the drop of revenues due to the economic crisis created new incentives to pursue efficiency.

This change is visible, first, in the hiring process. In 2006, only half (54%) of the firms had open systems of recruitment and received applications through their website. Now this practice is widespread: 91% of firms accept resumes online. The transition from the academic space to professional life also receives more attention. Unlike what happened in 2006, more than half of the firms had agreements to provide internships with various universities, a practice that allows for the early detection of talent.

In many firms, the incorporation of recent graduates is clearly structured. A partner of Marval O'Farrell and Mairal described this process in their firm:

> We are very demanding in the process of incorporation of young professionals, in how we set our requirements, and in how we hire. In fact, only one-fifth of the people who apply are taken. It is a process that begins in February of each year and ends with hiring decision in August. It's almost six months of internal debugging process. The selections include a legal exam, a language test and a psychophysical exam. Last year about 35 young professionals joined us, in a market that is in retraction. Those lawyers who are just entering spend six months rotating through different departments. After two years the best qualified enter a specific team, usually one included in the rotation plan. Thereafter they will rise in their category.[44]

Web pages typically include detailed information on the stages of the career and the existence of explicit criteria for promotion, as well as the availability of assistance in pursuing career path (coaching and mentoring), a trait that, unlike Brazil, for example, was rare in 2006 (Bergoglio 2010a).

As might be expected, the process of incorporating these mechanisms has been largely dependent on the firm. In more traditional firms, explicit evaluation procedures are a recent development, while younger firms have been quicker to enact changes. One of them—which also bans hiring family members—reports on its website the existence of upward review mechanisms, through which the work accomplished by supervisors and mentors is assessed.[45]

The discourse published on firm websites suggests that we are dealing with organizations where mobility within the hierarchy is based more on criteria connected with the merit than others such as family ties, gender, or simply time. The practice is however somewhat distant from these aspirations, as shown by the persistence of gender inequalities in the hierarchy of firms.

A 2006 study of the professionals in major law firms found that only 7.5% of partners were women, but they consisted of 45% of the associates. The detailed comparison of academic background and experience of 929 attorneys working in large firms showed that, regardless of professional achievement, gender remained influential as a promotion standard (Bergoglio 2007b). A recent study, which repeated the previous analysis, shows that gender inequalities have softened slightly, but are still clearly visible (see Table 2.5).

Furthermore, statistical analysis of the relative weight of various factors such as gender, academic background, and professional experience in mobility within the hierarchy of firms shows that, as in 2006, five years later, the promotion criteria that apply to men and women are not the same (Gastiazoro 2014).

In recent years, the Anglo-American law firm model has experienced many difficulties in its countries of origin. A long period of recession started in the United States in 2007 and the resulting problems faced by large international law firms have brought to light internal contradictions pervasive in this legal services organizational model. Today, legal services are increasingly determined by market standards, as well as by the existence of a legal culture of entrepreneurial roots. Therefore, the tensions between public and private interests typical of the legal profession[46] have increasingly been resolved in favor of private interests.

The emphasis on partners obtaining individual benefits has led to a lack of attention on appropriate risk-sharing arrangements that would contribute to the growth of the firm in the long run. This is a sensitive issue in organizations based on professional prestige. It has been noted

Table 2.5 Gender composition of large firms

	2006		*2011*	
Position	*Women %*	*Men %*	*Women %*	*Men %*
Founder		100.0		100.0
Consultant	0	100.0	7.1	92.9
Partner	7.5	92.5	11.3	88.7
Associate	45.4	54.6	52.1	47.9
Total	37.3	62.7	42.7	57.3
	N = 1222 professionals Source: Bergoglio 2007b		*N* = 1332 professionals Source: Gastiazoro 2014	

that eagerness to improve profits has led to the emergence of practices such as excessive increase in the number of associates—which weakens the mechanisms of formation and selection of staff—and lateral recruitment. These negative effects can be clearly seen in times of crisis (Ribstein 2010; Henderson 2013).

In the classical model, the big law firms have a pyramidal structure, where the rate of associates to partners is around four to one. Clients pay more for the services of young lawyers than the latter receive as compensation, which creates an incentive to incorporate more young professionals. This organizational style discourages lateral recruitment (recruitment of senior staff members who have spent formative years at other firms), as they move quickly to participate in the firm's profits.

In Argentina, as elsewhere, the economic crisis has meant that customers seek to reduce their legal expenses and thus are reluctant to finance the associate training process. It is not surprising that, faced with a stagnant market, where it is difficult to obtain sufficient workflow, Argentine firms have hired fewer new associates in recent years (Table 2.6).

Table 2.6 Associate/partner rate, 2006–2011

	2006		*2011*	
	Associate/ partner rate	*Lawyers in the firm*	*Associate/ partner rate*	*Lawyers in the firm*
Abeledo Gotheill	3.83	58	3.57	78
Allende y Brea	3.31	56	2.28	63
Beccar Varela	1.36	99	2.74	130
Bomchil	3.21	59	1.84	57
Brons & Salas	6.30	73	2.27	52
Bruchou, Fernández Madero	6.26	138	2.67	101
Bullo, Tassi, Estebenet, Lipera & Torassa	11.89	116	7.67	156
Cárdenas Di Cio	3.43	62		
Marval O'Farrell	4.55	305	4.26	314
Mitrani, Caballero Ojam y Ruiz Moreno			3.58	87
Nicholson & Cano	4.38	70	3.12	110
O'Farrell	3.92	59	2.13	54
Perez Alati,Grondona, Benitez, Arnsten & Martínez de Hoz	4.41	92	3.62	109
Total	4.16	1187	3.40	1311

As shown in the table, the mean associate-partner rate, which was at 4.16 in 2006, now stands at 3.40. The decrease can be observed in virtually all firms, and is especially noticeable in those that were well above average in 2006. The table also shows that half of the firms have a very low proportion of associates, just over two per partner. This striking decrease raises questions about how low-complexity professional work is organized.

It must not be forgotten that recently most firms have built internships systems, either directly or together with universities. Although it is difficult to get hard numbers on these issues, it could be assumed that large firms are shifting work previously performed by associates to law students in order to adapt to economic difficulties. The wide availability of students willing to complete a clerkship for minimum wage or even for free (Giaquinta and Viqueira 2014) makes this alternative attractive.

In large firms, the recruitment of experienced professionals is not a desirable alternative, as they participate in the profits of the firm without having contributed to its growth over the years. Moreover, these additions generate difficulties of adjustment to the uses of the firm. "Bringing in a lateral partner does not happen every day, and it is not something to take lightly. We must live together," said a managing partner.[47]

Despite these obstacles, the practice has spread among Argentine firms in recent years. The restructuring of practice areas meant the opening of new departments such as criminal, wills and estates, family and other legal fields oriented toward individuals, making it necessary to incorporate trained professionals. Unlike what happened in 2006, many firms now offer these options on their websites. As noted on resumes published on firms' websites, partners frequently have previously had work experience at other local firms.

This lateral recruitment is facilitated by the mounting generational tensions in the firms. In a restrictive context, where wages are comparatively low, growing discontent among young lawyers against extended work hours and the uncertain expectations of promotion in the hierarchy stimulate their desire to change firms. In addition, the traditional five-to-eight-year process of becoming a partner challenges younger generations accustomed to new technologies with immediate answers. A partner of the largest law firm in the country described this situation, which requires firms to make greater efforts to retain young talent:

> Today we are dealing with people who are much more short-term oriented than before. Ours was a generation willing to make great efforts to get a better future in an undefined term. Now the new generation has much shorter deadlines and they need more immediate satisfaction for their

> efforts. Ten years is a geological era. This translates into a thousand alternatives from our side: the possibility of working at home; the flex-time; the part-time; team lunches to see how you are, how you feel. The level of coaching and support is much greater than we had when we started.[48]

The critical look at the working model of large firms is not limited to young people. The managing partner of one of these firms commented on this subject at the time of his retirement:

> In firms like this you sell your life per hour. I always tried to do the reverse and keep time for me to think ... Selling life per hour creates a kind of alienation from time management, and I can now say, an inefficient plan of life. I did it for many years but it is not very efficient from the point of view of profit. You have to sacrifice personal time to reach the goal.[49]

Concluding Remarks

In short, large law firms have undergone major changes in recent years. They experienced a period of expansion during the nineties, when the country was carrying out economic liberalization policies, including privatization, open markets, and deregulation. The debt crisis in 2001, with the consequent renegotiation of contracts and arbitration at the ICSID, also represented a significant workload for professionals who provide legal advice to large corporations.

However, with the consolidation of the Kirchner administrations, firms representing big businesses have experienced a period of economic stagnation and decline in earnings. Their strategies to adapt to this situation have included the reorganization of their fields of specialization, including new criminal business law departments and other legal fields oriented toward individuals, including wills and estates, family, or motor vehicle accidents.

At the organizational level, the crisis prompted the search for greater administrative efficiency, which contributed to abandoning the family office model, typical to the region. Recruitment processes have become more open and tend to give more importance to professional capacity over personal relationships.

In recent years, firms have hired fewer lawyers, making the associate-to-partner ratio lower than other parts of the world. Instead, the recruitment of experienced professionals (lateral hiring) to lead new departments has been frequent, as well as the incorporation of law clerks to complete tasks previously assigned to recent graduates.

These years of stagnation, of absence of large transactions and falling professional revenues, have had two significant consequences. First, Argentine firms have lost relative weight in the region. This is visible in their presence in international directories: for example, in the latest edition of the directory of business law firms published by Martindale Hubbell, Argentina occupies 66 pages of the 516 devoted to Central and South America, while Brazil, in turn, takes 124 pages. The list compiled by Chambers and Partners shows the same difference: it mentions 68 Argentine law firms and 133 from Brazil.

Moreover, there are significant generational tensions in the internal organization of firms. Young people are increasingly critical of the extensive labor requirements and the need to postpone personal life when income levels are falling and promotion prospects are unclear. Criticism of the dynamics of work in large firms is not rare among senior professionals, suggesting that in Argentina, as elsewhere, the model of the big law firm has begun to show some fissures.

Appendix

Table 2.7 List of law firms included in the research

Name	*Established in*	*Lawyers in 2006*	*Total organizational levels*	*Lawyers in 2014*	*Dif. 2014–2006*
O'Farrell	1883	56	4	54	–2
Beccar Varela	1897	90	5	130	40
Marvel, O'Farrell & Mairal	1923	300	4	314	14
M & M Bonchil	1923	60	3	57	−3
Bullo, Tassi, Estebenet, Lipera & Torass	1925	114	3	156	42
Allende y Brea	1957	50	3	63	13
Abeledo Gotheill	1963	50	4	78	28
Brons & Salas	1973	69	5	52	−17
Nicholson & Cano	1976	68	3	110	42
Baker & McKenzie Buenos Aires	1981	59	2	71	12
Bruchou, Fernández Madero, Lombardi & Mitrani	1990	110	3	101	–9
Cárdenas, Di Cio y Tarcitano	1991	61	3		–61
Pérez Alati, Grondona, Benítez, Arnsten & Martínez de Hoz	1991	65	3	109	44
Mitrani, Caballero Ojam y Ruiz Moreno	2007		2	87	
Total		1,152		1,382	

Table 2.8 Law graduates from Argentine universities, 2002–2011

	2002		*2011*	
Graduated in	*N*	*%*	*N*	*%*
Public universities	7,437	74.68	9,401	69.39
Private universities	2,522	25.32	4,147	30.61
Total	9,959	100	13,548	100

Source: Anuarios 1999–2003 y 2012 de Estadísticas Universitarias, Ministerio de Educación, Secretaría de Educación Superior. The numbers include degree, masters and PhD students in the legal area.

Notes

1. Turner and Carballo (2010), and Micozzi (2013) have analyzed institutional legitimacy in Argentina.
2. The 2013 corruption index, prepared by Transparency International for 2013, gave Argentina 34 points on a 0–100 scale. The country is ranked at 106 out of a total of 177 audited. Article in *La Nación*, December 3, 2013, accessible at www.lanacion.com.ar/1644091-la-argentina-cayo-en-el-indice-de-percepcion-de-la-corrupcion
3. The Convertibility Plan was a response to the 1991 hyperinflation episode. The government established a fixed pegging of one-to-one parity between the peso and the US dollar. It also guaranteed full convertibility of pesos into US dollars. The government hoped to establish local and international credibility in the peg and to limit the local control over monetary and fiscal policy. The currency board regime intended to stabilize the peso, encourage both foreign and local investment, and foster sustained economic growth.
4. Many other Latin American countries signed bilateral investment treaties during the 1990s. Bolivia signed 16 treaties, Ecuador 18, Venezuela 22, Chile 48, Peru 28, and Mexico 15. Brazil also signed 15 treaties, but none were ratified (Minaverry 2013).
5. Income inequality, measured by the Gini coefficient, rose from 0.40 in 1954 to 0.53 in 1995.
6. Official data, published by the Sistema de Información, Monitoreo y Evaluación de Programas Sociales (SIEMPRO), Consejo Nacional de Política Social.
7. A *corralito* is a small fence or gate, commonly used to restrict the movement of a toddler.
8. Historical data on poverty, Instituto Nacional de Estadistica y Censos (National Institute of Satistics and Census, INDEC). Accessible at www.indec.gov.ar/nivel4_default.asp?id_tema_1=4&id_tema_2=27&id_tema_3=64

9. According to INDEC, in mid-2006, 31.5% of Argentines lived in poverty. See www.indec.gov.ar/nivel4_default.asp?id_tema_1=4&id_tema_2=27&id_tema_3=64
10. This was the case, for example, with the following companies: Correo Argentino, renationalized in 2005, Aguas Argentinas, in 2006, Aerolineas Argentinas in 2008, and finally YPF in 2012.
11. The Spanish original: "La figura presidencial continúa dominando hoy el escenario político de la misma forma que lo hacía a fines de 1983. El poder ejecutivo nacional inicia las principales políticas públicas, controla ampliamente la asignación de recursos presupuestarios, marca la agenda de los medios de comunicación y define el tempo de la política nacional" (Pérez-Liñán 2013, p. 389).
12. A study on corruption cases handled by the federal courts, during the period 1980–2006, showed that only 14 cases out of a total of 750 resulted in a conviction (Biscay 2006).
13. A recent ECLAC report summarizes the state of the country in the Latin American context: "Argentina was the main direct investor outside Latin America during the 1990s. Outward foreign direct investment (FDI) flows topped US$ 2 billion annually (25% of the total for the region) until the 2001–2002 crisis, which sent them plummeting. Although they later ticked up again they did not return to prior levels, even at current prices. The pattern for inward FDI has been the same: indeed, Argentina (together with the Bolivarian Republic of Venezuela and Ecuador) is one of only three countries in the region where inward FDI is now lower than it was a decade ago" (ECLAC 2014, p. 85).
14. In Treves' classification (Treves 1988), these are called *collective* law offices, in contrast to *associated* law offices. In the latter, the law firm, and not the solo practitioner, takes the case in an impersonal fashion and receives the corresponding fees. Treves also pointed out the existence of *business* law offices, where professional service is organized according to models from industrial production in order to adequately serve large economic and social institutions. The latter represents the type of offices we have called "legal firms" here.
15. Bruchou, Fernandez Madero, Lombardi & Mitrani was established in 1990. Cárdenas, Di Cio y Tarcitano, and Perez Alati, Grondona, Benitez, Arnsten & Martínez de Hoz were created in 1991 (see Table 2.7, Appendix).
16. Marval, O'Farrell and Mairal allied with Demarest e Almeida from Brazil and with Spanish firm Uria Menendez. Perhaps the most interesting case is Bomchil, which began the construction of a network of Latin American offices under his name in 1963 (The Bomchil Group, www.bomchilgroup.org), which now has members in 17 different countries.

17. Perez Alati formed in 1998 an alliance with Cuatrecasas (Spain), Goncalves Pereira and Castelo Branco (Portugal), and Machado, Meyer, Sendacz & Opice from Brazil. The group opened a shared branch in New York, while Marval O'Farrell and Mairal held an office in the same city.
18. Dezalay and Garth have observed this trait in Latin American law firms in general in the 1990s: "This practice shows Latin American business lawyer as a hybrid phenomenon with a variety of contradictory aspects. Thus, these law firms look and act like an American law firms, but they are basically family businesses" (Dezalay and Garth 2002, p. 302). The Spanish original: "Esta práctica muestra al abogado de negocios latinoamericano como un fenómeno hibrido con una diversidad de aspectos contradictorios. Así, estas firmas de abogados lucen y actúan como una firma de negocios estadounidense, pero los cimientos de dichas instituciones fundamentalmente son de familia" (Dezalay and Garth 2002, p. 302).
19. Comparing the present time with the 1990s, the partner of one of these studies commented, "[t]he firm tries to be more prudent. We do not hold our prior hiring policy, of calling not less than 20 lawyers per year. And also we analyze thoroughly before replacing when one is going" (Case 18, Senior Partner, Buenos Aires).
20. Dezalay and Garth (1995) have described how this type of gentleman lawyers are progressively replaced by a new type of professionals, oriented to business engineering.
21. Working in Chile, Ashton (2002) also found that international customers demand faster lawyers. For a detailed analysis of temporal changes in the organization of legal work, see Bergoglio (2010b).
22. In the same study, based on data from national household surveys, it was found that the percentage of lawyers working as employees rose from 38% in 1995 to 49% 2003. At the same time, the percentage of lawyers who worked as employers rose from 11% to 18% (Bergoglio and Carballo 2005).
23. Interview published by *Apertura*, August 2009, p. 48.
24. Bomchil represented the plaintiff in six of these cases; Pérez Alati, Grondona, Benitez, Arnsten & Martínez de Hoz, which had a branch in New York, five cases. Meanwhile, Marval, O'Farrell and Mairal, along with a subsidiary in the United States, carried out two cases. Data obtained on the ICSID website, http://documents.worldbank.org/curated/en/2013/01/17810575/icsid-caseload-statistics-carga-de-casos-del-ciadi-estadisticas
25. This happened in the following cases, whose counterpart is the Bolivarian Republic of Venezuela: Vestey (2006); Flughafen Zürich A.G. (2010); Valleverde (2012); Blubank (2012); Glasses Los Andes (2012); and Transban (2014).
26. For a detailed report on the situation of large firms in 2006, including their structure, internal organization, practice areas, and professional discourse, see Bergoglio (2010a).

27. Jorge Pérez Alati, name partner in Pérez Alati, Grondona, Benites, Arntsen & Martinez de Hoz (H), interview in *El Cronista Comercial*, October 10, 2014, accessible at www.cronista.com/legales/El-MampA-se-queda-sin-talento-20141001-0001.html
28. Guillermo Malm Green, partner at Brons & Salas, interview in *El Cronista Comercial*, May 8, 2012. Accessible at www.cronista.com/legales/Lo-mas-hot-en-jurisprudencia-20120508-0021.html
29. Alfredo O'Farrell, de Marval, O'Farrell y Mairal, interview in *Apertura*, August 2009, p. 28.
30. Taken from the English version of the company's web page, www.ebullo.com.ar/eng/seccion.php?idmenu=3&cat=9
31. Taken from the company's web page, www.estudio-ofarrell.com.ar/es/ss_areas/sss_laboral/index.php
32. The proportion of lawyers who graduated from private universities was 30% in 2011, according to official data from the ministry of education. See Table 2.8, Appendix.
33. See *Allende y Brea, medio siglo de un estudio jurídico innovador, La nación*, September 10, 2007. Accessible at www.lanacion.com.ar/942577-allende-y-brea-medio-siglo-de-un-estudio-juridico-innovador
34. For example, when submitting a new anti-hoarding law to the Congress that was strongly criticized by banks and business chambers, President Cristina Kirchner said, "We do not want entrepreneurs to ruin the Argentinians" ("No queremos que los empresarios nos fundan a los argentinos"). See "Cristina Kirchner respondió a las críticas de las empresas: 'No queremos que nos fundan a los argentinos,'", *Diario La Nación*, August 14, 2014, accessible at www.lanacion.com.ar/1718684-cristina-kirchner-respondio-a-las-criticas-de-las-empresas-no-queremos-que-nos-fundan-a-los-argentinos
35. Jorge Pérez Alati, name partner, Revista *Apertura*, August 2009, p. 46.
36. The Spanish in original: "si el problema se presenta con las autoridades, si hay que articular algún interés en los organismos estatales, Banco Central, Bancos Oficiales, Ministerios, administraciones provinciales por razones impositivas, autoridades comunales por tasas y gravámenes, de todo eso se encarga el abogado argentino. Este abogado, que figura en el directorio, que tiene amistades, que mantiene sus relaciones de Colegio y Facultad y las utiliza provechosamente, que conoce a los ministros, sabe cómo tratar a los directores de repartición y estimular el interés de un gerente bancario, resulta imprescindible" (De Imaz 1965, p. 146).
37. Analyzing the law firms employed by the largest Argentine companies, an economic magazine reports that Petrobras works with six firms, YPF with nine, Telefónica five, and Cargill three. Only Techint trusts its affairs to a single firm. Magazine *Apertura*, August 2009, p. 44.

38. Avelino Rolón, managing partner at Baker & McKenzie. Statements published by *El Cronista Comercial,* May 8, 2012. Accessible at www.cronista.com/legales/Lo-mas-hot-en-jurisprudencia-20120508-0021.html
39. Avelino Rolón, managing partner at Baker & McKenzie. Interview in *Auno*, No. 9, Vol. 3, March 2013, p. 30. Accessible at www.aunoabogados.com.ar/index.php/revista-auno-abogados/numero-9
40. Alfredo O' Farrell, managing partner at Marval, O'Farrell y Mairal, interview in *Apertura*, August 2009, p. 34.
41. Baker and McKenzie is currently the only international firm that has an office with more than 50 professionals. Other firms have small delegations: Cleary Gottlieb opened an office in 2009 with four lawyers, and Lewis and Baach has a delegation with one lawyer.
42. Avelino Rolón, managing partner at Baker & McKenzie. Interview in *Auno*, No. 9, Vol. 3, March 2013, p. 29. Accessible at www.aunoabogados.com.ar/index.php/revista-auno-abogados/numero-9
43. Local legal elites enthusiastically adopted the model of the big US law firms as part of a strategy to attract large corporate clients in various Latin American countries. See Ashton (2002) on Chile; Dezalay and Garth (2006) on Mexico, Bergoglio (2010a) on Argentina and Engelmann (2011) on Brazil.
44. *Auno*, Vol. 1, No.1, April 2011, p. 26–27.
45. The firm is Bruchou, Fernández Madero y Lombardi. See www.bfmyl.com/es/desarrollo-de-la-carrera
46. Parsons had pointed out the ambiguous character of the social position of legal work, which he considered as "an entity that, so to speak, penetrates the limits among private and public responsibilities. Their members work in both functions and the profession has a strong anchorage in both" (Parsons 1967, e.o. 1949, p. 326).
47. Horacio Esteban Beccar Varela, managing partner, *Auno,* No. 7, p. 31, September 2012.
48. Santiago Carregal, partner at Marval, O'Farrell y Mairal, *Auno*, No. 1, April 2011, p. 28.
49. Juan Cambiaso, *Apertura,* August 2009, p. 50.

References

Agulla, Juan Carlos. 1968. *Eclipse de una aristocracia*. Córdoba: Líbera.

Altimir, Oscar. 1997. Desigualdad, empleo y pobreza en América Latina: Efectos del ajuste y del cambio en el estilo de desarrollo. *Desarrollo Económico* 37 (145), April–June.

Ashton, Scott. 2002. *El Torneo De Abogados: Law Firms in Chile*, Contribution to the Lawyers of Latin America project, coordinated by Rogelio Pérez Perdomo,

Stanford Law School. Accessible 21 February 2014. http://liblog.law.stanford.edu/wp-content/uploads/2012/07/AshtonLawFirmsinChile.pdf

Bergoglio, María Inés. 2007a. El papel del abogado litigante. In *Los actores de la justicia latinoamericana*, ed. Luis Pásara, 57–85. Salamanca: Universidad de Salamanca.

———. 2007b. Llegar a socia? La movilidad ocupacional en las grandes empresas jurídicas. Análisis de género. *Anuario del Centro de Investigaciones Jurídicas y Sociales* 10: 599–614.

———. 2009. Diversidad y desigualdad en la profesión jurídica: Consecuencias sobre el papel del Derecho en América Latina. *Revista Vía Iuris*, 6 (January–June), ISSN 1909–5759. Facultad de Derecho, Ciencias Políticas y Relaciones Internacionales, Fundación Universitaria Los Libertadores, Bogotá.

———. 2010a. Transformaciones en la profesión jurídica en América Latina. Empresas jurídicas y nuevos discursos profesionales. In *Sociología del Derecho. Culturas y Sistemas Jurídicos Comparados*, Vol. I: Globalización y Derecho, Justicia y Profesión Jurídica, ed. José Antonio Caballero Juárez, Hugo A. Concha Cantú, and Héctor Fix-Fierro, 529–573. México: Universidad Nacional Autónoma de México.

———. 2010b. Cambios en la organización temporal del trabajo jurídico: La mirada de los abogados. In *Anuario XII del Centro de Investigaciones Jurídicas y Sociales*, 553–568. Universidad Nacional de Córdoba. isbn:978-987-03-1906-1.

Bergoglio, María Inés, and Jerónimo Carballo. 2005. Segmentación en la profesión jurídica: Cambios ocupacionales de los abogados argentinos, 1995–2003. *Academia. Revista sobre Enseñanza del Derecho de Buenos Aires*, 3 (5) (Autumn): 201–222. Departamento de Publicaciones, Facultad de Derecho, Universidad de Buenos Aires.

Biscay, Pedro M. 2006. La Justicia Penal y el control de los delitos económicos y de corrupción. *Sistemas Judiciales* Buenos Aires, a. 6 (11): 4.

Blue Bank International & Trust (Barbados) Ltd. v. Bolivarian Republic of Venezuela. ICSID Case No. ARB/12/20. Award rendered by the Tribunal on April 26, 2017.

De Imaz, José Luis. 1965. *Los Que Mandan*. Buenos Aires: Eudeba.

De la Maza, Iñigo. 2001. *Lawyers: From State to Market*. Master Thesis, Stanford Program in International Legal Studies, Stanford Law School. Accessible 17 December 2014. http://liblog.law.stanford.edu/wp-content/uploads/2012/07/delamaza-thesismay2001.pdf

De la Maza Gazmuri, Iñigo, Rafael Mery Nieto, and Juan Enrique Vargas Viancos. Forthcoming. "Big Law" en Chile: Un vistazo a las firmas de abogados, Contribution to the Stanford Seminar.

Dezalay, Yves, and Bryant Garth. 1995. Merchants of Law as Moral Entrepreneurs: Constructing International Justice from the Competition for Transnational Business Disputes. *Law and Society Review* 29 (1): 27–64.

———. 2002. *La internacionalización de las luchas por el poder*. Bogotá: ILSA/Universidad Nacional de Colombia.

———. 2006. De elite dividida a profesión cosmopolita. Los abogados y las estrategias internacionales en la construcción de la autonomía del derecho en México. In *Del gobierno de los abogados al imperio de las leyes. Estudios socio-jurídicos sobre educación y profesión jurídicas en el México contemporáneo*, ed. Fix-Fierro, Héctor, 185–253. UNAM. http://biblio.juridicas.unam.mx/libros/5/2261/9.pdf

ECLAC (Economic Commission for Latin America and the Caribbean). 2014. Foreign Direct Investment in Latin America and the Caribbean. 2013 Report. http://repositorio.cepal.org/bitstream/handle/11362/36861/S1420130_en.pdf?sequence=1D

Engelmann, Fabiano. 2011. Abogados de negocios y la Rule of Law en Brasil. In *Política, Revista de Ciencia Política*, 21–41. Santiago de Chile: Universidad de Chile. http://www.revistapolitica.uchile.cl/index.php/RP/article/viewFile/16274/16856

Fábrica de Vidrios Los Andes, C.A. and Owens-Illinois de Venezuela, C.A. v. Bolivarian Republic of Venezuela. ICSID Case No. ARB/12/21. Pending on August 22, 2017.

Flood, John. 2013. Institutional Bridging: How Large Law Firms Engage in Globalization. *Boston College Law Review* 54 (1). HLS Program on the Legal Profession Research Paper No. 2014-9.

Flughafen Zürich A.G. and Gestión e Ingeniería IDC S.A. v. Bolivarian Republic of Venezuela. ICSID Case No. ARB/10/19. Award rendered on November 18, 2014.

Gastiazoro, Maria Eugenia. 2014. *Profesiones jurídicas. De la dominación masculina al discurso de la diversidad*. PhD Thesis, Facultad de Derecho y Ciencias Sociales, Universidad Nacional de Córdoba.

Giaquinta, Lorena, and Sebastián Viqueira. 2014. Y ahora ¿Qué hago? Estrategias de inserción ocupacional de los estudiantes de la Facultad de Derecho y Ciencias Sociales de Córdoba. In *Contribución al XV Congreso Nacional y V Latinoamericano de Sociología Jurídica*. Rosario. Accessed October 2014.

González, Manuela G. 2012. Posgrados: Génesis y crecimiento en democracia. El caso de la FCJYS-UNLP. In *CD de ponencias del XII Congreso Nacional y III Latinoamericano de Sociología Jurídica*. Viedma. Accessed October 2012.

Heinz, John, Robert L. Nelson, and Edward O. Laumann. 2001. The Scale of Justice: Observations on the Transformation of Urban Law Practice. *Annual Review of Sociology* 27: 337–362.

Henderson, William D. 2013. From Big Law to Lean Law. *International Review of Law and Economics*. Vol. 3. Indiana Legal Studies Research Paper No. 271. http://ssrn.com/abstract=2356330

Henderson, William D, and Rachel Zahorsky. 2011. Law Job Stagnation May Have Started Before the Recession—And It May Be a Sign of Lasting Change - ABA Journal. Accessible 1 July 2011. http://www.abajournal.com/magazine/article/paradigm_shift

Micozzi, Juan Pablo. 2013. Ellos los representantes, nosotros los representados: Reflexiones sobre la representación y la conexión electoral en la Argentina contemporánea. *Revista SAAP* 7 (2): 401–411. ISSN 1666-7883.

Minaverry, Cecilia. 2013. *International Arbitration as a Dispute Resolution Mechanism: The Argentine Case in ICSID*. Publications of the Nestor Kirchner Fellowship. http://www.observatorylatinamerica.org/en/programs/pnk/158-publications-president-nestor-kirchner-fellowhip

Parsons, Talcott. 1967. Consideraciones de un sociólogo sobre la profesión legal. In *Ensayos de Teoría Sociológica*. Buenos Aires: Paidos. Original edition 1949.

Pérez Perdomo, Rogelio. 2010. Abogados, educación jurídica y globalización en América Latina. In *Sociología del Derecho. Culturas y Sistemas Jurídicos Comparados*. Vol. I: Globalización y Derecho, Justicia y Profesión Jurídica, ed. Caballero Juárez, José Antonio, Concha Cantú Hugo A., and Fix-Fierro, Héctor. http://biblio.juridicas.unam.mx//6/2813/21.pdf

Pérez Perdomo, Rogelio, and Lawrence Friedman. 2003. Latin Legal Cultures in the Age of Globalization. In *Legal Culture in the Age of Globalization: Latin America and Latin Europe*, ed. L.M. Friedman and R. Pérez-Perdomo. California: Stanford University Press.

Pérez-Liñán, Aníbal. 2013. Liderazgo presidencial y ciclos de poder en la Argentina democrática. *Revista SAAP* 7 (2): 389–399. ISSN 1666-7883.

Ribstein, Larry E. 2010. The Death of Big Law. *Wisconsin Law Review* 3: 49–815.

Rodríguez Jiménez, Sonia. 2010. El CIADI frente a Argentina, México, Ecuador y Bolivia. Una actualización. In *Arbitraje en Materia de Inversiones*, ed. Rodríguez Jiménez, Sonia amd Wöss, Herfried. UNAM. http://biblio.juridicas.unam.mx/libros/libro.htm?l=2815

Silver, Carole. 2001. Lawyers on Foreign Ground. In *Careers in International Law*, ed. Mark Janis and Salli Schwarz, 2nd ed., 1–21. ABA Publishing. Accessible 14 February 2015. http://works.bepress.com/carole_silver/8

Szwarcberg, Mariela L. 2011. *The Microfoundations of Political Clientelism: Lessons from the Argentine Case*. Kellogg Institute for International Studies. Working Paper # 377, July 2011. https://kellogg.nd.edu/publications/workingpapers/WPS/377.pdf

Transban Investments Corp. v. Bolivarian Republic of Venezuela. ICSID Case No. ARB/12/24. Pending on August 22, 2017.

Treves, Renato. 1988. *La Sociología del Derecho: Orígenes, investigaciones, problemas*. Barcelona: Ariel Derecho.

Turner, Frederick C., and Marita Carballo. 2010. Cycles of Legitimacy and Delegitimation Across Regimes in Argentina, 1900–2008. *International Social Science Journal* 60 (196): 273–283.
Valle Verde Sociedad Financiera S.L. v. Bolivarian Republic of Venezuela. ICSID Case No. ARB/12/18. Pending on August 29, 2017.
Vestey Group Ltd v. Bolivarian Republic of Venezuela. ICSID Case No. ARB/06/4. Award rendered by the Tribunal on April 15, 2016.

Maria Inés Bergoglio is a Professor at the Facultad de Derecho y Ciencias Sociales of the Universidad Nacional de Córdoba (Argentina). Professor Bergoglio is a prominent law and society scholar in Argentina and the rest of Latin America. Her research focuses on different aspects of criminal law, social stratification, comparative politics, and the legal profession.

CHAPTER 3

Big Law in Brazil: Rise and Current Challenges

Mariana Conti Craveiro and Manuel Gómez

Introduction

The chapter is aimed at assessing how the so-called Big Law market has been formed in Brazil, its current features as well as possible challenges for the future. To understand the Brazilian market for Big Law, though, it is vital to consider the institutional and general market framework in which it is embedded.[1] Thus, some assumptions shortly described below must be kept as background for the arguments discussed and/or further explained in the following sections. Some of these aspects are peculiar to Brazil, while others can be found also in different Latin American countries, as presented in the other chapters of this volume.

M.C. Craveiro (✉)
ContiCraveiro Advogados, São Paulo, Brazil

M. Gómez
Florida International University College of Law, Miami, FL, USA

M. Gómez, R. Pérez-Perdomo (eds.), *Big Law in Latin America and Spain*, https://doi.org/10.1007/978-3-319-65403-4_3

A Growing Number of Lawyers

According to information provided by the Brazilian Bar ("Ordem dos Advogados do Brasil" or "OAB"), by November of 2014, there were 839,758 lawyers in Brazil, as well as 42,418 trainees. The annual growth rate of lawyers in the country is about 60,000. The trainees are granted a special enrollment, with no prior exam. Such enrollment enables the trainees to perform some of the acts reserved for lawyers, according to the "Legal Profession Act" ("Estatuto da Advocacia", Lei 8906/94, art.9°). In any case, enrollment with OAB is a condition for becoming a lawyer in Brazil. It is important to stress that the bar exam has an average approval rate of only 13%. In other words, the universe of law-school graduates is much higher to the number of lawyers in the country, generating an increasing contingent of non-qualified professionals. A bill providing for the "paralegal" career has been approved by the House of Representatives and is under analysis of the Senate. This is one attempt of giving these graduates a formal status while they do not pass the exam.

This circumstance is a product of the massification of legal education, a movement initiated during the dictatorship—during the sixties and seventies—and which reached its peak in the last decade. There are currently 1,284 law schools in Brazil, but only a fraction of it (around 8%) is recommended by OAB. In terms of the geographical distribution of lawyers in Brazil, it follows the level of economic development of each state, so the numbers are as follows: São Paulo (SP) with 25,691 lawyers; Rio de Janeiro (RJ) with 127,313 lawyers; Minas Gerais (MG) with 85,492 lawyers; and Rio Grande do Sul (RS) with 60,512 lawyers.

Another key feature of the Brazilian market is the strict regulation of the legal activities by the Brazilian Bar (OAB). After a long process of incorporation initiated in 1843 with "Instituto dos Advogados do Brasil", OAB was finally founded in 1930 and, over the years, has played a very decisive political role in Brazil, especially during dictatorship periods. The Legal Profession Act ("Estatuto da Advocacia") provides for how the legal activity shall be performed in Brazil, granting OAB the monopoly of infra-legal regulation, surveillance and sanctions over these matters, by its disciplinary tribunals.

The Closed World of the Legal Profession in Brazil

Only lawyers can perform the activities considered as legal services in Brazil. To be a lawyer, one has to pass the Bar Exam and it is a breach of conduct for a lawyer to facilitate a non-licensed third person to provide legal services. A foreign law-graduate can become a lawyer in Brazil: it is necessary to validate the foreign law degree with a Brazilian University and, once this is obtained, to take and pass the bar exam. In this case, this foreign law-graduate is considered a lawyer apt to be part of a Brazilian law firm. According to the "Estatuto da Advocacia", law firms are a different form of legal entity, whose acts are registered with OAB and not in the Board of Trade. The whole idea behind the provisions of the "Estatuto" is that the law firm should not be handled as a regular "mercantile" business. As a consequence, the law firm denomination must be formed with the name of one or more partners, even if deceased. As a result, it is not allowed to use fantasy names.

Another important feature is that only lawyers can be part of a law firm and render legal services—and legal services only. Thus, no other professionals (including non-licensed law graduates, national or foreign) can be part of the firm. On the other hand, firms that render other category of services (e.g. accountants, realtors, etc.) cannot provide legal services in association with their original activities. Brazil, thus, differs from realities such as the Spanish (Marisa Mendez, in this book). Moreover, it is not possible to access capital markets or other forms of third-party capitalization since only lawyers can be shareholders.

Lawyer advertisement is very restricted. Practices that involve "touting clients", lobbying and promoting causes can be deemed as mercantile and, thus, a breach in the Code of Ethics.[2] The general idea is that the client must come to the lawyer, and not the opposite. Consequently, advertising must be done exclusively for information purposes and in specialized media (lawyers' magazines and website, for instance); law firms are not allowed to advertise in regular media and/or in association with other professionals or activities (Ordem Dos Advogados, Provimento 94/2000). With such restrictions, more emphasis is given to building a client base through reputation and acknowledgment from peers. As a result, being listed and/or well ranked in international prestigious publications becomes increasingly important to reach even big Brazilian clients. However, the culture of "ranking" in Brazil is not as consolidated as in other jurisdictions.

The Limited Presence of Foreign Lawyers

Regarding the presence of foreign legal service providers, according to OAB regulations (*provimentos*) 91 and 112, foreign law firms can act in

Brazil solely as consultants in the respective foreign law and, as such, their professionals are not considered lawyers for the purposes of the "Estatuto". Brazilian lawyers hired by international firms to work in the Brazilian offices are forbidden to advise in Brazilian law, even if they are enrolled in OAB. A foreign law firm is also not allowed to act in partnership with a Brazilian firm if it results in the former interfering in the management of the latter, as well as over its economic results. When both entities preserve their independence, their billing to the client, and other matters, the association would not be challenged.

The first association challenged by OAB was the agreement between Lefosse and Linklaters. CESA (Law Firms Association) presented a formal consultation to the OAB Federal Chapter to clarify the ethical limits of association between Brazilian law firms in association with international giants (e.g. Campos Mello/DLA Piper, Tauil & Chequer/Mayer Brown, Trench, Rossi & Watanabe/Baker & McKenzie), who in turn presented several legal opinions to support their arguments. The OAB Federal Chapter, however, confirmed the strict regulations of Provimento 91. Those international firms with limited authorization are allowed to adopt the same denomination used abroad, but they must enroll with OAB and periodically renew their authorization to operate in Brazil.

The Big Law Segment in Brazil

The expression "Big Law" refers to the segment that provides sophisticated legal corporate services, being the very elite of legal practitioners. In Brazil, the biggest local law firms in number of associates are not necessarily among the Big Law law firms. The notion of Big Law in Brazil is more related to the prestige and sophistication of the market, as well as of the services rendered. Indeed, as the most evident example, JBM e Mandaliti, currently one of the biggest firms in the country with almost 800 lawyers, is specialized in "mass litigation", that is, in the following up of law suits (consumer rights, labor claims) on behalf of corporate clients who seek low-cost outsourcing of such activities. Notwithstanding, given that JBM e Mandaliti does not employ elite lawyers nor serves elite clients, the firm is generally not considered as part of the Big Law segment.

The high-end corporate legal sector is made up of law firms that have on average about 250 lawyers while there is also a high number of very renowned firms in the same market with smaller numbers. The market for Big Law is, therefore, fragmented and its configuration depends on the service and the needs of the client. There are, for instance, certain solo practitioners and *juristas* for "artisanal" complex work, small and medium-sized boutiques excelling in niches, full service medium-sized law firms, and finally the big and sophisticated law firms.

Another key feature linked to the size of the firms is that the number of well-trained and qualified law students, who have graduated from top Brazilian universities and are skilled in foreign languages, is only a small percentage in the universe of law graduates. Due to this characteristic, competition is not so fierce for elite new lawyers as the general figures over the number of yearly new lawyers entering the market would suggest. In other words, Big Law firms in Brazil are frequently in need and search of new talents.

As previously mentioned, the "ranking" culture in Brazil is still incipient when compared to other countries. The "Análise Advocacia 500" has been published since 2009 and intends to present the 500 law firms "most admired" by the in-house teams of 1,500 Brazilian companies, but this, again, not necessarily brings a coincidence of the nominees to the most important actors in the Big Law market, in terms of reputation, revenues or transactions. Rankings published by the most prestigious international publications such as Chambers & Partners, Latin Lawyer, and IFLR are praised for international assessment of local firms and are becoming more relevant even to Brazilian clients.

The Big Law market is still concentrated in São Paulo and Rio de Janeiro, both capital cities being the hubs for high-end legal services to other regions. It is worth mentioning that most Brazilian Big Law firms have offices in both cities, as well as in Brasilia (seat of the Supreme Court and Superior Tribunals), while the foreign international law firms are mostly based only in São Paulo.

The Role of the Industrialization and Modernization of Brazil on the Rise of Big Law

The radical transformation in economy and society by the intense industrialization process of the late fifties led to the first relevant reshaping in the legal services market, with the necessity of providing legal assistance to the new industries and to Brazilian businessmen seeking association with foreign companies. Due to the increase in the number of law schools since the thirties, the rise of an urbanized middle class and new job opportunities, most Brazilian law graduates during the fifties simply aspired to work for one of the newly created companies. Others decided to pursue a solo career, and opened small offices that served mostly local clients. José Martins Pinheiro Neto, a former BBC war correspondent in London, was an exception in this latter group.

When foreign investment started to pour into Brazil during the fifties, contacts made by Mr. Pinheiro during the London years as well as his fluency in English and experience abroad were the fuel that made his firm the pioneer of the corporate legal sector in Brazil. As Mr. Pinheiro himself used to say, Pinheiro Neto Advogados has been the "training ship" of Brazilian legal elite. Former Pinheiro Neto associates are the founders of other firms currently among the main players in Big Law market, such as Machado Meyer Sendacz and Opice, Mattos Filho, and Lefosse. Indeed, Pinheiro Neto was the first Brazilian firm to be organized according to American standards, that is, adopting an entrepreneurial structure (so far as admitted by OAB strict regulations), having introduced the different departments within the firm, the hourly-based fees, career plan and other technological innovations. Also, no family members were allowed to work in the firm, which is a very unusual restriction in the region.

All this added to the extreme seriousness and commitment to excellence of Pinheiro, who conducted his team with an iron fist to make it internationally respected, and gave the firm the best reputation that it carries up to the present date, even after Pinheiro's death in 2005. In fact, the generational transition in the firm is widely known to be the most successful in Brazil, also credited to the innovative views of Pinheiro.

In parallel with Pinheiro Neto, Demarest & Almeida was created in São Paulo in 1948 and has benefited from the boom of foreign investment in the years that followed, becoming one of the Big Law players to date. Mr. Kenneth Demarest was an American lawyer who represented a foreign energy group in Brazil, and Mr. João Batista Pereira de Almeida, the legal director of FIESP (São Paulo Industrial Confederation). Both, as a consequence, had good contacts in the industrial community, especially with American companies that were coming to São Paulo. Their intention was to provide these companies excellent corporate legal services and, as Pinheiro Neto, to establish a law firm based in the American entrepreneurial model.

In Rio de Janeiro, João Pedro Gouvêa Vieira had already an established firm since the thirties, serving international clients especially in the telegraph and the navigation sectors. Having assisted Crédit Lyonnais in 1945 to become the first foreign bank in Brazil, the firm gathered an important clientele among the French companies that intended to enter the Brazilian market, for which the office is still recognized. During the industrialization upsurge of the fifties, the firm was thus very active in Rio de Janeiro and Gouvêa Vieira himself was a member of the Board of Directors in the National Bank for Economic Development (BNDE).

Similarly to Pinheiro Neto, Gouvêa Vieira, in Rio de Janeiro, formed a number of business lawyers who would in the future launch their own practices and now are important players in the Big Law market, such as Francisco Antunes Maciel Müssnich (founder of BM&A- Barbosa, Müssnich and Aragão). Unlike Pinheiro Neto, though, Gouvêa Vieira has been a family-controlled firm. Still in Rio de Janeiro, Siqueira Castro Advogados dates back from 1948, founded by professionals like left IP legend Momsem, Leonardos & Cia. The firm is one of the biggest Brazilian firms today, with 71 partners and 872 associates.

In line with the strategy of expanding its activities throughout Latin America, Chicago-based Baker & McKenzie opened its first Brazilian office in São Paulo in 1959, in association with the local firm Trench, Rossi & Watanabe. It was only in 1972 that a Brazilian partner based in Chicago, Ronaldo Veirano, was transferred to Rio de Janeiro to open a new firm office in the city. After 25 years, Veirano decided to open his own firm, Veirano Advogados, which is one of the most important Big Law firms in the country today.

The Golden Years and Their Impact on Big Law in Brazil

Brazil faced an energy crisis in 2001 that dropped Fernando Henrique Cardoso's popularity, rising Lula's chances of winning the 2002 Presidential elections. During the campaign, afraid of Lula's imminent election, foreign speculative capital started to exit Brazil, leading to a crisis and to the need of a new agreement with International Monetary Fund to calm down the market. As a consequence, even if leftist, Lula was forced to keep Cardoso's economic policy. The international rise in the commodity prices brought an important and constant surplus in Brazilian foreign trade balance throughout the decade. The international liquidity levels, already high in the nineties, kept as an incentive to foreign direct investment not only in existing industries but also in the development of new projects and plants.

With favorable overall economic conditions, Lula put into practice other income transfer programs such as Fome Zero and Bolsa Familia, granting millions of lowest-income Brazilians (the so-called classes C, D and E) access to the market, especially when retail businesses were concerned, improving consumption patterns. These conditions gave Brazil a privileged position when the 2008 world financial crisis hit and important moves in this "blooming" decade affected the consolidation of Big Law in Brazil.

First, the number of mergers and acquisitions (M&A) transactions increased substantially. Players that had not still entered the Brazilian market during Cardoso's years, despite the stabilization of the economy, now became eager to benefit from the new market conditions and growth rates. In most cases, the fastest way to "take part in the party" was to buy an already running business or at least a stake in that. On the other hand, private equity funds saw good opportunities in Brazilian companies that lacked funds or professional management to benefit from the good economic moment.

Second, with the high liquidity in international financial markets and the internal stability achieved since the late nineties, Brazilian capital markets became very attractive to investors as well as, increasingly after 2004, to Brazilian companies with a higher level of professional structure, that saw the opportunity to successfully open their capital and raise funds through equity offering opposed to the traditional debt financing. As a result, between 2004 and 2007, Brazil has seen an unprecedented boom of initial public offers (IPOs) and other capital market activity. With the 2008 international crisis, the rhythm of IPOs slowed down, but Brazil showed itself as a safe harbor and kept attracting investments.

Third, strong Brazilian companies increased their presence around the globe. As examples, AmBev merged with InterBrew to form InBev in 2004. The company later merged with Anheuser-Busch in 2008, forming the world's largest brewer. After the 2008 crisis, Lula's administration favored the creation of "National Champions", funding through BNDES a few big Brazilian groups in M&A transactions and expansion abroad, aiming to make them global players in their sectors.

Fourth, the Public-Private Partnership Law (11.079/04) as well as the PAC (Growth acceleration program) were aimed at improving infrastructure in Brazil, especially public transportation. The hopes that the infrastructure problems would be solved or at least reduced were increased by the nomination of Brazil as seat of both the FIFA Soccer World Cup in

2014 and the 2016 Summer Olympic Games in Rio de Janeiro. However, despite the high level of public expenditure and of private investment, not all the intended construction works and improvements were successfully completed.

A Closer Look at the Features and Challenges of Big Law

In response to the historical timeline described above, the actors in the legal services market in Brazil, as in most Latin American countries, have evolved from generalist lawyers—liberal professionals that formed the elite of the country—to specialized, sophisticated law practices structured to cope with the complex social and business environment of the globalized world. Interviews with partners of important law firms were conducted in parallel to a research in the specialized media and institutional presentations of the firms (i.e. websites, printed material) to understand this evolution in the corporate legal services niche (Big Law), the current design of such market as well as possible trends and challenges.

Turning Point of the Nineties

According to all the interviewees, the turning point for the Big Law rise in Brazil has been the nineties, when more law firms had to gain size and sophistication for the new demand in services. Not only the pioneer corporate legal offices have dramatically grown in size, but also a number of previously small and mid-sized firms, some founded in the seventies inspired in Pinheiro Neto and Demarest, such as Machado, Meyer, Sendacz e Opice (1972) and Tozzini, Freire, Teixeira e Silva (1977) emerged as big firms, with intense hiring (in some cases, firms growing four times in number of lawyers). Additionally new players came into the market—such as Mattos Filho, Veiga Filho, Moherdaui, Marrey Jr. Moherdaui & Quiroga (today, Mattos Filho); Barbosa, Müssnich & Aragão, Lilla, Huck, Malheiros; Veirano (no longer Baker&McKenzie in Rio de Janeiro); Goulart, Penteado, Iervolino e Lefosse (today, Lefosse)—and grew intensively throughout the decade.

The important changes in the economy during the Collor and Cardoso administrations brought a new scenario, with international clientele becoming more common and widespread. Importation, customs and tax law were the first areas affected by new policy. Thereafter, the stabilization of the economy permitted long-term investment projects, such as joint ventures with local partners and/or M&A deals. But the key factor is that privatization radically changed the landscape. Law firms were hired either by the government to conduct the process or by the interested foreign companies in their consortium with Brazilian counterparts as bidders. In both cases, intense manpower was required to organize and analyze the data rooms and other necessary procedures, up to the public bids and/or to contest them.

The regulation of the previously state-controlled areas, such as telecommunications, energy, oil, mining, and so on, demanded a high number of specialized lawyers, still lacking. Indeed, there was a significant shift from litigation to transaction services, the latter gaining a lot more percentage of work within the firms, and the average Brazilian lawyer was formed in the Law Schools with a litigation mindset, not the business-oriented or conciliatory ones that the new times demanded. Not surprisingly, the end of the nineties and the beginning of the 2000s represented the "boom" of the LL.M Brazilian candidates in the USA and/or the United Kingdom, seeking training to cope with the new challenges.

During this process, Brazilian legal practice was extremely impacted by the American contract models, especially for M&A deals. New technologies, especially the Internet, made more and more information available and definitely changed the pace and style of practicing law. Despite the boom in activity, however, Brazilian Big Law firms of the time were facing no competition from international firms. There was instead a collaborative atmosphere: strengthening contacts and ties with foreign law firms during the nineties secured a very important source of clients to Brazilian Big Law firms ever since.

According to some of our informants, the then recent Brazilian economic stability and the high demand of services abroad during the nineties made Brazil, by comparison, not so interesting as a market for legal services for the international firms as it became after the 2008 world financial crisis.

Mass Litigation

Another interesting aspect that recalls the impact of the nineties on the Brazilian legal market is that, in the aftermath of the privatization phase, the new owners of privatized companies had to face and deal with a high number of lawsuits inherited from the state-controlled years and the foreign clients desired that the same law firm that assisted them during the privatization followed up these lawsuits.

At first, some of the Big Law firms would render these services as part of their commitment to assist their clients, but the problem was that the costs to engage the team in such less sophisticated services became prohibitive. Some firms, then, decided to create a separate low-cost unit (some located in less expensive premises), with lawyers from a different school background (not top-tier law schools)—trying to lower the costs and keep the client at the same time satisfied and confident in the firm reputation of good quality. After some years, though, this solution proved to be not so ideal. Some partners who were responsible for these low-cost units decided to provide the same services independently from the mother-firms while these rapidly realized that they had to focus on sophisticated cases to avoid losing ground to specialized middle-sized (spin-offs were common) and boutique litigation firms. In other cases, the clients becoming more acquainted to Brazilian market simply realized that, for "mass" litigation services, they did not need the reputation of a Big Law firm and referred these matters to lesser known—and certainly less expensive—law firms.

Current Status: Fragmentation

In 2002, Brazilian economy was again facing a crisis, triggered by the imminent election of Luiz Inazio Lula da Silva. The privatization wave was over and some firms that hired intensively had to dismiss parts of their teams. On the other hand, even if no dismissal were made, the law firms were as booming as they had in previous years, which in turn reduced the incentives for some lawyers to remain in a Big-Firm structure. The know-how and expertise accrued by these professionals during their big-firm years decidedly counted to the success of individual and spin-off initiatives.

The pioneer traditional big firms had to develop their own expertise on a "trial and error" basis when facing the first challenges to becoming respectable international firms. Especially during the nineties, such firms were a cocoon of a generation of practitioners who benefited from this tutoring as well as from the broader access to information and schooling and, most of all, of the client basis of the big firms to become known (since with harsh marketing restrictions under OAB rules, assessing and conquering a client basis is the main difficulty for newcomers).

The tide began to change substantially in 2004, when the "Brazilian IPO boom" started. At first, the already traditional "big law firms" took advantage of their qualified position to provide such services and capital market teams were either formed or revamped within those firms. Brazilian capital markets had never been so dynamic. But after a while, spin-offs of these firms were presented as an increasingly more interesting alternative since a significant part of the services—that previously could be offered by only a "happy few"—have become "commoditized". Another factor for an accommodation in the market could be found in the more prominent role of the investment banks and private equity funds in the transactional matters and securities offerings, increasing the demand for such services. This was a signal for potential newcomers that there was still space in the Big Law market to be conquered by competitors of the traditional big firms, considering, specially, the pressure from clients to new billing systems.

Finally, it is important to highlight that due to the economic growth in other Brazilian regions, former regional firms from these locations grew in size and exposure, expanding to São Paulo and Rio de Janeiro. The keynote of their expansion has been the assistance to Brazilian companies seated outside São Paulo-Rio de Janeiro axis, that now had to face other circumstances, such as M&A deals, international investments and their own expansion abroad. The Brazilian Northeast region has probably experienced this movement the most.

A partial conclusion is that currently, in Brazil, a greater number of law firms dispute the same market when former "elite" and now "commoditized" corporate legal services are concerned. During the nineties, instead, the big Brazilian Big Law firms dominated the scene since the competitors could not provide the same level of professionalism, business-oriented structures and, particularly, know-how and track record. Differently from other Latin American realities, Brazil has a higher number of "big" law firms and middle-sized full service firms able to serve Big Law (more than 80 law firms with 50 or more professionals).

Specialized Firms and Boutiques

As it can be seen in other jurisdictions, along with the big full-service firms and their spin-offs, Big Law market in Brazil is also shared with boutique law firms. Within these, some are acknowledged by their reputation in a specific area of law while others are valued in niches, be it industry or clientele niches. Their (small) size should not be taken as a direct indicator of their relevance in the significant market and on the other hand, some boutiques are only considered as such by its niche of activity, since they can have high headcount figures.

One of the most important reasons why clients hire Big Law firms is their full service appeal, that is, the possibility of their being one stop shop. And this works mostly for complex transactions and litigation, where a solid and resourceful team is required to perform the volume inherent to these services (e.g. due diligence of over 500 employees). Keeping this infrastructure available, though, represents higher costs embedded in the fees. On the other hand, in a big team it is more likely that several different associates dealing with the cases serve that client. As a result, specialized boutique firms are increasingly more active, proving to be successful when rendering specific services at usually lower fees and/or more personalized client-attorney relationship. It is also not rare that boutique firms team up with the Big Law firms to provide in depth assistance in complex or sensitive cases.

Areas in which this is particularly true are high-end dispute resolution, business crime, tax, antitrust, intellectual property, environmental, bankruptcy and public/administrative law. Some boutique or individual references in these areas are shown in Table 3.1.

Other boutique firms specialize in industries, for instance, among others, Agribusiness (Santos Neto; Ramos Zuanon; Lazaretti, Moretti e Moraes) Aviation (Abdalla & Zimmermann Advogados, De Luca, Derenusson, Schutoff e Azevendo), Media and Entertainment (Bitelli Advogados; Cesnik, Quintino & Salinas; and, Schivartche Advogados). Finally, some boutique firms are focused in assisting a specific foreign clientele, with an appeal of greater awareness of its cultural differences and fluency in their respective mother language. These boutiques are a natural competitor to the "foreign desks" of the big firms, and are usually very active with the Bilateral Chambers of Commerce and other institutions in the respective community. As examples, Canada (Murray Advogados), France (Gouvêa Vieira and spin-offs), Germany, Switzerland, Austria (Stüssi Neves Advogados, Rothmann; Florenz; Bolz; Pacheco Neto, Sanden, Teicheire) Italy (Buccioli, Braz de Oliveira Advogados; Guarnera Advogados).

Individual Professionals

In addition to the firms, it is important to underline the importance and influence of some elite individual professionals who excel in providing Big

Table 3.1 Brazilian law firms by area of specialization (2015)

Dispute resolution	Sergio Bermudes; Ferro, Castro Neves, Daltro e Gomide; Andrade&Fichtner; L.O. Baptista, Schmidt, Valois, Miranda, Ferreira, Agel; Castro, Barros, Sobral, Gomes; Tepedino, Migliore, Berezowski
Business crime	Moraes Pitombo; José Carlos Dias (Dias & Carvalho Dias); Nilo Batista & Advogados Associados; José Roberto Batocchio; Celso Sanchez Vilardi (Vilardi & Advogados Associados); Arnaldo Malheiros Filho (Malheiros Filho, Meggiolaro e Prado Advogados); Alberto Zacharias Toron (Toron, Torihara e Szafir Advogados)
Tax	Krakowiak; Dias de Souza; Paulo de Barros Carvalho Advogados; Mariz de Oliveira e Siqueira Campos; Sacha Calmon e Misabel Derzi
Antitrust	Magalhães e Dias; Grinberg, Cordovil; Sampaio Ferraz; Advocacia José del Chiaro; Franceschini & Miranda.
Intellectual property	Dannemann, Siemsen (a big specialized firm, with 45 partners); Gusmão & Labrunie; Kaznar Leonardos; Montaury, Pimenta, Machado & Vieira de Mello; Advocacia Pietro Ariboni; Di Blasi, Parente & Associados; Bhering Advogados; Luiz Leonardos & Associados
Environmental	Milaré Advogados; Tabet Advogados
Bankruptcy/restructuring	Renato Mange Advogados Associados; Mandel Advocacia; Ramos & Zuanon Advogados; Sergio Bermudes
Public/administrative	Manesco, Ramirez, Perez, Azevedo Marques; Sundfeld Advogados; Tojal & Renault Advogados
Capital markets	Pinheiro Guimarães Advogados; Vaz, Barreto, Shingaki e Oioli Advogados; Perlman, Vidigal Advogados; Motta, Fernandes Rocha; Carvalhosa & Eizirik

Source: Chambers and Partners Latin America 2015

Law services, most of them being legal scholars in their field and, as such, an "authority". Others have been in the Big Law market for years, working in Big Law firms or boutiques, having gained the same level of deference from peers. Taking into consideration the weight of doctrine arguments to solve a dispute in Civil Law tradition, these experts are hired by law firms and/or in-house counsels to present legal/expert opinions, affidavits and are as well appointed as arbitrators in domestic and international procedures.

This caste is praised with the highest level of individual prestige, based on their intellectual and academic achievements. Accordingly, even though serving the Big Law, their "relevant market" is not exactly the same one shared by the Big Law firms of even boutique firms: their competitors are other scholars and professors acting in the same field of research and/or activity.

In-House Legal Team

As seen all over the world, one of the most significant changes in the Brazilian legal market in the past ten years has been, according to the interviewees, the shift of the in-house legal team to a more active position within the structure of the client companies. The in-house teams are now seen as a fundamental actor to the development of the business activities and no longer a deterrent to the initiatives formulated by the executives. As such, they have been revamped in headcount and professional qualification. Some practical consequences for the Brazilian legal market and, ultimately, for Big Law market in Brazil are that in-house teams tend to be formed and directed by professionals formerly working in Big Law firms, with expertise of dealing with complex issues. These professionals have the background to evaluate the competence and reputation of law firms when deciding to outsource services and, on the other hand, they can provide a higher percentage of the same services internally. It is opposed to the former scenario where the most part of legal services would be outsourced.

Foreign Firms

Finally, despite the restrictions, Brazilian Big Law market has been impacted by the local presence of the international firms since the exchange and cooperative work has become more intense, and, on the other hand, international firms could better sense the Brazilian reality, which currently does not correspond to the "gloomy" paradise depictured in the past five years, after the 2008 financial crisis. According to some interviewees, differently from other jurisdictions, Brazil has already a mature market served by consolidated local law firms with international levels of quality and professionalism and even if OAB would lift the barriers, the foreign firms would face real local competitors in the "big" Big Law firms, such as

Pinheiro Neto, Machado Meyer, Mattos Filho, Tozzini, Freire; Barbosa, Müssnich & Aragão among others. For the mid-sized full service Brazilian Law firms in the same market, however, the presence of other giants could or could not be a threat, since most Brazilian companies still prefer to handle their cases to smaller firms, where personalized relationships can be developed.

Lateral Hiring and Spin-Offs

As we said earlier, talented and skilled elite lawyers find no difficulty in entering the market and they have been favored, in the last 20 years, by a wealthy economic circle in Brazil. In the past 20 years, all the changes in the local and global legal market landscape affected the dynamics. Until 2002, lateral hiring and spin-offs were much less common in large Big Law firms and the professionals were still pursuing the partnership goal, being in the same firm for over a decade and sticking to such purpose. When the 2002 crisis hit, and it became clear that the fast growth of the late nineties could not be entirely absorbed, a generational issue arose in some firms, where "old" founders and partners who were still very active would not "lift the lid" for the younger generation. As a result, these "big-firm-trained" lawyers founded a series of spin-offs, as previously noted.

During the "Brazilian boom" of the last ten years, the good moment served as a trigger for lawyers to search the best opportunities available for them in the market, be it within their "original" law firm or in competitors and, as a result, the market became much more dynamic from the lawyers perspective. It is important to note, regarding this trend, that Brazil is still a personalistic market. That is, even in large Big Law firms, clients would have their "preferred" partner and in some cases stick to him/her regardless of the firm. This is not a rule since some clients are in fact bound to the firm, but such cases are becoming to be less and less common. Clients search the best service for the best price, and who can provide it, will take it.

In sum, it has become harder for the firms to hold their talents, since not only there are more competitors than in the 1990s but also the awareness and availability of lawyers to switch jobs is higher. The so-called "lockstep" progression scheme, requiring long years of devotion to a large firm, is proving itself less interesting for this generation.

Conclusion: Current Challenges and Possible Trends

There is a consensus among the lawyers that we interviewed that the main challenge to the Brazilian Big Law market in comparison to the "rise" years, and in particular after the 2008 world financial crisis, is the cost pressure. This affects the firms—especially the big ones—in multiple ways. Big firms can no longer count on the fidelity of their clients, who would more likely split their real sophisticated cases into different firms (other large firms or boutiques, depending on the area/specific need), handle most of their regular necessities by their now revamped legal departments and outsource their commodity/mass litigation services to firms outside the "Big Law" market.

Smaller competitors, who are now much stronger than a decade ago, have a more flexible structure and consequently lower costs, thus allowing different billing systems. They hire former large law firm professionals and, thus, offer similar results from a technical point of view, to the majority of the cases. In other words, one must now deliver much more for the same fees to hold clients. After initial years of struggling to keep the usual source of revenues (from the "one stop shop" concept), the largest Brazilian Big Law firms seem to be focusing themselves exactly in the "high end", sophisticated cases, providing services of high aggregated value. Of course, they do not "decline" more commoditized services, if the client wants them, but they are aware that this income cannot be the focus of their marketing efforts and/or revenues basis.

In this scenario, the headcount "pyramid" becomes less steep, with more partners but also more qualified personnel handling the cases, since a smaller percentage of less complex cases could be delegated to young, unseasoned associates, as it was commonplace. For middle-size full service law firms, there is an opportunity to gain from this shift in the bigger firms strategy, if they can really organize themselves in a more cost-effective way. Otherwise, they would also face the price pressure and, without the same reputation and "muscles" of the largest ones, would have a difficult time.

Boutiques, on the contrary, have been favored since not only clients have become more prone to hire them, but the big firms themselves increasingly do see them, in some fields, as important team workers. The main difficulty for boutiques, which makes their development probably slower, is that they rely mostly in their reputation as specialists to reach new clients: making the market perceive their value and to distinguish itself from small—but not qualified—law firms is a hard task, especially with all OAB restrictions, not to speak about the usually lower financial resources available for marketing initiatives.

Last, but not least, a very important trend is the relevance of "best-friendships" and agreements with foreign law firms to enhance mutual referrals. Past are the days when only Pinheiro Neto and a few other law firms were known abroad and automatically attracted foreign companies as the "go-to" law firms in Brazil. This trend seems in full force, facilitated by the international interest in Brazil in the last few years as and by the more active presence of Brazilian lawyers in international transactions, organizations (e.g. IBA).

Happily, and despite all the recent economic and political turmoil, Brazil Big Law market is still growing, with a high number of transactions, reorganizations, litigation and arbitrations, providing demand for high skilled professionals, not to mention the increase in the bankruptcy/turnaround, debt renegotiation and anti-corruption areas. In the next few years, the market may suffer a consolidation as the economy can experience a more intensive slowdown, even if is not foreseeable, for the interviewees, that a dramatic shift as the ones that hit Venezuela and Argentina will in fact take place.

Notes

1. See, Eliane Botelho Junqueira, "Brazil: The Road of Conflict Bound to Total Justice" in *Legal Culture in the Age of Globalization*, ed. Friedman and Perez-Perdomo (2003, Stanford University Press).
2. OAB Code of Ethics and Discipline, Art. 7°—The offering of professional services that result, direct or indirectly, in touting new clients is forbidden.

References

Arend, Marcelo. 2009. *50 anos de industrialização no Brasil: Uma análise revolucionária*. Porto Alegre: Universidade Federal do Rio Grande do Sul. http://www.ppge.ufrgs.br/redesenv/teses/2009/doutorado/29.pdf

Brandão, Ignacio de Loyola. 2002. *Pinheiro Neto Advogados: 60 years*. Dezembro Editora.

Chambers & Partners. 2015. http://www.chambersandpartners.com/41/2364/editorial/9/1

Comparato, Fabio Konder. 1979. Reflexões sobre o Método do Ensino Jurídico. *Revista da Faculdade de Direito da Universidade de São Paulo* LXXIV: 123.

Cunha, Luciana Gross ed altri. 2007. Sociedades de Advogados e Tendências Profissionais. *Revista Direito GV* 6: 111–118.

Junqueira, Eliane Botelho. 2003. Brazil: The Road of Conflict Bound to Total Justice. In *Legal Culture in the Age of Globalization*, ed. Friedman and Perez-Perdomo. California: Stanford University Press. also available in Kindle Edition.

Lacerda, Antonio Correia, and Alexandre Oliveira. 2009. *Influxos de investimento direto estrangeiro (IDE) no Brasil: Uma análise da desnacionalização da estrutura produtiva nos anos 2000.* São Paulo: VII Ciclo de Debates em Economia Industrial, Trabalho e Tecnologia – EITT.

Lamy Filho, Alfredo. 1972. A crise do ensino jurídico e a experiência do CEPED. *Revista do Instituto dos Advogados Brasileiros. Rio de Janeiro* 6 (18): 151–164.

Martins, Ana Luiza, and Heloisa Barbuy. 1999. *Arcadas: História da Faculdade de Direito do Largo de São Francisco.* São Paulo: Melhoramentos.

Moreau, Pierre (org). 2011. *Grandes Advogados*, Rio de Janeiro, Casa da Palavra (*The Book Brings a Series of Interviews of the Most Prominent Brazilian Lawyers in a Wide Array of Topics, from Legal Education to the Current Challengs of Brazilian Legal Market*).

Müssnich, Francisco Antunes Macial. 2007. *Cartas a um jovem advogado: Paixão, determinação e talento.* Rio de Janeiro: Elsevier.

Steiner, Henry J. 1971. Legal Education and Socio – Economic Change – Brazilian Perspectives. *The American Journal of Comparative Law*. http://www.jstor.org/discover/10.2307/839148?uid=3737664&uid=2129&uid=2&uid=70&uid=4&sid=47698979843057

Trubek, David M. n.d. Reforming Legal Education in Brazil: From the CEPED Experiment to the Law Schools at the Getulio Vargas Foundation. University of Wisconsin Law School, Legal Studies Research Paper Series, Paper No. 1180, http://ssrn.com/abstract=1970244

Venâncio Filho, Alberto. 2011. *Das Arcadas ao Bacharelismo: 150 anos de ensino jurídico no Brasil.* 2nd ed. São Paulo: Perspectiva.

Mariana Conti Craveiro is the founding partner of ContiCraveiro Advogados in São Paulo (Brazil). She holds a law degree, Masters in Law degree, and PhD in Law from the Universidade de São Paulo.

Manuel Gómez is an Associate Professor of Law and Associate Dean of International & Graduate Studies at Florida International University College of Law (United States of America). Professor Gómez's research and teaching focuses on comparative civil procedure, dispute resolution, the globalization of the legal profession and legal education and private systems of governance.

CHAPTER 4

Big Law in Chile: A Glance at the Law Firms

Iñigo de la Maza Gazmuri, Rafael Mery Nieto, and Juan Enrique Vargas Viancos

Introduction

A specter is haunting the legal profession—the specter of the market. Although not all the powers of the old legal profession have entered into a holy alliance to exorcise it. The opposite is true.

Everything seems to indicate that the legal profession has accepted the specter enthusiastically and has modeled its appearance to adapt to the needs imposed by the specter. At the beginning of the twentieth century, the prevailing image of the most successful legal practice was that of a lawyer who worked independently, close to the figure of a family doctor. However, at the beginning of the twenty-first century, the image of that legal practice has changed to what we call a *law firm*, which at least in an aspirational sense, is constituted as a company. The emergence of the law firms in the country is a recent phenomenon that has started no more than 40 years ago.

In the first part of this chapter, we intend to demonstrate that the traditional professional practice as well as the law firm responds to the supply and demand mechanism. A moderate offer of legal services determined by the entry barriers to the profession (specifically due to the small number of law schools) along with a demand from unsophisticated economic

I. de la Maza Gazmuri (✉) • R.M. Nieto • J.E.Vargas Viancos
School of Law of Universidad Diego Portales, Santiago, Chile

M. Gómez, R. Pérez-Perdomo (eds.), *Big Law in Latin America and Spain*, https://doi.org/10.1007/978-3-319-65403-4_4

actors, determined that the dominant model of the professional practice was individual, in small family offices or in "communities under the same roof."[1] On the contrary, a more vigorous offer (determined by the opening of the university system as of the 80s) along with a growing sophisticated and complex demand, favored the emergence of law firms.

In the second part of this chapter, we try to make a type of radiography of law firms in Chile. By mixing quantitative and qualitative indicators, we examine their lawyers and clients. The main conclusion is that this is an ongoing and successful process. Law firms are a reality that is increasingly more important. However, law firms are not mature enough to turn into corporations. It is still possible to see amidst the desired corporate practices, traces of old family offices or style of lawyers trained in a different world.

Individual and Associative Practice, a Century Apart

Carey & Co is to date the largest law firm in the country. Its website features a timeline with information regarding the history of the firm. "In 1905 Francis Carey opened an *estudio*[2] in Antofagasta and began to practice the profession independently ... In 2013, the firm had 25 partners, 152 lawyers and a total staff of more than 380 people."[3] The independent law practice was the standard at the beginning of the twentieth century in Chile. The *law firms*, the name given to the associative professional practice organizations described in this chapter, has been common in Chile since the beginning of the twenty-first century with a number close to 100 lawyers per firm.

1905

Supply and Demand for Legal Services

In 1905, the number of lawyers (or the supply of legal services) was low, partially due to the lack of educational institutions to study Law in Chile, which until the end of the nineteenth century was just the School of Law of Universidad de Chile and the Pontificia Universidad Católica de Santiago, which the School of Law was founded in 1889. Until the second half of the nineteenth century, the Chilean economy depended almost exclusively on agriculture and only 36,000 persons from the 800,000 inhabitants registered in the census of 1812 lived in major cities (Serrano

1994: 35). As Urzúa (1992: 170–171) suggests, in such an environment the social relations that took the form of a legal dispute must have been rather scarce.

This situation changed toward the end of the nineteenth century with the increase of saltpeter exports. Lawyers acted as intermediaries between the new saltpeter entrepreneurs and the state (Urzúa 1992: 173). Lawyers gained some importance as consultants and litigants in mining issues. The financial sector and somewhat later the banking sector, railway, brand protection and maritime transport added to the aforementioned (Silva Vargas 2004: 37–38). Insurance practice should be added to this list. This might explain the origins of Carey and other firms that were still very prominent in Chile back in those days.[4]

There is nothing strange that in the early twentieth century, which would become the largest the law firm was the office of a lawyer who practiced independently. And this is not strange because that was the way lawyers worked in Chile at that time. We have suggested that the independent practice of the profession can be explained by two reasons. The first relates to the limited supply of legal services and, second, to a very weak demand for such services.

Legal practice was not very important, at least when compared to the social prestige of a law degree or its relevance in politics. During the nineteenth century, a law degree was highly regarded, relating it to social prestige, power and wealth (Aylwin 1999; Bravo 1998; Galdames 1937; Serrano 1994). During the nineteenth century, a law degree was the fastest way to improve the social status of a person (Serrano 1994). The legal profession of was the "profession of power" (Bravo 1998: 96).[5]

The Lawyers' Practice

Some of the most important law firms in Chile have their origin in the last two decades of the nineteenth century, but it should be noted that they did not begin as what today we consider a law firm but rather as a group of lawyers who practiced the profession individually or, in some cases, with family members. In this sense, the practice of law in Chile at that time resembles the description provided by Pérez-Perdomo about Venezuelan lawyers during the 20s and 30s (1981: 209–212), that is, the individual practice of the profession in small offices in the city center. The main activity was lawsuit in courts and personal and sustained relation (similar to a family doctor) characterized the relationship with the clients. Lawyers were independent from the clients. Finally, the number of cases handled by each lawyer was rather small and their relationship with other lawyers more or less close.[6]

For example, Julio Philippi Izquierdo, who was one of the most important lawyers to Philippi, Yrarrazabal, Pulido y Brunner, recalls that during the 50s "The law firm did not have a rigid organization, no comfort, just one telephone on the wall at the end of the corridor and a lounge where the clients sometimes had to wait the whole morning before being received by a lawyer" (Silva Vargas 2004: 14).

This kind of practice was maintained in the most prestigious firms until the 80s. According to an observer, quoted by Dezalay and Garth (2002: 307):

> The legal profession maintained a very traditional approach. Most of the leading lawyers were lawyers in court professors who worked in small family firms. Just a few law firms with experience in international affairs but not necessarily with "more technical knowledge" compared to the other ones and ... preserved many of the traditional features of the family firms.

2013

In the 108 years that span between 1905 and 2013, there is a continuing growth in the number of lawyers due to the increasing availability of legal education, and on the other hand, the demand for legal services from the economic sector has also increased. As it may be obvious, this has significantly impacted the outlook of the legal profession, especially, the segment that we have called *big law*.

The Supply of Legal Services

During the period between the first decade of the twentieth century and the second decade of the twenty-first century, the number of lawyers continued to grow in Chile. While the population census of 1952 reported 4,239 lawyers (including 309 women),[7] in 1992, the census reported 9,946 lawyers. This is a moderate growth in relative terms: 70 lawyers per 100,000 in 1952 and almost 75 lawyers in 1992.

The explanation for the moderate increase is the limited availability of legal education. At the beginning of the twentieth century, there were only five places where you could study law in Chile: Universidad de Chile,

Instituto Literario de Concepción that would become the School of Law of Universidad de Chile,[8] Pontificia Universidad Católica de Santiago, the Curso de Leyes de la Congregación de los Sagrados Corazones, that would become part of the Pontificia Universidad Católica de Valparaíso[9] and the Curso de Leyes de la Ciudad de Valparaíso, that would become the School of Law of Universidad de Valparaíso.[10] This situation persisted until 1981, in which we find eight universities in Chile, of which only five, already mentioned, offered legal studies leading to a law degree. In the same year, the number of students in these schools amounted to 1,799 (Zabala Ortiz 1999: 94).

In 1981, the military government changed the rules. The purpose of the military regime was to create an open and competitive university system with high academic standards (Atria 1998: 614). To achieve this goal, private agents were encouraged to participate in the provision of university services and the State contribution to the funding policies of the universities was reduced (Fuenzalida 2003: 14).

Up to some extent (though rather paradoxically), the opening of the university system to the market favored the slogan of the left-leaning parties during the first years of the 1970s: "universal access to university." The total number of students enrolled grew from 116,474 in 1982 to 146,720 in 1992 (Bravo 1992a: 285); and from 276,852 in 2000 to 636,417 in 2014 (Higher Education Council).

In 2003 there were about 40 law schools that, according to the information provided by the Higher Education Council, taught 119 programs conferring a law degree.[11] By 2014, data from the Higher Education Council shows 49 Schools of Law and 127 law programs.[12]

Chart 4.1 shows the data of law graduates who had taken the oath as lawyers at the Chilean Supreme Court.[13]

Considering that the National Census of 1992 reported 9,946 lawyers and the number of lawyers is not registered in subsequent Population Census and if we add 31,897 new lawyers who have taken the oath since then and registered by the Supreme Court, the number of lawyers in Chile is close to 40,000; that is, about 230 lawyers per 100,000 inhabitants. The relative number of lawyers has doubled between 2006 and 2013.[14]

The Demand for Legal Services

The economic conditions changed from the saltpeter boom during the last decades of the nineteenth century, allowing the incorporation of

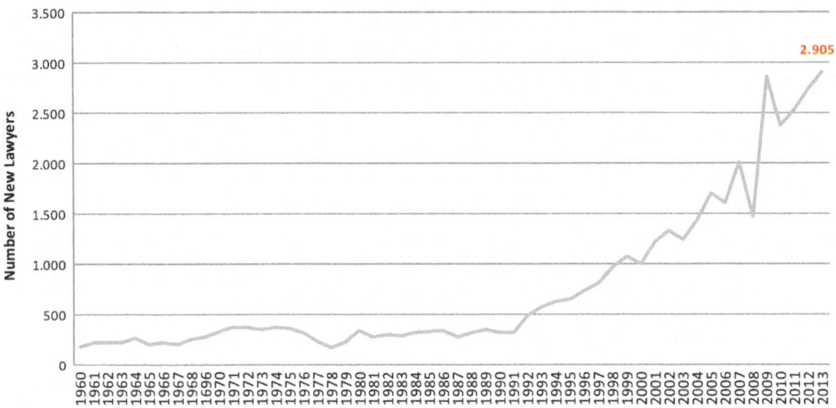

Chart 4.1 New Lawyers (1960–2013). Source: Chilean Supreme Court

new-sophisticated economic actors who increased the emerging demand for legal services.[15] The demand became stable: from the early twentieth century until the 70s, the industry had a moderate growth that responded to an increase in the number of professionals and the new requirements posed by the market.[16]

From the "debt crisis" and more clearly since 1986, the military government's economic policy was modified with a new package of measures. A set of new policies led to deep institutional and regulatory changes, particularly in the financial sector, granting a variety of incentives, including tax and credit, besides huge assets transfer in the re-privatization process. Special incentives to foreign investment and incentives were created to promote exports.

In that period, a way was open toward restructuring the economic groups, the emergence of new domestic and foreign agents, the dynamism of natural resources processing activities of natural resources and infrastructure and the growth of the exporting sector. In fact, the strategy after the "debt crisis" opened a business cycle that matured throughout the 1990s and which benefited from the positive macroeconomic growth, the favorable international context and the consolidation of the capital market.[17]

Finally, the great leap of the industry—regardless of the small size of the industry at a comparative level—took place in 1995, a period when Chile was in a remarkable economic situation. These were years of a quiet but dynamic growth, reinforced by a significant optimism. Major investment projects in sectors of natural resources and energy happened, and lawyers took advantage of the opportunities presented by the market.

The expansive demand and growing complexity stemming from the emergence of economic actors required legal services that exceeded the capabilities of the individual practice of the profession or in small family firms and seems to have stimulated the emergence and growth of a certain type of associative practice. For example, Jorge Carey Tagle (2009: 11), partner of Carey, notes:

> [W]e decided to refine our rules of internal governance following the organizational model of international firms based in London and New York, but adapted to our idiosyncrasy and reality.

Something similar occurred in the same period with Philippi, Yrarrázabal, Pulido y Brunner when they merged with Philippi e Yrarrázabal:

> [T]ogether with the increasing number of lawyers and a bigger staff, a change in the work modality also occurred. To the so called "communities under the same roof", a common expression to name an office shared by different lawyers as well as maintenance costs of the same, the specialized and team work began to prevail, what assumed the design and application of an income distribution system. (Silva Vargas 2004: 92–93)

The Law Firm as an Associative Practice

The opinions about Carey & Cia. and Philippi, Yrarrázabal, Pulido & Brunner allow us to observe the emergence of a type of associative practice of the legal profession with organizational structures that, sometimes, gradually resemble the pattern of large US law firms (Galanter and Palay 1991: 33–37):

> These lawyers are highly specialized and ordinarily divided into departments (for example, corporate, banking, real state, litigation). Work for clients includes planning, counseling, negotiation, and representation in a wide range of settings…
>
> These firms are hierarchical. The working groups that serve clients consist of senior and junior lawyers. The latter are hired on the basis of their

> qualifications directly form prestigious law schools. The work of these junior lawyers is supervised and reviewed by seniors. Training is imparted to young lawyers in the course of a prolonged (four to ten year) apprenticeship, normally ended either by promotion to partnership or by departure from the firm.

With some ambiguity, we use the term law firm to designate a kind of associative practice. The most relevant characteristics of these firms are usually the following: (a) it is a group of lawyers organized as a for profit legal entity having its own name; (b) the object of that legal entity is to provide a comprehensive set of legal services; (c) its structure is hierarchical and it is possible to distinguish partners and associates; and (d) it is very common that the management of the firm is in the hands of or partially depends on professional managers, who are not lawyers.

This model of associative practice has become important and common in Chile for the following reasons: (a) it is the type of legal service demanded by the most powerful economic actors and, therefore, it is the kind of profession that relates to the most important businesses; (b) it is a type of legal practice that tends to attract a significant percentage of the most talented graduates of law schools; and (c) their practice is very prestigious.[18]

The notion of law firm can be clarified if it is distinguished from the individual practice of lawyers, either solitary or in the so-called "communities under the same roof" in which a group of lawyers share an office and some of its costs (typically secretary, bills and rent) but they are not organized as a company.[19]

Some precautions are necessary. The dominant model of the elite lawyers' practice is not identical to the big law firms in the US. Our proposition, and our use of the term "Law Firm," is more modest. What we want to point out is that if we analyze the situation of those considered as the most important lawyers in Chile, a significant percentage of them work in a kind of associative practice that has the features we have previously assigned to law firms. Now, within the associative practice, some of them resemble the big US firms (although the size is quite smaller), others want to be like the US firms and others are rather *boutiques.*[20] What is relevant is that, at least in relation to the lawyers considered in this study, the individual practice or in communities under the same roof seems to be in withdrawal choosing a more structured organization.[21]

The available data from the Law Directory of Martindale-Hubbell provide an idea of the evolution of the main firms since 1970 in relation to their size (Chart 4.2).

The second part of this chapter explores the features of this kind of associative practice.

Chilean Law Firms: A Radiography

Some Methodological Questions

There are no universal specific criteria to classify firms by relevance, nor to define the limit from which they should be regarded as big firms. In the US, the main indicator to classify the firms is the amount of their annual income (which considers, e.g., the ranking of *The American Lawyer*), but the number of lawyers that are part of a firm is also used (is the criterion used by Law360). As noted, there is no consensus on the threshold for discriminating firms, and *The American Lawyer* produces two rankings: the AmLaw 100 and the AmLaw 200. The *Thomson Reuters Peer Monitor* considers 130 firms in its database and Law360 ranks 400 law firms.

The difficulty is even greater in the case of Chile since there is no public and equivalent information on revenues, costs and profits of law firms.

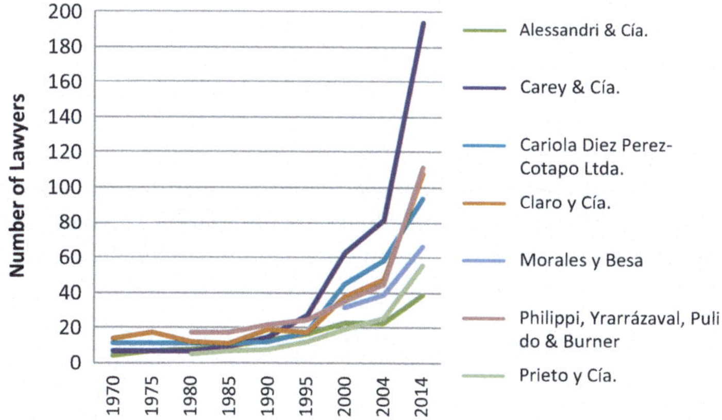

Chart 4.2 Evolution of the main Chilean law firms. Source: For data from 1970 to 2000: Martindale-Hubbell Law Directory. For 2004 data: Universidad Diego Portales (2004). For 2014 data: information taken from the relevant law firms' websites

Given that there is a widespread perception that certain firms of a rather modest size get high levels of profitability ("boutiques"), we had to find another standard of comparison, different from revenue or the number of lawyers, to define the scope of our study. The standard of comparison that we chose was the ranking or registry of the most prestigious lawyers—the "elite lawyers"—in the region, that is, *Chambers Latin America*.

There are 78 law firms in Chile mentioned in *Chambers and Partners*. Appendix 1 of this chapter shows the list of the firms.

In the first stage, the study focused on analyzing quantitative information of the firms that could be taken directly from their websites. Specifically, data on the number of lawyers of each firm, categories of the lawyers (partners and associates), gender distribution in the different categories of lawyers, universities of origin and postgraduate studies. Additionally, information was also gathered regarding the areas of professional practice and the languages of the websites. The information is updated to June 2, 2014. Of the 78 firms considered, 6 were excluded for lack of information in the web site. Thus, the universe of firms analyzed from their websites was 72.

The second part of the study consisted of semi-structured one-hour interviews of *senior partners* and/or managing partners of 20 firms. The list of law firms and partners interviewed are listed in Appendix 2.

The purpose of the aforementioned interviews was to obtain a more detailed information on the following issues: (a) firm governance (how and who makes decisions about the organization and functioning of the firm, level of professional management and role of the administrative structure, number and responsibility of non-legal professionals); (b) structure and change of position (optimal size of the firm, criteria to change position from associate to partner, degree of formalization of these criteria, gender aspects); (c) clients (type, ways to gain clients and relationships with them); and (d) future of the profession in Chile (current market behavior, perspectives and perceived threats and, specifically, its internationalization).

Law Firms, Lawyers, Clients and Competitors

Law Firms

(a) Size. Although law firms have increased in number over the last decades in Chile, they are still small when compared to the US or British firms as well as with some other Latin American countries.[22]

Moreover, it is worth noting that, as shown in Table 4.1, not only is the maximum number of lawyers comparatively low, but also only a very low percentage of firms exceed 80 lawyers (7%). However, the majority of the firms have less than 40 lawyers (86%) and more than 50% has less than 20 lawyers. Under these conditions, we must accept that in this chapter, the term law firm is used at Latin American scale, not US scale.

The determination of the firm size considered only the number of lawyers. The numbers change significantly if other employees of the firm are added. For example, Carey had 152 lawyers in 2013 but, in total, the staff of the company exceeded 380 persons.

In general, when asked about the size of the firms during the interviews, two comments were frequent. The first one is that the size of big firms in Chile should not increase, at least, not too much. The second comment was that firms with about 20 lawyers had thought or intended to increase their size.

Our impression is that the perception of the interviewees is that, while big firms will not grow too much in terms of the number of lawyers, there is still enough room in the market for other smaller firms to increase their size.

(b) Location. Two issues call attention in relation to the geographical location of the law firms considered. First, all the firms are all located in Santiago. None of the firms is located in a province. Second, the firms are concentrated in one zone of Santiago, most of them in east Santiago. Our perception is reinforced by a report in the journal *El Mercurio Legal*[23] according to which, the great majority of firms mentioned by Chambers & Partners are located in Las Condes (81.8%) and Providencia (6.5%) districts. The remaining percentage is located downtown Santiago, except for one firm located in Vitacura district.

(c) Partners and associates. A typical feature of law firms seems to be a hierarchical structure that distinguishes between partners and associates

Table 4.1 Firms according to the number of lawyers

Firm size	*Number of firms*	*%*
2–19 lawyers	42	58
20–39 lawyers	20	28
40–59 lawyers	2	3
60–79 lawyers	3	4
80 or more lawyers	5	7
Total	72	100

with a particular functional distribution between them.[24] When reviewing the different websites, we also find consultants and directors.[25]

The following Table 4.2 shows the percentage between partners, associates, of counsel and directors in the firms that have different lawyers' categories.

As regards partners, their asset seems to be their capacity to attract clients. The associates' asset is what may be called *leverage*. Thus, the role of the associates seems to be, at least in general, to assist the partners in the tasks entrusted to them. This explains the pyramidal structure of law firms: more associates than partners, a structure that becomes more pronounced with the increase in size of the firms. The reason for this may be that big firms tend to take care of corporate clients whose needs have been commoditized.[26] The thing is different when needs are not commoditized, which typically occurs in litigation *boutiques* that probably demand more work from the partners.

The category of partner and associate has some sub-classifications. For example, we were told that sometimes it is possible to distinguish between partners listed as such but not entitled to profit sharing and partners entitled to profit sharing. In relation to partners, particularly regarding payment for working hours (and very probably remuneration) is common to distinguish between *junior* or *senior* associates according to their experience or seniority.

Two comments can be made regarding the pyramidal and hierarchical structure of law firms. The first one relates to the degree of institutionalization of the firm, the second to the situation of associates from the perspective of the sociology of professions:

(1) The professional career. In terms of the degree of institutionalization, the most interesting question concerning the pyramidal structure of partners and associates relates to what we might call the "career" of a lawyer in the firm.

Table 4.2 Lawyers according to the category in the firm

Position	*Number of lawyers*	*%*
Partner	439	24
Associate	1,301	72
Of counsel	61	3
Director	13	1
Total	1,814	100

The interviews show a few things that should be highlighted. The first relates to what we might call the "degree of institutionalization of the career." In general, respondents expressed their agreement with the idea of an institutionalized career in the firm; however, the degree of institutionalization is highly variable. Some firms have established periods after which lawyers are assessed; others have manuals explaining the professional career and others just express their desire for some institutionalization.

Nevertheless, the interviews show some asymmetry regarding the institutionalization when income and change in category of lawyers is compared with process of leaving the firm. In the interviews, we perceived that the process of joining the firm and promotion is more rigorous than that of leaving the firm.

The process of leaving the firm is different for partners and associates. For the lawyers who do not become partners, the firms use a system that is common in many countries called *up or out*. But this mechanism is not always sufficiently institutionalized. When asked about the topic, one interviewee, a partner of one of the leading firms in Chile replied, "we inform about the process, but not directly." On the other hand, in general, the idea is to manage the process in a friendly manner since it is assumed that, in the future, the lawyer may be part of an in-house counselor at a company that may work with the firm. With respect to partners, our perception is that, although sometimes leaving the firm is structured (e.g., establishing retirement age at 65) the rule is not always observed. This probably has to do with the fact that some of the older members were the founders of the firm.

It appears that there is some correlation between the firm's size and the degree of institutionalization and the trend seems to be: the bigger the firm the higher the institutionalization degree of the career structure is and vice versa.

It is interesting to note that very often, respondents perceive this higher degree of institutionalization as one of the necessary requirements to attract talented lawyers to the firms. The idea is that these lawyers may project and predict their career in the firm from their entry. This seems to be a form of building loyalty, particularly during the first years.

During the interviews, one consideration came up often: the competition among law firms in Chile is not only for the best clients, but also for the best lawyers. And of course, access to the best lawyers requires firms to make attractive offers. An important part of this offer is the possibility to become partner.

(2) The loss of the liberal character of the legal profession. Our second comment relates to an important feature of law firms, particularly the biggest ones, in relation to the work of the associates, which implies the loss of the liberal character of the legal profession. Particularly, when you consider that one of the crucial features of liberal professions is its independence, which is understood as the control over the working conditions (Freidson 1986: 110–230). Actually, associates are more like employees performing their duties under the supervision of senior professionals and keeping a work schedule. In this sense, it seems that sociologists are not wrong when referring to the "proletarianization of the professions" (MacDonald 1995: 61–62) and the "bureaucratization of professional work" (Pavalko 1971: 180).

(d) Management of law firms. In recent years, firms have adopted more sophisticated organizational structures and responses to business needs, although the reality in the market is diverse. Some big firms have chosen more formal structures, headed by a general manager. In most cases, the general manager is not a lawyer and is experienced in engineering, or human resources, finance and accounting, communication and marketing.

On the other hand, smaller firms have a less professional organization, although the presence of other professionals with expertise in management, finance and accounting, such as business managers or accountant-auditors, is a trend that can be found in all firms.

Interviews have shown that in the case of larger firms, managerial duties are entrusted to professionals with special expertise in administration and finance. The peculiar thing is that the "client" of these professionals is the firm itself. Their job is the administration of the firm.

The presence of these professionals does not mean that the partners lose control over the administration. Although the mechanisms may vary, the partners are deeply involved in the administration of the firm. It is very common that a managing partner or administrator (not a lawyer), may be part of the board of directors of the firm. In general, the manager is subordinated to one or more lawyers and assists them in tasks that require their special expertise.

Moreover, both the number and the type of work of the administrator may vary. We have found firms with one manager and firms with a management department. Regarding the functions of a manager, the lawyer interviewed said that, in some cases, the administrator resembles a *house keeper* and, in others, they take on more complex tasks including financial issues and sophisticated administrative tasks such as the process of selection and promotion of lawyers to new categories, creation of new areas or departments in the firm, and marketing activities focused on advertising and visibility of the firm's name.

Third, once again, size matters. It seems to be an obvious correlation between the firm size and sophistication of its administration, although predominantly, the most important decisions are still made by lawyers. Management teams give a variety of assistance.

Briefly, the law firm model is not yet consolidated as company and, it is very common, even in very important firms, to find distortions caused by family relationships of partners or by the character of some of the partners.

One issue that deserves special attention about the impact on law firms' management is the incorporation of information technologies. The use of software to manage the hourly rate is now a regular feature in law firms, allowing them to improve efficiency in accounting billable hours, clients' billing and management control at the law firms. There are two software in the market that are distributed to the industry: TimeBilling developed by Lemontech and AddIn Horas developed by Tecnolex. A newer tool in the Chilean market is the legal case-tracking software, Case Tracking, developed by Lemontech, which allows case processing from the office or mobile devices. This technology has led to significant savings for lawyers.

(e) Other professionals in the law firms. A look at the firms' websites shows that there are not only lawyers, business managers and accountants, but also other professionals, intuitively at least, unconnected to law. Thus, as shown in Table 4.3, it is possible to find civil, chemical and pharmaceutical engineers, biochemists, journalists, and so on.[27]

(f) Clerks and paralegals. The firms not only hire lawyers and other professionals but also law students generally called "attorneys in fact" who carry out auxiliary tasks for lawyers. Because law students who are attorneys in fact have time constraints due to school, law firms also hire paralegals. Paralegals are persons with some kind of technical training in law who carry out tasks similar to those of the attorneys in fact.

(g) Areas of practice and services. The vast majority of the firms studied deal with all kinds of issues related to the company and its line of business, what is commonly known as "corporate issues."

Table 4.3 Professions in the law firms

Profession	*Men*	*%*	*Women*	*%*	*Total*	*%*
Chemistry and Pharmacy	2	4.3	6	12.8	7	14.9
Civil Engineer	6	12.8	0	0.0	6	12.8
Business	2	4.3	4	8.5	6	12.8
Accountant	4	8.5	2	4.3	6	12.8
Ing. Civil Mecánico	5	10.6	0	0.0	5	10.6
Bioquimica	1	2.1	3	6.4	4	8.5
Chemical Engineer	1	2.1	2	4.3	3	6.4
Mechanical Engineer	0	0.0	2	4.3	2	4.3
Bio technology	1	2.1	1	2.1	2	4.3
Bachelor of Arts	1	2.1	0	0.0		2.1
Architect	1	2.1	0	0.0		2.1
Civil Industrial Engineer	1	2.1	0	0.0		2.1
Journalist	0	0.0	1	2.1		2.1
Civil Constructor	1	2.1	0	0.0		2.1
TOTAL	26	55.3	21	44.7	47	100

On the whole, two types of firms can be distinguished given the areas of practice and the type of service they offer. On the one hand, there are *full-service* firms that intend to provide a wide variety of services to their clients ranging from consultancy on corporate and real estate matters, to issues of intellectual property and natural resources, including civil litigation and, in some cases, criminal litigation in these areas.[28] From the interviews, we concluded the only area that law firms exclude is family law. Such matters are referred to specialized lawyers.

Furthermore, we find the *specialized firms or boutiques* that deal with specialized issues or offer a specific service. In these kinds of firms, we find the *litigation boutiques* which exclusive service consists of representing clients in sophisticated litigation. But we also find boutiques that are devoted exclusively to intellectual property, trademarks, competition, tax issues, insurance, real estate, environmental issues, mining, family matters, and telecommunications, among others.

Through the interviews and from the review of the websites, we can conclude that the most frequent areas of practice of the selected firms are corporate, financial and real estate law. Moreover, when interviewees where asked about the areas they had developed more intensely in recent years, they pointed out regulatory, natural resources and, more marginally, intellectual property issues.

An issue that came up repeatedly during the interviews is something that could be called "commodification of legal services."[29] For example, we were told that issues such as the American depositary receipt (ADRs) placement or articles of incorporation, among many others, which were considered services that required a lawyer with special expertise and knowledge, today are considered as fungible goods that can be obtained in any law firm devoted to that area.

The respondents considered the progressive commodification of legal services as relevant, since in this type of service the competition is not exactly for the quality of the services or the prestige of the lawyers. Law firms are fungible with each other, and what really matters (and determines the most advantageous position among competitors) is the market price of these legal services that has dropped significantly.

(h) Payment method. The hourly payment is the usual payment method of big firms: they charge the clients the hours effectively worked in each case.[30] Thus, under this scheme, the invoice details the hours worked by each lawyer multiplied by the hour rate. The trend shows that the use of a cap is increasingly required by clients to avoid excessive billings. The *retainer fee*, that is, a fixed monthly rate, is still the payment method in some firms, but appears to be in retreat, which could go hand in hand with a decline in consultancy services like "family lawyer or firm" that takes care of all of the client's issues. On litigation, the *contingent fee* or *cuota litis* is the general rule, where an initial payment is determined, or payment at each procedural stage plus a premium for the result. Finally, it is possible to find the *flat-fee* payment method, usually related to a specific task, which may be deferred until the task is finished or paid in installments over the period.

(i) Internationalization. Morgan (2010: 83–91) offers some persuasive pages to explain why globalization has affected the activity of lawyers. No need to reproduce his reasoning here, particularly because the impact of globalization on an important US law firm is different from the impact of globalization on an important Chilean firm. Perhaps, we may resort to an unpretentious label: internationalization. And by that, we basically mean that firms—although with different emphasis—direct their services toward foreign clients.[31]

Regarding the supply of services to foreign clients, what is probably most applicable to Chilean lawyers is that some of the important clients, in economic terms, are foreigners requiring lawyers who could understand them, not only in terms of the language.[32] But language can be a good *proxy* of internationalization. As shown in Table 4.4, on the websites of the firms a high percentage of lawyers seem to speak at least one foreign language, English being the most common. According to the information provided on the websites of the firms, 1690 lawyers out of 1866 report to master a language other than Spanish (90%), English being the most common foreign language with almost 85%.

Another proxy of the level of internationalization can be found in those law firms offering their websites in more than one language. Table 4.5 shows that most firms have their website in Spanish and English (97%), and just a few have included the information in other languages.

The presence of international firms in Chile is an important issue. During the interviews, we only heard about Baker & Mackenzie and rather vaguely, a possible merger between Phillipi, Irarrázabal, Pulido & Brunner.[33] However, in general, interviewees noted that competition with international firms was almost nonexistent in Chile and hence, not perceived as a threat. However, this statement should be taken with caution. Of course, the Phillipi merge changes the law firms market in Chile. But it is not the only movement. The newspaper *El Mercurio* (November 3, 2014) reported that Ontier, a Spanish firm, plans to settle in Chile during 2015.[34] Moreover, Ecija, another Spanish firm specialized in technology mentions on its website that has an office in Chile.[35]

Table 4.4 Second language mastered by lawyers

Language	*Men*	*%*	*Women*	*%*	*Total*	*%*
English	983	58.17	444	20.27	1,427	84.44
French	94	5.56	32	1.89	126	7.46
German	36	2.13	28	1.66	64	3.79
Italian	22	1.30	7	0.41	29	1.72
Portuguese	14	0.83	5	0.30	19	1.12
Hebrew	7	0.41	6	0.36	13	0.77
Dutch	1	0.06	2	0.12	3	0.18
Chinese	2	0.12	0	0.00	2	0.12
Russian	0	0.00	2	0.12	2	0.12
Arabic	1	0.06	1	0.06	2	0.12
Norwegian	0	0.00	1	0.06	1	0.06
Wolof	1	0.06	0	0.00	1	0.06
Croatian	0	0.00	1	0.06	1	0.06
Total	1,161	68.70	529	31.30	1,690	100

Table 4.5 Language of the websites

Website language	*Number of firms*	*%*
Spanish	67	100
English	65	97
German	6	9
French	4	6
Portuguese	3	4
Japanese	2	3
Chinese	3	4
Italian	3	4
Hebrew	1	1

(j) The firm's "culture." In some of the interviews, both lawyers and managers referred to something rather vaguely called the "culture" of the firm. Thus, for example, when asked about the difference between one firm and an equivalent one in terms of size and organization, they said: "the culture of the office," what seems to mean a kind of hallmark of the firm.

Two anecdotes told by one of the lawyers interviewed trying to illustrate the culture of the firms may help explain the concept. The first relates to a merger between two firms. One of the partners asked for a cup of tea and considered unacceptable that it was not served by a uniformed waiter and in chinaware as it was before the merge. The urban legend goes that this has caused the merge to fail. The second anecdote also relating to a merger refers to two important firms that were trying to reach an agreement on their clients and all the economic aspects. However, the merge failed because they did not reach agreement on the order of names on the letterhead and the location where they would establish.

Lawyers

Who are the lawyers working in the main Chilean firms? To address this question, we have considered the following issues: (a) how lawyers are accepted in the firms and (b) who are they, specifically the composition of the members in terms of gender, undergraduate and graduate studies institutions, and membership of the Bar.

(a) Admission. Joining a law firm as lawyer may take place immediately after graduation from a law school or later. In the first case, interviews and other sources of information[36] showed that, in general, one of the most important aspects considered in the selection of a recently graduated lawyer are their academic grades. We were told, repeatedly, that firms are only interested in students who are among the best of their generation. In a couple of cases, we were told that if the candidate was a graduate from Universidad Católica or Universidad de Chile, the firm considers the 20% of the best graduates. With regards to other universities, the standard dropped to 10%. Other firms do make these distinctions. We also were told that it could be important that the applicant had been an attorney in fact of the firm. Another important aspect that seems to be relevant in the decision process is the English language proficiency.

The second possibility for entry into the firm is what might be called "lateral hiring," that is, hiring lawyers who already have some experience. The information we have regarding this type of entry is rather vague, a kind of anecdote. Having said that, the comments we heard is that this type of recruitment is disruptive for those who are "working their way up" in the firm, so it is not a frequent entry way but rather takes place when a new area is going to be open in the firm which is not possible to fill with lawyers currently working in the firm.[37]

(b) Who are the lawyers? We should start by circumscribing this question. We obtained information mainly from the websites that answers three things. The first one relates to the gender of lawyers, the second to the educational level and, the third one to the membership of the bar.

(1) Gender. In aggregate numbers, we find 1,866 lawyers. Of these, 1273 are men (68%) and 593 women (32%). If we break down these numbers and make a distinction between partners and associates, we find that, regarding associates, 744 (59%) are men and 512 (41%) are women; whereas, with respect to partners, the numbers change dramatically, where 94% (403) are men and only 6% (25) are women. Table 4.6 shows a breakup according to gender.[38]

Interviewees explained that it was not surprising that the numbers were similar for associates because, in their opinion, this relates to the integration of law schools. They were not surprised either about the disparity regarding partners. They explained that, while both male and female lawyers began under the relatively same conditions, women were affected by family issues, particularly motherhood, which prevented them from competing on equal grounds with men.[39]

(2) We got information on academic background of 1,571 lawyers. In total, 1,552 (99%) completed their undergraduate studies in Chile, as shown in the following Table 4.7.

Table 4.6 Lawyers according to gender

Gender	*Number of lawyers*	*%*
Lawyers		
Women	593	32
Men	1,273	68
Total	1,866	100
Associates		
Women	512	41
Men	744	59
Total	1,256	100
Partners		
Women	25	6
Men	403	94
Total	428	100

Our second finding is that a significant percentage of lawyers come from Pontificia Universidad Católica and Universidad de Chile. Of the 1,552 lawyers, 1177 (75.83%) completed their graduate studies at one of these law schools (Table 4.8).

These schools are the oldest and most prestigious law schools. A good question is why there is so much of a difference between them. Both are probably equally prestigious and, in general, the law school of Universidad de Chile requires entry scores slightly higher than those of the Pontificia Universidad Católica de Santiago.

Table 4.7 Lawyers according to the country where they completed their undergraduate studies

Country	*Men*	*%*	*Women*	*%*	*Total*	*%*
Chile	1,036	99.42	516	97.54	1,552	98.79
Spain	2	0.19	5	0.95	7	0.45
Canada	1	0.10	1	0.19	2	0.13
USA	0	0.00	2	0.38	2	0.13
Germany	1	0.10	0	0.00		0.06
Argentina	0	0.00	1	0.19		0.06
Brazil	0	0.00	1	0.19		0.06
France	1	0.10	0	0.00		0.06
The Netherlands	1	0.10	0	0.00		0.06
Colombia	0	0.00	2	0.38	2	0.13
Venezuela	0	0.00	1	0.19	1	0.06
Total	1,042	100	529	100	1,571	100

Table 4.8 Lawyers according to universities where they completed their undergraduate studies

University	*Men*	*%*	*Women*	*%*	*Total*	*%*
PUC Chile	433	41.8	220	43.0	653	42.07
U. de Chile	357	34.5	167	32.6	524	33.76
U. de los Andes	74	7.1	40	7.8	114	7.35
U. Diego Portales	42	4.1	34	6.6	76	4.90
U. Adolfo Ibañez	23	2.2	16	3.1	39	2.51
U. Gabriela Mistral	28	2.7	6	1.2	34	2.19
PUC Valparaíso	15	1.4	4	0.8	19	1.22
U. de Concepción	11	1.1	8	1.6	19	1.22
U. de Valparaíso	11	1.1	2	0.4	13	0.84
UAI (Viña del Mar)	5	0.5	7	1.4	12	0.77
U. Finis Terrae	9	0.9	1	0.2	10	0.64
U. Andres Bello	6	0.6	2	0.4	8	0.52
U. Austral	3	0.3	3	0.6	6	0.39
U. del Desarrollo	6	0.6	0	0.0	6	0.39
U. Central	6	0.6	0	0.0	6	0.39
U. de las Americas	0	0.0	2	0.4	2	0.13
U. de Taka	0	0.0	2	0.4	2	0.13
U. de la república	2	0.2	0	0.0	2	0.13
U. Alberto Hurtado	1	0.1	1	0.2	2	0.13
U. Bolivariana	0	0.0	1	0.2		0.06
UC del Norte	1	0.1	0	0.0		0.06
USACH	1	0.1	0	0.0		0.06
U. Santo Tomás	1	0.1	0	0.0		0.06
U. SEK	1	0.1	0	0.0		0.06
Total	1,036	100	516	100	1,552	100

A third aspect that is interesting to note is that there are three very prestigious law schools located in the provinces: Pontificia Universidad Católica de Valparaíso, Universidad de Concepción and Universidad de Valparaíso, which are located under some other universities that are less prestigious. Probably personal networks explain these differences.

(3) There is an increasing number of lawyers' with higher studies of law in Chile or abroad. This is particularly important when it comes to postgraduate studies abroad, something that is highly valued in the market due to the international networks that may be established, command of a second language (mainly English) and the ability to deal with multinational clients or attorneys of foreign firms. Table 4.9 shows the number of lawyers with a Diploma course, Master's degree or PhD.

Table 4.9 Lawyers with postgraduate studies

Graduate studies	*Number of lawyers*
Diploma	389
Master's	590
PhD	33

When asked about the country and the university where they completed the Master's degree course, the results show that most lawyers preferred to continue their studies in the US (46%) followed by Chile (30%), as shown in the Table 4.10.

In the interviews, we asked about how important it was for lawyers to have a postgraduate qualification from a foreign university. The answer, in general, was that programs could be academically interesting, but certainly the most valuable for a firm was that its associates worked in foreign firms, particularly US firms. Table 4.11 shows the 15 leading universities.

Clients

Concerning clients we considered three different aspects: (a) how firms advertise their services; (b) how clients come to the firms; and (c) who the clients are.

Table 4.10 Countries where lawyers completed their Master's degree

Country	*Number of lawyers*	*%*
USA	272	46.1
Chile	181	30.7
England	45	7.6
Spain	41	6.9
Germany	15	2.5
France	11	1.9
Australia	10	1.7
The Netherlands	4	0.7
Scotland	3	0.5
Canada	1	0.2
Argentina	1	0.2
China	1	0.2
Finland	1	0.2
Italy	1	0.2
South Africa	1	0.2
Sweden	1	0.2
Uruguay	1	0.2
Total	590	100

Table 4.11 Main universities where lawyers completed their Master's degree

University	*Country*	*Number of lawyers*	*%(*)*
Universidad Adolfo Ibáñanez	Chile	55	9.3
Universidad de Chile	Chile	52	8.8
New York University	USA	36	6.1
P.U. Católica de Chile	Chile	34	5.8
Duke University	USA	34	5.8
University of Chicago	USA	26	4.4
Columbia University	USA	25	4.2
Universidad de los Andes	Chile	24	4.1
University of California at Berkeley	USA	21	3.6
Northwestern University	USA	21	3.6
Harvard University	USA	19	3.2
London School of Economics	UK	18	3.1
American University	USA	15	2.5
Georgetown University	USA	12	2.0
Heidelberg University	Alemania	8	1.4

(a) Advertising. Article 13 of the former Code of Ethics of the Bar provided the following: "Any advertising directly or indirectly produced by the lawyer of the firm for profit or compliment of his own situation, undermines the traditional dignity of the profession." Things—including the traditional dignity of the profession—have changed. For now, the vast majority of firms considered in this study have a website that advertises their services.

The interviews showed that, at least in big firms, the presence of a journalist and in some cases a communications team in charge of the image and promotion of the firm is relatively frequent.

The interviewees reacted with some discomfort when asked how they advertised their services (perhaps a remnant of the "traditional dignity") and, in general, restricted it to their website and *brochures* or some kind of printed material. Sometimes, we were told that another advertising material consisted of *newsletters* or updated reports on topics of professional interest. Finally, we were also told that another advertising mechanism especially important with respect to foreign clients was to attend events organized by Bars abroad and make presentations on topics of their expertise.

Rankings, especially the ones included in this chapter, are extremely important for the firms.

Eventually, in terms of how customers come to the firm, the answer used to be related to the prestige of the firm or being referred by other customers.

(b) Tenders. The interviews revealed a kind of clients' sophistication. Traditionally clients and lawyers did not discuss fees.[40] That image seems to be fading. We were told that it is common that clients invite firms to bid in a more or less formal way, the provision of some legal services.

According to respondents, making the firms bid against each other in a beauty contest of sorts shows that the market has become more complex in terms that it has become much more competitive. We can add two comments. The first one is that—paraphrasing Anthony Kronman—there is a feeling that law has become a business like any other (1993: 370), and this should have some impact on the way the legal system regards the lawyers. The second refers to the possibility that the clients may exercise control over lawyers like in other places, seems to have increased, at least for the most important Chilean firms.[41]

(c) Who are the clients? The respondents frequently distinguished between more or less permanent clients (kind of clients' portfolio) and those who are occasional. A high percentage of clients are legal entities, not natural persons.[42] Heinz & Luhman's point out the increased importance of corporations as lawyers' clients applies to Chile. Natural persons generally entrust their issues to a more individual type of legal practice.[43]

Clients are in the vast majority private, not public entities. In the interviews, we did not find firms working predominantly for public agencies. Foreign companies are also frequent clients.

A Conclusion: Law Firms and the Big Law Future in Chile

As we have seen, the legal profession has experienced an impressive growth in recent years in the country. In parallel, the law firms have also increased significantly in number and size. Despite this huge expansion, the rate of lawyers and magnitude of the firms continues to be somewhat lower than that of other countries in the region and countries with similar level of development, but the existing gaps have been gradually reduced.

Will this development continue into the future? In our opinion, the answer must be put into context. On one hand, it appears that Galanter and Palay (1991: 31) are right when they say that in a Darwinian sense, legal forms are a success.[44] However, on the other hand, it appears that growth will slow down. The situation that gave rise to this phenomenon (a highly concentrated and elitist legal profession, with a volume and level of sophistication that was not in line with the size and economic development of the country) is a thing of the past. Today, our law market is much more settled and significantly more competitive.

The natural consequence of these higher levels of competition has been a downward trend in prices associated with legal services, or at least some of them. New dynamics have contributed to what we have already highlighted, as the award of certain standardized legal services put to tender and the internalization of some of the tasks previously entrusted to external firms into the company inspector's office. The lack of transparent information precludes a definitive judgment of the above, but various signs show that the profit margins of the biggest law firms in Chile have shrank and, most likely, the trend will continue.[45] This process has also contributed to a steady increase in operating costs of the firms and the financial burden of the same.

The growth strategy of the most successful firms, in most cases,[46] followed the model of structured firms where the work of a significant number of associates allows the firm to take care of clients and complex cases, maximizing the work of partners and, incidentally, profits. This model puts pressure on the steady growth of firms: associates should have the certainty that at least some of them will become partners, leading to a permanent increase in the number of the same; and new partners require more associates to produce the *leverage* needed to implement the model. This can generate idle capacity, what could be useful in any case, to take care of big businesses and prevent the entry of new competitors, but that is necessary to finance. To a large extent, the fact that all firms are now participating in tenders could be explained by the need to occupy this idle capacity.

Although we cannot rule out the emergence of new structured firms, it is likely that the number of these firms is close to reaching a balance in the country, so sudden changes in sector are not expected. Naturally, there is always the possibility, as it has happened in the past, that some of the consolidated firms enter into a declining phase or split up. The crises faced by some law firms in Chile are mainly the result of improper management of the expansion process (or, in other words, of the incentives for its members) or because of personal relationship problems and expectations of the partners.

No structural threats to the system under which these firms operate in Chile are envisaged, at least in the medium term. Unlike what is currently happening in the United States, the current economic situation in the country has been rather beneficial for law firms and no dramatic changes are expected beyond the economic slowdown in the country. The absence of a great economic contingency makes it unlikely that some movement may occur in terms of the demand for legal services seeking to introduce major changes regarding the way they are offered and, above all, financed.[47]

This goes without prejudice that the hourly rate has been reduced by the processes already mentioned several times: the "CAP" or maximum rate and tender of commoditized services. It is likely that both phenomena will continue and expand in the future without questioning the model.

The stability we claim for the model of big structured firms in the country, does not mean it is fully mature in terms that it will not experience changes in how it operates. We are not discussing if the system will remain in place or not, but how. We think that the following changes may occur in the future:

(1) The full institutionalization of existing firms will be achieved when the founding partners retire, since their weight within the firms is so significant that rules are made more flexible in their favor. Presently, in many firms the age limit for partners does not apply to the founders, reducing the turnover which is basic to the operation of the model. In other firms, the founding partners have a lot of power when making key decisions, including the distribution of profits, so it is expected that the way the decisions are made will change when they are no longer in the firm.

(2) The demand of an increasing competition in the market for legal services has led firms to be more rigorous in their mechanisms of entry, promotion and personnel matters in general, since they deem the quality of services provided as one of their main competitive advantages to be displayed. But this process is not consolidated yet, because although the market values quality, it also moves by other considerations, such as social, political, family or personal affinities, resulting in the same criteria subsequently altering or playing down more objective mechanisms for entry and promotion within the firms. Otherwise we could not explain the highest proportion of graduates from Universidad Católica in the firms analyzed (43% according to the Table 4.10) compared with those from Universidad de Chile (34%), when both have similar admission requirements and graduates from the latter are far more numerous than the first one. In the future, we expect purely meritocratic criteria and, therefore, more plural and heterogeneous composition of the firms.

(3) We said that all structured firms are made up of a team of professionals responsible for management issues. However, the authority that managers have now is limited. It is rather technical support to management that, in essence, remains under the control of the partners or some of them. The capacity of intervention for these managers in the most relevant decisions (e.g., those concerning the professional career of the members), are limited. This also must change in the future and it is likely to foresee that we will gradually find managers and other non-legal professionals gaining more power.
(4) Big firms are internationalized, in terms of the type of issues they deal with, which compels them to maintain fluid contacts with foreign clients doing business in Chile or vice versa and, essentially, with lawyers from other latitudes. Notwithstanding, there is still considerable room for greater integration with foreign firms in the future, a proof of which is the step taken in this direction by Philippi. The possibility that a big national firm is acquired or taken over by a foreign firm or that a foreign firm enters the Chilean market with own offices is not clear yet.

However, though they may be the most attractive, big firms do not exhaust the universe of associative practices. In Chile, the numbers indicate that they are rather few. The stability we have predicted with respect to big firms is not necessarily applicable to small ones. In general, the view of respondents is that there is room for new firms or for the existing ones to grow.

Appendix 1

Firms included in the study

Law firm	*Number of lawyers*
1 Acuña & Cía.	8
2 Albagli Zaliasnik	31
3 Alcaíno Abogados	20
4 Alessandri & Cía.	39
5 Aninat Schwencke & Cía.	34
6 Arteaga & Goziglia Cía.	16
7 Arthur, Humeres, Mejías &Toloza	0
8 Avendaño Merino Abogados	19
9 Baraona Abogados	16
10 Barros yErrázurizAsoCíados	90
11 Barros, Letelier y Gonzalez	22
12 Beuchat, Barros & Pfenninger Abogados	9
13 Boffil Mir & Alvarez Ltda.	76
14 Bulnes Urrutia & Bustamante	6
15 Carcelén, Desmadryl, Guzmán, Schaeffer &Tapia	12
16 Carey &Allende	28
17 Carey y Cía.	194
18 Cariola Diez Perez-Cotapo Ltda.	94
19 Clarke, Modet& Cía.	4
20 Claro y Cía.	108
21 Correa Gubbins	25
22 Covarrubias & Silva	3
23 Cruzat, Ortuzar & Macenna (Backer & Mc Kenzie)	43
24 Cubillos Evans	20
25 D y P Abogados, Estudio Juan Agustín Figueroa	18
26 DAC Beachcroft Chile (NO INFO]	5
27 Dalgalarrando Romero y Cía.	11
28 De Irurrizaga, Arnaiz & Cía.	9
29 Del Rio Izquierdo	9
30 EPT Tax Advisors	5
31 Estudio Carvallo	16
32 Estudio Villaseca	13
33 Etcheverry, GarCía, Bragado y Cía.	6
34 Eyzaguirre y Cía.	24
35 Fernandois & Cía.	8
36 Ferrada Nehme	36
37 Garay Guerrero	7
38 García Magliona & Cía.	12
39 Grasty Quintana Majlis & Cía.	24
40 Grupo Vial Abogados	13

Law firm	*Number of lawyers*
41 Guerrero Olivos	64
42 Hárasic & Lopez	8
43 Honorato, Russi & Eguiguren Ltda.	10
44 Jara, Del Favero & Cía. Ltda.	27
45 Johansson &Langlois	4
46 Larrain Rencoret & Urzua	17
47 Larraín y As oCíados Ltda.	37
48 Luis Lizama Portal Abogados & Cía.	10
49 Molina Rios Abogados	11
50 Morales y Besa	66
51 Noguera Larrain & Dulanto	20
52 Nuñez Muñoz & Verdugo	10
53 Ovalle Ugarte & Letelier	6
54 Palma Abogados	20
55 Pellegrini & Cía.	5
56 Philippi, Yrarrazával, Pulido & Burner	112
57 Porzio, Rios &Asociados	12
58 Prieto y Cía.	56
59 PugaMir	2
60 Puga Ortiz	38
61 Reymond & Fleischmann	14
62 Rodríguez, Vergaray Cía Abogados.	5
63 Sargent & Krahn	14
64Silva&Cía.	12
65 Urenda, Rencorret, Orrego, Dörr	20
66 Uribe, Hubner & Canales	29
67 Urrutia&Cía.	26
68 Vergara & Cía.	10
69 Vergara Galindo Correa Abogados	19
70 Vergara, Labarca & Cía.	7
71 Yrarrazaval, Ruiz-Tagle, Goldenberg, Lagos & Silva	20

Appendix 2

Persons interviewed

Law firm	*Interviewed*
Albagli Zaliasnik	Rodrigo Albagli [partner]
Aninat Schwencke & Cía.	Luis Alberto Aninat [partner]
Arteaga Gorziglia & Cía.	Ignacio Arteaga [partner]
Avendaño Merino Abogados	Luis Felipe Merino [partner]
Barros & Errázuriz	Fernando Barros y Cristián Barros (partners]
Carcelén, Desmadryl, Guzmán, Schaeffer & Tapia	Jerónimo Carcelén [partner]
Carey y Cia	Jaime Carey (partner]
Cariola, Diez, Pérez-Cotapo & Cía.	José Luis Letelier [partner]
Claro & Cía	José María Eyzaguirre (partner]
Correa Gubbins	Juan Ignacio Correa [partner]
Cubillos & Evans	Gonzalo Cubillos [partner]
Del Rio Izquierdo	Humberto Del Rio [partner]
Guerrero Olivos	Roberto Guerrero del Río (partner]
Harasic & López	Iván Harasic [partner]
Morales & Besa	Eugenio Besa (partner]
Nuñez Muñoz Verdugo	PatriCía Nuñez (partner]
Philippi, Yrarrázaval, Pulido & Burner	Camilo Jiménez [CEO]
Prieto & Cía.	Alberto González (partner]
Urrutia & Cía.	Alejandra Pérez [partner]

Notes

1. By "communities under the same roof" we mean groups of lawyers who share a physical space and its expenditures (e.g., rent, bills, administratives, etc.) but they are not organized as a company.
2. The lawyers' offices were call *estudios jurídicos.*
3. Carey website available at http://carey.cl/nuestro-estudio/historia/
4. For example, Claro & Cía., in 1880, Cariola, Diez, Pérez-Cotapos & Cía. in 1889, Phillipi, Yrarrázabal, Pulido and Brunner in 1904, Sargent and Krahn in 1899, and Estudio Arturo Alessandri in 1893.
5. It is probably a good indicator that from 1851 to 1952, 19 of the 20 democratically elected presidents of the Republic had a degree in Law. For his part, Eyzaguirre (1973: 406) refers to the great participation of lawyers in public posts and Galdames (1937: 128) points out that "The whole government was in the hands of lawyers." Although this is an exaggeration,

the truth is that their presence was hegemonic. The number of parliamentarians is probably a good indicator. Marcella (1973: 87) points out that from 1834 to 1888 there was 782 parliamentarians. The author could determine the profession of 226 of them: 186 were lawyers, 26 engineers and 14 physicians.

6. Part of the description seems to be comparable to any country in the world of that time.
7. National Service of Statistics and Census (1952).
8. As per the web site of the School (http://www.juridicasysociales.udec.cl/?page=historia): The origin of the law degree goes back to the year 1830, when the President of the so called "Instituto Literario" in Concepción, together with other professors of the Instituto Nacional, started a course of civil law in Concepción, through public enrolment. The teaching of law continued in the same Instituto Literario, subsequently named "Liceo de Hombres de Concepción," until the Curso Fiscal de Leyes de Concepción is created by Decree 753, dated May 5, 1865, which first classes began at the end of the same month.
9. Although the School of Law of the Pontificia Universidad Católica de Valparaíso was established in 1894 as Curso de Leyes de la Congregación de los Sagrados Corazones de Valparaíso, it became part of the University just in 1947.
10. As per the website of the School (http://www.derechouv.cl/portal/?page_id=51): Although the School of Law of the Universidad de Valparaíso was established in 1911 under the name "Curso de Leyes de la ciudad de Valparaíso," the first reference may be found in the Course of Law rendered in 1878 at the Liceo de Hombres de Valparaíso, presided by Eduardo de la Barra, whose name was given to such educational institution.
11. Ver http://www.cse.cl/ASP/WEB_CSEestad_resultado.asp?i4_especial. Last visited December 20, 2004.
12. Data from the website of the Consejo Nacional de Educación regarding university programs which allow getting a degree on law. *See* http://www.eligecarrera.cl/buscadores/formularios/index.aspx#/Carreras. Last visited November 12, 2014.
13. In Chile, the professional qualification to practice law is granted by the Supreme Court as established by the Código Orgánico de Tribunales, Title XV.
14. According to the Report on Justice in the Americas 2006–2007 (p. 569) the relative number of lawyers in Chile was 114 in 2006.
15. For Aníbal Pinto, the lawyers acted as intermediaries between foreign investors who controlled saltpeter and the state (quoted in Urzúa 1992: 173). Peña says that investors and the new businessmen of the nineteenth century contributed to consolidate the liberal characteristics of the profession in that period.

16. Another important piece of information provided by the lawyer Fernando Barros in a seminar organized by El Mercurio, 27 October in Santiago, refers to the boom of litigations during the 1960s and 1970s as a result of the expropriations.
17. For a documented description of the economic transformations introduced during the military government in Chile, see Meller 1998; Ffrench-Davis and Stallings 2001; Larrain and Vergara 2000.
18. We do not refer to the social prestige but that one within the legal profession. We do not have information about the law firms' prestige in Chile. We need to be cautious when considering the social prestige of law firms. A study by Michael Asimow about the way how law firms are shown in the movies, quoted by Galanter (2006: 1438), states that they are shown as "The embodiment of evil." As Asimow says:

    > Big firms are money machines run by greedy old men that eat their Young, are horrible places to work for halfway decent human beings. In conducing litigation, big firms always deploy their superior resources to unfairly thwart rightful claims brought by their adversaries. Big firms are always on the wrong side –generally that of the vicious corporations rather than the deserving plaintiff.
19. A classic study of the individual practice of the profession and in small firms in Jerome Carlin… As regards the communities under the same roof, although it is true that some use a name that is useful for the lawyers, it is what Falcao (1988: 428) has called *de facto* firms; that is, groups of lawyers that are not organized as companies.
20. The boutiques are firms that center their work in a specific area. For example, firms devoted to intellectual property, energy, environment, taxes or lawsuit. These are firms of highly specialized lawyers who provide a sophisticated service to their clients what is reflected in the work load and fees, generally higher than big firms or *full service*. Boutiques are characterized by an inverted pyramidal structure where the partner/associate ratio may be 1:1 or even 2:1.
21. In the interviews, lawyers and managers frequently said that according to them, the US Law Firm model had come to stay.
22. Baker & McKenzie, the biggest global firm has more than 4,200 lawyers. In the US, there are more than 20 firms with more than 1,000 lawyers and 250 firms that exceed the number of lawyers of Carey, the main Chilean firm. In Europe, the situation is not so different. The British firm Clifford Chance LLP has about 3,400 lawyers. Garrigues, the biggest Spanish and European firm exceeds 1,300 lawyers and there is an important number of firms that have more than 200 lawyers. At a regional level, *Marval, O'Farrell & Mairal* in Argentina has more than 250 lawyers; *Machado, Meyer, Sendacz e Opice*, in Brasil, has 350 lawyers; *Brigad & Urrutia* in Colombia has more than 150 lawyers; and *Muñiz, Ramirez, Pérez-Taiman & Olaya* in Peru exceeds 250 lawyers.

23. *El Mercurio Legal*, no 6, August 2014, pp. 56–59.
24. Related literature is abundant, it can be consulted. Gilson and Mnookin (1985), Galanter and Palay (1991), Kordana (1995), Wilkins and Gulati (1998), Galanter and Henderson (2008).
25. Their functions are not described in the websites. We think that this category is not so clear as partners and associates.
26. For a comparative analysis of commodification and standardization of legal services, see Engel (1977).
27. It is important to point out that the table was prepared with the information published on the websites. The interviews showed that data are not as accurate as expected. So, there is no doubt that journalists are underrepresented.
28. It is interesting to see that, at least the biggest firms are gradually developing the area of criminal law that historically was more restricted to the individual practice or to *boutiques*.
29. In Law, the term "commodification" may be used in very sophisticated contexts—see, for instance Radin (1996) and Smith (2009); however, the use we make of term in this paper is unpretentious. We just mean that some legal services, which used to be considered traditional and complex, today are regarded as standard commodities which demand depends exclusively on their price.
30. Rates are normally set in UF (Unidad de Fomento) for national clients and USD or Euros for international clients.
31. We think (we have no hard data to support this) that the internationalization may be expressed in another manner. The expansion of some Chilean economic groups to other countries in the region, has probably led entrepreneurs to entrust Chilean lawyers the legal organization of their business abroad. However, as far as we know, the Chilean law firms have no subsidiaries abroad as US or European firms do. Nevertheless—as in the case of Philippi—some of them reached good or *best friends agreements*.
32. One of the lawyers interviewed who work in a firm that characterizes by the high number of foreign clients, said that in the next trip to US, he would divert from the route to visit the area where the factories of one of his main clients are located. Not because he had to visit him but because he wanted to understand where the client was coming from and his business.
33. Later, specifically September 9, an announcement was made on the press about the merge with a Colombian firm (Prietocarrizosa) as of January 1, 2015 and partnership with a Spanish firm (Uría). *See* CincoDias (http://cincodias.com/cincodias/2014/09/09/economia/1410287241_309394.html) on September 10, 2014 reported it in the following way:

    "Los despachos de abogados Philippi (Chile) y Prietocarrizosa (Colombia), dos de las firmas amigas de Uría Menéndez, han anun-

ciado su fusión en lo que supone la primera unión de dos firmas líderes en sus países que se produce en Latinoamérica. Además, Uría Menéndez ha tomado una participación del 30% en la firma resultante. La fusión de las dos firmas latinoamericanas y la participación de Uría Menéndez convierten al nuevo despacho en la primera gran firma iberoamericana de abogados.
nueva firma empezará a operar el 1 de enero de 2015 bajo el nombre de Philippi, Prieto Carrizosa & Uría y contará con 220 abogados y oficinas propias en Santiago (Chile), Bogotá y Barranquilla (Colombia). Además, se beneficiará de la aportación que ofrecen los 530 abogados y las sedes de Uría Menéndez en Latinoamérica, Estados Unidos, Europa y Asia. Las responsabilidades ejecutivas se delegarán en un comité de Dirección formado por seis socios, que contará con un Senior Partner y un Managing Partner.
Se trata de la primera fase de un proyecto que responde al interés de las empresas de Europa, Asia y Norteamérica en los países que conforman la Alianza del Pacífico (Chile, Colombia, México y Perú). El auge de dicha alianza, que se configura ya como la octava economía del mundo, pone de manifiesto el potencial de crecimiento de los países que la conforman, que aúnan sus esfuerzos desde hace algunos años en beneficio de una integración económica. Estos cambios promueven a su vez la oportunidad de que las firmas de abogados ofrezcan sus servicios en ese marco transnacional. Por ello, la vocación futura es la de crecer hacia otros mercados, como Perú y México, y caminar hacia una integración plena con Uría Menéndez."

34. See http://diario.elmercurio.com/2014/11/03/economia_y_negocios/economia_y_negocios/noticias/21F4D9D5-E692-46DE-A9A1-CBD7B2CCD5DC.htm?id={21F4D9D5-E692-46DE-A9A1-CBD7B2CCD5DC}. Last visited 04/11/14.
35. See http://www.ecija.com/oficinas/santiago-de-chile/. Last visited November 4, 2014.
36. The three of us are professors at the School of Law of Universidad Diego Portales and one is the Dean of the same. In 2014, we had a course and invited different partners of the main Law Firms and, one of the topics of interest was to know how they selected the lawyers.
37. It is important to clarify that this comment is significant for the firms where lawyers can really work their way up. As we said, this is more the case in big firms. Therefore, our impression is that this comment is only applicable to them, as long as the career is institutionalized.
38. It is worth pointing out that all websites differentiate between partners and associates.

39. Another reason argued was that it is not uncommon that women accompany their couples to postgraduate courses they take abroad, after which it is difficult for them to resume their duties at the workplace.
40. One of the anecdotes we were told is that of a football team who during the 1980s met with one of the most important Chilean lawyers to discuss an issue regarding image rights. After the meeting and hiring the services of the lawyer, someone asked them how much the lawyer had charged. The answer was that they didn't dare to ask.
41. On lawyer's independence see Gordon (1988).
42. When the interviewees were asked to estimate the percentage of legal entities and natural persons they took care of, the percentage of legal entities was usually 90%.
43. Probably some precautions should be taken regarding the *boutiques* which demand is more plural.
44. Or as one of the interviewee put it: "the US model is here to stay."
45. We do not have specific data from big firms but the general income level of all the lawyers of the country is known. According to the data base of the Ministry of Education of Chile (www.mifuturo.cl), the average monthly income of a Law graduate after five years was CLP 1,726,665 in 2010 (equivalent to USD 41,440 a year at the exchange rate of that year), and CLP 1,709,343 in 2014 (equivalents to USD 34,187 a year at the exchange rate of September 2014).
46. The alternative was to set up the *boutique* law firms that work for a delimited professional niche, highly specialized, where the name of the lawyers is the most relevant aspect. The *boutique* firms, although smaller, can be highly profitable for the owners (typical of criminal cases). It is foreseeable that in the future, the greatest news will come mainly from the law firms established in this segment, and not from the structured ones.
47. There are no innovative initiatives in Chile as online legal offices or legal software.

References

Atria, Raul. 1998. La educación superior en Chile: la demanda por regulación. In *Chile en los noventa*, ed. Cristián Toloza and Lahera Eugenio. Santiago: Presidencia de la República. Dolmen Ediciones.

Aylwin, Mariana. 1999. *Chile en el siglo XX*. 9th ed. Santiago: Editorial Planeta.

Bravo Lira, Bernardino. 1992a. *La universidad en la historia de Chile, 1622–1992*. Santiago: Universidad Santo Tomas.

———. 1992b. Codificación civil en Ibero América y en la Península Ibérica. (1827–1917) Derecho nacional y europeización. In *Fuentes ideológicas y nor-*

mativas de la codificación latinoamericana, ed. A. Levaggi. Buenos Aires: Universidad del Museo Social Argentino.

———. 1998. Estudios de derecho y cultura de abogados en Chile 1758–1998: Tras la huella del ius commune, la codificación y la descodificación en el Nuevo Mundo. *Revista de Estudios Histórico-Jurídicos.* No XX. 85. Universidad Católica de Valparaíso. Ediciones Universitarias de Valparaíso.

Carey Tagle, J. 2009. *El crecimiento de las firmas de abogados en Chile: relato de una experiencia.* Escuela de Derecho, Universidad Diego Portales.

Dezalay, Yves, and B. Garth. 2002. *The internationalization of palace wars: Lawyers, economists, and the contest to transform Latin America states.* Chicago: University of Chicago Press.

Engel, David. 1977. The Standardization of Lawyers' Services. *American Bar Foundation Research Journal* 2 (4): 817–844.

Eyzaguirre, Jaime. 1973. *La Logia Lautarina y otros estudios sobre la independencia.* Buenos Aires: Editorial Francisco de Aguirre.

Falcao, Joachim. 1988. Lawyers in Brazil. In *Lawyers in Society: The Civil Law World*, ed. R. Abel and P. Lewis. Berkeley: University of California Press.

Ffrench-Davis, Ricardo, and B. Stallings, eds. 2001. *Reformas, crecimiento y políticas sociales en Chile desde 1973.* Santiago: LOM Ediciones.

Freidson, Eliot. 1986. *Professional Powers. A Study of the Institutionalization of Formal Knowledge.* Chicago: The University of Chicago Press.

Fuenzalida, Edmundo. 2003. Law and legal culture in Chile (1974–1999). In *Legal Culture in the Age of Globalization. Latin America and Latin Europe*, ed. L. Friedman and R. Pérez-Perdomo. Stanford: Stanford University Press.

Galanter, Marc. 2006. Tournament of Jokes: Generational Tension In Large Law Firms. *North Carolina Law Review* 84: 1437.

Galanter, Marc, and W. Henderson. 2008. The Elastic Tournament: A Second Transformation of the Big Law Firm. *Stanford Law Review* 60 (6): 1867–1920.

Galanter, Marc, and T. Palay. 1991. *Tournament of Lawyers. The Transformation of the Big Law Firm.* Chicago: The University of Chicago Press.

Galdames, Luis. 1937. *Valentín Letelier y su obra 1852–1919.* Santiago: Imprenta Universitaria.

Gárate, Manuel. 2012. *La revolución capitalista de Chile (1973–2003).* Santiago: Ediciones Universidad Alberto Hurtado.

Gilson, Ronald, and R. Mnookin. 1985. Sharing Among the Human Capitalists: An Economic Inquiry in to the Corporate Law Firm and How Partners Split Profits. *Stanford Law Review* 37: 313–392.

Góngora, Mario. 1981. *Ensayo histórico sobre la noción de estado en Chile en los Siglos xix y xx.* Santiago: Ediciones La Ciudad.

González Echenique, Javier. 1954. *Los estudios jurídicos y la abogacía en el Reino de Chile.* Santiago: Universidad Católica de Chile.

Gordon, Robert. 1988. The Independence of Lawyers. *Boston University Law Review* 68: 1–83.
Jocelyn-Holt, Alfredo. 1992. *La independencia de Chile.* Santiago: Editorial Mapfre.
Kordana, Kevin. 1995. Law Firms and Associate Careers. Tournament Theory Versus the Production-Imperative Model. *Yale Law Review* 104: 1907–1934.
Kronman, Anthony. 1993. *The Lost Lawyer: Failing Ideals of the Legal Profession.* Cambridge: Belknap Press of Harvard University Press.
Larrain, Felipe, and R. Vergara, eds. 2000. *La transformación económica de Chile.* Santiago: CEP.
MacDonald, Keith. 1995. *The Sociology of the Professions.* London: SAGE Publications.
Marcella, G. 1973. *The Structure of Politics in Nineteenth-Century Spanish America: The Chilean Oligarchy, 1833–1891.* Notre Dame: Department of History, Notre Dame University.
Mellafe, Rebolledo, and Mario Cárdenas. 1993. *Historia de la Universidad de Chile.* Santiago: Ediciones de la Universidad de Chile.
Meller, Patricio. 1998. *Un siglo de economía política chilena (1890–1990).* Santiago: Editorial Andrés Bello.
Morgan, Thomas. 2010. *The Vanishing American Lawyers.* Oxford: Oxford University Press.
Pavalko, Ronald. 1971. *Sociology of Occupations and Professions.* Itasca: F. E. Peacock Publishers.
Pérez Perdomo, Rogelio. 1981. *Los abogados en Venezuela.* Caracas: Monte Ávila Editores.
Philippi, Yrarrazabal, Pulido y Brunner. 2004. Historia de un estudio de abogados. En *Un estudio con historia y proyección*, Santiago.
Radin, Margaret. 1996. *Contested Commodities.* Cambridge: Harvard University Press.
Serrano, Sol. 1994. *Universidad y nación: Chile en el siglo xix.* Santiago: Editorial Universitaria.
Silva Vargas, F. 2004. Historia de un estudio de abogados. En *Un estudio con historia y proyección*, ed. Philippi, Yrarrazabal, Pulido y Brunner. Santiago.
Smith, N. 2009. Commodification in Law: Ideologies, Intractabilities, and Hyperboles. *Continental Philosophy Review* 42 (1): 101–129.
Susskind, Richard. 2013. *Tomorrow's Lawyers.* Oxford: Oxford University Press.
Urzúa Frademan, Raúl. 1992. La profesión de abogado y el desarrollo: antecedentes para un estudio. In *Derecho y sociedad*, ed. G. Figueroa. Corporación de Promoción Universitaria.
Wilkins, David, and M. Gulati. 1998. Reconceiving the Tournament of Lawyers: Tracking, Seeding, and Information Control in the Internal Labor Market of Elite Law Firms. *Virginia Law Review* 84: 1581–1682.

Zabala Ortiz, J.L. 1999. Evolución de la oferta de enseñanza del derecho en los últimos 25 años. In *La enseñanza del derecho: una visión crítica ante el nuevo escenario de acreditación*, ed. M. Claro Maturana. Santiago: Avid Universidad Miguel de Cervantes.

Iñigo de la Maza Gazmuri is a professor and a researcher at the Universidad Diego Portales in Santiago (Chile). He holds a Masters in Law degree from Stanford University, and a law degree from the Universidad Diego Portales. He has been the principal researcher and co-researcher in several projects related to law and economics, private law specifically contracts, new technologies, among others, funded by universities and institutions from Chile, Mexico and Spain.

Rafael Mery Nieto is a Professor and a Researcher at the Universidad Diego Portales in Santiago (Chile). Mery holds a Masters in Public Policy from the Universidad de Chile and a law degree from the Universidad Diego Portales. His research interests include regulation and governance, civil litigation and antitrust.

Juan Enrique Vargas Viancos is the Dean of the Universidad Diego Portales in Santiago (Chile) where he is also a Professor and Researcher. Professor Vargas holds a Master degree in Public Policy from the Engineering School of the Universidad de Chile, and a law degree from the Universidad de Chile. He is the former Executive Director of the Centro de Estudios de Justicia de las Américas, and his interest is focused on judicial reform and legal education reform in Chile.

CHAPTER 5

Big Law in Central America, Panama and the Dominican Republic: Growth Strategies in Small Economies

Carlos Taboada and Manuel Gómez

The research for this chapter was conducted with the generous support from Stanford Law School through its Center for the Legal Profession. The authors kindly acknowledge Deborah R. Hensler, and the other researchers affiliated to the "Stanford Law School Project on the Future of the Legal Profession" who are also authors of the different chapters of this book, for their insight and valuable commentaries throughout the process. We also thank the participants in the workshop held at Stanford Law School on October 17, 2014. We are also grateful to our interviewees and those who completed questionnaires designed for this project, who despite their very busy schedules and other professional priorities kindly agreed to share with it us their valuable experiences and insights with candor and interest. Ana Carolina Alvarez, Monica Brenes, María Alejandra Briones, Zoila Mora, Orietta Pérez, Maria Lizeth Prado, Gonzalo Robles, Marcela Vega and María Gabriela Zeledon collaborated with us during the research stage and provided invaluable assistance in helping us secure and conduct interviews, complete questionnaires and obtain required information.

C. Taboada (✉)
Consortium Legal in Managua, Managua, Nicaragua

M. Gómez
Florida International University College of Law, Miami, FL, USA

M. Gómez, R. Pérez-Perdomo (eds.), *Big Law in Latin America and Spain*, https://doi.org/10.1007/978-3-319-65403-4_5

Introduction

Costa Rica, El Salvador, Guatemala, Honduras and Nicaragua once formed a single Spanish colony and did not become independent until the nineteenth century, when Panama and the Dominican Republic also became independent. Since then, each of these countries have taken their own path, developed their own legal systems and confronted their own economic, political and social realities. Interestingly, in the eyes of many multinational corporations, these countries still form a somewhat homogeneous sub-region.

Treating these relatively small economies as a single sub-region within Latin America allows multinationals to take advantage of economies of scale. In any case, the geographical proximity, common language and regulatory proximity between these countries seem to justify the unitary approach. Except for the Dominican Republic, which is part of an island, the rest are all neighboring countries (Guatemala, El Salvador, Honduras, Nicaragua, Costa Rica and Panama) sharing at least one border with another. The official language in each of these countries is Spanish, and their legal systems are rooted in the civil law tradition, which they inherited from Spain.

In 1960, countries of this sub-region entered into a Central American Common Market Treaty. Since the late 1990s, a number of bilateral and multilateral agreements, mainly the signing of the *Dominican Republic-Central America Free Trade Agreement* ("DR-CAFTA") in 2004, and the *U.S.-Panama Trade Promotion Agreement* in force since 2012, have also contributed toward the integration efforts, and the harmonization of national laws and regulations regarding trade. Nevertheless, each of these countries is also different in terms of their political environment and their degree of social development. Costa Rica has the highest level of education and is also the only one without a national army. Guatemala, El Salvador and Nicaragua, on the other hand, having been ravaged by civil wars suffered the pernicious effect of military dictatorships. Natural disasters have also left a mark in the region, but that none of these setbacks has hindered a sustained rise of the sub-region's consolidated gross domestic product (GDP).

Particularly during the last two decades—the period that occupies our attention—the sub-region has seen an important increase in trade and investment. This has in turn triggered an increased demand for corporate legal services, which explains in part why local firms have embarked in a rapid transformation to compete with their foreign Big Law counterparts.

Even the largest Central American sub-regional firm cannot compete in size with an average New York- or London-based corporate law firm. However, their level of sophistication, internal structure, marketing and promotion strategies, and client management practices seem more and more alike.

Very much like the US-style Big Law firms, the leading Central American firms devote special attention to enter the leading international directories such as Martindale-Hubbell, Chambers & Partners (Chambers Latin America 2010, 2011, 2012, 2013, 2014, 2015), IFLR (IFLR 1000 2010), Latin Lawyer (Latin Lawyer 2001, 2003, 2006, 2009, 2010, 2012, 2013), Legal 500 (2012). They have also become active members of the international legal networks. The rise of cross-border transactions, in terms of both amount and complexity, has created opportunities for lawyers in the region to share knowledge and experiences with attorneys from other parts of the world. This has facilitated the transfer of knowledge, including the adoption by Central American law firms of organizational strategies, hiring practices, client management and other features typical of US-style Big Law. This process of modernization and organic growth has been marked by a steady regional expansion and integration, the adoption of Swiss *verein* structures, license or franchise models, their affiliation to alliances and networks, the opening of satellite offices in neighboring countries, mergers with former competitors, acquisitions of smaller firms and spin-offs of larger ones.

This chapter focuses on three types of law firms: (1) *international or foreign law firms* that have offices in Central America; (2) *regional multi-service firms* with offices in different countries within Central America; and (3) *top-tier* national firms and *specialized* (*boutique*) *law firms* that operate in Costa Rica, Dominican Republic, El Salvador, Guatemala, Honduras, Nicaragua or Panama. We are particularly interested in discussing how these law firms have emerged and transformed during the last two decades, what external forces have affected their growth and what impact—if any—they have had on the legal profession of the selected countries and beyond.

In 1998, F.A. Arias from El Salvador, and José Antonio and Pedro Muñoz from Costa Rica launched F.A. Arias & Muñoz, thus marking the beginning of the first regionalization wave, which soon thereafter included Aczalaw, Aguilar Castillo Love, Central Law, Consortium Legal, Garcia & Bodan and Lexincorp. The second wave was marked by the regional expansion of Pacheco Coto, and BLP from Costa Rica, LatinAlliance from El Salvador and the integration of LatamLex. It was also during this period that the so-called Big Four audit companies returned to the legal services industry in Central America. These and other important developments will be analyzed in this chapter, from the perspective of each individual country.

In terms of methodology, we have relied on in-depth interviews with senior and managing partners at representative law firms in each of the selected countries. We have also compared our data with the relevant information from the leading international legal directories such as Martindale-Hubbell, Chambers & Partners (Chambers Latin America), IFLR, Latin Lawyer and The Legal 500. Whereas the information contained in these directories is valuable, it is also important to note that in some cases it originates from the firms themselves, which in some cases might put in question its objectivity and accuracy. Therefore, we observe this information with caution, understanding that it provides a partial overview of the realities that were studied. The reports may not precisely reflect the actual characteristics and configuration of every law firm. As an example, not all firms provide complete information regarding language skills or graduate studies pursued by their members, and in some other cases, the list of members is not complete or up to date. This made our interviews particularly important given that they allowed us to obtain first-hand information about many of these firms and could also triangulate the data.

Another observation regarding these directories is that each of them has served a different purpose. In the case of Martindale-Hubbell, during the 1990s and up until about a decade ago, it was mostly used by Central American corporate law firms to promote their services with their US counterparts and in-house counsel from US-based multinational corporations and similar potential clients. We consider information from the Martindale-Hubbell directories of the years 2000, 2005 and 2010. It was useful in providing information regarding foreign language skills, as well as graduate studies completed by the listed attorneys at the time of publication.

Latin Lawyer, on the other hand, concentrates on the largest law firms in each jurisdiction. We have reviewed the 2005 and 2010 printed editions, and the 2015 online edition to monitor size and leverage information. The leading international directories such as Chambers Latin America, IFLR 1000, and The Legal 500 Latin America Edition; rank law firms, practice areas, and lawyers according to surveys completed by clients and firms. We have considered editions published since 2010 to review recent trends in law firm and attorney promotional efforts. The Latin American edition of Chambers & Partners was launched in 2009, and the

Latin American edition of The Legal 500 was first published in 2012. Therefore, we found it relevant to consider this five-year period. The order in which we present the countries is merely alphabetical and does not imply any hierarchy or special importance.

Our research has allowed us to observe with some accuracy, the evolution of high-end corporate legal service providers in Central America, characterized by increasing competition and a growing number of brands operating in different countries. In addition, we have monitored certain characteristics of the firms in terms of size, practice areas, leverage, lawyers training and language skills. We believe this information will provide guidance to understand how the so-called Big Law sector is evolving in Central America. Despite the commonalities that exist across the countries that make up our study, and the presence of a regional trend, we have decided to analyze each country individually and draw comparisons regarding some general or specific aspects, when relevant.

Costa Rica

In business strategy terms, Costa Rica shows the most intense competition within Central America. The number, size and characteristics of firms and the demand for services limited mostly on local advice results in a very competitive market. This may explain why in recent years, important players have looked at Costa Rica for expansion opportunities in Central America, or have chosen Costa Rican law firms to lead the way. On the other hand, this might also show an important degree of market saturation caused by the intensification of the internal competition, as well as the development of strong leaderships in the process of internationalization of law firms.

Costa Rica is generally recognized as a sophisticated legal market. The amount of foreign investments, the fact that it serves as the regional headquarters to some important multinational corporations, and its attractiveness to retired immigrants—and therefore higher amounts of individual wealth than its neighbors—may explain why Costa Rican law firms had to deal with complex operations earlier than their other Central American counterparts. Twenty years ago, most Costa Rican firms were traditional firms led by solo practitioners or small family-owned firms. The legal marketplace has developed tremendously and we have observed a number of large and medium-sized law firms (in relative terms to the size of the market), which have adopted corporate structures, networking and advertisement practices. These firms are competing regionally and some have even expanded to other continents. One notable firm, Pacheco Coto, opened offices in New Zealand, Spain and Switzerland.

Before the opening of the Costa Rican economy, in the mid-1990s, there were few important transactions, in terms of absolute value or complexity. The increase in foreign investment slowly led to the development and growth of those law firms that were able to adapt. In-house counsel units were small, and law firms providing assistance to foreign and multinational corporations were strong in corporate practice, and provided limited assistance in tax and labor issues, while litigation assistance was offered as required. When tourism and real estate investments increased, law firms developed new practice areas. The firms that had traditional leadership and kept their small-scale configurations were pushed to second place by the firms that started to adopt the benchmarks of US-based law firms such as corporate structure, use of technology and hourly billing, just to name a few. One of our informants explained that during this period "soliciting was based in quality". Costa Rica tried with a fair amount of success to be the leader in regional legal coordination for multinational corporations during this period. Companies like Wal-Mart or Phillip Morris, for example, created regional legal offices in Costa Rica.

It was during this period that Costa Rican attorneys looked to pursue their graduate education in the United States and United Kingdom, not only as a way to improve their legal skills and becoming trained to work with common law attorneys, but also to strengthen their English language and communication competencies. During this period, José Antonio Muñoz and Pedro Muñoz, actively promoted the creation of a Central American law firm. After finding local candidates to join the project in Guatemala, Honduras and Nicaragua, they agreed with Armando Arias from El Salvador as co-founding partner, to create a regional law firm under the name "F.A. Arias & Muñoz". In each country, a local entity would be created to provide legal services, and the co-founders would each control the local operation through a type of holding structure. This structure would later allow the creation of local and regional partner positions. The new regional firm started operations in 1998.

In Costa Rica, KPMG, the international audit company, had developed a very strong legal practice and was considered one of the best legal service providers. KPMG Abogados as it was called in Costa Rica, provided an international network and brand. They also developed state of the art procedures, standards and business skills training for their attorneys.

In the early 2000s, Facio & Cañas and KPMG were the largest legal service providers. After the Enron debacle in the United States, some of the local members of KPMG Abogados left to other firms or created new ones such as BLP and AFC, which would become leaders in the corporate and tax practice areas. At the time, there were more internationally recognized law firms in Costa Rica than in any other Central American country, lending to the notion that they had a more competitive legal service market. The expansion of this segment also prompted some mid-size firms such as Odio & Raven and Zurcher, Montoya & Zurcher to merge, therefore creating the largest Costa Rican law firm at the time. Costa Rica was also the first country in the region where fantasy named law firms such as Econojuris and Sigma appeared.

By 2005, the main practice areas were corporate, banking, intellectual property and real estate. Law firms increased activities as investment expanded. Greater volume and amount of transactions had a significant impact on the economy. Law firms participated more frequently in cross-border transactions and dealt with law firms from other parts of the world, mainly the United States and Europe, became more common. Therefore, relationships with United States and European Law firms also increased, as well as the transfer of knowledge. Surveyed partners observed an increase in institutionalization of local law firms, which embarked on a restructuring process following United States and Europe benchmark structures. Competition increased both locally and regionally. Boutique or niche firms focused on special practice areas also emerged. Some examples are AFC in tax law (formed by former KPMG Abogados attorneys), and Labor Law Corp in labor and employment law.

Regionalization of law firms led or co-led by Costa Rican law firms increased. In 2005, Laclé & Gutiérrez joined Consortium Legal ("Consortium") a legal conglomerate co-founded by five Central American firms, each among the largest in their own Country. In 2006, John Aguilar's practice merged with Francisco Castillo Love from Guatemala, to create another regional law firm under the trade name "Aguilar Castillo Love", following a similar model used previously by F.A. Arias & Muñoz by opening offices in other countries. In 2013, Pacheco Coto acquired the operations of Aczalaw in Guatemala, El Salvador and Nicaragua. In 2014, BLP opened offices in El Salvador and Nicaragua. In 2015, Gómez & Galindo incorporated to a new regional alliance called "LatamLex", while

BLP opened an office in Honduras and merged with Weinstok Abogados, a competition law boutique. Those firms that have been successful in regional integration have also tended to consolidate as local market leaders. The trend of using fantasy names has consolidated as most regional players have decided to adopt this type of branding.

More competition has led to an increase in service and quality standards but has also led to lower profit margins. Some of our interviewees explained that soliciting became based on price after the financial crisis of 2007. Firms were forced to improve efficiency to protect margins with lower prices. Therefore, those attorneys that had trained in audit companies may have had some advantage in dealing with processes and efficiencies. The "Big Four" audit companies were returning to take strong positions in the legal services industry. Ernst & Young and KPMG were ranked in the Tax Practice Area of Chambers & Partners in their first Latin America Edition in 2009. By 2014, they all had expanded their practice areas by developing strong campaigns to gain market share in corporate, mergers and acquisitions, and other services beyond the tax practice, not only in Costa Rica, but also in other Central American countries.

Law firms began to start looking for niche areas of practice to protect their margins, and they also had to develop strategies to protect their members from being recruited—or "poached"—by aggressive competitors. In terms of size, by 2000 the average size of the leading Costa Rican firms was 21 attorneys, but Facio & Cañas with 33 attorneys was by far the largest law firm at the time. In 2015, the average size of the five largest firms grew to 55 lawyers. By 2015, Facio & Cañas had been displaced by several new players including BLP (Costa Rica), Consortium Legal, Arias & Muñoz, Zurcher Odio & Raven, and Pacheco & Coto. These firms ranged in membership between 38 and 69, as we can see in Table 5.1.

It was also during this period that Costa Rican law firms turned to recruiting attorneys with foreign graduate studies and language skills and made sure that the competition and the overall market knew about it. This was, after all, an important requirement for any firm that wanted to embrace modernization and globalization. Table 5.2 shows these traits for the leading Costa Rican law firms as reported by Martindale-Hubbell during the years 2000, 2005 and 2010.

This table shows that, during the relevant period, the number of Costa Rican law firms that listed among its members, lawyers with foreign graduate education and other languages increased steadily. Moreover, a study of the Latin Lawyer 250 directories of 2005, 2010 and 2015 regarding

Table 5.1 Largest Costa Rican law firms by number of lawyers (2000–2015)

Largest law firms in 2000	
Facio & Cañas	33
KPMG Abogados	19
Lara Lopez Matamoros Rodriguez & Tinoco	19
Vargas Jiménez & Peralta	16
Zurcher Montoya & Zurcher	16
Largest law firms in 2015	
BLP (Costa Rica)	69
Consortium Legal (Costa Rica)	63
Arias & Muñoz (Costa Rica)	60
Zurcher Odio & Raven	43
Pacheco Coto (Costa Rica)	38

Source: Martindale-Hubbell 2000; Latin Lawyer 250, 2016

Table 5.2 Costa Rican law firm members with foreign graduate studies and foreign language skills as reported in 2000, 2005 and 2010

	2000	*2005*	*2010*	*Average*
Listed firms	39	39	41	40
Attorneys	306	360	337	334
English-speaking attorneys as listed	227	230	238	232
Other foreign language-speaking attorneys as listed	85	68	38	64
Listed attorneys with legal graduate studies (master or doctoral level)	96	124	96	105
Listed attorneys with legal graduate studies abroad	70	93	80	81
Listed attorneys with non-legal graduate studies (master or doctoral level)	9	26	19	18

Source: Martindale-Hubbell, 2000, 2005, 2010

the number of associates per partner also showed a slight increase in these numbers. A clear increase of listed law firms with regional presence can also be observed. This information shows that the growth of the larger law firms is closer to the growth of the GDP rather than the growth of law firms observed in Martindale-Hubbell, though there are important differences between both directories in terms of average size of listed law firms for the years 2005 and 2010.

These observations might reflect both differences in reporting methodologies of both directories or lack of precise reporting by law firms, and sample differences. But still, the top five law firms listed in terms of size show a higher growth rate than the rest of Martindale-Hubbell-listed law firms. This may suggest that larger law firms in the market are better at capturing legal services demand when compared to smaller firms. Higher demand may be allowing larger law firms to sustain their growth, probably indicating a virtuous cycle in which firms with better resources are able to market and promote the firms more effectively as well as attract better talent that allows for capturing more clients. This good reputation would keep fostering more client referrals, which would encourage the increase in size, above the market average. For this reason, it is our hypothesis that size may be a source of competitive advantage for law firms, based on a network effect. Most regional firms show an important increase in the number of lawyers between 2010 and 2015, while local firms tended to maintain their size.

Chambers & Partners, IFLR and Legal 500 were also consulted to monitor ranking trends of Big Law in Central America. We observed ranked firms and lawyers highlighted in the corresponding *leading lawyers* sections. We could observe that law firms are not only positioning their brands but also tend to promote the ranking of their individual lawyers. Slowly, more practice areas are being considered.

The ranking information allows us to create a strategic group map for Big Law in Costa Rica for 2015, considering the scope of services and the geographical presence. These three directories include a total of 36 ranked firms. These ranked firms are made up of approximately 560 attorneys. Depending on whether a law firm is ranked in several practice areas or only in a few, we call it "full-service" or "niche" law firm. We do not consider all advertised practice areas in order to concentrate those in which the firms have been able to be ranked. We counted the number of times a particular law firm has been ranked in any practice area ranking. Some practice area rankings might be repeated or overlapped. Chambers & Partners usually separates the ranking of Banking, Finance and Corporate practice areas. IFLR, on the other hand, merges these practice areas in a single category. Therefore, what is being measured is the number of times a law firm practice area has been ranked by any of the three considered directories.

Regarding the geographical presence, we consider the use of the same brand and location of their offices to group firms in three groups: local firms (only in Costa Rica), regional firms (with operations in different countries within Central America) or international firms (with one or more offices in countries outside Central America). The Big four law firms that were ranked (Deloitte, KPMG and Ernst & Young) are considered international firms. While most ranked firms are local, 13 firms are either regional or international. Very few local firms are able to show strength in multiple practice areas. Those that approach a full-service scope operate under regional or international brands. In total, 27 firms seem to concentrate on fewer practice areas. About 25 percent of the ranked firms (nine) promote two or three practice areas only. Only nine firms (25 percent) were able to show strengths in more than four practice areas. It is important to highlight that Costa Rican law firms have played an important role in promoting regional or international firms.

We identify four internationalization strategies in Central America. One strategy we call *organic growth*, which is when a law firm opens an office in another country. This might occur through lateral hiring from other firms, or through the acquisition of smaller operations. In any case, the definition of policies, standards and the decision-making processes are centralized in the founding firm, which serves as its headquarters. A second method is the bi-anchored strategy, which occurs when two law firms from different countries create a joint brand and expand organically to a third Country. In this case, the main decisions tend to be shared between the two founding law firms as partners of the regional or international firm, and then implemented to the rest of offices. A third mechanism is the *multi-anchor* strategy, which happens when multiple firms from different jurisdictions join to create a new brand and benefit from economies of scale, network effects and synergies among them. Important decisions are made by consensus, which are then executed at a local level. Finally, we have the *international licensing*, which is based on a license or franchise-type agreement between a local and a foreign or international law firm, in which case the policies and standards are defined by the licensor or franchisor.

Law firms from Costa Rica have played a leading role in the creation of, or incorporation to, regional and international firms. These include Aguilar Castillo Love, Arias & Muñoz, BLP, Central Law, Consortium Legal, Ernst & Young Centroamerica, LatamLex, Lexincorp and Pacheco Coto.

El Salvador

El Salvador has a concentrated market, with relatively new law firms and few multi-generational traditional family structures. Demand for well-trained attorneys increased to advice new investments promoted during the last decade or so. Relatively large firms with many partners have also emerged. The partnership between Armando Arias, and Jose Antonio Muñoz and Pedro Muñoz from Costa Rica was seen as a pioneer in terms of regional expansion.

Like in other parts of Latin America, the privatization of state companies also helped local law firms grow as the demand for sophisticated legal services increased and made legal service providers more important. Lawyers were expected to be bilingual and understand the standards set by US law firms. Bilingual local attorneys gained experience in complex financial transactions by becoming involved in activities related to multilateral loans provided by international agencies to repair local infrastructure, generally through the International Finance Corporation or the International Development Bank. Later on, most financial transactions that occupied the lawyers were related to the entry of multinationals (i.e. France Telecom, AES, among others) to the country.

As a result, El Salvadorian law firms became active members of international legal networks, increasing the professional exchange with foreign attorneys. As an example, F.A. Arias & Muñoz became member of Globallaw; Espino Nieto became member of State Capital Law Group and the Club de Abogados; and Romero Pineda joined the Bomchill, Terralex and Lex Mundi networks. After 2005, family law firms began to institutionalize. Once regionalization consolidated, the competition became particularly fierce due in part to a reduction in the amount of foreign investments. Other competitors appeared in the local and regional market, led by a younger generation of lawyers, who found little room to compete with established firms. Economic growth limited the initial projections of success within the country, thus encouraging regionalization. While investment in general slowed down, investment funds and international companies continued looking for local acquisitions and opportunities, which in turn contributed to offset the low economic growth and allowed local firms, especially the largest, to continue developing.

During the last five years, important lateral movements have occurred. Benjamin Valdez left Central Law to form a boutique law firm, which later merged with Consortium Legal. Pacheco Coto acquired Aczalaw, and partner Ricardo Cevallos left Consortium Legal to lead BLP office in El Salvador. During recent years, corporate, mergers and acquisitions, banking and intellectual property have been the practice areas with more demand for Big Law in El Salvador. Established firms are in a strong competitive position to serve investors with English-speaking attorneys and foreign specialized training. But stronger competition has also caused hourly rate reductions and fierce price wars. The following table shows the largest law firms in El Salvador between 2000 and 2015 (Table 5.3).

Regarding the trend among elite Latin American lawyers of having a graduate diploma from a foreign law school and knowing another language, members of El Salvadorian firms are no different from the rest of the region. The following table shows the relevant data for the years 2000, 2005 and 2010 (Table 5.4).

Between 2000 and 2010, the Central American firms listed in Martindale-Hubbell had an average membership of eight attorneys. The

Table 5.3 Largest law firms of El Salvador by size (2000–2015)

Largest law firms in 2000	
F. A. Arias	18
Romero Pineda & Asociados	14
Guandigue Segovia & Quintanilla	13
Espino Nieto Umaña & Asociados	9
Delgado & Ceballos	6
Largest law firms in 2015	
Arias & Muñoz (El Salvador)	40
Romero Pineda & Asociados	25
Consortium Legal (El Salvador)	16
Sáenz & Asociados	16
Central Law (El Salvador)	14

Source: Martindale-Hubbell 2000; Latin Lawyer 250, 2016

Table 5.4 El Salvador law firm members with foreign graduate studies and foreign language skills as reported in 2000, 2005 and 2010

Martindale-Hubbell information—El Salvador	*2000*	*2005*	*2010*	*Average*
Listed firms	20	18	15	18
Attorneys	127	152	126	135
English-speaking attorneys	68	106	81	85
Other foreign language-speaking listed attorneys	12	16	14	14
Legal graduate studies (master or doctoral level)	7	24	34	22
Legal graduate studies abroad	7	22	28	19
Non-legal graduate studies (master or doctoral level)	5	10	4	6

Source: Martindale-Hubbell 2000, 2005, 2010

percentage of attorneys with English language skills in those firms was well above 60 percent, while those who spoke another language represented 10 percent. The percentage of attorneys with graduate studies in a foreign law school was 14 (compared to 16 percent of lawyers who pursued graduate studies in a domestic law school). Finally, the percentage of lawyers with graduate multidisciplinary training—understood as non-legal graduate studies—was 4.5 percent on average during the same period.

Another interesting characteristic of this period was the increase—in absolute numbers—of law firms with foreign operations, but a slightly decline in the number of listed attorneys. The average size of firms as well as the number of partners in the last five years is almost the same. Declining GDP growth for this period might explain the lack of growth these firms are experiencing. The number of associate-to-partner ratio in El Salvador has remained at 1:2.

Another interesting characteristic of El Salvadorian high-end corporate law firms is that, differently from their counterparts from the rest of the sub-region, most ranked firms from El Salvador have operations outside that country. Also, the number of niche firms is low relative to the number of multi-practice firms. This might be explained by one important characteristic of this market: law firms from El Salvador have been active in the creation of regional firms. After Costa Rica, El Salvador law firms had a leading role in the creation of six regional firms: Arias & Muñoz, Central Law, Consortium Legal, LatamLex, Latin Alliance and Lexincorp.

Guatemala

Despite having the largest population and economy in the sub-region, Guatemala's growth has been rather slow. The signing of the peace treaties and the ratification of the Central American Free Trade Agreement (DR-CAFTA) are perhaps the most important economic events in the last two decades. Upon ratifying the DR-CAFTA, Guatemala joined the rest of the region in boosting their trade with the United States and, simultaneously, committed to a number of required legal and institutional reforms meant to promote a better regional integration. Unsurprisingly, the impact for legal service providers was significant.

What is unique about Guatemala's corporate legal services market is its fragmentation. It has many small firms. Until the 1990s there were many small firms, and only five firms with 10–20 members. The largest player during those years was Rodriguez, Archila, Castellanos, Solares

& Aguilar S.C. The most important merger that occurred during that period led to the opening of Arenales Skinner-Klee, a firm that resulted from the merge of the practices of each of the co-founders. With these few exceptions, multinational corporations and foreign clients tended to rely heavily on family firms. These clients tended to work with only one firm, and only hired highly specialized boutique firms for specific cases, such as complex labor matters or high-stake litigation. During this time, there was low competition due to the limited number of large firms with the capacity to provide full legal services to multinational clients.

The financial crisis of the late 2000s, prompted foreign clients to pressing their Guatemalan lawyers to drop the hourly rate and work for fixed fees. The so-called beauty contests, whereby a wealthy client put different firms to compete for a single matter or a portfolio of cases, became the norm and is nowadays the general practice. Foreign and multinational clients are also distributing their legal work among several firms, instead of just giving it to a single provider like in the past. As a result, the commoditization of certain services started to make the offer of those services less attractive, which reduced the profit margins of Guatemalan law firms.

The aftermath of the financial crisis saw the emergence of new practice areas in the Guatemalan high-end corporate legal sector, and the larger firms quickly began advertising their services for corporate, banking, tax, labor, administrative and arbitration. Firm Rankings also forced firms to improve. The need to hire members with English language skills and foreign graduate studies became very important, as it also occurred with the organization, structure, management, technology and other processes related to the practice of law. Despite such apparent urge to modernize and adapt to the demands of a globalized legal market, there is still a lack of sufficient differentiation in practice areas, organizational structure changes, career plans or succession plans in most Guatemalan firms.

Size is also an interesting feature that distinguishes the Guatemalan legal market from the rest of the sub-region. Most high-end Guatemalan firms have between 10 and 20 attorneys. In order to remain competitive, the local firms that have not expanded beyond Guatemala have had to optimize their management and organizational skills, as a way to differentiate themselves from other players. That has been the case of Carrillo & Asociados, Mayora & Mayora and QILS Abogados, which a few years ago merged with “4Abogados”. In 2008, Carrillo became the largest in the country after merging with a smaller firm.

Regarding the growth in the number of law graduates in the country, it has gone from 8,000 in 1990 to 20,000 by 2015. At the highest level, the number of law firms competing for the business generated by multinational corporations has also increased. Some of these new firms have resulted from the spin-offs of traditional local leaders. For example, 4Abogados was formed under the leadership of Alejandro Cofiño, who had departed Consortium—Rodriguez, Archila, Castellanos, Solares & Aguilar. In 2015, 4Abogados merged with QILS Abogados. Pacheco Coto from Costa Rica acquired Guatemala’s. Parallel to this, multinational corporations have also invested resources in developing and expanding their in-house legal departments, thus reducing the demand for outside counsel, who are only used for matters that require highly specialized skills or resources that the corporation does not have. The growth of Guatemalan law firms can be appreciated in Table 5.5.

Regarding the special training and skills of the lawyers who work for the leading Guatemalan firms, the number of English-speaking attorneys is about 85 percent—a proportion that seems to be constantly increasing—while the percentage of those speaking another foreign language seems to be decreasing. Lawyers with graduate legal studies represent an average of 30 percent, which is similar to what occurs in El Salvador. However, most of the Guatemalan lawyers who pursued graduate studies in law did so by studying abroad. There also appears to be an increased

Table 5.5 Largest law firms of Guatemala by number of lawyers (2000–2015)

Largest law firms in 2000	
Carrillo & Asociados	10
Mayora & Mayora	7
Rodríguez, Archila, Castellanos, Solares & Aguilar	7
Bonilla, Montana, Toriello & Barrios	7
Melini & Asociados	6
Largest law firms in 2015	
Carrillo & Asociados	36
Consortium Legal (Guatemala)	28
Qil+4 Abogados	27

Source: Martindale-Hubbell 2000; Latin Lawyer 250, 2016

Table 5.6 Guatemala law firm members with foreign graduate studies and foreign language skills as reported in 2000, 2005 and 2010

Martindale-Hubbell information—Guatemala	*2000*	*2005*	*2010*	*Average*
Listed firms	23	25	21	23
Attorneys	94	162	156	137
English-speaking attorneys	77	139	139	85
Other foreign language-speaking listed attorneys	20	30	22	24
Legal graduate studies (master or doctoral level)	24	55	45	41
Legal graduate studies abroad	17	42	30	30
Non-legal graduate studies (master or doctoral level)	6	10	15	10

Source: Martindale-Hubbell, 2000, 2005 and 2010

interest in pursuing interdisciplinary (non-legal) studies. The data is shown in Table 5.6.

Finally, the associates to partner ratio has slightly increased in these firms, but shows a low leverage ratio. The number of attorneys in these firms grew approximately 70 percent between 2005 and 2015. Consequently, the average size for these firms increased to 20 attorneys. These firms were able to grow at a higher rate than the GDP growth for the same period. Six firms have maintained leading positions in the Latin Lawyer ranking by size. Similar to what has been observed for Martindale-Hubbell, very few new entrants seem to have been able to challenge existing market positions.

Honduras

Honduras has a smaller legal services market for multinational corporations, with fewer listed firms in comparison with other countries in the region. F.A. Arias & Muñoz opened offices in Honduras, and Rusconi, Valdes & Asociados, both from El Salvador, opened an office in 2002 but it was later closed. In the early 2000s, other firms were also considering opening offices in Honduras. Similarly to what occurred in other countries, the traditional players of the Honduran legal market were family-owned firms, which also began to institutionalize but much later than the family firms from the neighboring countries. Law firms were forced to think about efficient services, as clients became more demanding after the 2007 crisis. Corporate, banking and intellectual property practices were considered the most important practice areas.

The leaders of the Honduran legal market are the same firms that dominate the sub-region: Aguilar Castillo Love, Arias & Muñoz, Consortium Legal and Garcia & Bodan. Firms such as Lexincorp and BLP gained prominence after some important lateral hires, and other emerging firms like Advocatus, grew as a result of strategic alliances. The approximately 20,000 members of the Honduran bar have saturated the market, thus forcing the fees down. Unlike the multinational and foreign corporations, which prefer to work with some of the regional players, the domestic business sector still prefer to work with traditional local firms like Lopez Rodezno and Casco Fortin. Table 5.7 shows the growth of the Honduran high-end legal service sector between 2000 and 2015.

As we can see, the size of the largest firms in Honduras is similar to small to mid-size firm in other countries. Notwithstanding, a reduced number of lawyers does not necessarily put those firms at a disadvantage in terms of quality because their members tend to be well qualified and able to operate in a sophisticated environment. Regarding additional skills such as foreign languages and graduate studies, according to information obtained from Latin Lawyer and Martindale-Hubbell, the number of English-speaking lawyers in Honduran top firms is close to 60 percent, whereas those who speak other languages make up 13 percent of the population. Regarding the type of professional credentials brandished by

Table 5.7 Honduras largest law firms by size (2000–2015)

Largest law firms in 2000	
Medrano Irias	14
Lopez Rodezno & Asociados	9
Ortez, Colindres & Asociados	9
J.R. Paz & Asociados	9
Bufete Duron	6
Largest law firms in 2015	
Consortium Legal (Honduras)	25
Aguilar Castillo Love (Honduras)	13
García & Bodán (Honduras)	13
Arias & Muñoz (Honduras)	12
Bufete Mejía & Asociados	8

Source: Martindale-Hubbell 2000; Latin Lawyer 250, 2016

Honduras's high-end corporate lawyers, at least 20 percent have completed graduate studies in law, which the majority having done so abroad. The five largest listed law firms reported in Martindale-Hubbell in the years 2000, 2005 and 2010 evidence higher averages of language skills compared to the general sample of all listed firms, as well as a higher percentage of foreign legal graduate training (Table 5.8).

Finally, the associate-to-partner ratio has ranged between two and three to one. Firms listed in Latin Lawyer appear larger than the ones listed in Martindale-Hubbell in 2010. There also appears to be a decrease in the number of attorneys and average size of Honduran firms, between 2010 and 2015. The political and economic environment during this period might help explain this contraction. In 2015, four of the six listed firms were regional or international. The strategic group map for Big Law in Honduras in 2015 includes 22 law firms with approximately 170 attorneys.

Nicaragua

During the 1990s, the corporate legal services industry of Nicaragua was very small and dominated by solo practitioners. The first local law firm to base its fees on an hourly rate was Alvarado & Asociados, under the leadership of Gloria María de Alvarado. The largest firm in the country was Taboada & Asociados, and it belonged to three international networks: State Capital, TAG Law and World Services Group. Along with Garcia & Bodan, they were the only firms organized under a corporate structure. The rest of the firms were family owned or cost-sharing partnerships.

Table 5.8 Honduras law firm members with foreign graduate studies and foreign language skills (2000, 2005 and 2010)

Martindale-Hubbell information—Honduras	*2000*	*2005*	*2010*	*Average*
Listed firms	13	21	24	19
Attorneys	68	92	85	82
English-speaking attorneys	36	70	53	53
Other foreign language-speaking listed attorneys	9	15	9	11
Legal graduate studies (master or doctoral level)	7	21	23	17
Legal graduate studies abroad	6	16	17	13
Non-legal graduate studies (master or doctoral level)	3	3	3	3

Source: Martindale-Hubbell, 2000, 2005 and 2010

Toward the end of the decade, an upsurge of new investments increased the demand for legal services in Nicaragua, which in turn motivated the local leading firms to grow. When F.A. Arias & Muñoz entered the Nicaraguan market in 1998, several prominent solo practitioners began hiring younger well-prepared attorneys and adopted corporate structures similar to those of common among foreign law firms. The local firms undertook a coordinated effort to promote new regulations and policies to attract foreign investors, which would also benefit the Nicaraguan corporate bar in the long run. During the last decade, the leading firms have grown and become multi-service operations but their main areas of practice are still corporate, administrative law and government regulation. The advent of the DR-CAFTA pressured law firms to acquire the necessary capacity to advice clients on international trade and related matters. Molina & Asociados is an example of this. Some Nicaraguan firms like Garcia & Bodan, also expanded their operations beyond the national borders. Others, like Taboada & Asociados joined some of the nascent Central American firms. In the case of Taboada, the merger was in 2005 with Consortium Legal, the Central American multi-country multi-service law firm. Between 2000 and 2010, other local firms joined regional organizations such as Aczalaw and Lexincorp. Since 2013, joining a second regionalization wave, Pachecho Coto, BLP and LatamLex started operations in Nicaragua, by signing agreements with local partners. Table 5.9 gives a general synopsis of law firms' growth in Nicaragua.

In terms of individual skills, the average of English-speaking lawyers in the listed firms was about 67 percent. In total, 32 percent of those firms'

Table 5.9 Nicaraguan law firms by size (2000–2015)

Largest law firms 2000	
Taboada & Asociados	15
Mayorga, Valdivia, Rivas & Escobar	9
Delaney & Asociados	9
Alvarado & Asociados	7
Estrada & Asociados	7
Largest law firms in 2015	
García & Bodan (Nicaragua)	31
Consortium Legal (Nicaragua)	29
Arias & Muñoz (Nicaragua)	16
Alvarado & Asociados	14
Central Law—Molina & Asociados	11

Source: Martindale-Hubbell, 2000; Latin Lawyer 250, 2016

members also had graduate legal studies, the vast majority in foreign countries, consistent with the regional trend toward the globalization and modernization of the legal practice. The average size of these firms was nine attorneys, similar to the top five law firms in Honduras in the year 2000. English was spoken by 65 percent of their members. Even Alvarado & Asociados and Taboada & Asociados showed a high percentage of members holding legal graduate degrees, comparable to the highest averages in Central America for that year, the average considering the top five listed firms was below 20 percent. The average size of these firms in 2010 is 13 attorneys showing no significant growth in comparison to the year 2005. But Consortium—Taboada & Asociados grew to 30 attorneys, almost 2.5 ahead of the following listed firm. The average percentage of attorneys with graduate legal studies keeps rising in Nicaragua, at least for the largest listed firms. Table 5.10 presents a summary of the information corresponding to firms and attorneys listed in the printed editions of Martindale-Hubbell directories of the years 2000, 2005 and 2010.

Panama

Panama's corporate legal sector is unique in several ways. The unique geographical location of the country, which serves as the gateway to a significant amount of international trade that everyday crosses from or to Asia and other parts of the world, has forced the local legal sector to become efficient and highly skilled. Panama is also the headquarters of a robust financial sector, and a modern and flexible corporate legal framework. These and other conditions have incentivized foreign capitals to make

Table 5.10 Nicaragua law firm members with foreign graduate studies and foreign language skills as reported in 2000, 2005 and 2010

Martindale-Hubbell information—Nicaragua	*2000*	*2005*	*2010*	*Average*
Listed firms	12	14	15	14
Attorneys	76	104	83	88
English-speaking attorneys	45	90	47	61
Other foreign language-speaking listed attorneys	14	20	5	13
Legal graduate studies (master or doctoral level)	7	32	47	29
Legal graduate studies abroad	16	26	37	26
Non-legal graduate studies (master or doctoral level)	5	11	7	8

Source: Martindale-Hubbell, 2000, 2005 and 2010

their ways into the Central American country, or at least use it as a bridge for their global operations. Foreign investors have traditionally found Panama attractive in part because of the tax benefits, secrecy laws and other advantages typically found in most off shore markets. Such conditions have compelled the traditional local firms to find ways to offer inexpensive, fast and reliable corporate legal services that can compete with the most sophisticated foreign legal advisers.

As a result, there has been a culture among Panamanian corporate lawyers of strong corporate organizational skills, discretion, efficient client management strategies, global competencies and competitive fees. Some of the traditional leading law firms such as Alfaro Ferrer & Ramirez, and Alemán Cordero Galindo & Lee became known—throughout the region and in some other parts of the world—as the "go-to" firms for a broad range of corporate, tax and banking transactions. Their fast, cost efficient and reliable services helped corporate clients and foreign lawyers in a variety of matters, from structuring the most complex financial and tax planning operations to the simple incorporation of bearer-share corporations and other vehicles used by foreign parties to take full advantage of the country's offshore regulations.

The clientele of these Panamanian firms included not only multinational corporations and wealthy foreign clients, but also other Latin American law firms who referred business to them or acted as intermediaries between the Panamanian lawyers and the foreign clients. The basis for these relationships was one of mutual trust. The Panamanian firms did not accept "walk ins" but only clients who were referred either by other clients or by people they knew and trusted. Furthermore, given the heightened scrutiny on financial and corporate transaction imposed by foreign countries such as the United States through its Office of Foreign Assets Control (FATCA), or by industry standards such as the "known your client" policy so common among banks and other financial institutions, Panamanian lawyers have had to devise mechanism to monitor their own members and also the firm's clients.

The provision of general corporate services has been so profitable for some of the larger firms that they have set up entire departments exclusively devoted to handle the record-keeping of bearer-shares companies and other corporate entities on behalf of their clients. Fully bilingual employees staff these departments and work around the clock to meet the needs of the firm's clients. For years, many Panamanian lawyers took advantage and reaped the benefits of their country's reputation as tax haven. However, recent scandals involving allegations of money laundering, political corruption and fraud such as the one stemming from the so-called Panama papers had a negative effect on the country's reputation. Although the scandals implicated only a small number of firms, it had a negative halo effect on the rest of the legal community. Notwithstanding, the country's swift actions and the legal community's self-imposed ethical standards and reputation helped cleared up the country's name as a reliable forum.

Despite these recent difficulties, the prior two decades were marked by a rapid growth of the Panamanian corporate legal market. Multinational corporations, foreign banks, insurers, manufacturing companies, and shipping and transportation conglomerates established their regional headquarters or at least some corporate presence in Panama. This obviously generated a steady flow of legal work for the local firms, which in turn were pressured to devise effective strategies to attract and retain foreign clients by offering them high-quality work at a low cost. During that period the most prominent local firms began paying more attention to their recruiting and retention policies, and also built regional and international alliances that helped them protect their market share. Some of the most important signs of the regional integration of the Panamanian corporate legal market were the arrival of Central Law, Aguilar Castillo Love, and Arias & Muñoz. More recent efforts include the joining of LatamLex by Lovill, a spin-off of Morgan & Morgan. Notwithstanding these important efforts, considering the importance of Panama in the sub-region, the opening of regional firms and the integration of Panamanian lawyers into existing ones have been slow and limited.

The low presence of regional law firms is compensated by one of the most interesting characteristics of Big Law in Panama. Thirteen of the Panamanian firms ranked by Latin Lawyer and Martindale-Hubbell have opened offices outside Central America, thus revealing their efforts to internationalize beyond their sub-regional market. Panamanian law firms were pioneers in Latin America in expanding their own local brands to different countries and even to other continents. This is explained by the strong offshore legal practice developed in Panama. The country's flexible and modern corporate law, its territorial tax and other features have allowed their corporate legal offshore practice to grow significantly. Strong offshore practices allowed for the opening of two kinds of offices outside Panama. The first type being representation offices that were created to assist local clients in places such as London, São Paulo or Shanghai, mainly to advise foreign clients on Panamanian and other offshore structures. The second type of offices they have opened—mainly in other offshore jurisdictions such as Belize, British Virgin Islands, Seychelles and Uruguay—are meant to provide support to a comprehensive off shore legal advice strategy, which distinguishes Panamanian firms from all other Latin American counterparts.

Panamanian firms therefore are very international. The management of thousands of companies as part as their offshore portfolio, as well legal advice on shipping services, financial transactions and other matters is their main competitive advantage. Panama is a world leader in ship registry, a reason that has allowed Panamanian firms to have offices in Europe and Asia to attract and serve an international cadre of shipping clients. On the other hand, the structural characteristics to the Panamanian economy have fostered the development of strong banking, trade, migration and real estate practice areas. Panamanian law firms have evolved to provide assistance to international clients investing in Panama.

Finally, diversification is another characteristic visible among Panamanian law firms. ARIFA and GALA have developed Trust Companies. Morgan & Morgan has gone further by creating a Bank and a Commercial Real Estate Development Company that built one of the most modern office towers in Panama City. In terms of size, Panamanian law firms started bigger than the rest of Central America and have had a substantial increase in

Table 5.11 Panamanian law firms by size (2000–2015)

Largest law firms in 2000	
Morgan & Morgan	31
Icaza, González-Ruiz & Alemán	25
Arias, Fábrega & Fábrega	24
Galindo, Arias & López	31
Benedetti & Benedetti	13
Largest law firms in 2015	
Morgan & Morgan	79
Arias, Fábrega & Fábrega	58
Galindo, Arias & López	46
Icaza, González-Ruiz & Alemán	36
Alfaro, Ferrer & Ramírez	30

Source: Martindale-Hubbell, 2000; Latin Lawyer 250, 2016

size, but there have not participated in any mergers with other firms of the sub-region. Table 5.11 shows the growth of the leading Panamanian law firms between 2000 and 2015.

Regarding their internal structure and the individual profile of their members, Panama has more law firms and attorneys listed in Martindale-Hubbell and Latin Lawyer than all the other countries in Central America. This is startling considering that some of the other countries had a higher GDP, more foreign trade and a larger population. Panama's corporate legal sector also stands out from the rest of the sub-region in terms of the internationalizing features of its lawyers. The percentage of English-speaking Panamanian business lawyers is higher than the regional average. Members of the leading firms also hold more foreign graduate studies than their counterparts in the neighboring countries. Table 5.12 shows these figures as reported by Martindale-Hubbell.

The strategic group map for Big Law in Panama in 2015 includes 31 law firms, with approximately 441 attorneys (Table 5.13).

Local firms represent almost half of the ranked firms, compared to those with regional or international operations. The high number of international firms is explained by the fact that many of these firms have opened offices in other countries. A few firms—less than 25 percent—have been ranked in more than six practice area categories. Considering the internationalization strategies of Panamanian firms, most firms have grown organically. Among the 15 regional or international law firms currently ranked in Panama, 14 have been founded or co-founded by local firm.

Table 5.12 Panamanian lawyers by foreign language skills and graduate studies (2000–2010)

Martindale-Hubbell information—Panama	*2000*	*2005*	*2010*	*Average*
Listed firms	51	64	77	64
Attorneys	374	510	496	460
English-speaking attorneys	321	435	345	367
Other foreign language-speaking listed attorneys	60	44	48	51
Legal graduate studies (master or doctoral level)	126	234	138	166
Legal graduate studies abroad	119	215	132	155
Non-legal graduate studies (master or doctoral level)	9	23	28	20

Source: Martindale-Hubbell, 2000, 2005, and 2010

Table 5.13 Ranked Panamanian law firms (2015)

Panama 2015	*Local firms*	*Regional firms*	*International firms*	*Total*
13–18 Ranked practice areas			5	5
7–12 Ranked practice areas			2	2
1–6 Ranked practice areas	16	1	7	24
Total	16	1	14	

Dominican Republic

During the decade of the 1990s, there were no clear leaders in the corporate legal sector of the Dominican Republic. Increase in foreign investment fostered the development of new firms and the growth of those able to capture the new opportunities. Local firms began to handle more cases and the demands of multinationals and foreign clients prompted the creation of new practice areas for firms that traditionally offered mostly domestic corporate and litigation services. The influx of foreign capital in tourism, for example, was an incentive for the growth of real estate practice groups within the larger firms.

By the year 2000, the increase in foreign investment allowed local firms to forge close relationship with important foreign firms. This allowed local firms to incorporate operational benchmarks set in foreign legal markets, including the adoption of organizational and management structures typical of the US-based Big Law firms. Some foreign firms such as Squire Sanders (now, Squire Patton Boggs) opened offices in the country. One of the most important innovations of those years was the implementation of the hourly rate instead of the traditional fixed fee arrangements. Having a graduate law degree from a foreign university and speaking English became a requirement among the top law firms, since they wanted to meet the demands of important clients. The financial crisis brought alternative financing sources from The World Bank, IFC and other multilateral organizations, which also created unprecedented opportunities for the larger local firms. By 2015, the Dominican corporate legal sector had experienced a significant growth, as we can see in Table 5.14, which shows the average size of the top firms as ranked by Martindale-Hubbell and Latin Lawyer.

Even though Dominican lawyers became more responsive to the pressures of globalization, for the most part the structure of their firms remained very traditional. One characteristic of the corporate legal services industry of the Dominican Republic is the number of firms that have

Table 5.14 Dominican Republic law firms by size (2000–2015)

Largest law firms in 2000	
Russin, Vecchi & Heredia Bonetti	21
Troncoso & Cáceres	19
Pellerano & Herrera	18
Dhimes & Marra	14
Headridk, Rizik, Álvarez & Fernández	12
Largest law firms in 2015	
Pellerano & Herrera	42
Headridk, Rizik, Álvarez & Fernández	41
OMG	39
Russin, Vecchi & Heredia Bonetti	16
Squire Patton Boggs Peña Prieto Gamudi	15

Source: Martindale-Hubbell, 2000; Latin Lawyer 250, 2016

opened satellite offices in multiple locations within the country. This is even more counterintuitive if one considers that the territory is relatively small. Notwithstanding, the significant amount of legal transactions related to tourism and real estate have more than justified the investment.

According to Martindale-Hubbell, almost 80 percent of the members of Dominican law firms speak English, and approximately 65 percent speak other languages. This is certainly the highest average in the sub-region. Regarding legal graduate studies, approximately 27 percent of the listed attorneys have pursued legal graduate studies, and 23 percent of them in foreign countries. Table 5.15 presents a summary of the information

Table 5.15 Dominican lawyers by foreign language skills and graduate studies (2000–2010)

	2000	*2005*	*2010*	*Average*
Listed firms	31	30	50	37
Attorneys	285	332	519	379
Average Martindale-Hubbell listed firm size	9.19	11.07	10.38	10
English-speaking attorneys	216	280	428	308
Other foreign language-speaking listed attorneys	109	269	397	258
Legal graduate studies (master or doctoral level)	38	135	142	105
Legal graduate studies abroad	28	120	128	92
Non-Legal graduate studies (master or doctoral level)	6	24	32	21

Source: Martindale-Hubbell, 2000, 2005 and 2010

corresponding to firms and attorneys listed in the years 2000, 2005 and 2010, according to the printed editions of Martindale-Hubbell directories.

Finally, the strategic group map for Big Law in the Dominican Republic includes 23 ranked firms that represent approximately 341 attorneys. The average law firm size of these 23 firms consists of 15 attorneys. Most law firms are ranked in less than four practice areas, suggesting a stronger niche competition than in other countries within Central America.

Conclusion: The Regional Outlook

Central American high-end corporate law firms seemed to have embraced the Big Law culture more recently than in some other parts of the continent. The first law firms to adopt a corporate law firm structure and the organizational platform of Big Law in Central America did so in the 1990s. These firms featured more foreign-trained attorneys, higher levels of academic preparation and better knowledge of foreign languages. With the increase in the number of attorneys, the number of law firms rose as well. Economic integration inspired business integration, among clients and among firms. Regional firms were founded as competition started to increase. Globalization and regional integration has led to faster transfers of knowledge from abroad, and also from the sub-region to other parts of the world. Local attorneys are becoming more sophisticated as they have more opportunities to participate in international legal teams, international networks, and in a variety of professional development opportunities (Taboada 2002, 2004, 2009, 2013).

Privatization and industry consolidation triggered a number of acquisition transactions that allowed the transfer of foreign practices and standards to the countries that were studied. As markets opened to private investment and foreign trade, and the free-trade agreements were signed, local law firms increased their contact and relations with US and European-based law firms.

We also observed an increase in specialization. This was shown by the growth of niche or boutique firms, and the growth of practice areas offered by law firms in the last 20 years. Compared to other jurisdictions and regions, however, Central American law firms have not developed as much practice areas or specialization. While some professional directories such as Chambers & Partners have listed up to 70 areas of practice in the United States,[1] Central American law firms have qualified only for 17 areas of practices, and not all apply to the seven countries that constitute the focus of this chapter. Our numerous interviews throughout the sub-region reflected that corporate clients expect their lawyers to know the client's business. This means that lawyers are required to gain business skills to be able to better communicate with their clients. Still, non-legal graduate training, including business training, seems to be low within Central America. But more firms are adopting continuing education programs that include business and professional skills training.

As economic agents, law firms providing services to big business adapt to economic trends. Within Central America, we found that higher growth rates in law firms were in positive correlation with higher GDP growth rates. Inversely, we found that in those economies that suffered low growth rates, law firms were not able to grow, and some even reduced their size.

Panama and Costa Rica have shown a better economic and competitive environment that allowed local firms to grow significantly in the last ten years, compared to the other jurisdictions that were analyzed. These are the two most competitive markets in Central America. They serve as base for the largest law firms, which members are equipped with better language skills and graduate studies than the average. The degree of development of the legal services industry is recognized by a higher number of ranked law firms. Nicaragua, El Salvador and Honduras on the contrary, have faced harder economic and competitive conditions, which has in turn affected the growth capacity of law firms operating in those countries. The legal markets of the Dominican Republic and Guatemala have shown an intermediate level of development, which is also a characteristic of the business environment in which they operate.

From a business strategy perspective, the period of study shows the development of the high end legal service industry from its an early stage (start-growth) to the consolidation phase. The increase in the availability of talent, growth of number of attorneys and proliferation of law firms targeting multinationals has increased competition and rivalry, which is being evidenced by the price pressures faced by law firms from all the jurisdictions within the areas of study. In recent years, we observe an increase of spin-offs from traditional firms, the creation of new firms, the merging of firms and more integration of existing ones. This provides a clear evidence of consolidation within the market of legal services in the region, where the offer is growing faster than demand.

The corporate legal service industry's current characteristics show low entry barriers, and a fragmented industry structure with many firms offering corporate legal services. Surveys evidence higher corporate legal service consumer power strengthened by low change costs and greater access to information. Clients are demanding more quality and lower prices. Big law in Central America is facing an important challenge in the growth of in-house legal departments. First, they compete for the same talent law firms require. Secondly, it affects demand for legal services which otherwise would be provided by law firms. An increased number of clients improving their legal departments suggest further reduction of profit margins for law firms.

Along with what is being observed in other parts of the world, it is questionable whether current business models are sustainable in the long term. Changes in the way legal services are provided in Central America are likely to occur as law firms adapt to these challenging industry conditions. The leverage statistics of the law firms that were studied are relatively low, and seem to be reducing as time goes on. Big Law in Central America and Dominican Republic faces a number of challenges driven by increased competition and higher client expectations. Multinational corporations have continued to expand their in-house legal units, which have forced business lawyers to lower their costs, and devise strategies to remain attractive to their clients and viable in economic terms.

The emergence of new business models and organizational strategies by Central American law firms seems unavoidable to guarantee their sustainability. This will surely include diversification strategies for some. Ancillary businesses are also likely to be offered more frequently. As it has occurred in other markets, more firms will be tempted to offer consulting or accounting services, becoming multidisciplinary service companies. Others will go further by investing or developing non-related businesses. The lack of regulatory restrictions in Central America makes this scenario possible in the short term. From a technological perspective, more firms have adopted new tools to promote, offer and deliver their services. This might impact the traditional office concept, as it is staring to occur in other jurisdictions.

In sum, Big Law in Central America and the Dominican Republic is constantly evolving. The talented teams that guide these firms have been able to navigate through the challenges of the turbulent waters threatening the legal services market, and appear to have the skills to readapt in order to survive and thrive.

Notes

1. See, Chamber & Partners http://www.chambersandpartners.com/practice-area-definitions-usa (consulted, June 15, 2015).

References

Chambers Latin America. 2010, 2011, 2012, 2013, 2014, and 2015. London: Chambers & Partners Publishing.

IFLR 1000: The Guide to the World's Leading Financial Law Firms. 2010. London: Euromoney Institutional Investor PLC.

Latin Lawyer 250. 2001, 2003, 2006, 2009, 2010, 2012, and 2013. London: Law Business Research Ltd.

Martindale-Hubbell International Law Directory. 2000, 2002, 2010. Chicago: Martindale-Hubbell.

The Legal 500. 2012. London: Legalease.

Carlos Taboada. 2002. *Central America Market Research*. Survey Presented at the Annual Meeting of Strategic Planning of Taboada & Asociados.

———. 2004. Central America Market Research. Thesis to Obtain the Degree of Masters of Business Administration, Adolfo Ibañez University.

———. 2009. *Central America Market Research*. Survey Presented at the Annual Meeting of Strategic Planning of Consortium – Central America Lawyers.

———. 2013. *Central America Market Research*. Survey Presented at the Annual Meeting of Strategic Planning of Consortium – Central America Lawyers.

Carlos Taboada is a partner at Consortium Legal in Managua (Nicaragua), Professor of Business Strategy at the INIDEM Business Law School and Professor of Civil Law at the Universidad Americana. Taboada holds a master's degree in Business Administration from the Universidad Adolfo Ibañez and a master's degree in Corporate Law from the Universidad Americana and the Universidad de Valladolid.

Manuel Gómez is Associate Professor of Law and Associate Dean of International & Graduate Studies at Florida International University College of Law, USA. Gomez's research and teaching focuses on comparative civil procedure, dispute resolution, the globalization of the legal profession and legal education, and private systems of governance.

CHAPTER 6

The Rise of Big Law in Colombia

Everaldo Lamprea and Mariana Díaz Chalela

Introduction

The emergence of Big Law firms during the past two decades transformed the practice of the law in Colombia. However, little or no attention has been paid to this phenomenon. Tellingly, the two books that are considered by many as the "gold standard" studies on the legal profession in Colombia flatly ignore law firms.[1]

Germán Silva's study on the legal profession—scattered in four volumes—devotes special attention to the judicial branch. To a lesser extent, Silva explores the academia, the bureaucracy and small, family-owned *studios* led by well-known litigants as places that shape how the law is practiced. Albeit Silva's book was published in 2001—when major law firms like Brigard & Urrutia or Cavelier were consolidated and in some cases exhibited some features of Big Law firms—Silva dismisses the large firm as an interesting site to study the legal profession in Colombia. Similarly, Garcia's edited book on lawyers and the legal profession in Colombia, published in 2010—a time when Big Law firms were leading the non-state practice of the law—fails to include law firms as a case study.

It is useful to cite Silva's argument at some length to understand why he—and probably García as well—failed to introduce law firms in their studies of the legal profession in Colombia:

E. Lamprea (✉) • M. Díaz Chalela
Universidad de Los Andes, Bogotá, Colombia

M. Gómez, R. Pérez-Perdomo (eds.), *Big Law in Latin America and Spain*, https://doi.org/10.1007/978-3-319-65403-4_6

> Litigants' offices are mainly small workplaces. Even though there are some large law firms in Colombia, for instance in the area of intellectual property, this organizational model [law firms] is completely exceptional... As a general rule, small offices, which have an individualistic character, dominate [Colombia's legal profession]. Even in the most famous offices, there is not an actual *law firm organizational structure*; prestige originates from the individuality of one of the office's owners. Clients do not concur because it is a law firm, but because one of the owners is famous. In those offices, and in less famous ones, expenses are shared, but not profits, which are individual. Those firms lack a space where cases are collectively discussed—as it happens in U.S. law firms—and they also lack a system whereby cases are distributed among members.[2]

One could argue with Silva and García whether the landscape of the legal profession described in their books was an accurate depiction of legal practice in Colombia. As several of my interviewees argue, by 2001 the consolidation of the Big Law firm model was well under way. At the time, it was clear that family-based bureaus composed by one or two famous litigants were not at the forefront of the legal profession; on the contrary, firms like Brigard & Urrutia had already incorporated a Big Law model that challenged small-scale or family-owned firms.

According to this model, clients went to Brigard & Urrutia not because a famous litigant owned the place. In fact, by 2001, it was clear that Mr. Brigard and Mr. Urrutia were two partners, who led a complex organizational structure composed by several other partners, associates, junior lawyers and so on. Thanks to this institutional arrangement, firms like Brigard & Urrutia were capable of offering legal advice in a diversified array of legal fields. Additionally, profits were shared among partners, and cases were distributed and discussed in a way that resembled a typical Big Law American law firm.

But independently of the merits of Silva's and Garciá's studies, it is undeniable that by 2015 any book devoted to tackle down Colombia's legal profession must incorporate law firms as an important site to observe how the law is practiced. However, we lack studies that explore the impact of law firms in the transformation of the legal profession in Colombia during the past two decades. This chapter tries to close that significant gap in the local literature.

Drawing from interviews with partners at large Colombian law firms, and using a database provided by one of the participants of my research, this chapter presents a general description of Big Law in Colombia. Furthermore, it tries to answer the following question: what were the variables that unleashed the emergence of Big Law in Colombia? This chapter argues that the "opening" of Colombia's economy championed by the Gaviria administration (1990–1994) provided the main incentives for the emergence of Big Law in Colombia. However, it also shows how some lawyers pioneered Big Law by transforming family-based firms into highly specialized firms that share profits among partners and offered reliable, long-step legal careers for young lawyers.

This chapter shows how local and global legal education plays out at Colombia's leading law firms. It shows that three elite law schools—Los Andes, Javeriana and Rosario—predominate at the "big four" firms. It also shows how having an LLM and, more importantly, acquiring some experience at US or UK law firms became a powerful booster for the careers of young lawyers. Finally, this chapter explores some challenges to the traditional Big Law model in Colombia. On the one hand, it discusses how the arrival of large international firms like Garrigues, where ambitious and sophisticated lawyers can have long-step career and become partners at a multinational organization, may challenge the job offers at traditional local firms like Brigard & Urrutia, where mobility to the top of the organization seems to be blocked.

This chapter also considers the merger of Colombia's second largest firm—Prietocarrizosa—with Chile's Philippi Yrarrázaval, Pulido & Brunner, and Spain's Uría Menéndez. This is the first merger of its kind in Colombia. It created a 220-strong lawyer firm with offices in Santiago, Bogotá and Barranquilla. Additionally, Uría Menéndez, after acquiring 30% of the new firm, provided its extensive network of offices and more than 500 lawyers. It discusses whether this type of mergers set a significant challenge to large, well-established, and local Big Law firms in Colombia. Furthermore, it touches on a fairly recent phenomenon among big law firms in Colombia: pro bono work.

The Legal Profession in Colombia

The importance of the legal profession in Colombia's history cannot be overstated. As legal historian Victor Manuel Uribe has showed, during the late eighteenth and early nineteenth centuries, lawyers played a decisive role in the administration of Spain's affairs in the Nueva Granada, the South American colony that became the Great Colombia after independence in 1810.[3] Furthermore, during the independence wars (1810–1824) against Spain, lawyers were instrumental to give shape to the revolutionary and secessionist efforts. Not surprisingly, the Spanish crown tried to crush insurgence in the Nueva Granada by prosecuting and executing lawyers.[4]

As Silva argues in his study, since the nineteenth century the legal profession has been closely associated with the attainment of political power. Having a law diploma from one of the traditional universities was considered as a marker of *prestige and status*, which was instrumental to obtain high-ranked posts within the bureaucracy, including the Presidency. Starting with Francisco de Paula Santander (1819–1827) and ending with Álvaro Uribe Vélez (2002–2010), most Colombian presidents have boasted a law diploma.[5] Since the 1990s the economists' technocratic expertise has challenged the lawyers' traditional monopoly over policy-making. However, one fact remains true: the legal language is still the predominant language of power in Colombia.

Yet, as both Silva and García highlight, it is surprising that despite the breadth of its influence, the legal profession in Colombia lacks a proper institutional arrangement for its self-governance. Unlike many other countries—including several Latin American ones—Colombia lacks a self-regulating body such as a lawyers' bar association. This, as Silva underscores, is an entrenched historical trend (p. 170). In 1984, the Ministry of Justice tried to revert this situation by passing a bill—Law 64 of 1984—which created a proper National Bar Association (Colegio Nacional de Abogados) endowed with faculties to regulate the legal profession, issue licenses for practitioners, and function as a disciplinary body. However, the bill was defeated at Congress and never became a law.

Article 26 of the 1991 Colombian Constitution established that "legally recognized professions might be organized into professional associations … occupations, the arts, and work that do not require academic training are to be freely exercised, except for those which involve a risk to society." However, the Constitution—and subsequent laws—failed to create a mandatory association or bar requirement for lawyers, even though the practice of the law has the potential to create a "risk to society."

But even though Colombia lacks a proper Bar Association, there are a number of unions and guilds that represent the interests of some sectors of the legal profession. Since 1976, ASONAL JUDICIAL has functioned as the official union of the judicial branch, representing the interests of judges, prosecutors and judicial staff. (179) In the past, ASONAL has staged many strikes in order to demand better salaries and benefits for its associates. In 2015, ASONAL opposed a constitutional reform that tried, among other things, to eliminate the Judicial Council or Consejo Superior de la Judicatura, an agency—which also operates as a higher Court—within the judicial branch that is tasked with the regulation of the legal practice of judicial employees.[6] The Colombian Constitutional Court struck down the reform and maintained the Judicial Council as the regulatory body of the legal practice.[7] The Judicial Council has been lately in the eye of the storm, after corruption scandals involved some of its members.

Litigants have formed several guilds that operate as venues for the discussion of issues related to specialized legal fields. Some of these guilds have influenced the drafting of new procedural codes in areas such as commercial, civil and labor law. However, being small and specialized niches, they usually lack academic and political clout. Additionally, in large cities like Bogotá, Medellín and Cali, high-ranked judges and prosecutors have formed elite associations. These associations differentiate themselves from ASONAL JUDICIAL by being elite-oriented. However, unlike ASONAL, they are incapable of exerting pressure on the government. As the specialized guilds, they also lack academic prestige.

The 1991 Constitution endowed the Judicial Council (Consejo Superior de la Judicatura) with faculties to regulate the requirements needed to become a legal practitioner. There are only two formal requirements that legal practitioners have to comply with. On the one hand, all lawyers must be part of the National Registry of Lawyers (Registro Nacional de Abogados), a database managed by the Judicial Council. On the other hand, all practitioners must carry a Professional ID (Tarjeta Profesional), issued also by the Judicial Council. However, in order to hold a professional ID or to be part of the judicial branch's database, practitioners are only asked to demonstrate that they graduated from a law school recognized by the Ministry of Education.

In 2009 Congress issued Law 1234, whereby it determined that all university students—including law school students—must take a national exam prior to graduating. However, Law 1234 did not establish that *passing* the exam was a prerequisite for practicing a profession. As a result of this loophole, students who fail to pass the national exam are allowed to practice the law.

According to sociolegal scholars like Mauricio García, the fact that the Colombian government failed to regulate legal education and legal practice by means of a functioning bar association and a nationwide bar exam explains to a large extent why there has been an uncontrolled growth of law schools and law school graduates since 1992, when Congress passed a law (Law 30) that bolstered the creation of private universities.[8]

Prior to Law 30 of 1992—the watershed event in the recent history of legal education in Colombia—both Congress and government tried to regulate different aspects of legal education. In 1918, a legislative act endowed the government to limit the practice of the law only to practitioners who have obtained a proper law diploma. In 1928, Law 62, a statute passed by Congress, ruled that only certified lawyers—those who had a legitimate diploma—could take criminal, civil and administrative law cases. Prior to 1928, any person, even those who lacked a law degree, could represent the interests of a plaintiff.

In 1936 a governmental decree (Decree 260 of 1936) established that all private law schools that wished to operate in Colombia had to design their curriculums under the tutelage of Colombia's largest public university (Universidad Nacional de Colombia).

Starting in the 1970s and ending in the late 1980s, the government handed down several decrees that regulated the creation of new law schools and also of law schools' curricula. However, the government's intervention in how lawyers were educated changed dramatically after Congress passed Law 30 of 1992, a statute that overhauled legal education based on a principle entrenched in the 1991 Constitution: the universities' autonomy.

As Salamanca explains in detail, Law 30 of 1992 created several legal incentives for the creation of new, low-quality law schools across the country.[9] As a result of these incentives, in the following years there was an explosion in the number of law schools and law school graduates. For instance, whereas in 1993 there were approximately 32 law schools, by 2007 there were more than 72.[10] The number of law school graduates also doubled during the same period. In 1994 there were approximately 36,000 law students in Colombia. By 2007 there were more than 70,000. Additionally, Law 30 of 1992 created incentives for the establishment of new private law schools, most of which fail to observe basic quality standards. At the same time, well-established public law schools lost an important share of their market. Whereas in 1949 public law schools represented 54.5% of the total number of law schools in the country, by 2007 that number plummeted to 29%.[11]

According to some accounts, Colombia is one of the countries with the highest ratios of lawyers to population. By 2009 the number of lawyers per 100,000 inhabitants was 35,445 second only to Costa Rica (see Chart 6.1).

The upsurge in the numbers of law graduates and the mushrooming of private law schools transformed legal education and legal practice in Colombia. Prior to Law 30 of 1992, well-established universities were the gatekeepers of legal practice. The case of the Externado University law school is meaningful. Traditionally, this private university founded in the nineteenth century used to "own" an important portion of the judicial branch, and more particularly of higher courts' seats. However, during the past decade the Externado power has eroded. Since 1992, three or four of

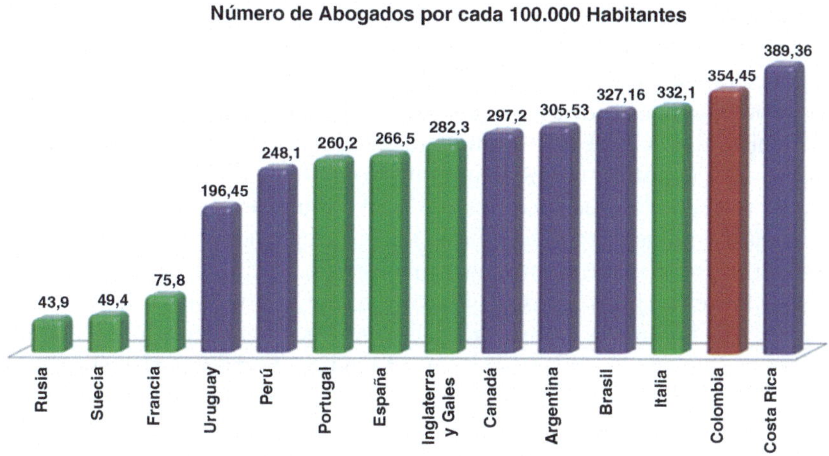

Fuente: Centro de Estudios de justicia de las Américas, Reporte sobre la justicia en las Américas 2008-2009. comisión Europea para la Eficiencia de la justicia, Sistemas Judiciales Europeos: Eficiencia y calidad de la justicia Edición 2010.
Nota: Las cifras presentadas corresponden al último año reportado por las autoridades de cade pais y hacen referencia exclusivamente al número de profesionales en derecho, no incluye asesores legales (*"legol advisors"*).

Chart 6.1 Ratio of lawyers per 100,000 inhabitants

the nine Constitutional Court Justices have been graduates from that law school. However, from 2013 until 2017, only two out of the eleven justices that sat on the Court were Externado graduates. A similar phenomenon took place at the Supreme Court and at the Administrative Court (Consejo de Estado). As things stand now, only 9 of 62 higher Court judges (6 in the Administrative Court, 3 in the Constitutional Court, and none in the Supreme Court) are graduates from Externado law school.[12]

Other well-established law schools have not filled the free room left by the waning of the Externado's power. For instance, there are currently only two Los Andes Law School graduates—the highest-ranked law school in Colombia according to several measurements—sitting at a higher court. Throughout the Court's history there have only been four Los Andes graduates out of 37 elected justices.

The arrival of new law schools to the commanding heights of Colombia's judiciary can be interpreted as the democratization of an "old boys" club. However, some analysts have underscored that the new judicial elite has a poorer legal training than the old one.[13] Additionally, there are good indications that the newcomers are more prone to be captured by politics. An example of the politicized practices that have taken over the judicial branch is what the media calls the "merry-go-round" between higher courts.

Since higher courts have the faculty to nominate candidates to fill seats at other higher courts—for instance, the Supreme Court and the Administrative Court can nominate candidates to the Constitutional Court—some justices are now jumping from one higher court to the next. Under this scheme, qualifications and legal training are secondary criteria to nominate candidates to the highest courts in the land. Other recent example of this trend is the scandal that involves a Constitutional Court Justice (Jorge Pretelt) who is accused of having accepted bribes in order to "massage" a case before the Constitutional Court. As it has been argued by some authors, since the latest appointment of Constitutional Court Justices, the standards used to nominate and appoint the members of the Constitutional Court have been heavily politicized, allowing lawyers like Pretelt to become a justice at Colombia's highest (and most esteemed) Court.

But unlike what has happened at the judicial branch where scandals like the so-called Preteltgate have damaged the prestige of higher Courts, Big Law firms are not willing to open their doors to "shady" newcomers. As I will discuss later, junior and senior lawyers working at prestigious law firms are—almost invariably—graduates from a handful of traditional and well-established private law schools (Los Andes, Rosario, Javeriana, and to a lesser extent Externado). This has been a solid trend during the past two decades, and does not show signs of changing course.

Mapping Big Law in Colombia: The Big Five

In this project we define Big Law firms as those specialized in "the provision of complex legal services usually in the context of business transactions, by organizations incorporated as law firms, to high-end business clients, regardless of the size of the provider."[14]

Since the early 1990s Colombia has witnessed the transformation of traditional law firms into sophisticated *Big Law* conglomerates. That is the case of Brigard & Urrutia, Colombia's oldest—it was founded in 1937—and largest law firm. Additionally, during that same period several new firms were created based on the model of Big Law. Gomez-Pinzón and Posse Herrera are two examples of that trend. Finally, other traditional and highly respected law firms, like Cavelier, did not make the leap into Big Law but remained safely anchored in the old model. Yet, the cost paid by traditional law firms like Cavelier is their current irrelevance in the legal market.

Before delving into the variables that drove the emergence of Big Law firms in Colombia, we present in this section the overarching landscape of law firms in that country.

According to *The Legal 500* ranking, "the so called 'Colombian big four' formed by Brigard & Urrutia, Gómez-Pinzón Zuleta, Posse Herrera Ruiz, and Philippi Prieto Carrizosa Ferrero DU & Uría remain market leaders…"[15] Those four law firms had, indeed, the strongest claims to be the only Big Law firms in Colombia. While Brigard & Urrutia, Gómez-Pinzón Zuleta, Posse Herrera Ruiz and Prieto Carrizosa belong to a league of their own, their dominance is currently being challeged by the arrival of powerful international law firms. In 2017, *The Legal 500* ranking pointed this change in the market: "the dominance of the traditional 'top four' – Brigard & Urrutia, Gómez-Pinzón Zuleta, Posse Herrera Ruiz and Philippi Prietocarrizosa Ferrero DU & Uría (formerly PrietoCarrizosa) – is perhaps, no longer to be taken for granted, with Baker McKenzie S.A.S. in particular, claiming a place at the top table. The arrival (and/or consolidation) of other international firms, including Dentons Cardenas & Cardenas, DLA Piper Martinez Beltran, Garrigues, Norton Rose Fulbright and most recently, CMS Rodríguez Azuero Contexto Legal Abogados, has hiked competition for qualified and experienced talent, and is increasingly altering the dynamics of the local market." The traditional 'big four' have now become the 'big five' with international giant Baker Mckenzie leading the way for foreign law firms.[16]

For instance, in terms of number of employees the "big five" are, by far, the largest firms in Colombia, with Brigard & Urrutia topping the list. Moreover, the "big five" look fairly similar in terms of number of employees. For instance, Brigard & Urrutia employs 129 lawyers, whereas Posse Herrera Ruiz has 122 employees. Baker Mckenzie, by 2013 was not part of Big Law league, however with its income and size growth, it has become the third largest firm, following Brigard & Urrutia and Philippi Prieto Carrizosa. Baker Mckenzie went from having 63 employees in 2013 to having 97 by 2017. In terms of employment capabilities, the difference between the "big five" and the rest of the top ten largest firms in Colombia are marked (see Table 6.1).

The majority of the top eight law firms offer services in all areas of practice. However, only Garrigues offers services in all areas (up to 20 areas). Among the 'big five', Brigard & Urrutia offers services in most areas with 16 different areas of practice, while Philippi Prieto Carrizoa only offers services in up to 13 areas (see table 6.2).

Table 6.1 Number of employees: Associates and Partners (2017)

	Firms	*Partners*	*Associates*	*Total employees*
1	Brigard & Urrutia	16	113	129
2	Philippi Prieto Carrizosa Ferrero DU & Uría	16	99	115
3	Baker Mckenzie	10	87	97
4	Posse Herrera Ruiz	19	103	122
5	Gómez Pinzón Zuleta Abogados	15	95	110
6	Pricewaterhousecoopers Slt Lta	6	56	62
7	Dentons Cárdenas y Cárdenas	12	35	47
8	Garrigues	9	31	40
9	Lloreda	8	55	63
10	Cavelier Abogados	7	40	47
11	Ernst and Young SAS	8	55	63
12	Olartemoure	2	64	66
13	Godoy Córdoba	7	52	59
14	Norton Rose Fulbright	8	15	23
15	Brigard y Castro	3	6	9
16	Araújo Ibarra y Asociados	5	20	25
17	Holland and Knight Colombia	7	44	51
18	López Asociados	3	53	56
19	Arrieta Mantilla y Asociados	5	12	17
20	CMS Rodríguez Azuero Contexto Legal Abogados	9	37	46
21	Esguerra Asesores Jurídicos	6	18	24
22	Arce Rojas Consultores	2	38	40
23	Lewin & Wills	7	11	18
24	Clarke Modet and Company Colombia	0	16	16
25	Durán y Osorio Abogados Asociados	5	19	24

Information taken from: Revista Dinero 'Así son las firmas de abogabos más grandes de Colombia', *Revista Dinero*, August 17 2017, http://www.dinero.com/edicion-impresa/caratula/articulo/bufetes-de-abogados-mas-importantes-de-colombia/248692

Table 6.2 Number of areas of practice for top eight Colombian law firms (2017)

	Firms	*Areas of practice*
1	Brigard & Urrutia	16
2	Philippi Prieto Carrizosa Ferrero DU & Uría	13
3	Baker Mckenzie	14
4	Posse Herrera Ruiz	14
5	Gómez Pinzón Zuleta Abogados	14
6	Pricewaterhousecoopers Slt Lta	15
7	Dentons Cárdenas y Cárdenas	13
8	Garrigues	20

Information taken from: Revista Dinero 'Así son las firmas de abogabos más grandes de Colombia', *Revista Dinero*, August 17 2017, http://www.dinero.com/edicion-impresa/caratula/articulo/bufetes-de-abogados-mas-importantes-de-colombia/248692

Codes for areas of practice

International Trade and Customs	*A*
Arbitration and Dispute Resolution	B
Derivatives and Structured Products	C
Due Diligence	D
Environmental Law	E
Corporate	F
Antitrust & Competition	G
Financial Law	H
Real Estate	I
Labor	J
Mining, Gas, Oil, Energy	K
Tax	L
M&A	M
Project Finance & Infrastructure	N
Capital Markets	O
Inheritance Law and Family Firms	P
Telecoms	Q
Intellectual Property	R
Administrative & Constitutional Law	S
Environmental Law	T

Not surprisingly, the "big five" are, by far, the most profitable law firms in Colombia. However, Brigard & Urrutia outperforms the rest of the group. It can be inferred that the outstanding economic performance of Brigard & Urrutia is the product of—among other variables—the comprehensiveness of its legal services and its size. Contrastingly, the profits of the remaining firms are very similar. It is reasonable to argue that Philippi Prieto Carrizosa Ferrero DU & Uría, Baker Mckenzie, Posse Herrera Ruíz, and Gómez-Pinzón Zuleta are similarly large law firms in terms of profit, whereas Brigard & Urrutia is a super large firm.

Yet, as it can be seen in Table 6.3, in terms of profitability the difference between the "big five" and the up-and-coming Pricewaterhousecoopers, Dentons Cárdenas y Cárdenas, and Garrigues is remarkable.

Although not comparable in size, comprehensiveness and profitability with US and UK Big Law, Colombian law firms have experienced a sustained growth that was unthinkable 20 years ago. What variables drove the emergence of Big Law firms in Colombia? In the following sections we will try to address this question from the perspective of the lawyers who spearheaded this particular transformation in Colombia's legal education and legal practice.

Table 6.3 Top eight Colombian law firms by revenue (2017)

	Firms	*Earnings (US$ millions)*
1	Brigard & Urrutia	34
2	Philippi Prieto Carrizosa Ferrero DU & Uría	26.5
3	Baker Mckenzie	26.1
4	Posse Herrera Ruiz	21
5	Gómez Pinzón Zuleta Abogados	20.3
6	Pricewaterhousecoopers Slt Lta	12
7	Dentons Cárdenas y Cárdenas	8.6
8	Garrigues	8.4

Information taken from: Revista Dinero 'Así son las firmas de abogabos más grandes de Colombia', *Revista Dinero*, August 17 2017, http://www.dinero.com/edicion-impresa/caratula/articulo/bufetes-de-abogados-mas-importantes-de-colombia/248692

The Early 1990s: The Economic Opening

According to all of our interviewees, the early 1990s marked a turning point for the emergence of Big Law in Colombia. This is not surprising, since that period was a transformative juncture for Colombia's political and economic institutions. On the one hand, in 1991 a new Constitution was proclaimed. This new Constitution introduced institutions such as the Constitutional Court and the attorney's general office; it also transformed a heavily centralized political system—established by the 1886 conservative Constitution—into a decentralized one. At the same time, the 1991 Constitution introduced a charter of basic rights and an informal and expedited judicial mechanism whereby citizens could claim their fundamental and socioeconomic rights—the tutela injunction.

But on the other hand, during the early 1990s, Colombia's economy experienced a major transformation. César Gaviria's administration (1990–1994) inaugurated what was labeled as the "economic opening" (*apertura económica*). During the "opening" the government conducted a structural readjustment of Colombia's economy. Many public utilities and public services companies were privatized. But most importantly, trade barriers and capital controls were rapidly eliminated. Public deficits were slashed and inflation controlled. Privatization policies, trade liberalization and free capital movements attracted more foreign direct investment.

The "opening" meant bad news for important sectors of the economy. For instance, prior to economic liberalization trade barriers protected local industrial and agricultural production, focused on supplying the domestic market. After the "opening," cheaper agricultural and industrial goods entered the market, creating havoc for domestic agricultural and industrial sectors, totally unprepared to compete in a globalized market. Consequently, several sectors of Colombia's agriculture (rice, cotton, corn) and industrial production (cars, textiles, pharmaceuticals, and manufactured goods such as shoes and leather goods) experienced a crunch. Whereas Colombian costumers had access to cheaper goods, many local companies went broke.

However, for some sectors the "opening" brought affluence and unprecedented business opportunities. One of those sectors was the provision of legal services by law firms. As Sergio Michelsen, currently a partner at Brigard & Urrutia—Colombia's largest law firm—explains:

> In the course of twenty years legal practice was completely transformed… Try to picture the abysmal difference… In 1986 I was working at Cavelier. I conducted the largest M&A transaction at the time, 1 million dollars. And in 2006 I conducted Colombia's largest M&A transaction ever, 7.8 billion dollars…

Referring to the organizational transformations that occurred during that period, Michelsen explains:

> Prior to that [the 1990s *opening*] legal practice was limited to the individual lawyer who knew a little bit of tax law, a little bit of labor law, a little of corporate law, and so on, and who counseled his clients from that generalist perspective. After the 1990s, that's when everything took off. That's when we did the first international stock emissions, the first ADRs [alternative dispute resolution], when we did the first important M&A transaction, when we did the first finance projects in Colombia.

Jaime Herrera, a partner from Posse Herrera Ruiz, describes the groundbreaking influence of the "opening" on the emergence of Big Law in Colombia:

> A turning point [for law firms] was the economic opening championed by the Gaviria administration, which placed Colombia in the map. That was especially true for some sectors that had no previous access to the private sector both at the local and at the international level. In particular, from 1992 onwards there was a philosophical shift because it was allowed that private entrepreneurs, both local and foreign, could own public utilities firms. Thanks to that legislative breakthrough we were able to counsel big energy projects, and at the same time we were able to keep our clients from the financial sector, helping them to consolidate their business in areas that are still important for our legal practice.

According to Alejandro Linares, partner of Gómez-Pinzón Zuleta, the "opening" changed the type of legal practice offered by law firms. Instead of being mere intermediaries or simple providers of legal services, law firms became business facilitators and brokers.

However, in Colombia the "economic opening" did not create Big Law singlehandedly. It was thanks to the leadership of a handful of pioneering lawyers that some family-based law firms made the leap into Big Law. Arguably, the most important actor in this transformation process was Brigard & Urrutia. During the early 1990s the generational change that took place within Brigard & Urrutia sent shock waves throughout Colombia's law firms. Sergio Michelsen describes the transformation that took place at Brigard & Urrutia during the early 1990s as follows:

> Brigard & Urrutia changed in very important ways, especially in two points. First, it was basically a family-based firm. When I arrived [in 1992] we had Carlos Urrutia senior, Carlos Urrutia Jr., Álvaro de Brigard, Francisco Urrutia and Carlos Umaña, who was related both to Álvaro de Brigard and to the Urrutias. I was the first partner who was not related to anyone. Prior to that ours was a very family-based firm, like Lloreda, Cavelier, or Cárdenas. But that was the way things were back then, not only in Colombia, but also in Latin America. And then we had this groundbreaking moment. I was made partner, and then, at about the same time, Mónica Reyes (who later quitted the firm) was also made partner, and that's when the firm opened up. After that Carlos Urrutia senior and Álvaro de Brigard passed away, and we opened up even more… Another important change is that, today, everybody is made partner based exclusively on merits. Even Carlos Urrutia was an associate, like myself. That is quite different from family-based firms, where you are made partner just because you are family. Starting from that point, we insisted, rather intuitively first, on offering careers within the firm. We encouraged people to go abroad, study, and have experience at a firm, and then we encouraged them to come back. After that we institutionalized the career for associates and partners, and that completely changed our perspective. And second, another groundbreaking change was that we divided the firm according to teams. When I started, people worked a little bit on all kinds of things. A little bit on project finance, a little bit on capital markets, a little bit on oil and mining law, a little bit on corporate, you name it. And after a while we stopped and said: "Hey, each lawyer cannot be all-knowing here, we have to create teams", and that's when all teams grew exponentially.

Alejandro Linares, a partner at Gómez-Pinzón Zuleta, considers that Carlos Urrutia Jr. "understood where the world was heading to…"

According to Linares, Urrutia got rid of the "heavy burden of the past" and paved the way for the emergence of Big Law. Unlike other family-based firms like Cavelier and Cárdenas & Cárdenas, Brigard & Urrutia, under the leadership of Carlos Urrutia Jr. and of new partners like Sergio Michelsen and Carlos Umaña, abandoned the mindset that was typical at the time.

Asked about the mindset transformation that made possible the emergence of Big Law in Colombia, Linares considers that what sets apart Brigard & Urrutia, Posse Herrera Ruiz and Gomez-Pinzón Zuleta from family-based firms like Cavelier is that while the former are willing to share profits among partners, family-based firms are not interested in "having real partners, or in inviting other people to share the pie." According to Linares, Big Law firms are based on an equity rationale, that is, on a distribution of profit.

Based on that scheme, Brigard & Urrutia, and emerging Big Law firms like Posse Herrera Ruiz and Gómez-Pinzón Zuleta offered a "long-step" career for many ambitious young lawyers. The chances of forging a career from junior associate to full-fledged partner attracted the best legal minds in the market. Most of these promising young lawyers were working at the time [late 1980s and early 1990s] at family-based firms like Cavelier & Cárdenas & Cárdenas. That was precisely the case of lawyers like Segio Michelsen and Jaime Herrera. Both Michelsen and Herrera cut their teeth at Cavelier, but later left in order to begin more attractive legal practices at Brigard & Urrutia and Posse Herrera Ruiz, respectively. Herrera recounts this experience as follows:

> When I was hired by Cavelier, it was Colombia's biggest firm. And that is a very interesting case. Nobody in Colombia had the international vision that Germán Cavelier had nor the organizational structure or the capacity to deal with so many subjects and international cases... It was really a model in terms of organization, systematization and infrastructure... But the question is this: Why Cavelier did not grow? Basically because many of the most talented lawyers working at Cavelier at the time lacked incentives to develop their careers there; that is why they decided to move on and create their own firms. Many of the most important lawyers in Colombia were trained at Cavelier Abogados. If ten years ago you took the ten biggest Colombian firms—we did that exercise back then—six of them were created by former Cavelier lawyers.

As Alejandro Linares argues, the creation of law firms that were based on the US model of profit-sharing and that were organized according to specialized areas of practice constituted one of the most important "legal transplants" that have occurred in Colombian law. Lawyers like Carlos Urrutia Jr., Sergio Michelsen, Alejandro Linares and Jaime Herrera felt that the times were changing for legal practice. Consequently, they championed at their firms the transplant of procedures, organizational practices and legal culture that was predominant at the US and UK law firms where they worked after completing their LL.M. This transplant led to the decline of traditional, family-led law firms like Cavelier and Cárdenas & Cárdenas.

Local and Global Legal Education

According to all of my interviewees, the three dominant law schools at their law firms are, in no particular order, Rosario, Los Andes and Javeriana. Alejandro Linares, a graduate from Los Andes Law School and Harvard Law School (LLM), argues that his firm (Gómez-Pinzón Zuleta) hires mostly people from Los Andes, Rosario and Javeriana. However, there are important differences between Los Andes and the other two law schools. Whereas Los Andes offers the weakest legal training, its graduates have the best English and rapidly familiarize themselves with the practices, networking and legal culture of Big Law firms. Since a great number of transactions are conducted in English, Los Andes graduates are sought after by law firms like Gómez-Pinzón Zuleta. However, in terms of legal training, Rosario and Javeriana graduates outperform those from Los Andes.

Felipe Quintero, a young lawyer who is currently a local partner at Garrigues (a large Spanish firm that opened an office in Bogotá in 2013), offers a similar account. According to Quintero, who is also a graduate from Los Andes and from Harvard Law School (LL.M.), Los Andes law school graduates may be more interesting for a firm because they have "better English and a more attuned international sensibility." However, legal training is as important as fluency in English. For Quintero, a Rosario graduate with good English will always outperform—in a job application—a Los Andes graduate with equally good English. Not surprisingly, Quintero reports that most of Garrigues hiring comes from Rosario and Javeriana.

However, Los Andes, Rosario and Javeriana are "the big three" law schools within law firms. Carlos Urrutia Jr.—the powerhouse of Big Law in Colombia—is a graduate from Los Andes Law School. According to Alejandro Linares, Los Andes graduates are a usually a good fit for Big Law firms because they are trained under the American model of law schools. That explains why Los Andes graduates can solve research problems better than other lawyers. Contrastingly, legal training at law schools like the Externado is more Europeanized and memory-based.

According to all of my interviewees, having an LL.M. from a prestigious US law school is an important requisite for making a career within Big Law firms. However, that was not the case in the 1990s. For instance, Carlos Urrutia Jr. lacks an LL.M. Yet, that was not an obstacle for his rise to the top of corporate law in Colombia and Latin America. As Felipe Quintero explains, even though most experienced partners lack an LL.M., nowadays partners expect that associates complete an LLM prior to becoming candidates for a partnership.

Having an American LL.M. became, during the past decade, a "must" for ambitious associates who want to climb the ladder of their firms. But, according to all of my interviewees, what their firms value the most is that their associates obtain experience at a large US or UK firm after completing their LL.M. Albeit passing the bar exam is welcomed, having experience at a global Big Law firm remains the most important qualification.

We searched several firms' webpages in order to find data regarding their partners and associates' US training. The results are given in Table 6.4.

Table 6.4 Big Lawyers and LL.M. graduates from top ten law schools (2017)

Law firms	*N Lawyers*	*Lawyers with LL.M. from foreign universities*	*LL.M. from top ten law schools*
Brigard & Urrutia			
Partners	16	11	8
Associates	113	29	11
Philippi Prieto Carrizosa Ferrero DU & Uría			
Partners	16	7	1
Associates	99	18	5
Baker Mckenzie			
Partners	10	4	4
Associates	87	10	3
Posse Herrera Ruíz			
Partners	19	10	3
Associates	103	19	10
Gómez Pinzón Zuleta Abogados			
Partners	15	6	3
Associates	95	22	7

As we can perceive, an LL.M. from a top American university is not as important as my interviewees have said. Among the top 10 American law schools where Colombian Big Law lawyers have studied, I found that New York University counted with 21 alumni, Columbia with 12 and Harvard with 6. Among top UK universities, LSE counted with 7 alumni, UCL with 4, and Oxford with 1.

Challenges and Opportunities: Mergers, International Law Firms, and Pro Bono Work

For Colombian law firms the arrival of UK, European and US global Big Law constitutes a threat but also a chance for healthier growth. An illustration of this phenomenon is the arrival to Colombia, in 2013, of Garrigues, one of Europe's largest law firms. As Felipe Quintero—a local partner—argues, firms like Garrigues offer to a new generation of lawyers working at the traditional "Colombian big four" a new chance to climb the ladder of an organization that is predominantly global. The ceiling of firms like Brigard & Urrutia is so distant and elusive that many young lawyers have good reasons to doubt whether they will become partners some day, argues Quintero.

On the other hand, firms like Garrigues can attract the most sophisticated lawyers available by offering them better salaries, more job security and the chance of becoming not only local partners but also global equity partners. That is precisely the path that Quintero is now following. Furthermore, according to Quintero, the arrival of big global players can be a waking call for "the big four." If those local firms offer partnerships to their most competitive lawyers they may be capable of retaining their human capital.

However, the creation in January 2015 of Philippi, Prietocarrizosa & Uría became one of the most important developments for Colombia's "big five" law firms. The merger of Colombia's second largest firm—Prietocarrizosa—with Chile's Philippi Yrarrázaval, Pulido & Brunner and Spain's Uría Menéndez created a 220-strong lawyer firm with offices in Santiago, Bogotá and Barranquilla. Additionally, Uría Menéndez, acquired 30% of the new firm, and provided its extensive network of offices and more than 500 lawyers. In January 2016, PPU merged with Peruvian firms Ferrero Abogados y Delmar Ugarte who provided 29 new partners and 99 new associates, becoming Philippi Prieto Carrizosa Ferrero DU & Uría (PPU).

The emergence of PPU is relevant insofar as it constitutes the first major merger between Colombian and foreign law firms. Unlike the model represented by Garrigues, PPU presents itself not as a foreign firm that is branching out in Colombia, but as the first "Iberoamerican law firm," as it is publicized in PPU's webpage.[17] Being the first Iberoamerican law firm means that the driving force behind PPU is two well-established Latin American law firms that are joining forces in order to provide legal services for a whole region, and not only for a particular country or domestic economy. As PPU's website explains:

> With this merger is expected to efficiently respond to the new demands for professional services involving the growing economic relationship between the countries of the Pacific Alliance (Chile, Colombia, Mexico, and Peru), added to the growing interest of companies from Europe, Asia, and North America in the Latin American region. Therefore, the firm's future plans include deploying its presence into other markets such as Peru and Mexico. The experience gained by the three firms, along with technical and professional quality, and geographic diversity, will allow Philippi, Prietocarrizosa & Uría provide counseling with increased direct presence in a region that has attracted interest from both local and multinational companies.

After the merger, PPU was estimated to be able to hire up to 220 attorneys in the Colombia office, more than two times the number of attorneys of Brigard & Urrutia, Colombia's largest firm. However, PPU offers the same 13 areas of practice that Prietocarrizosa offered in the past and 3 less than Brigard & Urrutia.

Two years after the merger, PPU still is the second largest firm in terms of profit, while Birgard & Urrutia maintains its dominance in the Colombian market. As far as employees goes, PPU is third to Brigard & Urrutia and Posse Herrera Ruíz. This shows that although the merger brought PPU closer to Brigard & Urrutia it did not affect the market in the way it was estimated. Furthermore, international firms as Baker Mckenzie are fairly near PPU in terms of profit, with PPU reporting 26.5 million USD and Baker Mckenzie reporting 26.1 million USD in earnings.

With the PPU merger also came the union between the up-and-coming Cárdenas y Cárdenas and global giant Dentons. According to *The Legal 500,* Dentons is the sixth largest firm in terms of revenue and, following its merger wtih chinese law firm Dacheng, the biggest one in number of employees.[18] While the impact of the new Dentons Cárdenas y Cárdenas reamins to be seen, it is likely that in the following years we could witness more mergers between Colombian and foreign law firms.

The completion of these mergers would be influenced not only by the domestic and regional economic performance, but also by the de-escalation of Colombia's internal armed conflict and by the successful conclusion of the peace talks between the Colombian government and the guerrillas.

Baker and Mckenzie is another example of how Big Law has changed within the past couple of years. Baker and Mackenzie acquired family-run firm Raisbeck, Lara, Rodriguez, and Rueda in 1979, but it wasn't until 4 years ago that it started eroding the Big Law scenario. While in 2013, Baker Mckenzie was nowhere near the 'big four', it has now entered the Big Law game, and has transformed the 'big four' into the 'big five'. With offices in over 50 locations worldwide and total revenues of 2.67 billion USD, Baker Mckenzie offers its partners mobility across offices and acces to a global legal market.[19] Claudia Pardo, Baker Mckenzie's regional chair for Latin America highlights Baker's global impact: "Baker McKenzie has demonstrated a solid commitment with the Latin American region over decades. We are pleased to celebrate the 80th anniversary of the Bogota office where we have been offering innovative legal advice to local and multinational companies anticipating challenges combining deep local expertise with an unmatchable regional and global footprint."[20]

Finally, one of the biggest challenges to Big Law in Colombia, has been the introduction of pro bono work. Since 2009, the 'Pro Bono Foundation' has been promoting pro bono work among law firms. Today it has 46 members, including the 'big five'. The 'Pro Bono Foundation' acts as a link between pro bono clients and law firms, and promotes pro bono work across the legal field. The 'Pro Bono Foundation' also has a program in which law students are able to have internships in law firms, while doing pro bono work.

Although the rise of pro bono has made an impact on the social commitment of law firms, it has also faced many challenges. We discussed some of the challenges of doing pro bono work in Colombia with members of the 'Pro Bono Foundation', for most of them, although the good outweighed the bad, integrating big law and pro bono work is still an ongoing process. While law firms do take pro bono cases, they are often handed down to junior associates or interns who, by themselves, decide the legal strategy. Furthermore, students who apply for the pro bono interships are also looking to get a job offer at the firm and end up relegating their pro bono assignments.

The legal market in Colombia is rapidly changing and is often adjusting to global experiences. More often than not, we are seeing how international law firms have entered the Colombian legal scenario, via mergers or by opening their own offices. With the de-escalation of the Colombian conflict and the promotion of foreign investment, we expect big law in Colombia to rise. It remains to be seen whether local law firms adjust or explore new law firm models.

Notes

1. These books are: Germán Silva García, *El Mundo de los Abogados y de la Justicia—La Profesión Jurídica*, Externado, Bogotá, 2011. Mauricio García Villegas (Edit), *Los Abogados en Colombia*, Universidad Nacional, Bogotá, 2010.
2. Silva, op cit (Vol. I), pp. 144–145.
3. Victor Manuel Uribe, "The Lawyers and New Granada's Late Colonial State," in Latin American Studies, Cambridge University Press, 1995.
4. Victor Manuel Uribe, "Kill all the Lawyers! Lawyers and the Independence Movement in New Granada, 1809–1820", in *The Americas*, 1995.
5. Silva, op cit (Vol. I), pp. 193–2130.
6. Colombian Congress. Acto Legislativo 02 de 2015. http://wp.presidencia.gov.co/sitios/normativa/actoslegislativos/ACTO%20LEGISLATIVO%2002%20DEL%2001%20JULIO%20DE%202015.pdf
7. Colombian Constitutional Court. Ruling C-053/16.
8. Garcia-Villegas, "Colombia, Tierra de Abogados," *El Espectador*, May 1, 2010, http://www.elespectador.com/impreso/nacional/articuloimpreso 201004-colombia-tierra-de-abogados
9. Freddy Alexander Salamanca, "Reseña Histórica de la Regulación de la Enseñanza del Derecho", en Mauricio García Villegas (Ed), *Los Abogados en Colombia*, Universidad Nacional, Bogotá, 2010.
10. Mauricio Garcia-Villegas, "Sociología de la Profesión Jurídica," *Pensamiento Jurídico* No. 26 (September 2009): 237–251.
11. Ibid.
12. Juan Esteban Lewin, "EL Cambio En El Poder Judicial," *La Silla Vacía*, October 21, 2013, http://lasillavacia.com/historia/el-cambio-en-el-poder-judicial-detras-de-las-peleas-de-montealegre-45923
13. Ibid.
14. Rogelio Perez-Perdomo and Manuel A. Gómez, "Big Law in Venezuela: From Globalization to the Chavista Revolution," n.d.
15. The Legal 500, "Colombia: Legal Market Overview," n.d., http://www.legal500.com/c/colombia

16. The Legal 500, "Colombia: Legal Market Overview," 2017, http://www.legal500.com/c/colombia
17. See http://en.ppulegal.com/posts/philippi-prietocarrizosa-&-ur%C3%ADa-starts-operating-today-january-1st-as-the-major-large-ibero-american-law-firm
18. *The Legal 500,* The Global 100: The Richest Law Firms In The World (2016), September 26 2016, http://abovethelaw.com/2016/09/the-global-100-the-richest-law-firms-in-the-world-2016/
19. Baker Mckenzie, 'About Us', 2017, http://www.bakermckenzie.com/en/aboutus).
20. Baker Mckenzie, 'Baker Mckenzie Celebrates 80 years in Colombia', August 25 2017, http://www.bakermckenzie.com/en/newsroom/2017/08/80-years-in-colombia).

Everaldo Lamprea is Associate Professor of Administrative Law at the Universidad de Los Andes in Bogotá (Colombia). Lamprea holds a JSD and JSM degree from Stanford University, an LLM from Georgetown University and a law degree from the Universidad de Los Andes. His research focuses on administrative law, comparative law, state regulation and empirical legal studies.

Mariana Díaz Chalela, Managing editor of the Latin American Law Review, and Teaching Assistant at the Universidad de los Andes Law School in Bogotá (Colombia).

CHAPTER 7

Global and Traditional: A Profile of Corporate Lawyers in Mexico

Rodrigo Meneses-Reyes and José Antonio Caballero

Introduction

In Mexico, during the past ten years the number of lawyers has increased from 191,000 to 321,000 (INEGI 2014). This figure reflects two phenomena. On one hand, there has been a sustained growth in educational offerings in the legal field. On the other hand, there has been a notable increase in the number of lawyers entering the market, compared to previous decades. How has the market received these new lawyers? Have their studies provided the necessary skills for incorporation into the market? (Pérez Hurtado 2009).

According to many observers, changes in Mexican law have had a profound impact on how it is practiced in Mexico (López-Ayllón and Fix-Fierro 2000), with two matters frequently cited to this effect. The first was the signing of the North American Free Trade Agreement (NAFTA), which marked Mexico's formal entry into global free trade.[1] The second was a process of replacing significant elements of the nation's legislation. Within this, notable events have included the emergence of state regulatory agencies (the Economic Competitiveness Commission, the Energy

R. Meneses-Reyes (✉) • J.A. Caballero
Department of Legal Studies, Centro de Investigación y Docencia Económicas, Mexico City, Mexico

M. Gómez, R. Pérez-Perdomo (eds.), *Big Law in Latin America and Spain*, https://doi.org/10.1007/978-3-319-65403-4_7

Regulatory Commission and others) as well as the reform of nearly all-federal legislation over a period less than 20 years (López-Ayllón and Fix-Fierro 2000).

In both cases we may assume there have been repercussions on the legal profession. However, to what extent have things really changed for lawyers? Our hypothesis is that, contrary to what may be expected, the changes have been quite limited. In fact, what we observe is that regularities remain and show a high resistance to change. In terms of conditions, the legal profession in Mexico appears to be a space where we see the convergence of a larger group of lawyers, whose education and practices have remained stable, and a smaller group of lawyers whose training and practices have been diametrically transformed. In general the two groups do not interact. The few settings where these interactions do occur tend to be where providers of transformed services seek traditional services. In other words, transformed or elite lawyers seek traditional lawyers only for specific or particular services, while traditional lawyers rarely seek out elite lawyers.[2]

In the following pages we will attempt to describe the way in which stability and change have interacted in Mexico in recent years, and how they have modified some aspects of the practice of law in Mexico. To this end, we will begin by reviewing the regularities represented in the formation and regulation of the legal profession. Next, we will address changes in the profession, looking at the experiences of elite lawyers who were chosen for interviews for this study. In the final section, we will present some conclusions based on our findings, with the intention of outlining the main characteristics of the legal market in Mexico.

A Profile of Lawyers in Mexico

In the past ten years (2004–2014), Mexican legal world and the practice of law have had significant changes. First, we describe the way lawyers are trained in Mexico and how it has changed. In the second subsection, we establish the general characteristics of the legal profession. Finally, we present some considerations with respect to the contemporary debate on the regulation of the legal profession in Mexico.

Forming Lawyers in Mexico

In the ten years between 1997 and 2007, the population of law students grew 41% (from 170,210 students to 240,000) and the number of institutions authorized to offer a law degree grew 156% (from 364 to 930) (Pérez Hurtado 2009: 50–51; Fix-Fierro and López-Ayllón 2006: 115).

This increase in the number of schools and educational programs aimed at forming lawyers seems to have had an important impact on the number of professionals currently practicing law in Mexico. In fact, as we will see in the following section, in just ten years (2004–2014) the number of professionals stating they had studied law grew 68% across the country; moreover, this process has been accompanied by the emergence of academic programs increasingly specialized in teaching particular branches of law.

For example, according to the recently published Catalogue of Undergraduate and Graduate Programs by the National Association of Higher Education Institutes and Universities (ANUIES, its acronym in Spanish), of all the higher education programs in law, including classroom learning as well as distance learning programs, as well as both public and private institutions ($N = 252$), 10% represented educational programs specialized in areas such as law and finance ($N = 8$), law and economics ($N = 6$) or corporate and international law ($N = 2$).[3]

Despite the value of these results, it is still true that we know little about the content of what these law students cover during the course of their studies. We also have little recent information about their expectation of employment. Two empirical studies do exist that allow us to examine these issues. The first is a survey of 339 law students in Mexico City (Fix-Fierro and López-Ayllón 2006). The second is a very thorough study that surveyed law professors and students across the country (Pérez Hurtado 2009).

In the first place, we should note the circumstances faced by the students at the time they were enrolled in a law program. The data shows that 41% of students work while studying. Of this group, it is especially notable that only 55% of those who work do so in areas related to law (Pérez Hurtado 2009: 161 and 165).

Moreover, with regard to the area where they aspire to develop their legal career after their studies, "just over one-third (34.5%) hope to enter the private sector while those who wish to enter the public sector intend to do so, in nearly equal parts, in the legislative branch (14.7%), in public administration (13.3%), in the judicial branch (14.4%) and in the legal justice system (14.4%)" (Fix-Fierro and López-Ayllón 2006: 126).

A question for those surveyed who were working was "how useful is the knowledge acquired in law school for your current job?," 71% answered "very little," 24% said "little" and 5% said "not at all" (Fix-Fierro and López-Ayllón 2006: 124). Taken together, these numbers suggest that, for nearly a quarter of law students in Mexico, their studies are useful only slightly or not at all in carrying out their daily activities and probably they were not relevant as training in the legal profession. About an equal number of law students begin to insert themselves in the labor market to practice in their chosen fields of law in the private sector (corporate and civil), despite the fact that just over 40% plan to enter the public sector.[4]

In another study based upon interviews with undergraduates and lawyers, Ana Laura Magaloni starts with the assumption that it is necessary to modify how law students are trained. This starting point is aspirational. The author asserts that many elite students have different aspirations than their peers did several years ago. In this sense, litigation and public service seem to have been displaced by international law and transnational practice (Magaloni 2006: 62).

Magaloni (2006: 63–64) also states that the dominant model is reproduced in nearly the entire country. The differences that may exist have more to do with the specific characteristics of the schools than with the content of the instruction offered. Therefore, it appears that the same type of lawyer is developed no matter where one is in Mexico. A good example of the standardization of legal training is seen in the textbooks that are used in the process. One matter that stands out is the use of textbooks and manuals written more than 50 years ago, such as those by Ignacio Burgoa,[5] Gabino Fraga[6] and Felipe Tena Ramírez.[7]

In all three cases it is possible to buy new editions, despite the fact that these are works produced in the distant past. The use of textbooks such as these reveals that many courses have not substantially changed for many years (López-Ayllón and Fix-Fierro 2000: 597). The case of administrative law is especially notable given that in the past 20 years nearly all aspects of Mexico's administrative legislation have been changed, as well as the government agencies responsible for its application.[8] However, the text by Fraga remains currently in use. In the matter of textbooks, standardization combined with tradition has meant that reality has been set aside. While the evidence about the use of textbooks may be weak, the conclusions seem to corroborate the sensation expressed by a quarter of the students interviewed by Fix-Fierro and López-Ayllón, implying that their studies will have a limited impact. Magaloni's position is similar: law schools do not appear to be reacting to the multiple changes occurring in the country and continue to produce traditional lawyers.

Lawyers in México (2004–2014)

According to information from the National Population Council (CONAPO), in Mexico in 2004 there were an estimated 103 million inhabitants, while in 2014, INEGI reported that the number had risen to 112 million, which reflects a population increase of 9% in the period discussed here (2004–2014). What draws our attention is the fact that during the same period, the number of lawyers living in Mexico has increased from 191,000 reported lawyers in 2004 (INEGI 2004) to 321,000 reported lawyers in 2014 (INEGI 2014). As we can see, during the same decade the number of professionals who claim to have studied law increased 68%, revealing the apparent popularity of studying law in México.

However, during the decade we are examining, not only the number of lawyers has changed, but also their distribution and working conditions. On one hand, the number of women who state they have studied law has moved from 52,525 in 2004 to 131,610 in 2014, an increase of 14.5% in women's representation among those practicing law in Mexico. On the other hand, the number of graduates with an undergraduate law degree employed within the legal field has increased. In fact, in this category we see that in 2004, the number of lawyers who claimed they were not working in the legal profession was 51.9%, a number that fell to 36% in 2014.

In short, the information reported here suggests that during the past ten years, not only has the number of people who studied law increased, but also the number of lawyers who practice law daily. But under what working conditions is law practiced in Mexico? According to the information in Table 7.1, we may establish that lawyers currently work an average of 40 hours a week, while earning an approximate average US$ 5.40 (MXN 73 pesos).

It is also possible to identify that the number of "employer/lawyers" (those who head up a law firm or office), along with the number of "self-employed lawyers" (those who work individually), saw a slight decrease between 2004 and 2014, while the percentage of "salaried lawyers" (those who work for a firm, office, company or public institution) rose 13.10% during the reported period. Finally, it becomes important to note that it is precisely those segments, "self-employed lawyers" and "employer/lawyers," that appear to have a higher income for their work (83 and 86 Mexican pesos, respectively).

Table 7.1 A decade of change in the legal profession in Mexico (2004–2014)

	2004[a]	*2014*[b]
Number of lawyers	191,000	321,000
Percentage of female lawyers	27.50	42
Percentage of male layers	72.50	58
Average age (years)	37	37.4
Percentage of lawyers not practicing law	51.90	36
Average salary (hourly)	N/D	73 MXN pesos
Hours worked (weekly average)	41.5	40
Percentage of lawyers who are self-employed	37.80	33
Percentage of lawyers who are employers	12.90	7
Percentage of salaried lawyers	45.50	58.60
Hours worked by self-employed lawyers (weekly average)	40.9	N/A
Hours worked by employer/lawyers (weekly average)	39	N/A
Average salary of self-employed lawyers (hourly)	N/D	83 MXN pesos
Average salary of employer/lawyers (hourly)	N/D	86 MXN pesos

[a]Source: INEGI, national employment survey, first semester 2004

[b]Source: INEGI, national survey on employment and occupation, first quarter 2014

In all, the reported information in this section seems to suggest that the legal profession has experienced important changes in Mexico during the past decade, creating a labor market where there is greater professional competition given the increase in the supply of legal services (the number of lawyers), an ever-growing level of female participation in the industry and with the trend toward lawyers in salaried labor relationships, probably in government offices or in increasingly large law firms.

The Regulation of the Legal Profession in Mexico

It is no exaggeration to say that the legal profession in Mexico is essentially unregulated (American Bar Association 2011: 1–2). To enter the labor market one merely needs to conclude their studies in a higher education institution that is authorized to grant an undergraduate degree in law, and then receive authorization to exercise the profession. This last step does not imply an evaluation of the aspirant; it is simply a formality that allows a new lawyer to begin practice throughout the country. There are also no significant requirements for lawyers to become associated in order to offer services jointly (American Bar Association 2011: 39). But in some cases it is even possible for legal services to be offered by those who do not have a legal degree (Pérez Hurtado 2009: 25ff). This is the case in labor law, for example, where a law degree is not required to represent workers in litigation related to labor rights.[9]

Criminal law is one of the few areas where the legal profession is regulated. The Federal Criminal Code establishes a series of crimes related to the law profession. The crime of divulging secrets obliges lawyers to maintain confidentiality regarding the information they receive from their clients.[10] In a specific clause it includes crimes known as those of lawyers, employers and litigants. Here it describes certain conducts, such as making false accusations, falsifying events, conflicts of interest or abandoning a defense, among other cases.

However, despite these existing criminal penalties, the prosecution of wrongdoing by lawyers is quite rare and statistical reports rarely mention such a case. In these conditions, the scope of criminal codes as a mechanism for regulating lawyers is, in the best of cases, very limited.

As a trade, the legal profession is poorly situated. The trade associations and guilds that affiliate lawyers are, in most cases, far from being instruments of representation or defense for the group they claim to represent. There is no census of the guilds and organizations of lawyers in Mexico. The data seems to suggest that most organizations are poorly representative and tend to be short-lived (American Bar Association 2011: 10–11). The few organizations of lawyers that have maintained a certain degree of stability over time have few members and are seen as elitist organizations.[11] Generally, there is little interest in industry representation.[12]

The current debate about regulating legal practice centers on the creation of obligatory trade associations.[13] It is common to hear representatives of lawyers associations and legislators refer to this issue.[14] However, the proposal to organize does not appear to have a clearly defined regulatory mechanism that could be implemented or the manner in which to make such a move effective. One fundamental problem in the matter of creating a guild or colligate organization of lawyers' associations has precisely to do with the aforementioned weaknesses of such groups.

Beyond obligatory association, ideas for other forms of regulation appear scarce. In some cases, the idea of strengthening mechanisms for professional responsibility has been mentioned.[15] In all, the issue of regulation of the legal profession remains one of the pending issues to be resolved regarding the practice of law in Mexico.

Globalization and the Legal Profession in Mexico

In the mid-1990s, there was an important change in the market for legal services with the signing of the NAFTA. This change produced a discussion about the possibility of foreign lawyers practicing law in Mexico. The change also gave rise to the development of a new model of specialized legal services, dealing with law firms specialized in providing services to transnational companies. While the Mexican market already had a few firms of this nature, the first years of the 1990s opened the way to the growth of much greater competition in this area.[16]

Many of these new competitors appeared as branches of international law firms, especially from the United States. One important characteristic of these types of firms was that they generally did not offer clients services related to representation in litigation in national tribunals. For these cases, they typically referred clients to other firms or subcontracted these services. It was most common to see these firms when litigating trade cases. Perhaps the only area in which tradition has retained ground has been with regard to gender. The presence of female lawyers either in Mexican firms or in Mexican branches of international firms remains quite low.

For some sectors of the profession it became indispensable to speak English. The effects of this change may be appreciated in how contracts are phrased and in how services are offered and fees paid. The practice of administrative law also experienced changes. The constitutional and legal reforms of the mid-1990s brought with them new regulatory agencies covering issues of competition, energy and telecommunications. The characteristics and settings of these new agencies forced changes in significant swaths of Mexican administrative law. The change in these laws and the onset of free trade opened a niche which some firms took advantage of, specializing in these topics and offering their services to international and national businesses.

However, the arrival of new competition, and generally the changes produced by free trade, did not immediately impact the market for traditional legal services. Nonetheless, many lawyers resented the change and potential new competitors. The first reaction consisted of attempts to establish limits and barriers to prevent the participation of foreign law firms and lawyers in Mexico. Some legal organizations even opted to expressly prohibit their members to associate with foreigners offering legal services in Mexico (Dezalay and Garth 2005: 319, and interview with a corporate lawyer).

In this way, the contemporary panorama of the legal profession in Mexico reveals a market essentially divided into two segments. In one segment are the traditional small firms where legal advice is offered to people and companies on matters of litigation, as well as drawing up contracts and preparing documents related to company operations. The other part is made up of firms that specialize in advising businesses who have interests in both international and national markets.

It is important to describe the way in which the Mexican lawyers have experienced, perceived and affected the process of change in the profession. To do this, this part will be divided into four sections. In the first, we will explain the impact that the signing of the NAFTA has on the reconfiguration of law practice in Mexico. In the second, we will discuss the changes that the Mexican legal system has experienced in recent years and how this process has also impacted the legal services environment. Next, we will describe the differences, in terms of stratification and specialization, which exist in the Mexican legal services market. In the fourth section, we will analyze the size and organization of law firms in Mexico.

The Free Trade Agreement and the Globalization of the Mexican Lawyer

Among existing studies on the legal profession in Mexico, there appears to be consensus around the fact that, since the signing of NAFTA, there have been many changes in the way that law is conceived of and practiced. In particular, this process seems to be the basis for two sizable transformations. On one hand, the entrance of foreign law firms into the national market, and on the other, the possibility for Mexican lawyers to become inserted into the international market. One of the lawyers who were interviewed said:

> I left the university and began practicing in the same year that Mexico signed the Free Trade Agreement. In a way, I feel like the generation of lawyers we could call the NAFTA generation. [In this sense] the signing of NAFTA was perhaps the most significant moment for Mexico within this global phenomenon we are calling "globalization." So, the most important effect of the

> free trade agreement on the practice of corporate law has been the "internationalization" of exercising our profession.

This internationalization of how Mexican law is practiced, however, does not only refer to the appearance of new international actors or clients who will reconfigure the legal services market, but also to the need to better understand foreign legal systems, especially that of the United States:

> I remember when I went to get a Master's degree in a North American university, people here asked me why I wanted to go learn about the legal systems in other countries if I was a Mexican lawyer. Practicing law was seen as something eminently local. The legislation even had provisions that reflected this view such as the Law of Professions article, which impeded the practice of law in Mexico by those who did not have Mexican nationality.

This change in professional practice has implied changes in the demands of preparing lawyers. According to another one of our interviewees:

> Indeed, a masters degree in law from the United States opens an important door, it is highly valued. The lawyers who do not have a high-level preparation are not able to compete. Because it is not only about knowing the Mexican legal system, it is knowing those of other countries. How can you explain the Federal Labor Law without context? You need to know their system and vice versa in order to explain things well to your clients.

As such, the need to have a greater level of knowledge of other legal systems seems to be based on the expectation of being hired by an international client, but also recognizes the potential impact that legal and commercial operations conducted in Mexico may have upon operations in other parts of the world, and vice versa:

> For those of us who work in international corporate law, to be working on operations where one company acquires several dozen subsidiaries around the world in one fell swoop, and to close the deal at one on the morning in Mexico City because the financing is coming from London, and to have bulging frequent flyer accounts, has all become normal, its part of the job.

Perhaps the dimensions of this process are better summarized in the words of one interviewee, who felt that having comparative understanding of judicial systems as well as the ability to speak another language in addition to Spanish have become indispensable capital for doing business:

> It goes without saying that to provide legal advice in the new world of business requires fluency in foreign languages, particularly in English. Before, for example, the study of comparative law and understanding diverse judicial systems was an academic issue more than a practical one, and knowledge that was earlier alien to the formal preparation of a lawyer, such as a solid preparation in finance, is today greatly desirable, if not indispensable. My firm, for example, which has traditionally recruited from law schools around the world, is now more interested in lawyers who have gotten MBAs after their law studies, or other similar degrees in finance or administration.

However, it seems that the scope of this process to "internationalize" Mexican lawyers has had relatively limited impact. Indeed, as one interviewee suggested, from a structural perspective it seems that the prestige of local firms and their capacity to foster alliances with international firms is what determines, in large measure, the possibilities for Mexican lawyers to collaborate with international actors:

> The relationship and good name connected with other practices plays a fundamental role. For example, we now see more mergers and associations with American firms in Mexico. The question is whether the more local practices can access important clients. And the truth is no, we almost always enter as local experts for a particular issue. But we are still not entering the market as project leaders. We are local experts, we know the laws and who to talk with, but no more than that.

The New Normative Configuration of Law in Mexico

In addition to signing NAFTA, another process experienced by Mexican lawyers is the dizzying wave of economic and legal reforms that have reconfigured the Mexican legal system. In effect, as has been well illustrated by various authors (López-Ayllón 1998; Fix-Fierro 2014),[17] during the past 30 years the Mexican legal system has experienced an unprecedented transformation. Indeed, in the words of some interviewed lawyers, it seems that this legislative reform process has an even greater impact that NAFTA on the professional practice of law in Mexico:

> The complexity of the Mexican legal system has grown, through new laws and new criteria [...] even new social values, and I would say this has had the effect of requiring a greater degree of specialization. Its now impossible for a single lawyer to have deep knowledge in certain fields, such as in competition, communication, money-laundering [...] new fields have appeared in recent years and they can not be covered by firms operating they way they have until now.

This process has not only impacted the way in which law firms organize themselves around a given topic, it has also contributed to the configuration of new spaces for the supply and demand of legal services. In fact, it appears that some topics have reached such a degree of specialization that some large companies have opted to subcontract specific law firms for carrying out concrete tasks:

> This is also interesting for big businesses. There had been in Mexico a tendency for legal matters in large companies to be dealt with internally. Big companies created their own internal law firms, because they had enough volume, and so doing in-house services was justified. However, with this new complexity and specialization, the large companies began recognizing that they could not, or preferred not to, cover all their needs for legal services and the result has been to turn to the big law firms. The big law practices have this specialization on one hand and on the other, a significant impact on the Mexican economic system.

Size and Organization of Law Firms in Mexico

As stated by Bergoglio (2010), it is possible that the growth tendency in both the number of law school graduates and the proportion of lawyers who effectively practice law in Mexico reflects the changes brought by the democratization process in Mexican state institutions experienced since the 1990s. Indeed, as posited by Fix-Fierro and López-Ayllón (2003), in Mexico the democratization process has led to a series of initiatives and reforms that tended to modernize and strengthen the judicial powers within the country, represented the permeation of a larger quantity of resources into the administration of justice as well as the emergence of the state as a new professional field for lawyers.

However, the same democratization process was paired with the configuration of an increasingly liberalized market and of a new regulatory scaffolding, parallel processes which have been accompanied by the more frequent existence of large law firms, predominantly foreign, who seek to consolidate the services offered in the country. As such, according to Bergoglio (2010), in 1999 there existed in Mexico just 5 law practices with over 50 lawyers, while by 2005 the number of law firms with over 50 lawyers was 19, of which 63% were foreign companies looking to enter the local market.

In this sense, it appears that little has changed in the market for law firms in Mexico during the past ten years. Indeed, according to an international directory of lawyers,[18] there currently exist 116 law firms in

Mexico, of which 13 employ 50 or more lawyers. Also, the average number of lawyers employed at firms who operate in Mexico is 20.53; however, those law firms with 50 or more lawyers employ an average of 90.5 lawyers (min. 50, max. 185).

In this context, we must point out that according to Bergoglio (2010) until 2005, the law firms with 50 or more lawyers in Mexico had an average of 74 lawyers on the payroll. In all, the information reported here suggests that while during the last decade the number of firms with more than 50 lawyers has not increased, the number of lawyers employed by these firms has passed from an average of 74 lawyers per practice in 2005 to 90.5 in 2014 (Chart 7.1).

In terms of the types of work they carry out, according to the data the main area that law firms say they specialize is corporate law (38%), followed by general law practice (18%) and administrative law (9%). However, the profile of law firms with 50 or more lawyers employed seems to be more specialized and concentrated in corporate law (23%) and intellectual

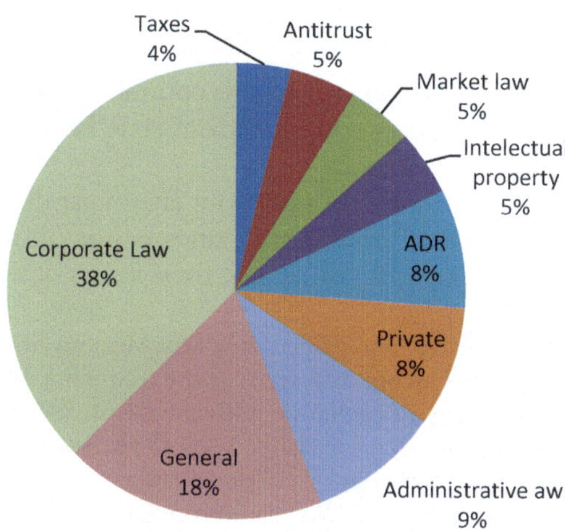

Chart 7.1 Areas of specialization of law firms in Mexico (2014). Source: This data comes from the directory http://www.martindale.com/all/c-mexico/all-law-firms-1.htm?ne=422&n=4294966079&c=N, and the list has been cleaned and systematized to exclude offices of the same firm located in different cities of the same country. Also, 27 firms have been excluded from the graph due to difficulties in categorizing them.

property, general practice (civil and criminal law) and alternative dispute resolution (15% each).

In all, given the nature of the sources consulted, it is impossible to know if the majority of law firms in Mexico are in fact concentrated in the area of corporate law. Nonetheless, the data does give a good indication of the weight or prestige these types of legal services have acquired in recent years.

Specialization and Stratification in the Legal Services Market

It is precisely this tendency toward the specialization of legal services that is the factor that appears to have had the greatest impact on the development of two types, or strata, of legal services. Some more traditional firms have continued representing cases in all areas while others, more globalized, specialize in concrete areas and tend to play support roles for large foreign corporations that arrive in the country. Corporate lawyers not only tend to emphasize their particular specialties, they also tend to emphasize how "Americanized" they have become. In the words of one interviewee: "As corporate lawyers, in the past several years we have shifted from being a more European type of lawyer, which was common before, a sort of half-lawyer/half-philosopher, to a more American-style lawyer, a lawyers who is half-lawyer/half-businessperson."

Despite this, some interviewees point out that what distinguishes "traditional" lawyers from the "globalized" ones is not only this matter of self-appointment but also, and principally, their forms of working:

> There are profiles of firms. One glance now at a Mexican firm will tell you who has foreign clients. **The big difference is the frequency and the quality of the information that you exchange with the client**. You need to formulate budgets and projects with more clarity. You can put small added costs, but always with an average hourly cost. Traditional lawyers tend to charge at the end, they have small incomes and charge everything at the end. But American clients don't like this, you need to specify how much you will spend.

Conclusion

In this chapter we have presented some preliminary work from an analysis of the current situation for the legal profession in Mexico. Our focus is on reviewing the way the market for legal services has changed in light of economic openings and legislative changes in Mexico. In this sense, the first finding that stands out is the role played by the signing of NAFTA in the process of transforming the contemporary legal profession in Mexico. Certainly, NAFTA seems to have had a dramatic effect in the appearance of new economic actors and in the configuration of a new market that demanded a particular type of legal services. However, it would appear that from a broader perspective, the overall effect of NAFTA on the legal market is marginal. In other words, there are apparently few professionals who have succeeded in inserting themselves in this "global" market. The traditional lawyer, monolingual, with limited studies, without specialization and with ample forensic experience, remains dominant.

On the other hand, the Mexican legal system has experienced great transformations in the past 30 years. Recent reforms such as the liberalization of the energy market, and the subsequent fiscal reform, have come to constitute new market for legal services, which tends toward specialization. In this territory new "boutique" practices have appeared, which offer a particular knowledge to the large corporations who enter the country. However, this market also appears to be monopolized by large multinational law firms who simply subcontract local services to be able to claim "local knowledge." It would seem then that specialized Mexican lawyers still face great difficulties in entering a global market and competing, on equal terms, with their international peers.

An even more compelling question has to do with the manner in which many traditional elements in the legal profession have kept their distance from change. Firstly, education stands out. Universities present themselves more as institutions who defend tradition, unable to transform themselves despite the changes surrounding them. Therefore, the majority of new lawyers graduate without the knowledge or the skills needed to enter the new legal services market. Secondly, we see the legal services market. The traditional model of services, non-specialized, deregulated, informal and bounded by relationships of trust rather than by rules of professional responsibility, has been able to maintain operating in a manner that is relatively isolated from the changes occurring. The irony in this case is that the number of cases resolved under this model is much larger than the number resolved by lawyers whose services and structures have transformed. This is not the case in the amounts earned during each operation. In the case of the former, family, labor, criminal or commercial matters mostly involved the recovery of small payouts. In the latter case, they are dealing with business deals involving millions of dollars.

In some ways, the above description resembles a portrait of Mexican society. On one end there is a small, well-educated group who is familiar with the expatriate world and processes significant resources. On the other, there are the majority of people, poorly educated, with few resources and unfamiliar with the global world. Just as in the case of legal services, the privileged minority has incidental need of the services of the marginalized majority.

In the present study we analyze the present situation for the legal profession in Mexico. Our focus is on reviewing the way the market for legal services has changed in light of economic openings. The change brought with it many new developments in how legal services are offered. It paved the way for specialization of one segment and appears to have generated incentives for specialization. However, in other areas the changes are much less pronounced. Traditional law firms remain and their market does not appear to have changed markedly. In respect to practitioners, their changes also appear to be limited.

Notes

1. The first serious attempt to open markets was in 1986 with the signing of the General Agreement on Tariffs and Trade (GATT).
2. Fix-Fierro and López-Ayllón (2006) suggest a similar division in the legal profession.
3. This increase in the number of educational programs focused on training lawyers has been supported by an extraordinary increase in the number of institutions that currently teach law. In fact, according to a report by the Center for the Study of Legal Teaching and Learning in Mexico, a private institution, the number of institutions teaching law grew from 691 in 2004 to 1608 in 2014.
4. The following section allows us to verify the constancy of this tendency.
5. Burgoa, Ignacio. *El Juicio de Amparo*, Porrrúa, México. First edition 1943 and most recent re-edition 2013.
6. Fraga, Gabino. *Derecho administrativo*, Porrúa, México. First edition 1934 and most recent re-edition 2006.
7. Tena Ramírez, Felipe. *Derecho constitucional mexicano*, Porrúa, México. First edition 1944 and most recent re-edition 2011.
8. An example is the Federal Public Administration Law. This law sets norms that organize the entire federal government. The law was first published in 1976 and has been modified on 49 occasions. Between 1994 and the present date there have been 34 reforms that have included the creation of new public agencies and the assignation of new powers.

9. In the area of criminal law, until the constitutional reform published on July 18, 2008, it was possible for those being processed to be represented by "persons of trust" in criminal trials. Evidently, as a person of trust, it was perfectly viable to offer legal services without a law degree.
10. Articles 210 and 211 of the Federal Criminal Code.
11. Here are three groupings which are relatively stable but are far from representative: The Mexican Bar, the College of Lawyers, the Illustrious and National College of Lawyers and the National Association of Business Lawyers. According to the Bar's website (www.bma.org.mx visited in June 2015), they have 3000 members. The Illustrious and National has less than 500 members. The ANADE shared data on its lawyers in 2013 and had around 700 lawyers.
12. As asserted by Meneses (2017), it is possible that this situation has changed recently in certain regions of the country, especially given the increase in the number of crimes and homicides that Mexico has experienced since 2006. However, in structural terms, it appears that the willingness of lawyers to form trade associations has not changed radically.
13. On February 20, 2014, an initiative for a constitutional reform was presented to promote the organization and obligatory certification to practice certain professions, law among them. See http://www.senado.gob.mx/sgsp/gaceta/62/2/2014-02-20-1/assets/documentos/Inic_PRI_Reforma_Constitucional.pdf accessed in October 2014.
14. See Cruz Barney, Óscar. "The reestablishment of obligatory association of the law profession in Mexico: a necessary step." In *Abogacía Española.* General Council. International Section. http://www.abogacia.es/2014/09/19/el-restablecimiento-de-la-colegiacion-obligatoria-de-la-abogacia-en-mexico-un-paso-necesario/ visited in October 2014.
15. CIDE Report: *Justicia Cotidiana.* In http://www.justiciacotidiana.mx/swb/JusticiaCotidiana/conclusiones visited in September 2015.
16. Free trade and the modification of foreign investment regimes were fundamental for this change (Dezalay and Garth 2005: 314 and following).
17. To illustrate the dimensions of the process of legislative transformation, it is worth noting that "to date, the text of the Constitution of 1917 has been modified 573 times by 214 reform decrees. Nearly two thirds of these reforms were after 1982 and nearly one fifth of all reforms were published just during the Administration of President Felipe Calderón (2006–2012). The government of President Enrique Peña Nieto, who took office on December 1, has also begun his mandate with various constitutional reform initiatives, of which some have already been approved and published (education, competitiveness, economic, telecommunications, energy) and others are in the process of approval by the States (transparency, elections)" (Fix-Fierro 2014).

18. This data comes from the directory http://www.martindale.com/all/c-mexico/all-law-firms-1.htm?ne=422&n=4294966079&c=N, and the list has been cleaned and systematized to exclude office of the same firm located in different cities of the same country.

References

American Bar Association. 2011. Index for the Reform of the Legal Profession for Mexico, June 2011. Rule of Law Initiative of the American Bar Association and USAID, Mexico.

Bergoglio, M. 2010. Transformaciones en la profesión jurídica en América Latina. Empresas jurídicas y nuevos discursos profesionales, Sociología del Derecho. Culturas y sistemas jurídicos comparados, Volumen I, Globalización y derecho, justicia y profesión jurídica, UNAM-IIJ, México, 529–572.

Dezalay, Y., and B. Garth. 2005. *La internacionalización de las luchas por el poder. La competencia entre abogados y economistas por transformar los Estados latinoamericanos.* México: UNAM-IIJ.

Fix-Fierro, H. 2014. Engordando la Constitución, disponible en http://www.nexos.com.mx/?p=18375

Fix-Fierro, H., and S. López-Ayllón. 2006. Muchos abogados pero poca profesión? Derecho y profesión jurídica en el México contemporáneo. In *Del gobierno de los abogados al imperio de las leyes*, ed. H. Fix-Fierro and S. López Ayllón. México: Instituto de Investigaciones Jurídicas UNAM.

López-Ayllón, S. 1998. *Las transformaciones del sistema jurídico y los significados sociales del derecho en México.* México: UNAM.

López-Ayllón, S., and H. Fix-Fierro. 2000. "¡Tan cerca, tan lejos!". Estado de derecho y cambio jurídico en México (1970–1999) (parte A) Boletín Mexicano de Derecho Comparado, XXXIII (97).

Magaloni Kerpel, A.L. 2006. Cuellos de botella y ventanas de oportunidad en la reforma a la educación legal de elite en México. In *Del gobierno de los abogados al imperio de las leyes*, ed. Héctor Fix Fierro. México: UNAM-IIJ.

Meneses, R. 2017. Lawyering on the Margins: Drug-Cases and the Legal Profession in Mexico. *International Journal of the Legal Profession.* [Forthcoming].

Pérez Hurtado, L.F. 2009. *La futura generación de abogados mexicanos. Estudio de las escuelas y los estudiantes de derecho en México.* México: Instituto de Investigaciones Jurídicas UNAM.

Rodrigo Meneses-Reyes is a professor and a researcher at the Centro de Investigación y Docencia Económicas (CIDE) in Mexico City (Mexico). He holds a doctoral degree in law from the Universidad Nacional Autónoma de México and a master's degree from the International Institute of Sociology of Law (IISL-Oñati). Meneses specializes on law and society, law and poverty, administration of justice and empirical legal studies.

José Antonio Caballero is a professor and a researcher at the Centro de Investigación y Docencia Económicas (CIDE) in Mexico City (Mexico). He holds a doctoral degree in law from the Universidad de Navarra and a master's degree in Law from Stanford University. Caballero specializes on judicial reform, legal education and the administration of justice in Mexico.

CHAPTER 8

Lawyers and Globalization in Peru (1990–2014): Challenges in the Shadows

Gorki Gonzales Mantilla

Introduction

The aim of this chapter is to discuss the changes produced in the last two decades in the Peruvian legal market. It also explains these changes in the broader context of the institutional reforms that are part of the process of globalization.

The chapter provides an assessment of the importance of globalization as a complex phenomenon and of the need to understand the changes in the historic process that informs practices and cultural paths. In this context, the equality deficiency and the exclusion from public institutions' design are elements that have to be reckoned with in order to appreciate the importance of the legal practice.

I would like to thank Moisés Sotelo, Jean Paul Saucier and María José Gonzales for their collaboration in the data collection and for having discussed with me the ideas laid down in this article. The usual disclaimer applies.

This chapter is a corrected and expanded version of "Abogados y Globalización en el Perú (1990–2014)". En: *Anuario Parlamento y Constitución*. Universidad de Castilla, La Mancha y Cortes de Castilla, La Mancha. España. Año 2015 – N° 17.

G. Gonzales Mantilla (✉)
Pontificia Universidad Católica del Perú, Lima, Peru

M. Gómez, R. Pérez-Perdomo (eds.), *Big Law in Latin America and Spain*, https://doi.org/10.1007/978-3-319-65403-4_8

Furthermore, it analyzes lawyer's activities that are attempting to adjust to the requirements of professional demands from international markets and global transactions. The law firms, their organization, their articulation with the global market and the political implications derived from the activity of these corporations are the focus of our discussion and reflections.

The Legal Profession and Globalization as a Complex and Intricate Process

A set of transformations have altered the bases of the modern social order, specifically since the 1990s. In terms of radical changes, it is comparable to Renaissance or the Spanish Conquest in the sixteenth century (Supiot 2012: 243) in Peru.

Globalization refers to the way in which the goods and services are produced and how the international markets operate in the world economy (Santos 2001). In this new order, the powers of the industrialized countries' economy have "achieved an unprecedented domination as international actors" (Santos 2001: 152–153), at the point of having displaced, subordinated and maybe blurred local political orders (Stiglitz 2006: 48).

Globalization has a "polycentric" structure (Teubner et al. 2010: 68) because it involves all dimensions of social life. This includes the economy, politics and culture in general. It causes changes in each sector, and each change shapes changes in other sectors. It creates values and norms that are meant to legitimize power relations in the communities.

In such a context, legal norms aim at representing the interests championed by globalization, and they are also instruments that warrant the changes sought by that process. When it comes to the effects of globalization on the legal field, lawyers are central institutional actors that give meaning to the impacts globalization has on everyday life.

Having lawyers with excellent knowledge of the law and of the legal field is crucial for the community. The legal profession has impacts on the guarantee system that gives meaning to rights and freedoms. In other words, the legal profession justifies and limits the exercise of private and political powers as a part of the dynamics directed at legitimizing the political system.

The consequences brought by globalization in the legal area constitute a challenge for the legal profession. This new reality and the practical interests underlying globalization call for the adaptation of our professional legal culture but also impact the way lawyers understand and apply the law. The legal profession must have the ability to reckon with the new relevance of certain knowledge, techniques and skills necessary for globalization. Nevertheless, these challenges take place in a context marked by social stratification that is also clearly present in the legal field. The social and economic gaps that mark the history and the reality of the communities of our country are an inevitable consequence of globalization, the legal culture and the role lawyers play in their profession.

In the following lines, I explore the evolution of such realities that have marked the legal profession for the last two decades in Peru. More precisely, the chapter aims at identifying and analyzing the most outstanding changes that have taken place in the legal profession in this new context.

Legal Culture and Legal Practice as Precursors of Globalization

In the early 1990s, Peru was going through a deep crisis that reached all facets of the national life. The disastrous economic performance, caused by the misguided policies of the 1880s, alongside political violence triggered by terrorism, puts the limelight on the law and legal institutions' limitations to face this turmoil (Gonzales Mantilla 2000: 17–25).

These features refer to the last phase of the process that brought the globalization process to Peru. However, contextualizing globalization through certain historical features of Peru's history is an essential condition to understand Peru's legal culture and its connection with globalization.

The beginning of Peru's institutions dates back to the emergence of the republic. Political institutions and the economy were weak due to the war of independence (Contreras Carranza 2011: 12). In addition, the republican state did not offer a real nation-building model for its society. Instead, it offered disintegration and fragmentation that is still part of our socially excluding structures (Bernales and Rubio 1981: 31)

In such a context, the formalism of legal education contributed to depeening the gap between theory and practice, which was prevalent in the legal profession. The knowledge shared in the law faculties provided weak answers to the questions necessary to understand our reality.

Lawyers' activities take place in a world of apparent neutrality. Formalities and rituals of the profession seek to protect specific interests and legitimize practices inconsistent with values entrenched in the Constitution (Gonzales Mantilla 2008: 30–32). The turning point of this way of understanding the legal profession dates back to the late 1960s. During that time, the military regime of Juan Velasco Alvarado undertook new changes and transformations. From that moment onward, a new institutional and social framework emerged in Peru (López 1995: 549).

Legal education and the legal profession The country's landscape was to substantially evolve: crisis of the oligarchy, reforms of the military regime, state's expansion in the 1970s, failure of populist and liberal politics (1980–1985) and the economic and political collapse provoked by the *Aprista* regime in a context of political violence (1985–1990).

There were numerous difficulties presented by the reality of the institutional context in which lawyers of that period were operating, including a growing informality which generated underground institutional practices and greater potential for corruption ramification; a growing number of human rights violations by the state, including enforced disappearances, torture and extrajudicial executions (early 80s); a scarcity of resources to provide for people's basic needs; and inadequate policies to address poverty in general and extreme poverty in particular. All of these features defined and marked the Peruvian public and private spheres of the 1990s.

Such features lead to a situation in which the practice of the legal profession is contingent upon the circumstances and reality. In this context, the legal profession was marked by the widespread practice of solo practitioners, but it can also be noted that others operated as "small firms of a handful of lawyers collaborating in order to save administrative costs", which were "mainly associations of lawyers independent from each other without a shared accounting book or ethical code".[1] Legal practice was limited to classical spheres of the law (private law, procedure, labor, taxation, criminal, etc.) and legal marketing was non-existent.[2] There was no full-fledged service provider vision, except for the three or four Lima-based firms that were highly organized.[3]

This situation was not affected by the increased demand on the legal education market. Between 1980 and 1986, students registered in law faculties increased from 16,412 to 35,503.[4] In six years, the number had doubled. The legal profession was already one of the most "populous" professions in the country, reaching the approximate figure of 45,198 according the 1995 National Census (Encuesta Nacional de Hogares).[5] However, that quantitative growth was not followed by a qualitative improvement of the lawyers. The dominating legal culture did not realize the need to reassess its principles in a context of institutional crisis.

Lawyers are thus contributing directly or indirectly to the low credibility of the legal system by participating, among others, to practices such as corruption. Lawyers practiced in such an environment; they were part of the problem and gave shape to such issues and made them last in time. Legal practice was directed at litigation (essentially micro-litigation), not connected to the "developed world". It was permeated by a formalistic view of the law, on many occasions disconnected from public values. Such features of the legal profession explain why lawyers were an integral part of the institutional crisis.

Legal Culture and the Authoritarian Globalization of the 1990s

Alberto Fujimori's *coup* on April 5, 1992 (Gonzales Mantilla 1998: 51–52), marked the end of the institutional framework of the 1979 Constitution. The new period to come was defined by Fujimori's will to continuously stay in power through the instauration of an authoritarian democracy.

The coup brought the closure of the Congress, repression of political parties, destitution of the judiciary and closure of the public prosecutor's office and of the Constitutional Tribunal (*Tribunal de Garantias Constitucionales*). Fujimori's coup declared that the reason for the closure was to "completely reorganize the judiciary, the Judicial Council (*Consejo Nacional de la Magistratura*), the Constitutional Tribunal (*Tribunal de Garantias Constitucionales*) and the Public Prosecutor's Office in order to achieve an honest and efficient administration of justice".[6]

The declaration concluded with the dismissal of 134 judges and prosecutors: 33 judges of the Superior Court of Lima, 8 judges of Callao, 19 provincial prosecutors of Lima, 10 provincial prosecutors of Callao and 6 trial judges. During the following days, more decree laws were enacted in order to dismiss more judges and prosecutors.[7]

The population's low confidence in the judiciary appeared to back such decisions (Brandt 1990: 151). This perception became stronger years later. By 1993, 72% of Lima's population believed the exercise of judicial power was not reliable. Furthermore, it is worth noting that more than 50% viewed corruption as the main problem, followed by political interference with the judiciary (12%) and the judiciary's low budget (9%).[8]

The Fujimori's regime intervened at all levels of the state institutions, led to the dissolution of political parties and established a populist strategy in order to directly link the president with the people without any institutional mediation. In this context, freedom of speech was sidelined as the regime bribed most of the media.

A great deal of the regime's power was due to its alliance with the military. The latter played an instrumental role in the political sustainability of a social context that claimed order, peace and security. This made the implementation of the structural reform of the Economic Adjustment Program possible. An evidence of the globalizing steps taken in that period by Peru can be found in the active presence of the International Monetary Fund, the World Bank and the Inter-American Development Bank in the country. This would mark a turning point for the legal profession.

The adjustment politics and the concentration of powers deepened the institutional crisis, leading to the broadening of the poor segments of society and endemic corruption that would finally cause the fall of the regime. Concerning this, the economist Pedro Francke underlined that "at the end of the decade (...) half of the Peruvians were below the poverty line" (Francke 2001: 30).

The structural adjustment model of Fujimori's regime caused the total deregulation of markets, privatization of state agencies and an extreme liberalization of foreign trade (Gonzales de Olarte 1998: 9–10). One result of this model is the 1996 agreement for the restructuring of the external debt. At the beginning of the 1990s, the debt amounted to 6 billion US dollars, but with this agreement the sum rose above 16 billion US dollars (Gonzales de Olarte 1998: 44–45).

The social backdrop had also deteriorated due to escalating informality. Indeed, the state's lack of response to social demands—which included rights and guarantees—pushed many to the margins of the legal system in order to face the state's inability to respond. This phenomenon is multidimensional and has had impacts on most social, economic and political spheres of the country, and it is intrinsically linked to the realities of poverty and exclusion (Delgado Narro n.d.).

Thus, certain changes were put forward to redefine the state's role, limit its interference with the economy, privatize the economic activities and promote a free market. According to the regime, this process had to be centralized through an institutional framework that consolidates the reforms. To achieve that goal, it was necessary to strengthen the legal system in order to guarantee rights, specifically property and contractual rights. It was also important to create bodies and instruments capable of promoting the conditions necessary for the protection of the legal system in a predictable manner and to promote the growth of a legal culture backing the values of structural adjustments (Bullard 1997: 243–244).

The globalization process of the 1990s generated a set of economic, social and political demands, which in many cases deepened poverty, inequality and vulnerability of substantial parts of the country. With these consequences in mind, lawyers' practice and the way they conceive the law have come to play an instrumental role in the legitimization of institutions. However, we are not speaking of homogeneous practices. As mentioned above, the deep social fragmentation caused by the economic policies created the ideal circumstances for poverty to take root, putting social mobility at risk in a context where rights were obliterated (Francke 2001: 30). These factors have indubitably shaped the legal culture that was championed as part of the changes put forward by the regime in power in the 1990s.

The legal culture focuses on the promotion of free markets and the protection of private property and contractual obligations but overlooks inequalities and social exclusion. The law thus becomes a tool to justify economic changes and that neoliberal conception of the law is backed by weak, recycled legal and economic views such as the glorification of the law—as a set of clear rules—or the belief that economics determines the meaning of "life" or "rights". These positions converged in the view that it was necessary to legally legitimize the economic reforms above social demands and the values of liberal democracy (Gonzales Mantilla 2010: 299).

Having these observations in mind, the ways in which the legal profession contributed to legitimize the main features of the economic reforms of the 1990s become intelligible. Large law firms sought to optimize their services in order to ensure the legal system would uphold the economic reforms. After all, the interests of their clients were intrinsically related to the results sought by the reforms. However, not all lawyers achieved this level of integration with the reforms: the lawyers that were not able to offer corporate services or to establish relations with foreign law firms are not as well positioned as the ones that were able to offer services corresponding to the demands of globalization. The "unadapted" lawyers—that constitute the majority of the members of the profession—practiced at the margins of the transformations brought by the reforms. Those are some of the negative effects of globalization: an institutional crisis, uncertainty, poverty and informality. This sheds some light on the inevitable fragmentation of the legal profession.

The legal culture generated by globalization is also influenced by corruption. Corruption has found a strategic opportunity to proliferate in public institutions. It is worth noticing that corruption has been continuously present in Peruvian history, but it has reached endemic proportions during the 1990s.

The clearest example of the relations between reforms and corruption is drug trafficking. Its expansion in the country's economic life is an example of corruption as an inevitable result involving different state entities: police, armed forces and the judiciary. The link between drug trafficking and law practice is unavoidable when it comes to discussing the impacts of globalization on our legal culture.

Even though it is quite difficult to provide estimates when it comes to corruption, Professor Alfonso Quiroz notes that between 1990 and 2000, corruption "has been consistently high or really high in spite of cyclic fluctuations". In the same period, corruption's economic impact represented about 30–40% of the budget expense and between 3% and 4% of GDP (Quiroz 2013: 554). In any case, the period between 1990 and 2000 had the highest indicators of corruption. The funds diverted as a result of corruption in Fujimori's regime represented approximately 20–29% of the annual budget and 2.1–3.9% of the GDP.

More precisely, as a result of the economic policies directed at privatization, approximately 78% of 4359 billions of dollars of revenue generated by the privatization of state entities between 1992 and 2000 were spent to pay external debts, weapons and "political" expenses (Quiroz 2013: 494). An instance of the tentacle-like spread of the regime's corruption was the unveiling of a network of about 50 corrupt judges all over the country (Quiroz 2013: 477).

But corruption operates in a broader and more complex manner. It is about different practices shaping beliefs and commitments regarding what is correct and legal. Corruption goes beyond mere measurable practices; it also refers to a "cultural category" with different meanings according to each person. Such meanings evolve in time and can only be grasped while understanding the specific sociocultural and historical background (Huber 2005: 23).

The connection between corruption and legal practice in the 1990s was very consistent. Due to its presence in the institutions, it is likely to have become a "controlled variable" in the context of institutions shaped by globalization. This adaptation of corruption became a feature of the Peruvian legal culture and involved lawyers from all segments of the profession.

The Legal Labor Market in a Context of Democratization

The reforms undertaken in the 1990s by the Fujimori regime correspond to an authoritarian conception of globalization. This view prioritizes the market and the interests of transnationals in commercial relations, before democracy's interests, and the need to improve education and opportunities for the poorest (Sen 2007: 18–19). Corruption and the manipulation of the public institutions were also a product of these reforms. In any case, the legitimizing discourse of the reforms was discursively relying on the law and legal practice.

The return of democracy should have implied several challenges at different levels. Regarding the strengthening and reorientation of institutions in constitutional terms, it was necessary to consider the basic principles of equality and social justice (Sen 2007: 19). This would not be possible without the paradoxically constructive aspect of legal knowledge and the legal profession.

This reality had to be faced by the constitutional democracy beginning with the government of President Valentin Paniagua, who assumed the charge of the government of National Reconstruction from November 20, 2000, and later by President Alejandro Toledo who was elected on July 28, 2001.

To be a member of the legal profession, it is necessary to hold a law degree for which the candidate has to undergo an examination evaluating whether she or he has sufficient knowledge of the practice of law. Law faculties administer this evaluation. The exam consists of a case analysis, or it can also consist of the defense of a research project before a committee comprised three professors. The lawyer title has to be registered at the closest Superior Court of Justice and at the relevant bar.[9]

These requirements do not guarantee the quality of the legal profession's practice. The institutional crisis—which also concerns law faculties—points to the necessity of analyzing these conditions' value from a strictly formal point of view, since their function is merely formalistic.

In any case, it is important to know what the main definitional features of the legal profession are from the fall of Fujimori´s regime onward. This analysis includes the influence of institutional reforms on the legal profession.

The Legal Profession: Economic Growth and the Expansion of the Legal Market

A broad list of consequences from the 1990s will mark the framework of the practice of law in the context of the return of democracy. As Nelson Ramirez points out, the profession faced new pressures: "Thousands of pension cases, the creation of a consumer complaint agency and the bankruptcy proceedings, now working in an administrative—not judicial—context, large investments in several sectors which test … the judicial system's behavior".[10]

Such an institutional framework was directly concerned by the approval of several legal regimes between the late 1990s and the following decade. These include statues on corporations (Ley General de Sociedades), administrative procedures (Ley de Procedimiento Administrativo General), arbitration (Ley de Arbitraje), public contracts (Ley de Contrataciones del Estado), competition (Ley de Libre Competencia) and bankruptcy (Ley del Sistema Concursal).[11] This body of rules is clearly based on the economic requirements of the model championed by the regime in power during the 1990s. This very system of rules thus becomes a priority field of practice for the legal profession.

However, the return of democracy brought with it a set of expectations that broadened the field of legal practice. Democratization also strengthened awareness of, and concern for, constitutional protections. The Constitutional Tribunal intensified its activities, and there was an opening up of constitutional law practice with the increased significance of the Constitutional Tribunal's activities.[12]

At the same time, the judiciary became more concerned with overseeing the other branches of the state, in particular the legislative branch.[13] This oversight has taken unprecedented steps in recent years, particularly when it comes to the oversight engendered by the Tribunal's implementation of the decisions of the Inter-American Court of Human Rights and the creation of specialized judicial bodies. These developments have significantly altered the modern landscape of the legal profession.[14] The reform of Codes of Civil Procedure has "also … an important impact in that a newfound interest for oral procedures changed the classical paradigm of defense".[15]

As anticipated, the economy's growth in its relation with the international market was a background for legal profession's expansion. The forced changes from the 1990s will have to be reduced through the institutional demands of democracy. In fact, legal practice, in spite of being institutionalized, opened itself to new international opportunities.

The urgency and expansion of the demand for legal services were part of the economic recovery process starting with the return of democracy in Peru. At that point, there was a convergence between the development of multinational economy and the opening of Peru's institutions to infrastructure and capital investments.

The macroeconomic figures speak from themselves: the Peruvian economy has kept a steady growth track since the year 2000. The early 2000 economic recession—which mainly struck developed countries—marks a period where Peru's GDP positively grew into the following decade (Table 8.1). Free trade agreements, such as the treaty signed with the United States, take place in that context. Said agreements imply different regulatory spaces which evidence the value and centrality of the legal profession to ensure the enforcement and implementation of free trade as a matter of policy.

Table 8.1 Peruvian GDP growth rate between 2000 and 2010

Year	*% GDP growth*
2000	3.0
2001	0.2
2002	5.0
2003	4.0
2004	5.0
2005	6.8
2006	7.7
2007	8.9
2008	9.8
2009	1.1
2010	8.8

Source: INEI. Principales Indicadores Macroeconómicos. 2011 http://www.inei.gob.pe/estadisticas/indice-tematico/economia/ http://www.inei.gob.pe/estadisticas/indice-tematico/economia/

In 2011, Peru's GDP growth rate was 6.9%, 6.3% in 2012, 5.3% in 2014, and in 2014 it fell to 2.35%. However, it is worth noticing that we are dealing with a growth-based model focused primarily on exports and services. This neoliberal model emerges from the economic reforms and has led to clear disparities in terms of the distribution of the benefits from economic growth. Sectors profiting the most from this bonanza are mainly the most productive sectors, such as the construction sector, marketing, finance and mining. This clearly explains why poverty has not diminished in spite of the economic growth: "inequalities appear to be unshakeable even though its causes have varied during time".[16]

The construction industry has undergone constant growth for several years, mainly construction relating to housing, shopping malls, rehabilitation and improvement of the road system and infrastructure. This industry has moved from a growth rate of 6.39% of the GDP in 2001 to a rate of 17.44% in 2010. In 2011, the industry was at 11.3% and fell to 10.6% in 2012 and to 8.56% and 2.26% in 2013 and 2014, respectively. In spite of that decline, the growth observed in that field is still higher than in any other similar sector in Latin America. Furthermore, such numbers are expected to reflect substantial growth for years to come.

On the other side, from 1999 to 2013, mortgages and bank deposits have almost quadrupled, while the financial system (including commercial and investment banking) has grown by a factor of between 4.25 and 4.7, in mortgages and deposits, respectively.[17] The finance and insurance sector has also been quite dynamic with a growth rate of 9.07% in 2013. In the same year, savings have increased 21.4%. The loan portfolio also evidenced significant growth: 21.1% in mortgages, 12.3% in consumer credit, 18.2% in business credit and most particularly credit directed at the mining sector (57.6%), manufacturing industry (20.5%), transport and communications (20.4%), agriculture and livestock (19.4%), which has mainly taken place in national currency.

The expansion of the mining industry has had a significant impact on the legal profession. The mining industry's importance is shown by the fact that it represented 14.5% of GDP until 2007. It has also opened an indispensable field of practice for lawyers. The formalistic nature of the Peruvian legal system imposes many intricate steps to be followed for public institutions to grant the permits and authorizations necessary to initiate any project. In that respect, it is often mentioned that investors have to hire more lawyers than engineers.[18]

The truth is that natural resources from mining represented 59% of all exports from the country in 2011. In the domestic economy, excluding Lima, the mining sector grew 28% in the same year.[19] Public investments in this sector have risen to 2.9% of GDP between 2000 and 2005 and 4.4% of GDP between 2006 and 2011. In 2011, the industry employed more than 820,000 workers. In 2013, the mining industry registered an annualized growth rate of 2.91% and reached historical levels in the extraction of copper, liquid hydrocarbons and natural gas.[20]

Therefore, there is no doubt that the conjunction of economic changes has resulted in the creation of new social, professional and business segments related to the extraction industry. But the private sector holds sway over a weak and undecided state apparatus which is unable to put its house in order, nor to improve its functioning.

This conjunction appears to be the main economic impetus for the increased demand for legal services. This demand also explains the incursion of foreign law firms into the national legal market. A survey led by *Peru Top Lawyer* and the magazine *Rumbo Ecónomico* seems to illustrate such observations. The survey was directed at business people operating in Peru in 2012. At that point, the annual economic growth was close to 7%, and it had become clear that law firms were the key players of most of the important financial transactions within these growing sectors, to the extent that the number of high-quality firms had tripled, while domestic firms have also managed to expand their networks nationally and internationally.[21] Table 8.2 provides an overview of the per capita geographical distribution of lawyers in the country.

As evidenced by the table, the lion's share of the lawyers can be found in Lima and Callao. The remaining lawyers are mainly located in la Libertad, Cusco, Arequipa, Lambayeque and Puno. It is worth noticing that the important number of lawyers in Lima relates to the capital's high demographics, but such a concentration is also explicable by the centralization of political and economic power in Lima that has been a feature of Peruvian landscape since the emergence of the republic.

Furthermore, the different regional numbers of lawyers *per capita* show that regional growth has had an impact on the number of lawyers practicing in many departments. However, the main decisions are taken in Lima where the most prominent law firms are located. These decisions are directly linked to the most important mining, oil and gas projects that take place in regions outside Lima.

Table 8.2 Lawyers by department in 2015[22]

Rank	*Department*	*Lawyers*	*Inhabitants*	*Lawyers per capita*
1	Lima	59,968	9,685,490	162
2	Cusco	5449	1,308,806	240
3	Tacna	1324	337,583	255
4	Arequipa	4839	1,273,180	263
5	Lambayeque	4487	1,250,349	279
6	Moquegua	636	178,612	281
7	La Libertad	6356	1,836,960	289
8	Puno	4106	1,402,496	342
9	Ica	1965	779,372	397
10	Huánuco	2043	854,234	418
11	Callao	2375	999,976	421
12	Ancash	2677	1,142,409	427
13	Ayacucho	1400	681,149	487
14	Junín	2748	1,341,064	488
15	Apurímac	915	456,652	499
16	Madre de Dios	198	134,105	677
17	Ucayali	633	489,664	774
18	Tumbes	293	234,638	801
19	Piura	2002	1,829,496	914
20	Cajamarca	1617	1,525,064	943
21	Amazonas	287	421,122	1467
22	Loreto	606	1,028,968	1698
23	San Martín	370	829,520	2242
24	Huancavelica	185	491,278	2656
	Totales	107,479	30,512,187	284

Variables and Actors in a Stratified Legal Context

The open nature and the expansion of the "new" labor market emerged from the economic reforms marked by inequalities. This aspect impacts lawyers' positions in the market and their practice.

A Professional Context with Asymmetries and Inequality

Professionally, lawyers have a strategic position due to their relation with the legal system and the social order. The activities they perform allow them to act at the intersection of private and public functions (Bergoglio y Carballo 2005: 202).

From a certain point of view, lawyers' community is based on a culture with a specific set of skills (Silva García 2001:TII, 104) to face conflicts and legitimize certain social and individual structures of power. Thus, lawyers are usually endowed with a broad set of conceptual tools and interrelated skills.

Legal discourse and the legal practice are implicitly articulated. The connection between practice and discourse takes place beyond state structures and factual realities. Thus, discourse and practices connect structures and realities through a common language that includes the same concepts and categories. However, coherence—a value for this conception of the legal profession—is being questioned by reality. The social, economic and cultural changes undergoing in Peru since the last decades are the pillars of a stratification process of the profession.

The 1990s' neoliberal economic policies aimed at promoting direct foreign investment in education. The Legislative Decree 882, the 1996 Education Private Investment Promotion Act (Ley de Promoción de la Inversión Privada en la Educación) made this possible. This statute does not provide any quality control standards and the proliferation of low-quality universities followed.

Legal education became the second most popular professional degree program in the country, with 36,477 registered students in the year 2000. Before the decree came into force in 1996, there were only 14 public university law faculties and 6 private ones, whereas by 2008, these numbers respectively increased to 20 public and 14 private law faculties (Gonzales Mantilla 2008: 68–69).[23] The lack of regulatory control over the proliferation of law schools clearly has had negative impacts on the quality of legal education and thus on the legal practice as a whole.[24]

All of the above-mentioned elements explain why the legal market is saturated. By 2014, there were about 130,000[25] lawyers registered with a Peruvian bar.[26] About 72,521 lawyers practiced in Lima and Callao, which represents one lawyer for every 250 inhabitants.[27] This proposition means that in Peru—a country plagued by security issues—there are currently more lawyers than policemen.[28]

Consequently, there are now fundamental differences among lawyers. The university where they are trained and the socio-economic provenance of their clients are elements of stratification. Such differences have an impact on the ability to conceptualize legal issues and the strategies used to deal with cases.

The legal profession has been shaped by globalization since the 1990s. The globalized feature of the profession impacts to a greater or lesser extent all actors. In the meantime, informality and corruption are not left behind: they are part of the new reality of the legal profession.

Actors of the Legal Field
One of the most evident expressions of stratification in the legal profession is the association of lawyers through large law firms that adopt a structure similar to the companies they are looking to represent. This process, described in the United States in the middle of the twentieth century (Mills 1973: 164), becomes a reality during the 1990s in Peru and defines part of the actual legal profession.

Aside from the lawyers that play an active role in the changes put forward by the economic reforms, most lawyers do not get to be part of that process. It could be argued that the legal profession is characterized by a hierarchical structure with a low level of internal mobility. It is sometimes possible that some opportunities not taken by the highest segments of the profession may trickle to the next level, but such cases are exceptions.

At the lowest point of the stratified profession are the "excluded" lawyers, who did not manage to integrate into the process of economic changes. They are however part of the process in that they represent the negative effects of globalization, as it exists in our country.

The stratification of the profession has not suddenly emerged; it is part of a process beginning in the 1990s with the economic reforms. It is a factor that contributed to the fracture our weak political institutions, deepening social inequalities and exclusion, including the legal field.

Globalized Lawyers: Features and Nuances

An overview of the main features defining the best Peruvian law firms (which are mainly the oldest and most prominent of the country), according to Legal 500 Chambers and Partners' reports, allows us to grasp the reality—and the nuances—of the current legal market. Table 8.3 shows in alphabetical order the largest law firms, with more than 25 lawyers.

The law firm's size reflects the magnitude of their clients' operations and the type of clients they deal with. This aspect impacts the firm's organization and methods.

Being allied with international law firms became a distinctive feature for local law firms in this context. However, it is not necessarily an indicator of the globalized nature of a firm, as it can also be a consequence of the firm's portfolio of clients. In anyway, the association with foreign colleagues can open a window of professional opportunities.

The growth of the legal market brought by globalization pushed multinational corporations to request complex services provided by large firms. Said corporations "are looking for counsel from law firms where

Table 8.3 Peru's largest law firms

Law firm	*N. partners*	*N. associates*	*Total*
Barrios & Fuentes	9	27	36
Benites, Forno & Ugaz	12	35	47
Echecopar (member of Baker & McKenzie)	33	71	104
Ferrero Lawyers	11	17	28
Garcia Sayan Lawyers	15	22	37
Grau	18	19	37
Hernandez & Cia	12	18	30
Lazo, De Romaña & Gagliuffi	7	23	30
Miranda & Amado Lawyers	21	94	115
Olaechea	51		51
Muñiz, Ramirez, Perez-Taiman & Olaya	22	70	179
Osterling	13	14	27
Payet, Rey, Cauvi, Perez & Mur	17	48	65
Rebaza, Alcazar & De Las Casas Financial Lawyers	9	34	43
Rodrigo, Elias & Medrano	40	90	140
Rubio Leguia Normand	11	32	49
Total	364	734	1,098

Source: Legal 500 chambers and partners

they will find lawyers from all the fields their business requires" (Interview with Julio César Pérez Vargas).

An instance of such law firms can be found in Echecopar, which has been at the forefront of the Peruvian legal profession since its foundation in 1950. In November 2012, Echecopar became an affiliate of Baker & Mackenzie. This alliance marked a turning point for legal services in Peru, particularly because of the international prominence of Baker & Mackenzie. The firm actually is at the top of the law firm rankings of the world.[29] What is more, Baker & Mackenzie is the only law firm with presence in all the Latin American countries of the Pacific Alliance. The Pacific Alliance represents 35% of the economic production of the region (www.bakermckenzie.com).

It is important to grasp how Baker & Mackenzie stresses the relationships its lawyers have established particularly with private sector stakeholders but also with key political, local and judicial authorities of the Pacific Alliance countries (www.bakermckenzie.com). Lawyers' responsibilities are understood by their positions in the institutional system.[30] As advertised by Baker & Mackenzie, its lawyers maintain ties with political activities in order to enhance their professional goals, and thus it becomes clear they have an interest in the design and application of different policies (Lasswell y McDougal 1999: 75–76).

The association with Baker & Mackenzie provided Echecopar with an invaluable international standing.[31] Grassroots knowledge and experience allied with global resources generated a new mindset in the legal profession in order to face a growing demand and to evolve alongside with that demand. This alliance has not led to a change in the internal structure of the local firm nor in the decision-making processes which are still in the hands of the local partners, who are now better equipped.

Not all associations have reached the level of integration of Echecopar, although it is the case of Payet Rey Cauvi Perez & Mur,[32] which has reached an agreement with the Spanish firm Uria Menendez in 1997, one of the most prominent firms in Europe. It was founded in the 1940s and has more than 500 lawyers in 16 offices in the main markets of Europe, America and Asia. In September 2014, Uria Menendez decided to expand its presence in the Latin American market with a five-year plan that would make the firm, according to Managing Partner Luis de Carlos, "the only global Iberoamerican firm that will bill half of its hours in Spain and the other half in the rest of the world" (www.expansion.com/2015/02/27/juridico).

According to Julio Cesar Perez, partner and member of the 70-lawyer team of Payet, Rey, Cauvi and Perez & Mur, "the practice of the profession has been modified by the changes of the last decades". And " the most prominent lawyers have adapted to the new structures through strategic alliances" (Interview with Julio Cesar Perez Vargas).

The representation agreement involves the continuous presence of a lawyer from Uria Menéndez in the Peruvian firm (www.uria.com/es/oficinas/lima). It is likely that such a relationship will generate opportunities to answer to new demands of the legal market. Being connected with such a large law firm is likely to impact the profile of the local firm's clients.

Other firms—even though they have not developed international strategic alliances with international firms—have found other means to answer to the needs of a globalized market. In such cases, most law firms share a set of common features.

An important shared feature by all the firms at this level is their client's profile. Representing and advising have to be suited to highly specialized corporations with complex economic activities. Such clients operate all over the world and thus need preventive advice that follows legal transformations in the jurisdictions where their client's business is taking place (Bergoglio y Carballo 2005: 204).

Most of the firms' work is connected to investment and financing projects taking place in the context of the privatization processes and the opening of the local markets to international dynamics that have marked the economic landscape of the country during the past two decades. This allowed firms to build interesting client portfolios in crucial sectors of the economy such as the fields of petroleum, gas, capital markets, labor law, real estate, trademarks, electricity, telecommunications and fisheries. As a result of the above, firms have gathered clients from the major capitals of the world, such as New York, London, Madrid, Toronto and from other main economic centers from Asia and Latin America. In a country that has become favorable to international business, the affinity of these firms with the requirements of the legal market can be described in the following line: "Our business is the business of our customers" (http://www.mafirma.com.pe/index.php/nuestra-firma/el-estudio).

Law firms in this segment seek to be perceived as "top partners to connect investors with global markets and international investment to integrate the great cycle of growth and internationalization taking place in Peru" (www.mafirma.com.pe/index.php/nuestra-firma/el-estudio). According to the same page, the services provided by the firms seek growth hand in hand with the corporate management of their clients in order to create wealth for their businesses.

This way of operating characterizes a path taken by the legal profession and defines the basic values underlying the commitment of all these law firms to their clients (Interview with Carlos Carpio, from Rodrigo, Elias & Medrano). This firm, established in 1965 (www.chambersandpartners.com/latin-america), was the first in the country to reach foreign markets. In 1973, he set up an office in Madrid under the name of *L.C. Rodrigo Lawyers* in order to provide "networking services to Spanish clients interested in investing in Peru or vice versa" (estudiorodrigo.com/portada/es). In this case, the firm focused on the areas of litigation, corporate, insurance and tax law. This firm also reflects the common practice of this segment of the legal profession, that is, the idea of being present "in all areas of the law" (estudiorodrigo.com/portada/es).

Along these lines, some of these firms were created from the merger of other firms. As Nelson Ramirez Jiménez, Emeritus Partner at Muñiz, Ramirez, Perez-Taiman & Olaya, says, his firm was the result of successive mergers of four smaller firms: "The partners were aware that the whole is greater than the sum of its parts, and that working alone had no place in the market where the firm emerged". Along these lines, it was necessary to offer a well-rounded range of services to corporations (Interview with Nelson Ramírez Jiménez).

The services of these firms should offer solutions that answer the Peruvian and international legal issues.[33] It is necessary in Peruvian market, since in this type of market "firms with a global presence are preferred and from that perspective, they tend to be prioritized even at the national level. That is to say that it does not happen often that large corporations directly hire local firms" (Interview with Nelson Ramírez Jiménez).

As part of the globalization of the legal market, some foreign actors have penetrated the national market without being connected to a local partner. Garrigues, a Spanish firm operating in Lima since April 2014, is probably the most significant and recent case (www.garrigues.com/es). This firm is highly successful in terms of billing and has offices in New York, Shanghai, London, Sao Paulo, Mexico, Madrid, Barcelona and Brussels, among others (Méndez, in this volume).

The presence of this firm reflects the interest to get closer to investments in emerging markets and to be accessible to clients expecting legal service corresponding to the standards of their country of origin.[34] However, it is very likely that such a demand will expand and that those services will end up competing with local law firms. In fact, in spite of its late arrival in the Peruvian market, it has a "growing portfolio of clients in the finances sector, infrastructures, investment funds, mining, education, telecommunications (including those of the Peruvian state)" (*Gestion* from October, 10, 2014).

Some have endeavored to enter the Peruvian legal market in a much easier way than Garrigues. Competition in Spain has been harsh since there are more than 25 foreign firms with local lawyers practicing in that country. This explains why small- and medium-sized law firms have been looking toward expanding their business in Latin America, particularly in Peru (*Expansion*, February 28, 2015). In that respect, it is worth mentioning the incursion of Ontier (pe.ontier.net/equipo/es) and Broseta (www.broseta.com/international/latinoamerica). While Ontier was established through the physical presence of local lawyers, Broseta is trying to work through a partnership with Benites, Forno & Ugaz.

During the past two years, other—rather small—Spanish firms have sought to open their own offices in Peru. This has been the case of *Gaona Abogados* and *Bufete Marín*. Local lawyers, however, staff both foreign firms.

The Globalization of Lawyers "From Below"

As foreseen by many, inequality and exclusion were part of the processes leading to globalization in Latin American countries (Santos 2001: 155). Stratification caused by that model of economic development shapes the legal market and the legal culture.

The lower segments of the profession have clearly suffered from globalization. These lawyers have failed to integrate successfully to the extent that economic reforms and the openings to international markets have not generated benefits to their practices.

The stratification of the legal profession did not emerge out of nowhere. The impact of the economic reforms of the early 1990s is a factor that led to the breakup of our weak political institutions, the deepening of social inequalities and exclusion. The legal profession was not spared by these dynamics.

This explains stratification in the legal profession as well as the development of a type of legal practice that is related to the world of informality. For years and in several cities, lawyers have been offering their services to people walking around the surroundings of courthouses. The clients that would retain their services were mainly low-income people needing to protect their rights and these lawyers were willing to offer affordable services.

In Lima, the creation of the Association of Itinerant Lawyers (Asociación de Abogados Ambulantes–AAA)[35] clearly shows what was taking place in the legal profession during the economic reforms of the early 1990s. Like street vendors, these lawyers were equipped with a typewriter and ready to draft legal briefs and other legal documents according to the client's needs on the spot.

Such a practice reproduces informality as a social phenomenon and contributes to uphold a situation where there is a lack of rules that guarantee the proper operation of institutions. That reality takes its roots in the historical design of the judiciary and gets worse with the institutional breakdown of the 1990s. Legal practice thus becomes the theater of discretion and favors (Mujica 2011: 88). In order to gain clients, lawyers involved in such practices skillfully demonstrate their knowledge of the judicial system and their proximity to civil servants of the judiciary.[36]

The lawyers in this segment mainly draft legal documents. They hardly manage the whole case. Consequently, their participation in a case is partial. Such a level of commitment defines the whole litigation process at that level: full of uncertainties, compartmentalized without a perspective that values the rights at stake as a whole.

In a recent press release, the AAA states that it represents about 20,000 lawyers operating in Lima.[37] Even if that number may be wrong, it speaks to the internal segmentation of that part of the profession. In other words, nowadays, many of these lawyers work in small crowded offices, in the surroundings of the courthouse, but this does not mean that they may not go on the streets to find clients (Interview with Oscar Soria Limaylla and Robert Torre Tenorio).

In any case, the fees charged by the lower end of these lawyers speak to the deep stratification in the legal profession in Peru. A claim to enforce a right to alimony can cost between 17 and 20 dollars if the client is female and up to 35 dollars for a male. In civil or commercial matters, the fees vary between 70 and 100 US dollars (Interview with the lawyers Oscar Soria Limaylla and Robert Torre Tenorio). This situation reflects the weak belief in equality, justice and access to justice in a system that tolerates and sponsors such contrasts (Piketty 2015: 10).

The legal profession has to face, besides precariousness and informality, the effects of the proliferation of law school, which have substantially increased the number of lawyers on the market. AAA lawyers are not enthusiastic about this reality (Interview with the lawyers Oscar Soria Limaylla and Robert Torre Tenorio), since the segment it represents is the most affected by the increase in the population of lawyers. Law graduates from the numerous new law schools seek their clients among people with fewer resources, who are located at the margins of the globalization process.

The Increased Demand and Specialization Requirements in a Context of Economic Growth

The growth in demand due to new globalized dynamics led to the increase in lawyers and law firms nationwide. However, these increases also put into limelight the influence of centralism in the administration of the social, economic and political development throughout our history as a republic.

The tendency to centralize these features is reinforced by the way globalization operates. It is worth noticing that, almost 80%—that is to say 375 of approximately 470 firms that are registered nationally—have their main offices in Lima (Interview with the lawyers Oscar Soria Limaylla and

Robert Torre Tenorio). This has to do with the fact that more than half of the lawyers nationally are concentrated in Lima, but it is certainly a particular example of how economic relations and transactions have shaped the legal profession.

Certain specific examples of this economic process can be observed in reputable law firms whose reputation is based on their ability to adapt their practice to the demand for legal services tailored to the evolving complexities of rapid economic growth.[38] Success in this field is determined by the use of legal innovation and technical skills to accommodate the demands of globalization. Professionalism, quality of customer service, professional diligence and commitment to the clients also become key factors to succeed in our legal market. The firms meeting such high standards are located in Lima where a common "corporate" culture prevails.

However, the corporate character of that culture requires specialization, because expertise underlies the ability to come up with a broad array of solutions to problems to legal issues that shape an expanding demand. This is the characteristic feature of these law firms.

Reforms brought by globalization were instrumental in the creation of new fields of practice. For instance, there is a new need to regulate issues related to the extraction of natural resources.[39] Specialization is thus a condition imposed by globalization. Specialization is clearly influenced by the demands of globalization.

A poll taken in March 2014 showed that the areas of specialization that are shaping the offer of legal services are the areas generally associated with economic development (Table 8.4):

Table 8.4 Segmentation of the legal profession by fields (number of lawyers)[40]

Fields	*% of Lawyers*
Criminal law	25
Private law	24
Labor	17
Administrative	14
Constitutional	7
Corporate/commercial	5
Others	5
Taxation	3
Total	100

The areas of the law with the main number of lawyers are criminal, private and labor, but administrative law and commercial law have lately taken a prominent position. In criminal law, the services offered are associated with new "corruption opportunities" related to the growth of public and private investment. Such investments have led to the emergence of new and more complex schemes of corruption.

Private law maintains its focus on the litigation market, which has likely grown in the recent years as a result of the increase of economic transactions and contracts stimulated by major international business.

The legal market appears to have a specific relation to the deregulation process the labor market underwent during the 1990s. Furthermore, the increase in the offer of legal services in administrative law is related to the new role of the state with respect to supervisory and regulatory bodies.

The importance of corporate and commercial law, particularly in Lima, which is demonstrative of the prominence of corporate economic activity and the business they maintain with their international counterparts should not be overlooked. From a globalization standpoint, these fields concretely delineate the practice of the legal profession, as is evidenced by the following table portraying the main fields of practice of some of the leading law firms in Lima (Table 8.5).

This overview, limited to four of the main Lima-based law firms, speaks to the level of interconnectedness between legal services offered and the needs of a globalized market: banking and finances, corporate organization and restructuring, competition and antitrust, environmental, natural resources and energy, electricity, oil, gas, insurance, intellectual property and taxation. These specialties illustrate the new realities of the legal market.

The mentioned areas are fields of practice of most of the main Lima-based law firms; however, large law firms do not absorb every legal specialty. There are law firms that are well known for practicing in one main area of the law. This is the case of Monroy, or Benites, Forno & Ugaz for their activity in litigation or Laub & Quijandía specializing in natural resources, oil and gas.

As stated above, lawyers from these firms must focus on "the ability to solve complex issues in a timely manner and identify problems in different areas" (Interview with Jorge Toyama). They must also know when to refer matters to other experts. To some extent, technical and legal expertise go hand in hand with management and leadership skills (Interview with Carlos Caro Coria).

Table 8.5 Main fields of practice of four leading law firms

	Law Firms			
Main specialties	*Rodrigo, Elías & Medrano*	*Miranda & Amado*	*Echecopar (Baker & McKenzie)*	*Muñiz, Ramírez, Pérez-Taiman & Olaya*
Banking and finance	X	X	X	X
Organization and restructuring	X	X	X	X
Competition and antitrust	X	X	X	X
Corporate, mergers and acquisitions	X	X	X	X
Environmental law	X	X	X	X
Dispute resolution	X	X	X	X
Natural resources & energy: electricity	X	X	X	X
Natural resources and energy: oil & gas	X	X	X	X
Insurance	X	X	X	X
Intellectual property	X	X	X	X
Labor and employment	X	X	X	X
Projects	X	X	X	X
Public law and regulation	X	X	X	X
Real estate	X	X	X	X
Taxation	X	X	X	X

Source: Legal 500 http://www.legal500.com/c/peru/legal-market-overview

Specialization is a feature that "is a standard to be considered as a competent lawyer" (Interview with Carlos Caro Coria) and determines the results a corporate law firm must deliver to their clients (Interview with Carlos Carpio). Specialization outlines the profile of the lawyer needed in these types of firms. A focused specialization, related to new technologies, fluency in foreign languages and post-graduate studies in foreign universities (with a preference for Anglo-American universities), appears to be some requirements to be a lawyer at one of those corporate law firms.

However, the growing complexity of the legal demand, the importance given to technology, the broadening and focusing of legal knowledge led to the sidelining of the generalist lawyer who has now become suspicious. These factors have cast shadows on the need to have a legal profession not deprived of a humanistic approach (Silva García 2001:II, 116)

A humanistic vision is not synonymous with a lack of specific knowledge, weak expertise, lack of analytical skills applicable to specific issues or inefficiency in overall performance. There are risks in replacing a humanistic view by a merely technocratic perspective stripped of professional values. This would lead to a critical situation considering the important position held by law and lawyers in our societies (Table 8.6).

As evidenced by the table, corporate and commercial law are the most profitable fields according to 23% of the interviewed lawyers. However, these fields only represent 5% of practicing lawyers (see Table 8.4). Taxation is in a comparable situation: it only represents 3% of the lawyers but it is considered the most profitable field by 20% of lawyers. According to César Pérez Vargas, commercial law is deeply influenced by globalization in that commercial transactions involve the use and knowledge of different laws and languages.[42] Criminal law's ranking is striking: 22% of interviewed lawyers consider criminal law as the most lucrative field. This reflects institutional weaknesses that emerged through globalization. There are strong links between the practice of criminal law and certain criminal activities that have appeared in the context of a globalized economy.

The 2014 Chambers & Partners ranking highlighted the importance of area specialization in the business of law firms. The most outstanding are banking and finance, corporate law, mergers and acquisitions, arbitration, competition and anti-monopoly, as well as money laundering. The case of specialized firms in a single branch such as energy, environmental and

Table 8.6 Perception of the profitability fields[41]

Fields	*% Perception of profitability*
Corporate/Commercial	23
Criminal	22
Taxation	20
Private	14
Labor	11
Others	4
Administrative	3
Constitutional	3
Total	100

Source: Gaceta Jurídica, Revista La Ley. Los abogados en el Perú, Lima, marzo del 2014

labor law is also valued. A section of the rankings is also dedicated to real estate issues as well as to intellectual property.[43]

Specialization in the legal field has many distinctive features in the context of growth of corporate law firms, in number of lawyers, billing and also in terms of expansion toward provinces and international legal markets (Interview with Ricardo Herrera Vásquez).

The Organization of Law Firms in a Globalized Context

Globalization also has an impact on organizational structures and strategies directed at the expansion of law firms. In a globalized context, there is now a need for an overall specialized work method and, of course, there is also a need to offer specialized services when it comes to defining what kind of law firm is sought. Specialization must permeate all dimensions of the firm: the lawyers, interns, administrative staff, organizational values and the image the firm seeks to project in the legal market.

It is worth mentioning that not long ago, most law firms mainly consisted of solo practitioners. Lawyers barely had an assistant or a secretary, who was usually a typist. Exceptionally, two or more lawyers could share an office in order to save on costs, but they would hardly have a common business.[44] In that market, there was almost no room for specialization, and customer service did not reach the quality levels offered by today's firms.[45]

Offering legal services in a globalized context requires a set of skills that are not strictly legal. Today's clients have complex needs that go beyond the lawyer's skills. Clients now also need support in human talent management, since they have to project and plan their work in teams. It thus becomes indispensable to create and optimize organizational structures at all levels.

Most law firms' culture—including the ideal of specialization—values academic credentials, but experience is also preciously valued. Indeed, senior partners are at the apex of the law firms. This table is based on the data provided by 34 law firms located in Lima and shows the following (Table 8.7):

Hierarchies within these law firms roughly follow this scheme: senior partner, partner, senior associate, associate, junior associate, paralegal and intern (Interview with Julio Cesar Perez Vargas). There are also professional, administrative and other non-legal specialized employees that play an important role in the provision of well-rounded and complete services to clients. These employees strengthen the quality of the legal services because legal services—in order to be thorough—require support from other disciplines such as: economy, anthropology, history, engineering, psychology and accounting. The new way of organizing law firms has to be compatible with the flexibility needed to cooperate and interact with these or other disciplines.

Some have stressed that the legal profession was not a complex legal market[47] since it was limited to general legal advice, regardless of the quality of the service, and that there was no real concern to establish a structure capable to offer a service of quality. However, today's lawyer has to master technical skills and also managing, administrative, finance and communication skills.

The legal profession is articulated through work organization. The division of tasks, specialization, corporative focus, automation of administrative functions and the standardization of certain practices, including customer services, are features of a culture that lawyers are committed to and that they share as a requirement to the smooth functioning of the firm.

In this new form of organization, the division of labor deepens, and informality in the working methods ceases to exist. But the division of labor can also serve to reproduce the organizational hierarchy in the profession. This is a consequence of over-specialization and it can contribute to exacerbating inequalities (Bergoglio and Carballo 2005: 204).

Another new feature of the legal market has surprised the Peruvian legal culture. Mainly in large firms, a competitive professional labor market has emerged. Loyalty to the firm is not what it used to be. Nowadays, lawyers—as emphasized by Ricardo Herrera—can move from one firm to the other, which was "an inconceivable thing to do … my firm was my only job for life, this is where I would retire from, or I might end up opening my own firm" (Interview with Carlos Caro Coria).

On the other hand, law firms mainly decide to adopt a corporate structure as is evidenced by a survey to 34 law firms (Table 8.8).

Table 8.7 Firm's composition[46]

Total top 35	*Partners*	*Associates*
Lawyers	364	734
Ratio partners/associates	10	25

Table 8.8 Corporate structures of law firms

Limited liability company	29
Closed corporation	3
Individual limited liability company	2
Total	34

Source: Personal information from the web pages

The clear preference for limited liability companies is explicable due to its advantage in terms of the protection it provides to personal assets of its partners, but it is also worth noticing that such a corporate structure has important impacts on the internal mobility of lawyers of the firm.

The Case of Boutique Firms

Alongside this structured offer of multi-specialized legal services, boutique law firms are swimming against the tide in spite of the fact that they are also byproducts of a globalized context. The spirit of boutique firms also puts forward specialization but in a rather limited fashion in that boutiques do not purport to be specialized in many fields. Boutiques seek to be highly specialized in fewer intertwined areas of the law, which become their niche.

Boutique law firms are part of the growth and specialization process of legal services offered in the country. Some of them have managed to be regarded as the most successful firms operating in the areas of markets regulation, competition and corporate criminal law.

Among the most representative firms of this segment it is possible to observe some common traits: a small team of lawyers, a high level of specialization combined to relevant academic training and a rich specialized professional experience. It is worth noticing that the lawyers of these firms are quite influential in the legal market and highly valued for the quality of their services.[48]

The type of work associated with a boutique firm contributes to enhancing the specialization of the lawyers; their practice is limited to a handful of interconnected areas of the law. Thus, specialization in a few fields has impacts on how the lawyer grasps another interconnected field, which enriches the lawyer's overall expertise, and thus the firm's overall level of specialization. This is probably one of the most valuable advantages provided by boutique law firms.

There are some organizational features that are specific to boutiques. Their smaller size shapes their institutional management. It is thus quite likely that operative costs will be lower when it comes to a boutique. However, specialization involves a high level of commitment from the lawyers working in a boutique.

A certain extent of horizontality is also a new element that marks this segment of the legal market. It appears lawyers now tend to value the idea of working on interesting projects, rather than focusing on advancement opportunities.[49]

This leads us to a cultural aspect that has impacted the organization of law firms. Changes in legal paradigms that go beyond mere legal reforms are expressed in the way the law is conceived by lawyers and how they practice it. This has been a constant reality through the last 20 years in Peru.

3. The Legal Practice in a Globalized World and the Public Interest

Business and corporate activities are not matters that can be studied in a purely private perspective. Individual interests need to be guaranteed by public institutions, and in order to be legitimate, they must be articulated so as to not compromise the public values that give sense to a constitutional democracy. This ethic also applies to law firms.

Globalization and the Public Meaning of the Legal Profession

The legal profession's new focus cannot ignore that the law is, above all, a public profession. In that manner, the corporate structure of a law firm should be a means to face the challenges of a reality whose ends are always public. Furthermore, globalization is a process that reinforces the public nature of the interests championed by law firms. Changes brought by globalization affect our communities by restricting or broadening rights and liberties and by creating new means to develop humanity's potential, but globalization can also restrict these rights, liberties and human potential for development. These issues are fundamental to the meaning of public interest as a complex structure of institutional guarantees protecting the exercise of rights and liberties of citizens and moral persons.

Such realities call for a commitment to the public dimension of the legal profession. Lawyers represent their clients before the legal system, but they also represent the legal system before their clients (Gordon 1999: 173). This might be a rather idealistic view of the profession, but in any case, it can be considered as an ideal programmatic target which enhances the efficiency and competitiveness of the legal profession. If the lawyers' work becomes completely disconnected from any public goal, the legal market risks becoming a mere backdrop for a panoply of unregulated or underregulated conduct seeking to advance clients' interests at all costs irrespective of any countervailing public values (Gordon 1999: 175).

This view becomes clear if we have in mind the proliferation of social conflicts that took place over the last two decades in Peru. These conflicts are partially consequences of a conjunction of factors that date back to the creation of the republic. In their recent manifestations, such conflicts are part of the complex dynamics of globalization that led to the presence of important capitals and multinational corporations seeking to invest in the extraction of natural resources.

The profitability of such economic activities has lately been compromised by the lack of compliance with prior agreements with the communities involved. In fact, according to the data from Defensoría del Pueblo, in May 2015, there were approximately 211 social conflicts around natural resource extraction activities (152 active and 59 latent). The latest cases emerged in Áncash, where people from the San Marcos Province report that Antamina, a mining company, is not respecting its agreements relating to environmental issues. In Cajamarca, the people from Hualgayoc, an important mining center, demand that the Health Direction (Dirección de Salud) relinquish the blood test screening results for abnormal lead concentrations in the local population. In Ica, workers of the Shougang Mining Company demand for their petitions to be heard. In Lambayeque, active and retired workers petition the sugar company Tumán to pay for overdue salaries.

As an example, the most recent social clashes have caused many deaths and injuries. Such is the case of Islay, in Arequipa, where the Tía María mining project is led by the Southern Peru Corporation. Six years of conflict surrounding the mining project has left dozens injured and five dead. Similar events have occurred lately, among others, in Bagua, Conga, Espinar, Pichanaki and Ocuviri.[50]

According to the Defensoria del Pueblo, since 2006, 257 people have died and 4318 were injured in the context of social conflicts.[51] The government turned a blind eye to these events, and corporations were clearly conscious of the tensions they were stoking. In that respect, the foundational aspect of the public nature of the legal profession should take on its full meaning.

It goes without saying that when the most prestigious law firms of the country advise global corporations in the natural resource extraction sector, they do not do so without putting aside their own interests. Lawyers have the ability to influence business decisions or to limit expectations even if they do not have the last word. In the gap separating corporate and community interests, lawyers have a lot of work to do and probably bear a share of responsibility for bridging that gap.

Globalized lawyers are part of a reality that requires a constructive commitment. If they do not take such commitment, extractive activity will be affected by unstable dynamics that may convert the industry into an exceedingly expensive and inefficient business. In the worst-case scenario, these conflictive social and labor relations will likely destroy the foundations of public trust necessary to continue investment and development.

Big Law Firms Face Corruption: Globalization in the shadows

Corruption is one of the greatest challenges that the practice of the legal profession must face as a priority in the context of globalization. Due to the increase of social, legal and political demands, as a result of the complexity and speed of globalizing exchange, it is necessary to offer institutional structures with flexible but firm values. This should ensure that the effects of this new reality do not surpass the established values of ethical coexistence, indispensable in a community.

However, the last decades show the enormous contradiction between the optimistic discourse that globalization offers, especially in the field of legal profession. The impact of corruption on the legal and institutional practice has become a problem that has put even the governance of Peru at risk. In this scenario, lawyers have played a decisive role in many cases.

The link between corruption and the performance of globalized legal firms has had a particular significance in the case of Odebrecht, due to its enormous economic and political impact. It is a bribe net promoted by the company of Brazilian origin that involves officials and politicians from Brazil, Argentina, Venezuela, Angola, Mozambique, Guatemala, Mexico, Panama, Dominican Republic, Colombia, Ecuador and Peru. In December 2016, the United States Department of Justice revealed that in these 12 countries, the company had paid $788 million in bribes in exchange for contracts awarded between 2001 and 2016. For cases in the United States, The Justice Department imposed a fine of $3.5 billion on Odebrecht.[52]

This fact is part of a wider network of corruption that operated almost 20 years ago through the state-owned oil company Petrobras from Brazil. Main brazilian constructors had agreed to give them the tenders of their works in exchange for millonaire bribes. This same corrupt practice was replicated by the builders throughout Latin America. This is the mega case known by the investigations as "Lava Jato".

The US Department of Justice's report initially estimates $29 million USD in bribes paid by Odebrecht to Peru authorities between 2005 and 2014. For that reason, several investigative processes have been opened in the Parliament of the Republic, in the Office of the Prosecutor and the Judiciary, involving former officials, politicians and even the three former presidents of the Republic of the last 15 years.

The Odebrecht case is one of the most serious corruption processes in the history of the country. Preliminary investigations have shown the involvement of main law firms as interested and responsible actors in the definition of acts of corruption. The case of a prominent corporate lawyer, who is a senior partner of a very important law firm sheds light on the link between the legal practice by law firms and corruption allegations. This lawyer has been acused of participating in the creation of an offshort company aimed to conceal and launder assets, allegdly obtained from a $ 3 million USD bribe to a former Cusco governor by Odebrecht. After few days of being held in preventive custody, the lawyer accepted his responsibility and entered a plea guilty claiming benefits for cooperation.[53] Currently, other 26 prestigious law firms are expected to be investigated for their connections with Odebrecht.[54] However, not all the investigations are based on corruption allegations.

The role lawyers play is also visible in the arbitrations that Odebrecht had with the Peruvian state. This allowed the subscription of complementary contracts that substantially exceeded the agreed amounts in the original contracts. It is estimated that out of a total of 42 arbitration disputes over the last 13 years, the state-appointed arbitrators voted mostly for Odebrecht as well as the arbitrators appointed by the company. The decision taken by the presidents of the arbitral tribunals were also mostly in favor of the company: 34 times in favor of Odebrecht and only 8 in favor of the state.[55]

Due to arbitration awards, the Odebrecht company earned about $254,656,753 dollars from the Peruvian state, between 2003 and 2016. Everything indicates that this result was obtained due to a mechanism used in a systematic way by the enterprise: poor contracts with incomplete clauses, along with other anomalies in the management of contract enforcement processes.[56] And in most cases, were the lawyers of important legal firms, who made it possible the organization of these processes, concluding in favor of Odebrecht.

Conclusion

The role played by lawyers in society aims at constructing certain individual and institutional powers as legitimate and unavoidable. Their discourses have the ability to influence—sometimes in a determinative manner—the way law is shaped and the justifications underlying the exercise of certain powers and rights. This is why the legal profession is highly relevant in countries like Peru.

Indeed, it is undeniable that globalization, besides its own cultural and ideological baggage, acquires its own meaning according to each reality where it takes roots. Social inequalities, poverty and institutional weakness are factors that intertwine with the impact of globalization and thus multiply its devastating effects on the social fabric.

The rationale behind the lawyer's practice implies a strategic power which enables them to have ascendency on any civil servant, businessman, union leader or person that has to take a decision involving the law. Lawyers even get to create the law, in many different manners through such ascendency. Yesterday's legal advisor often becomes a politician or vice versa, with all the transparency issues that this might involve for public institutions (Lasswell and McDougal 1999: 75–76). Hence, the negative effect of the reforms brought by globalization on the institutional bases of democracy becomes clearer, especially when lawyers are involved.

The legal advocacy of certain private interests and the dissemination of discourses marked by their emphasis on efficiency sideline public values that should be represented and protected by the law (Fiss 2007: 266). These types of practices have a deleterious effect on the rule of law and thus have negative consequences on public institutions (García Raggio 2004: 104).

An example of such negative effects is corruption, which might have become a normal feature of how businessman, state agencies and lawyers interact. Corruption would have thus become part of the legal profession in a context of globalization.

The cultural legal changes brought by globalization have clear repercussions when it comes to specialization. This is a significant issue since it leads us to reflect on "the public value" of the law as an indispensable feature of legal culture open to the impacts of globalization, particularly when it comes to taking account of the importance that must be given to the interests of local communities in that process. An unbalanced approach in that context can have a very negative impact if specialization becomes a mere tool of economic requirements and thus disregards the legal needs of local communities. Specialization cannot become a simple compartmentalized approach that disdains constitutional principles and values as a foundation of legal culture.

The meaning conveyed by the conglomeration of law firms that were the product of globalization transposes the preexistent stratification and fragmentation of our society. The lawyers of those firms represent less than 1% of the members of the legal profession. However, the economic impact of their practice for the whole country is colossal, particularly when it comes to the process of economic and legal globalization. These features speak to what the legal profession has now become but particularly to how the structural inequalities of society are legitimized by legal practice.

It is necessary to analyze the relationships emerging from the professional arrangement which is also institutional. It is clear that we are facing a very complex professional reality in that the composition of the legal profession comprises nuances that are the products of the globalization process in the most negative sense. This is the case of informality and corruption that are, for many lawyers, part of a daily practice. Finally, we can also refer to solo practitioners, small groups of lawyers sharing offices to save on costs, who sometimes have considerable client portfolios, but it is still difficult to assert that they are part of the globalization process, even though they probably are indirectly part of that process.

Notes

1. Interview with Mr. Nelson Ramírez Jiménez, Senior Partner Emeritus at *Estudio Muñiz, Ramírez, Pérez-Taiman & Olaya abogados*, October 10, 2014.

2. Interview with Mr. Ricardo Herrera Vásquez, Senior Partner at *Estudio Muñiz, Ramírez, Pérez-Taiman & Olaya abogados*, October 12, 2014.
3. Interview with Mr. Nelson Ramírez Jiménez.
4. Secretaría Ejecutiva de la Comisión de Coordinación Interuniversitaria (ANR). Boletín Perú: Estadísticas Universitarias 1960–1986. Lima, Año IX, N° 10, junio de 1988. Gonzales Mantilla (2008).
5. Instituto Nacional de Estadística. Características del Empleo Urbano. Población profesional ocupada por principales profesiones, 1995. 4.3.2:http://proyectos.inei.gob.pe/web/biblioineipub/bancopub/Est/Lib0177/n00.htm.
6. http://www.blogcyh.com/2012/04/causas-del-autogolpe-del-5-de abril.html#sthash.ViERqrZj.dpuf.
7. The dismissals took place with the decree laws No 25423, 25425, 25442, 25443, 25446, 25471, 25492, 25529, 25563, 25580 and 26618. See Gonzales Mantilla (—) 56.
8. See *Debate, Revista del Instituto Apoyo*. Vol. XVI, N° 17, December 1993–January 1994, pp. 43–47.
9. According to Law N° 30220 (Ley Universitaria) and the Organic Law of Judiciary and the Law 27020, Art. 285.
10. Interview with Mr. Nelson Ramírez, Ibid.
11. Interview with Carlos Carpio, partner at Rodrigo, Elías & Medrano. May 30, 2015.
12. Interview with Mr. Nelson Ramírez.
13. Interview with Mr. Nelson Ramírez.
14. Interview with Mr. Nelson Ramírez.
15. Interview with Mr. Nelson Ramírez.
16. http://blog.pucp.edu.pe/item/101618/milagro-peruano-crecimiento-desigualdad-pobreza-y-democracia.
17. According to Ernst & Young, see:http://gestion.pe/mercados/mirada-al-sector-bancario-ultimos-15-anos-2111606.
18. According to Mr. Francisco Tong, Partner at Rodrigo, Elías & Medrano, such formalism is an unreasonable practice of the public administration. The administration requests between 200 and 400 permits to operate in this field. See: http://gestion.pe/economia/se-necesita-mas-abogados-que-ingenieros-abrir-mina-peru-2100008.
19. "Impacto económico de la actividad minera en el Perú". Sociedad Nacional de Minería, petróleo y Energía. Documento elaborado por Macroconsult. See : http://www.snmpe.org.pe, Primera Edición, junio de 2012, pp. 2–3.
20. http://www.inei.gob.pe/media/MenuRecursivo/boletines/01-produccion-nacional-dic-2013.pdf.
21. See:http://rumboeconomico.com/index.php/rankings/item/87-los-mejores-estudios-de-abogados-estudios-penalistas-y-boutiques-legales-del-peru-2013.

22. Based on data collected from: http://laley.pe/not/1215/los-abogados-en-el-peru/; http://www.web.onpe.gob.pe/modMarco-Legal/Resoluciones/RJ-011-2015.pdf. Pasco has not been considered for the purposes of this table, since it does not register more than 100 lawyers.
23. It is important to underline that in 2008, the private law schools (34) overpass the public ones (20).
24. Interview with Mr. Nelson Ramirez.
25. http://laley.pe/not/1215/los-abogados-en-el-peru. No official information exists.
26. http://www.conab.org/colegios.
27. http://laley.pe/not/1215/los-abogados-en-el-peru. No official information exists.
28. According to The National Statistics Institute, in 2012, there were only 34,805 policemen working in police stations: http://www.inei.gob.pe/media/MenuRecursivo/censos/cenacomResultadosDefinitivos/index.html. Also http://peru21.pe/opinion/hay-policia-cada-953-habitantes-lima-2181945.
29. http://gestion.pe/impresa/estudio-echecopar-se-asocia-baker-mckenzie-2013856.
30. Gonzales, Gorki. "Los abogados y la crisis del sistema legal". Diario El Comercio. Lima, 30 de marzo de 2003, p.A-33.
31. See: http://www.echecopar.com.pe/content/index.php?pID=1547.
32. http://prc.com.pe/en/the-firm.
33. http://www.bfu.pe/nosotros.php?p=0&d=89.
34. http://archivo.larepublica.pe/20-01-2015/abogados-sa.
35. http://elpacificador2008.blogspot.com/2009/03/reflexiones-de-un-abogado-en-el-dia-del.html and also: http://elobservador.perublog.net/2008/01/21/el_colegio_de_abogados_de_lima/
36. Interview with Oscar Soria Limaylla and Robert Torre Tenorio, both members of the "AAA". Interviewed on February 25, 2015.
37. The significant number is directly proportional to the degree of influence on the ability to define the election of the dean of the Lima Bar Association. See on this issue : http://aeronoticias.com.pe/noticiero/index.php?option=com_content&view=article&id=55182:asociacion-de-abogados-academicos-triple-aaa-organiza-cena-de-lanzamiento-de-julian-palacin-al-cal-este-viernes-24-de-julio&catid=97:noticias-cal&Itemid=635
38. http://www.legal500.com/c/peru and http://www.chambersandpartners.com/171/49/editorial/9/1#RankedLawyers_Tab.
39. Interview with Jorge Toyama on October 21, 2014.
40. SOURCE: Gaceta Jurídica, Revista La Ley. Los abogados en el Perú, Lima, March 2014. Survey based on data collected from 1010 lawyers operating at the national level.

41. Based on data from Gaceta Jurídica. Revista La Ley. Los abogados en el Perú, Lima, marzo del 2014.
42. Interview with Julio César Pérez Vargas on October 23, 2015.
43. http://gestion.pe/empresas/chambers-partners-publica-ranking-mejores-abogados-y-firmas-2109232.
44. Interview with Mr. Paul Paredes, October 20, 2014.
45. Interview with Mr. Carlos Caro Coria, October 17, 2014.
46. SOURCE: Data collected from websites of the 35 best law firms according to Chambers & Partners´ ranking.
47. Interview with Mr. Carlos Caro Coria on October 17, 2014.
48. See: http://www.bullardabogados.pe/blog/wp-content/uploads/2012/09/bfe_Chambers-and-Partners2012.pdf, también en: http://rumboeconomico.com/index.php/rankings/item/87-los-mejores-estudios-de-abogados-estudios-penalistas-y-boutiques-legales-del-peru-2013 y en: http://www.ccfirma.com/principal/distinciones/archivos/distincion16.pdf.
49. See: http://www.larepublica.co/asuntos-legales/las-boutiques-le-quitan-mercado-las-grandes-firmas-legales_112921. See also: http://www.bullardabogados.pe/nosotros.htm.
50. Véase el Diario El Comercio en línea: http://elcomercio.pe/peru/pais/conflictos-sociales-panorama-infografia-interactiva-noticia-1824294?ref=flujo_tags_25465&ft=nota_3&e=titulo.
51. http://larepublica.pe/politica/5305-baguazo-radiografia-de-un-conflicto-sin-culpables-en-su-sexto-aniversario.
52. See http://semanaeconomica.com/tema/la-corrupcion-de-odebrecht-en-el-peru/.
53. See https://ojo-publico.com/433/detienen-a-expresidente-regional-de-cusco-y-a-abogado-de-estudio-Rebaza-por-coima-de-odebrecht.
54. See http://diariocorreo.pe/politica/caso-odebrecht-esta-es-la-lista-de-estudios-de-abogados-de-la-constructora-brasilena-750637/.
55. See https://idl-reporteros.pe/arbitrajes-a-la-odebrecht-lavajato/.
56. Ibid.

References

Basadre, Jorge. 1968. *Historia de la República del Perú 1822–1933. Sexta edición aumentada y corregida*. Lima: Editorial Universitaria.

Bergoglio, María Inés, and J. Carballo. 2005. Segmentación en la profesión jurídica. Cambios ocupacionales de los abogados argentinos, 1995–2003. *Academia: revista sobre enseñanza del derecho de Buenos Aires* 3 (5): 201–222.

Bernales, Enrique, and M. Rubio. 1981. *Perú: Constitución y sociedad política*. Lima: DESCO, Centro de Estudios y Promoción del Desarrollo.

Brandt, Hans-Jürgen. 1990. *En nombre de la paz comunal. Un análisis de la justicia de paz en el Perú.* Lima: Fundación Friedrich Naumann – Centro de Investigaciones de la Corte Suprema de Justicia de la República.
Bullard, Alfredo. 1997. Las acciones de interés público en defensa de la libre competencia y la protección al consumidor: el caso peruano. In *Las acciones de interés público. Argentina Chile, Colombia y Perú*, ed. Felipe González, 243–244. Santiago de Chile: Universidad Diego Portales.
Contreras Carranza, Carlos, ed. 2011. *Compendio de historia económica del Perú IV: economía de la primera centuria independiente.* Lima: IEP/BCRP.
Delgado Narro, Augusto R. n.d. La Informalidad en el Perú. Centro Nacional de Planeamiento Estratégico. http://tasadeinteres.org/La-informalidad-en-el-Peru.pdf
Fiss, Owen. 2007. *El derecho como razón pública.* Madrid: Parcial Pons.
Francke, Pedro. 2001. Políticas Públicas y Pobreza en el Perú de los noventa. In *Ajuste estructural en América Latina. Costos sociales y alternativas.* Buenos Aires: CLACSO, Consejo Latinoamericano de Ciencias Sociales. http://biblioteca.clacso.edu.ar/clacso/gt/20101003014732/3cap02.pdf
García Raggio, Ana. 2004. Ciudadanía y política en el orden global emergente. En: *La política en conflicto.* Buenos Aires: Prometeo Libros.
Gonzales de Olarte, Efraín. 1998. *El neoliberalismo a la peruana. Economía política del ajuste estructural 1990–1997.* Lima: Instituto de Estudios Peruanos.
Gonzales Mantilla, Gorki. 1998. *Poder Judicial, Interés Público y Derechos Fundamentales en el Perú.* Lima: Pontificia Universidad Católica del Perú – Universidad Diego Portales de Chile.
———. 2000. *Pluralidad cultural, conflicto armado y Derecho en el Perú.* Lima: Fondo Editorial de la PUCP.
———. 2008. *La enseñanza del derecho o los molinos de viento. Cambios resistencias y continuidades.* Lima: Pontificia Universidad Católica del Perú.
———. 2010. La enseñanza del derecho como política pública. En *Derecho PUCP. Revista de la Facultad de Derecho de la PUCP.* 65.
Gordon, Robert W. 1999. La práctica del derecho empresarial como servicio público. In *La enseñanza del derecho y el ejercicio de la abogacía*, compilador by M. Böhmer. Barcelona: Gedisa.
Huber, Ludwig. 2005. *Una interpretación antropológica de la corrupción en.* http://cies.org.pe/files/active/0/LHuber-Corrupcion.pdf
Lasswell, Harold and M. McDougal. 1999. Enseñanza del derecho y políticas públicas. In *La enseñanza del derecho y el ejercicio de la abogacía*, compilador by M. Bohmer. Barcelona. hub Gedisa.
López, Sinesio. 1995. Estado, régimen político e institucionalidad en el Perú (1950–1994). In *El Perú frente al siglo XXI*, ed. G. Portocarrero and M. Valcárcel. Lima: Fondo Editorial de la Pontificia Universidad Católica del Perú.

Mills, Wright. 1973. *White collar: Las clases medias en Norteamérica*. Madrid: Editorial Aguilar.

Mujica, Jaris. 2011. *Micropolíticas de la corrupción*. Lima: Asociación Nacional de Rectores.

Quiroz, Alfonso W. 2013. *Historia de la corrupción en el Perú. Traducción de Javier Flores Espinoza*. Lima: Instituto de Estudios Peruanos e Instituto de Defensa Legal.

Santos, Boaventura de Sousa. 2001. Derecho y democracia: la reforma global de la justicia. In *El caleidoscopio de las justicias en Colombia*, ed. I. Tomo. Bogotá: Conciencias – Ediciones UNIANDADES. Universidad de Coimbra/Instituto Colombiano de Antropología e Historia/Universidad Nacional de Colombia/ Siglo del Hombre Editores.

Sen, Amartya. 2007. *Primero la gente. Una mirada desde la ética del desarrollo a los principales problemas del mundo globalizado*. Barcelona: Ediciones Deusto.

Silva García, Germán. 2001. *El mundo real de los abogados y de la justicia. Las prácticas jurídicas*. Tomo II. Bogotá: Universidad del Externado de Colombia/ ILSA.

Stiglitz, Joseph E. 2006. *Cómo hacer que funcione la globalización*. México: Taurus.

Supiot, Alain. 2012. *Homo Juridicus. Ensayo sobre la función de la antropología del derecho*. Buenos Aires: Siglo XXI Editores.

Tarello, Giovanni. 1995. *Cultura Jurídica y Política del Derecho*. México: Fondo de Cultura Económica.

Teubner, G., S. Sassen, and S. Krasner. 2010. *Estado, soberanía y globalización*. Estudio preliminar por Laura Saldivia. Bogota: Siglo del Hombre/Universidad Javeriana/Universidad de Los Andes.

Websites

Abogados S.A. 2015. http://larepublica.pe/20-01-2015/abogados-sa

Aeronoticias. 2015. Asociación de Abogados Académicos (Triple AAA) organiza cena de lanzamiento de Julián Palacin al CAL este viernes 24 de julio. http://aeronoticias.com.pe/noticiero/index.php?option=com_content&view=article&id=55182:asociacion-de-abogados-academicos-triple-aaa-organiza-cena-de-lanzamiento-de-julian-palacin-al-cal-este-viernes-24-de-julio&catid=97:noticias-cal&Itemid=635

Backer & Mckenzie. 2014. Alianza del Pacífico. http://www.bakermckenzie.com/files/Uploads/Documents/Latin%20America/br_la_pacificalliance_dec14_spanish.pdf

Baguazo: radiografía de un conflicto que tras seis años aún no tiene culpables. 2015. http://larepublica.pe/politica/5305-baguazo-radiografia-de-un-conflicto-sin-culpables-en-su-sexto-aniversario

Benites, Forno, and Ugaz Abogados. 2015. Nosotros. http://www.bfu.pe/nosotros.php?p=0&d=89

Broseta. 2015. Corresponsales en Latinoamérica. http://www.broseta.com/internacional/latinoamerica/red-latinoamericana/

Bullard Falla Ezcurra +. Nosotros. 2012. http://www.bullardabogados.com.pe/nosotros.htm

Caro & Asociados. 2015. Distinción. http://www.ccfirma.com/principal/distinciones/archivos/distincion16.pdf

Chambers & Partners publica ranking de los mejores abogados y firmas. 2014. http://gestion.pe/empresas/chambers-partners-publica-ranking-mejores-abogados-y-firmas-2109232

Chambers & Partners. 2015. Tax – Peru. http://www.chambersandpartners.com/171/49/editorial/9/1#RankedLawyers_Tab

"Comenzamos de cero, fichando a los talentos experimentados". 2014. http://gestion.pe/empresas/comenzamos-cero-fichando-talentos-experimentados-2110857

Condenan a 10 años de cárcel a Blanca Nélida Colán. 2003. http://www.larepublica.pe/24-01-2003/condenan-10-anos-de-carcel-blanca-nelida-colan

Conflictos sociales: el panorama en esta infografía interactiva. 2015. http://elcomercio.pe/peru/pais/conflictos-sociales-panorama-infografia-interactiva-noticia-1824294?ref=flujo_tags_25465&ft=nota_3&e=titulo

El Comercio. 2012. La élite legal peruana según "Chambers and Partners". http://www.bullardabogados.pe/blog/wp-content/uploads/2012/09/bfe_Chambers-and-Partners2012.pdf

El Pacificador. 2009. Reflexiones de un abogado en el Día del Abogado. http://elpacificador2008.blogspot.pe/2009/03/reflexiones-de-un-abogado-en-el-dia-del.html

Estudio Echecopar se asocia con Baker & McKenzie. 2012. http://gestion.pe/impresa/estudio-echecopar-se-asocia-baker-mckenzie-2013856

Estudio Echecopar. 2015. Noticias. http://www.echecopar.com.pe/content/index.php?pID=1547

Estudio Rodrigo, Elías, and Medrano. 2015. Áreas de Trabajo. http://www.estudiorodrigo.com/portada/es/index.php/areas-trabajo/index

Expansión. 2015. Latinoamérica, campo de batalla para los bufetes. http://www.expansion.com/2015/02/27/juridico/1425057797.html

Garrigues, Uría y Cuatrecasas confirman su liderazgo en España. 2015. http://www.expansion.com/juridico/actualidad-tendencias/2015/07/06/559a8ee822601d6c5c8b459a.html

Garrigues. 2015. Página Principal. http://www.garrigues.com/es/Paginas/Home.aspx

Gestión. 2014. Una mirada al sector bancario de los últimos 15 años. http://gestion.pe/mercados/mirada-al-sector-bancario-ultimos-15-anos-2111606

I Censo Nacional de Comisarías. 2012. Resultados Definitivos. http://www.inei.gob.pe/media/MenuRecursivo/censos/cenacomResultadosDefinitivos/index.html

INEI. 1995. Características del Empleo Urbano. Población profesional ocupada por principales profesiones. http://proyectos.inei.gob.pe/web/biblioineipub/bancopub/Est/Lib0177/n00.htm

La Ley. 2014. Los Abogados en el Perú. http://laley.pe/not/1215/los-abogados-en-el-peru

La República Colombia. 2014. Las boutiques le quitan mercado a las grandes firmas legales. http://www.larepublica.co/asuntos-legales/las-boutiques-le-quitan-mercado-las-grandes-firmas-legales_112921

La República Perú. 2008. Ex vocal supremo Alejandro Rodríguez Medrano salió en libertad. http://larepublica.pe/17-07-2008/ex-vocal-supremo-alejandro-rodriguez-medrano-salio-en-libertad

Miranda & Amado. 2015. La Firma. http://www.mafirma.com.pe/index.php/nuestra-firma/el-estudio

Ontier Perú. 2015. Página Principal. http://pe.ontier.net/equipo/es/

Payet, Rey, Cauvi, Perez Abogados. The Firm. http://prc.com.pe/en/the-firm

Perú21. Hay un policía por cada 953 habitantes en Lima. 2014. http://peru21.pe/opinion/hay-policia-cada-953-habitantes-lima-2181945

Pikkety, Thomas. 2015. *La economía de las desigualdades*. Buenos Aires: Siglo XXI Editores.

Principales Indicarores Macroeconómicos. 2011. http://www.inei.gob.pe/estadisticas/indice-tematico/economia/

Producción Nacional. 2013. http://www.inei.gob.pe/media/MenuRecursivo/boletines/01-produccion-nacional-dic-2013.pdf

Rumbo Económico. 2013. Los Mejores Estudios de Abogados, Estudios Penalistas y Boutiques Legales del Perú. http://rumboeconomico.com/index.php/rankings/item/87-los-mejores-estudios-de-abogados-estudios-penalistas-y-boutiques-legales-del-peru-2013

Se necesita más abogados que ingenieros para abrir una mina en Perú. 2014. http://gestion.pe/economia/se-necesita-mas-abogados-que-ingenieros-abrir-mina-peru-2100008

Sociedad Nacional De Minería, Petróleo y Energía. Impacto económico de la actividad minera en el Perú. Documento elaborado por Macroconsult. Primera Edición. 2012. http://www.snmpe.org.pe

The Legal 500. Peru: Legal Market Overview. 2015. http://www.legal500.com/c/peru

Uría Menéndez. Presentación. 2015. http://www.uria.com/es/oficinas/lima#

Interviews

"Entrevista con Carlos Caro Coria. Socio Fundador del Estudio Caro & Asociados". October 2014

"Entrevista con Carlos Carpio. Socio del Estudio Rodrigo, Elias & Medrano". October 2014
"Entrevista con César Azabache, Socio del Estudio Azabache Caracciolo". October 2014.
"Entrevista con Jorge Toyama. Socio del Estudio Miranda & Amado". October 2014.
"Entrevista con Julio César Pérez. Socio del Estudio Payet, Rey, Cauvi, Pérez". October 2014
"Entrevista con Nelson Ramírez. Socio Emérito del Estudio Muñiz". October 2014
"Entrevista con Paul Paredes. Socio del Estudio Cano Paredes Abogados". October 2014
"Entrevista con Ricardo Herrera. Socio Principal del Estudio Muñiz". October 2014

Gorki Gonzales Mantilla is Professor of Law at the Pontificia Universidad Católica del Perú in Lima (PUCP). He holds a doctorate in Constitutional Justice and Fundamental Rights from the Universitá di Pisa-Italy, and a master's in Laws from the PUCP. His research and publications are focused on problems regarding the administration of justice in Peru from the perspective of history, philosophy and political theory. He is also interested in legal education and its relationship with legal cultures.

CHAPTER 9

Big Law in Spain: A Dynamic Ecosystem

Marisa Méndez Sordo

Business Law and Lawyers in Spain

Spain is the seventh largest European country with a population of just over 46 million people,[1] and enjoys the 13th largest global economy. Spain is a parliamentary monarchy divided into 17 autonomous communities and two autonomous cities. There is a national law with regional variations allowed by the constitution. The regulatory framework, which is quite intricate, comprises more than 100,000 active rules and regulations decreed both by the central state and the autonomous communities. To put it in perspective, the legal system of a federal state like Germany, with twice the population, only has a tenth of the number of rules and regulations as Spain.

At the beginning of the twentieth century, there were roughly 6,000 registered lawyers in Spain.[2] In 1980, there were over 27,000, and ten years later, the number had increased to 55,000 lawyers. On December 31, 2013, there were 250,000 registered lawyers, and of those, nearly

The author would like to thank Juliana Hess for the editing work and her valuable contribution to this paper.

M. Méndez Sordo (✉)
IE Law School, Madrid, Spain

M. Gómez, R. Pérez-Perdomo (eds.), *Big Law in Latin America and Spain*, https://doi.org/10.1007/978-3-319-65403-4_9

150,000 are practicing lawyers. It is noteworthy to mention that around 45% of those belong to the Madrid and Barcelona bar associations. Overall, there are 290 lawyers per 100,000 people.[3] Appendix 1 shows the increase of lawyers since 1998.

Spanish law schools graduate approximately 13,000 students per year, a number that has remained steady and that contributes to the continued growth in the number of active lawyers in the country. Of these graduates, about 37% go into private practice at one of the more than 90,000 law firms currently operating across the 50 provinces and two autonomous cities.[4] At the same time, the number of new law firms also continues to rise. The growth in number of lawyers and number of new law firms is due to various reasons, one being the boom experienced during the "Golden Years" of the Spanish Economy. This growth continues despite of the critical economic situation the country is currently facing. Both the "Golden Years" and the state of the economy will be explained below.

Until recently, Spain was the only member of the European Union (EU), where obtaining a law degree from a recognized university was the only prerequisite to becoming a practicing lawyer. As a result of changes implemented in 2013, this road has become longer and more competitive. Now, three new requirements were put in place: a master's degree, a law firm internship and a bar exam. The changes were essential in order for the sector to remain competitive vis-à-vis the demands of increasingly sophisticated clients and of an increasingly intertwined global market place.

The *Consejo General de la Abogacía Española*[5]—the Spanish equivalent of the American Bar Association—provides a series of stipulations for the practice of law in Spain by foreign lawyers depending on their nationality. The main distinction lies in whether or not the individual is an EU citizen.

Generally speaking, the professional tracks in Spain do not really differ from those of other jurisdictions. There is a distinction between the sole practitioner track and the organizational track. The latter breaks down into legal organizations (partnerships and legal companies) and non-legal organizations (in-house or public/government sector).[6]

Big law facts and figures. There are about 91,000 registered law firms in Spain. Of these, approximately 89% of them have only three members or less. It is the remaining 11% that are relevant to this overview. It is this small percentage of firms that focus on providing specialized "business law" services mainly to mid and large enterprises and wealthy individuals.

This subsection of the market is quite dense. Law firms in this market subscribe to different operation and competition rules, whereby recruitment of professionals, branding and marketing of services, business development practices, track record and corporate governance structures play a significant role in the status of the firms and their leadership within the market.

This subsection can be further broken down as follow:

- Large firms: firms with 150 lawyers or more. Currently, 16 law firms fit in this category.
- Mid-sized firms: firms with 50 to 149 lawyers. There are at least 30 firms in this category.
- Small and boutique firms: firms with 49 lawyers or less. The former can be multidisciplinary or niche firms.

As new firms emerge, others grow and others fall victim to a turbulent economic environment. The market is constantly changing with younger or less established firms such as Roussaud Costas & Durán moving into the top 20 firms of the market alongside traditional and well-established firms such as Garrigues, Cuatrecasas or Uría, while others fall off the list.

In terms of revenues generated, according to 2013 available data, the 50 largest firms[7] generate about €2 billion per annum. Of this amount, seven law firms are responsible for half of the market share or €1,038,000.

It is important to note that while there has been a shift in recent years toward more strategic and financial transparency to allow greater access to quantitative information (such as revenues, number of lawyers and leverage ratios), there is no real way to verify all the information and firms of all sizes and ranking still wary of the resulting information. Reasons for this wariness include[8]:

- Revenues may or may not be earned exclusively from the provision of legal services.
- Revenues may or may not be generated exclusively by lawyers.
- Figures reported by domestic firms have not distinguished between revenues generated from purely domestic matters versus matters generated overseas or through their foreign operations. This puts the Spanish operation of international firms at a disadvantage, since the results provided by them are generally tied exclusively to their Spanish business.

- Information such as revenues and the number of lawyers does not mean much unless analyzed in a bigger context. Understanding the relationship between these figures and a firm's margins, profits per partner, partner/associate rations, etc. is key to understanding the real financial health of any firm. Even then, an exact comparison becomes extremely difficult given the lack of uniformity in corporate and operational strategy, billing and recording structure, etc.

Despite the above limitations and the obstacles naturally posed by the fact that these are all private outfits—and therefore limited in their obligation to disclose information—Spanish researchers and industry analysts embrace the move toward more transparency across the industry. And even with the limited amount of information, a clear set of issues and trends have been identified and analyzed. For the purposes of this chapter, we have analyzed all law firm-related information publically available with respect to the Top 20 law firms from 1996 to 2013 in order to give the reader more context. We used revenues and number of lawyers as our base and then proceeded to compare and analyze the information from the perspective of each of the types of legal practices found within this group: domestic firms, international law firms and legal arms of the Big Four.

The players. As of July 2014, about 70 domestic or independent law firms of 30 lawyers or more drive the Spanish market along with 15 English firms, eight American firms,[9] two Anglo-American, one Latin American, five of other European firms, one Australian and, the latest newcomer, a Chinese firm. In addition, "the Big Four" accounting firms also play a role—something that is described in depth below.

It is important to note that the Spanish independent firms have led the European rankings in terms of billings and number of lawyers in continental Europe during the last 15 years.[10]

Three Spanish law firms are market leaders and have had an enormous impact on the history of modern-day Spain. These firms are known as "the Trinity". They are Cuatrecasas, Gonçalves Pereira (founded in 1917), Uría Menéndez (1940) and Garrigues (1941). Their history is closely intertwined with the country, and there is no part of the evolution of the Spanish legal market that does not involve one or all three of these firms. They are an example of adaptability and inspiration to many young firms, and a true show of strength of the Spanish legal market in the face of adversity and foreign competition.

Later in the chapter, we will briefly describe their history and the role of three key individuals in their development and the development of the market. These individuals are Antonio Garrigues Walker, Rodrigo Uría Meruéndano and Emilio Cuatrecasas Figueras.

Comparative figures: In terms of profitability, Spain is the third largest European legal market with earnings of approximately €911 million. The other top European earners include Germany which ranks first with €1.5 billion in earnings, France is second with earnings of €964 million and The Netherlands fourth with earnings of €843 million. Other countries such as Norway, Ireland and Italy also make the list of top earners but with a significant gap between them and the top four previously mentioned.[11] Readers should note that those figures do only take into account earnings of largest European law firms but still reflect the gaps between jurisdictions. Refer to Appendix 2 for a complete list of continental Europe's top revenue-generating jurisdictions.

The World of Spanish Big Law

Big Law in Spain enjoys many of the benefits and faces many of the common challenges of Big Law in all other comparable jurisdictions. Firms in Spanish Big Law face competition for both talent and clients and from smaller, specialized and hyper-specialized boutique firms. Size, relationship history or law firm strategy do not seem relevant to clients who customarily hire different firms to advise on the various aspects of any given matter. For example, a firm established in 2011 dedicated exclusively to representing investors in connection with losses over financial toxic products already has more than 100 lawyers and is expected to generate around €20 million in revenue once all claims are settled.[12] The fiercest competition though, is most apparent at the "commoditized work" level, which accounts for the largest volume of legal work provided. Excellence in the quality of legal advice rendered (among other criteria) is a given, so price becomes the defining criterion. The ongoing pressure for more competitive pricing has created a very diverse market, where all types of law firms are active. Nothing suggests this trend will change.

Despite the gray and overlapping areas, there is an understood distinction in the Big Law market in terms of the type of service provider. The types of service providers are: (1) domestic firms, (2) international firms and (3) the legal arm of the Big Four accounting firms.[13]

Big Law's structure and career path. Like in most other traditional legal markets, law firms are largely organized under a pyramid structure with few senior partners leading larger numbers of lawyers. The various standard levels are junior associate, senior associate, of counsel, salaried partner and equity partner. And similar to other jurisdictions, the shrinking of the pyramid has resulted in the path to partnership becoming increasingly difficult with longer years in practice required prior to consideration and fewer individuals achieving the coveted status.

One area where Spanish Big Law does differ from some comparable jurisdictions and Latin American legal markets in the area of partnership track is that of international experience or training. Whereas law firms in other jurisdictions almost always require their rising stars to spend time overseas (primarily the UK and US) training at a law firm or client or pursuing additional legal courses or degrees, Spanish law firms and the market, in general, place as much value on other professional experiences and academic training such as time spent in government or public roles, and the pursuit of business studies and PhD programs. A perfect example of such reality is the globally recognized partnership Gomez-Acebo & Pombo, which by the beginning of 2015 had 62 partners on its roster: 23% of them hold an LLM from a foreign[14] university, and 18% of partners hold a PhD program or have spent time in public roles or both.

Big Four and Big Law. Something that surprises many outside of the jurisdictions where Big Law is reserved for law firms only, is the role of the "Big Four" within Spain's legal market (among several important (European jurisdictions). The penetration of the market by these now major players took place in the 1990s when the then "Big Five" identified an opportunity and decided to leverage their brand, international capabilities and existing relationships to enter these previously exclusive legal market. Their strategy was far-reaching as they looked to compete with traditional Big Law in various areas of law in addition to tax, and their approach was bold: they successfully lured top partners from big traditional firms with the promise of an international practice, a more innovative approach to the business of law and a pipeline supported by their already existing clients all around the world. Unlike in the US, their reputation did not suffer all that much as a consequence of the 2001 Enron-Arthur Andersen scandal. In fact, the remaining four have not only enjoyed steady growth over the last decade, their growth has resulted in greater returns than those of the leading Spanish law firms throughout the economic crisis,[15] and the strength of their services across various areas of law is continuously praised by clients and peers as reflected in various legal directories.[16]

In-house counsel and government lawyers. In addition to lawyers in private practice, there are two other types of lawyers who play a relevant role in the "business law" context: in-house counsels and government lawyers. And unlike other jurisdictions, their role is quite coveted and respected.

In-house counsel. The role of in-house counsel is pivotal in the business law universe in Spain. Like anywhere else, they are primarily "the client" and decision-makers when it comes to outsourcing work, but they are also internal agents of change. The later role, key to the development of legal departments, is primarily a phenomenon resulting from the move of lawyers from in-house to law firms and vice-versa. This phenomenon enables them to (1) have a clearer understanding of the shortcomings of the department and (2) bring the best practices with them. A recent trend that signals market evolution is that of communication between in-house and private practice lawyers via open forums and/or formal exchanges, where concerns and best practices are shared and discussed.[17]

In terms of the size of legal departments, Spanish companies are no different from their counterparts. In recent years, in-house legal teams have experienced significant growth, particularly those within highly regulated industries such as financial services and telecommunications. And like in many other jurisdictions, the outsourcing of legal work is highly dependent on the matter at hand, the complexity of the work, the volume of the work and in "Bet the company" matters, on the brand of the legal service provider. The one thing that affects the perception of the role of in-house counsel and is often the subject of discussion is that of their independence and their loyalty to the rule of law as opposed to loyalty to the employer. Many argue and question their ability to wear both hats and separate the two.[18]

Government lawyers: All lawyers working for the Spanish State, from constitutional lawyers to those providing assistance to the State, as well as those working for the State's regulatory agencies fall under one body: *"Cuerpo de Abogados del Estado"* (roughly translated into "State Lawyers Corps"). The members of this group are highly regarded for both their technical skills and their ample knowledge of the ins-and-outs of the government. They are also highly coveted by the private sector. Currently, about 54% of these professionals are on leave of absence from their government jobs and working at both law firms and listed companies.[19] There is no research-based or formalized data about their role in Big Law, but much can be concluded when six major international law firms currently have an "on-leave-of-absence" government lawyer leading their Spanish operations—as managing partners. These firms include Clifford Chance, Hogan Lovells, Baker & McKenzie, Linklaters, Ashurst and Latham & Watkins.

Madrid and Barcelona. The Spanish cities of Madrid and Barcelona play a central role in the Spanish legal market. Understanding their composition and dynamics provides good insight into its operation and composition. Madrid, in addition to being the capital of Spain, is also the country's largest city and the heart of the Spanish legal market with about 26% of registered law firms based there. Barcelona is the second largest city in Spain. It is also the capital of the autonomous community of Catalonia and the second most important legal market with about 15% of registered law firms having their base operations there. Of the 75 top-grossing business law firms, 72 have offices in Madrid, 44 in Barcelona and 42 have an office in both cities.

A comparative study of these two markets by Barcelona-based Esade business school yielded interesting and very informative findings[20]:

- There is an important distinction between the markets and industries which both cities serve. Madrid is home to the key financial and regulatory players of the Spanish economy as well as the headquarters of most IBEX 35[21] companies, thus playing an important role in Spain's international affairs. Barcelona (and the greater Catalan market, which it serves) on the other hand is more domestic focused and is home to the very popular family-owned Spanish middle-market companies, although some large Spanish conglomerates are also headquartered here.
- The above findings explain the fact that all international law firms with a presence in Spain have offices in Madrid, while only one-third have a presence in Barcelona. Moreover, most of the legal work with international implications is also performed by lawyers and law firms based in Madrid.
- Unlike the more open Madrid market, the Catalan market is more traditional and closed-off. Clients in this market are fiercely loyal to lawyers and law firms with ties to Catalan society.
- Legal fees in Madrid are significantly higher than in Barcelona.

Despite Barcelona's second-place status, the city plays a vital role in Spain's regional and global affairs in its own right thanks to its prominence in various fields including architecture, art, fashion, media and entertainment, and science among others.

Table 9.1 shows the evolution of revenues of top 20 law firms between 1996 and 2013

Table 9.2 reflects growth trends with respect to the number of lawyers for the 2013 Top 20 law firms.[22]

Graph 9.1 shows information relating to the number of lawyers and revenues according to the type of firm.

The Graph and Tables above provide some interesting insights:

- Domestic law firms (otherwise known as independent law firms) such as Garrigues, Cuatrecasas and Uría Menéndez still dominate the Spanish legal market both in numbers and in revenues.
- The total combined revenue for the top Spanish law firms is twice that of the revenues generated by the legal arm of the Big Four and more than three times the revenue generated by the international firms.
- The growth experienced by the domestic firms over the years has been quite significant compared to that of the international firms and the Big Four.
- International law firms—mostly those of UK origin—appear to attain largest revenues with smaller teams.
- Spanish domestic/independent law firms have done a marvelous job at defending their place in the market vis-à-vis their counterparts in other major European jurisdictions such as Germany, France and the Netherlands. International law firms have secured a sizeable share of these markets and have jeopardized the longevity of their domestic/ independent firms. In some cases, stealing market share not only with respect to international matters related to domestic deals but also domestic work.

What makes this phenomenon possible in Spain is subject for debate. Many would speculate that much of it could be cultural and based on tradition. Generally speaking, Spanish society has been close-knit and resistant to change, especially when foreigners bring about the change. There is also the fact that much of the Spanish business world is still largely family owned and operated. There are long-standing family ties that date

Table 9.1 Top 20 Spanish law firms by revenue (2013)

Firm	*Origin*	*Year established*	*1996*	*2000*	*2004*	*2008*	*2012*	*2013*
Garrigues	Domestic	1941	55.9	119.0	175.0	296.8	337.6	307.0
Cuatrecasas Gonçalves Pereira	Domestic	1926	27.6	84.1	133.5	240.6	245.6	198.2
Uría Menéndez	Domestic	1946	20.6	64.9	100.4	174.8	180.2	160.5
PwC tax and legal services	Big Four	1933		54.8	74.8	115.8	128.2	139.5
KPMG Abogados	Big Four	1971	8.2	20.4	38.5	67.2	92.1	82.1
Deloitte Abogados	Big Four	1969	5.0	12.3	28.0	50.2	72.5	76.9
EY Abogados	Big Four	1978	14.0	37.6	48.0	57.4	68.0	74.0
Baker & McKenzie	International	1965	7.8	20.9	40.4	58.8	59.1	55.2
Gómez-Acebo & Pombo	Domestic	1971	16.7	26.1	40.2	61.1	61.2	53.8
Clifford Chance	International	1989	10.5	34.3	47.6		50.1	51.6
Cremades & Calvo Sotelo	Domestic	1994				33.0	43.6	46.2
Linklaters	International	2000		6.0	16.3		37.0	41.1
Roca Junyent	Domestic	1996		10.2	23.8	40.3	29.4	30.5
Hogan Lovells	International	2005				20.1	26.9	30.5
Ecija	Domestic	1997			5.7	17.8	24.7	25.2
Pérez-Llorca	Domestic	1983	1.1	3.0	8.1		19.3	25.2
DLA Piper	International	1999			4.3	17.3	23.7	24.4
Auren Abogados	Domestic	1998					21.9	22.0
Ashurst	International	2001					19.3	21.6
CMS Albiñana & Suárez de Lezo	International	2005	6.6	11.1	12.5	19.7	19.8	20.1

Table 9.2 Growth trends of the 2013 top 20 law firms—number of lawyers

Firm	*Origin*	*Date established*[23]	*1997*	*2000*	*2004*	*2008*	*2012*	*2013*
Garrigues	Domestic	1941	484	790	1360	1954	1539	1417
Cuatrecasas Gonçalves Pereira	Domestic	1926	245	508	585	884	911	909
PwC Tax and Legal Services	Big Four	1933	158	507	546	824	712	730
KPMG Abogados	Big Four	1971	93	170	264	423	522	543
Uría Menéndez	Domestic	1946	115	174	317	497	534	530
EY Abogados	Big Four	1978	177	363	350	352	400	452
Deloitte Abogados	Big Four	1969	69	125	237	418	389	383
Gómez-Acebo & Pombo	Domestic	1971	110	149	173	279	270	277
Auren Abogados	Domestic	1998					121	257
Baker & McKenzie	International	1965	40	137	155	189	190	217
Roca Junyent	Domestic	1996	22	85	149	226	174	186
Cremades & Calvo Sotelo	Domestic	1994			60	125	174	184
Práctica Legal	Domestic	1989			145	174	148	173
BDO Abogados	International	1992				182	182	168
Barrilero	Domestic	90s	48	81	142	161		150
Clifford Chance	International	1989	48	134	146	164	126	146
Ecija	Domestic	1997			46	146	115	122
Rousaud Costas Duran RCD	Domestic	2003				68	105	121
Linklaters	International	2000			54		103	117
Pérez-Llorca	Domestic	1983	16	23	43		99	110

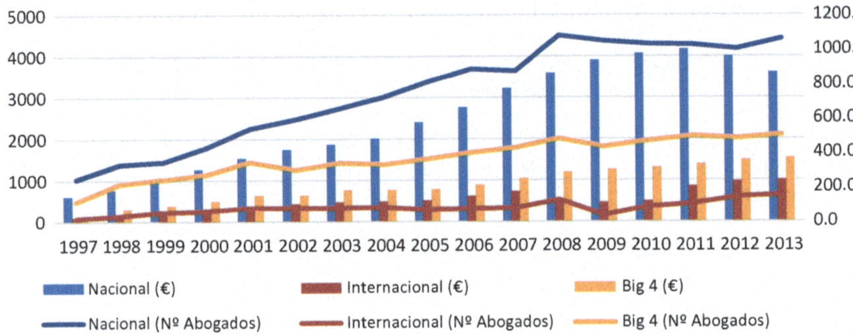

Graph 9.1 Evolution of turnover and numbers of lawyers. Top 20 2013

back centuries, and this could influence the strength of a business relationship making it very hard for foreign law firms and foreign lawyers to break up a long-standing relationship. Tradition and personal relationships remain strong features of Spanish society. There is also the fact that the younger generations of law firm leaders have enabled change by effectively importing and adapting best practices of successful law firms in jurisdictions such as the UK and the U.S. A shift toward a more business-minded, pragmatic way of practicing law, in response to both the threat posed by international law firms and the evolution of clients due to globalization, has also played a significant role in how Spanish domestic firms have developed over the last several years. We should not forget that Spaniards have a distinguished track record in the area of business and trade. It is only fitting to assume that their natural instinct to engage in global matters has led them down the path of success over their international counterparts, especially in their own territory.

It is worth pointing out that since the arrival of the first international law firms in 1965, all but one of the firms currently operating in the country have competed with Spanish firms for international matters with a Spanish law component and for domestic work. The exception is the American law firm Davis Polk & Wardwell.[24] So far, 26 of these major international firms have descended upon the Spanish market, confirming the relevance of the market and of its connection with Latin America. The latter has resulted in the setting up of many Latin American desks to be managed from Spain and by Spaniards—an added opportunity for growth for both domestic and international firms.

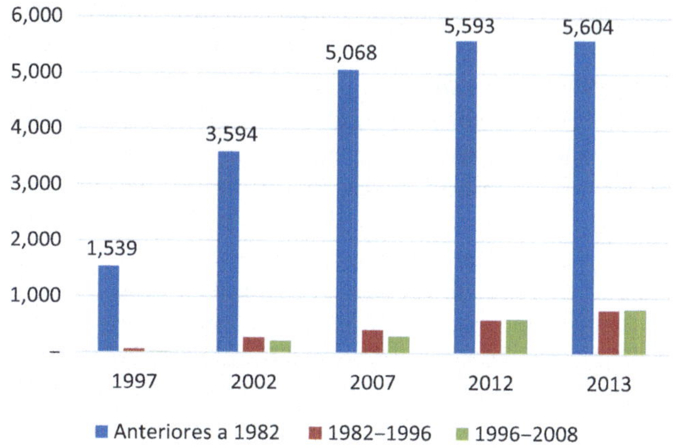

Graph 9.2 Total revenues of top 20 law firms (2013) according to founding year

Finally, it is worth looking at the dates of foundation of the largest firms. When analyzing revenue growth of the 2013 Top 20 law firms from the perspective of the year of establishment, the next graph clearly reflects the leadership of those firms established prior to Spain's "Golden Years" (Graph 9.2).

The Old Boys' Club and the Birth of Big Law

When analyzing the Spanish legal market, it is hard to separate the historic evolution of the country from the developments and evolution of the profession. As governments have changed, as the economy has evolved and as the standing of the country has changed within Europe and in the world arena, the law of the land and those who interpret it and enforce it have had to adapt as well, specially the lawyers that work within or on behalf of the business sector. These changes have become increasingly important and more apparent now that Spain is fighting for its well-being against a precarious economy, an aging population and what many call an outdated type of government. So in order to understand Big Law and the legal market, in general, and its evolution, it is essential to familiarize oneself with the country's most recent history.

Spain had a divisive and bloody civil war in the 1930s. After 1939, when the civil law officially ended, the country was profoundly divided between loyalists to the Republic (led by the monarchy) and the Nationalists (led by the military and General Francisco Franco). Franco and his followers had won the war, but what they had in their hands was not the glorious country of years and centuries past but a fractured and impoverished society, a weakened economy and an isolated country. Uncertainty was the common denominator across the public and private sector. It would not be until the 1950s when the winds turned for the legal profession and the country in general. Despite it being a dictatorship, Franco managed to bring about some prosperity to the country. As far as the legal market is concerned, this period proved to be particularly interesting and defining, as several key regulations with great impact on the country's economy were enacted. This prompted a busy period of conversion, harmonization and compliance for the corporate sector, thus creating high demand for legal work.

The Old Boy's Club

The first period for this study can be called *the Old Boy's Club*. It goes from the early 1950s to the late 1970s. This is a particularly interesting period for the legal profession. It was then when the first signs of modern-day private and commercial practice appeared within the profession, despite the dictatorship of Francisco Franco. For example, at the beginning of this period, the legal profession was still largely dominated by solo practitioners, but by the end of this period, multidisciplinary law firms with capacity for large volume and complex work was in vogue. Also at this time, important government reforms were introduced, and the first signs of policy shift toward a democratic state were seen.

In addition to very significant legislative changes, a series of events of commercial and international nature contributed to a new era of prosperity and economic growth for the country that would carry the country through the mid-1970s. These included the signing of a series of commercial agreements with the US (1953), its admission to the United Nations (1955), the approval of new policies favoring public investment and foreign direct investment, the liberalization and modernization of industry, and the revenue generated by tourism. Consequently, international conglomerates from across industries started to turn their attention to Spain as they discovered opportunities for investment and expansion. One of the first to arrive was Henry Ford, who would personally negotiate with Franco regarding the opening of a car factory in Valencia. This factory alone created 6500 jobs and set the pace for renewed hope for economic prosperity. Other American companies including Coca-Cola, Westinghouse and General Electric followed.

This would see the beginning of a very lucrative and significant chapter in the history of the country's legal sector. The resulting need for understanding, interpreting and implementing new rules and regulations triggered a wave of innovation within the profession, a need for business prowess, for complex problem-solving skills and for a more dynamic client-lawyer relationship.

All these changes and the opening of the country to foreign investment and foreign companies represented a great opportunity for the legal sector. In truth, these "sophisticated clients" felt that very few legal outfits and lawyers were prepared to handle the volume and demands resulting from working with them. Of all commercial law firms in Spain, it would be Garrigues J & A, Armero, Vega-Penichet and Melchor de las Heras that would dominate the market with respect to foreign clients and foreign investment work. It has been estimated that these law firms (the "Old Boy's Club") came to control as much as 95% of the work in this area. And because the number of "approved" firms was limited, these firms found themselves learning to trust each other, work together and lean on each other to take on work whenever a conflict of interest arose. The group was joined by an American law firm, Baker & McKenzie, in 1965, becoming the first of many international law firms to set up operations in the country.

Another occurrence that generated opportunity for the legal profession at this time was the involvement of Spanish companies and the Spanish government in several disputes before international courts. One particularly prominent case was the Barcelona Traction, Light & Power Company Limited[25] (the plaintiff) versus the Belgian government and the Spanish Regime (the defendants) litigation before the International Court of Justice, in the Hague. The battle lasted 12 years (1958–1970) and involved nearly all of Spain's great jurists of the time (many of whom were solo practitioners) and many of who, in line with customary practice, combined private practice with academia.

The Trinity. As previously mentioned, there is no part of the history of the modern-day Spanish legal market that does not include three prominent Spanish firms otherwise known as "The Trinity": Garrigues, Cuatrecasas Pereira Gonçalves and Uría Menéndez. These three firms have been closely tied to Spain's recent history in more ways than one.

Their lawyers have advised the Spanish government, industry and foreign investors. They have also served as informal ambassadors of Spain, have forged close relationships with world and international corporate leaders, and have single handedly contributed to the evolution and entrance of the Spanish legal market into the twenty-first century. To put it in perspective to the outside reader, these firms carry the weight of Cravath Swaine & Moore, Paul Weiss and Davis Polk in the US, Slaughter & May in the UK, DeBrauw Blackstone and NautaDutilh in the Netherlands, and Hengeler Muller in Germany. Here is some history:

Garrigues. Founded in 1941 by the brothers Joaquín and Antonio Garrigues Díaz-Cañabate, Garrigues is Spain's largest law firm in terms of number of lawyers, number of offices (38 offices in 11 countries) and revenues. It is also the largest law firm in Europe (not including law firms in the UK). Joaquín was a renowned professor of commercial law and played an important role in the modernization of Spain's corporate code. Antonio combined the practice of law with intense public activity: "general director during the Republic, Ambassador during Franco´s Regime and Minister of Justice in the first Government of the monarchy".[26]

It would be Antonio Garrigues' appointment as Ambassador to the US that would set the stage for the modernization of the firm. Upon his departure for the US, his son Antonio Garrigues Walker took over the management of the firm. The young Garrigues would use his trips to the US to visit his father as research trips. He would then return to Spain and implement much of what he had learned about successful legal practices in the US. One area where he made a mark was in the area of professional development and career path of associates. Thanks to him, Garrigues was one of the first Spanish firms to implement equity partnership, to develop a structure for career path development and to institutionalize the concept of international alliances and networks. It was thanks to him that Garrigues opened the first-ever Spanish law firm office overseas with the opening of the firm's New York branch in 1973.

Many would argue that there are two main reasons why Garrigues has and continues to enjoy a leading role within the Spanish legal market: its focus on corporate law and its vision for a more international practice.[27]

Cuatrecasas Pereira Gonçalves. The oldest of the three, Cuatrecasas, as it is commonly known, dates back to 1917. It was first established in Barcelona by Francisco Vigil as a small administrative agency. Two years later, Emilio Cuatrecasas Buquet joined the firm. Vigil died in 1923 and Cuatrecasas then acquired the firm from Vigil's widow for the equivalent of €450. Over the next 50 years, the firm would secure its leadership in tax law, strengthen its Catalan client portfolio and expand into the Madrid market. By 1977, Emilio Cuatrecasas Figueras, the grandson of the founder, joined the firm. Under his leadership, the law firm would transform from a tax law boutique firm to one of the largest and most prestigious multidisciplinary firms in all of Europe.

Emilio first rose to firm leadership in 1980 through his appointment as managing partner of the Barcelona office. The reference model was J&A Garrigues, and the guidelines of the corporate strategy to follow were drafted in a document named the "White Paper",[28] which included some of the following: to maintain the firm's leadership in the area of tax and utilize this as a springboard for expansion into other areas of service, to strengthen the firm's international partnerships, the creation and implementation of strong quality control measures and the promotion of cross-selling practices. Also, the development of a sound continuing education program for its legal professionals, the proactive fostering of a stronger client-law firm relationship and the development and implementation of the firm's IT infrastructure which included know-how and document management.

Cuatrecasas Figueroa was joined by Rafael Fontana in 1983 in order to help him achieve his vision for the law firm. Fontana joined from the firm, Arthur Andersen. The firm would go on to be recognized as a leader in internal organization and as a pioneer in the legal industry usually leading change and innovation among its peers—a reputation that holds true until today.

Uría Menéndez. Uría Menéndez is recognized worldwide for cementing the concept of independence among Spanish law firms, and domestically for its very strong ties to the government and the ruling parties since the reinstitution of democracy in the country post dictatorship. It was established in 1940 by Rodrigo Uría González, a commercial law professor and co-founder of "Revista de Derecho Mercantil"[29] a renowned legal publication. He was joined by his son, Rodrigo Uría Meruéndano, and by Professor Aurelio Menéndez in 1970. It was Uría Meruéndo—who after a stint at the New York office of US law firm Curtis, Mallet-Prevost, Colt & Mosle in 1974—would lay the ground for Uria's success. Upon his return to Spain in 1975 he set out to implement much of what he had learned about law firm management and during his time in the US. He would soon be appointed as managing partner, and in this post, he took care of honing in his "obsession" with hiring top talent. He was convinced that only the best talent would attract the best clients. He would go on to acquire smaller law firms on the premise that he was acquiring exceptional talent. A great example of his prowess and determination would be the acquisition of Bufete Armero in 1998 after the death of its founder.

Because of Uría Meruéndano's "obsession" with talent and his vision of independence through the creation of a strong network of "best friend" law firms across key legal jurisdictions, he was able to lay the foundations for the strong practice that the law firm Uría Menéndez is today.

On the Road to Democracy

When General Franco died in November of 1975 and King Juan Carlos I took power as the new Chief of State, together with Adolfo Suárez, as head of government, the country was ready and hungry for change. And while both were political appointees left in place by Franco as his successors, both took a rather centrist stand. The King pushed for modernization, and Suárez introduced a series of reforms, which would decisively initiate the transition toward democracy including a referendum of the Constitution in 1978. Suárez would go on to become the first democratically elected prime minister post dictatorship during the 1976 elections.

By this time, another law firm that would go on to play a key role in the evolution of the legal industry had been established. In 1971, Fernando Pombo and Ignacio Gómez-Acebo founded Gomez-Acebo & Pombo. This firm and those already in existence enjoyed a growth period fueled by the economic prosperity prompted by the winds of democracy. Key events such as Spain's economic expansion, the integration of the Spanish economy into the European economy and a referendum that resulted in the enactment of a new constitution and therefore a new government would all prove significant for the legal profession as a whole. As it would be expected, many of Spain's great lawyers would go on to play a prominent role in the events that took place at this time.

It was the case of Jose Mario Armero, who played a key—and dangerous—role in helping legalize the Communist Party so that they could run for the first democratic elections and his efforts in the promotion of Prince Juan Carlos in the US. Also, we find Antonio Garrigues who served as Minister of Justice and Aurelio Menéndez who joined the government as Minister of Education. In the government, we come across other lawyers who would be very relevant in Big Law business during the following period: Jaime García Añoveros and Pedro Pérez-Llorca, Minister of Finance and Minister of the Presidency, respectively, and Miquel Roca Junyent, one of the Seven Fathers of the Constitution.

The proclamation of the Spanish Constitution in 1978 was followed by specific tax and commercial regulation, which required more professionals and larger and cohesive structures, as well as the development of international relations. The meetings of the International Bar Association (IBA) facilitated the first informal contacts between the members of this networks and lawyers from different jurisdictions, which, in turn, helped facilitate more stable and formal collaborations. It is in these international forums where we could have met two Spanish lawyers whose names have become synonymous with Spanish internationalization: Ramón Mullerat, who was President of the Council of the Bars and Law Societies of the EU (CCBE) and occupied important positions in the IBA and Fernando Pombo, who would become President of IBA in 2007.

This period also marked the beginning of a change in structure and organization by many of the traditional law firms, following the example of partnerships in common law jurisdictions, mainly the US. Antonio Garrigues Walker of the Garrigues law firm recounted how he decided to establish the figure of the equity partner in his firm:

> I didn't have any examples to follow. I simply asked partners at some of the largest law firms in the U.S., and they told me which structure they felt I should establish if I was interested in the firm's survival. And that I did just that, even though at the beginning, some of my lawyers did not understand the benefits of partnership. Nowadays it is completely institutionalized.[30]

In a similar fashion, back in 1973, Rodrigo Uría González, Aurelio Menéndez and Rodrigo Uría Meruéndano agreed to constitute the firm as a partnership and established a professional career track to partnership in the 1980s to prevent "brilliant lawyers from leaving".[31]

It would be those law firms that followed a new strategy, that sought to strengthen their competitive position, and whose members somehow played a role in the development of the country that would succeed in those days. Newly formed partnerships emphasized the importance of mastering the English language, of contributing to the development of the country, and of nurturing and establishing strong international networks.

The Transformation (1982–1996)

As Spain experienced uncertainty, turmoil and a new renaissance under a democratic government, the legal sector was faced with a brand new challenge: the arrival of international law firms. How to defend their market, remain independent and survive a turbulent economic period became Spanish domestic firm's priority.

In 1982, the Socialist Labor Spanish Party (PSOE) came to power for the first time. The economic and social landscapes were both in dire conditions.[32] The country witnessed the closure of companies, especially those in the iron, steel, shipbuilding and appliances industries, a strong economic adjustment and the devaluation of the currency. Then, Spain's entry into the European community opened up the country to various positive effects, such as access to foreign investment, increase in public investment and privatization of public companies. Those outcomes encouraged and accelerated the Spanish economy, increasing its GDP and reducing rates of unemployment and inflation. This situation of growth was truncated by the entrance of Spain into recession, which took the country into an economic and ethical crisis[33] that prevented progress until 1995.

Legal regulation of business and commercial activity did not cease during this period and some of the changes to commercial and finance law include the Exchange and Check Law in 1985 (*Ley Cambiaria y del Cheque*), the Patent Law in 1986 (*Ley de Patentes*), the Intellectual Property Law in 1987 (*Ley de Propiedad Intelectual*), the Revised Text of the Stock Exchange Act in 1988 (*Ley de Reforma el Mercado de Valores*), the Competition Act in 1989 (*Ley de Defensa de la Competencia*) and the Law on Unfair Competition in 1991 (*Ley de Competencia Desleal*).

This period also witnessed a vital transformation in the way law firms provided legal services. It was the time to take the profession more seriously and rethink, inter alia, whether the structures, the corporate strategies, the training and specialization of professionals, and the client relationship systems were the right ones to compete. Those changes arrived very slowly. [34]

There was so much curiosity about how lawyers were transforming their way to offer their services that an article in 1987 in a business magazine[35] stated:

> In the last decade, mercantilist lawyers have undergone a profound transformation in which the *toga* remains simply as a historical hint of the old times, together with the Courts and *multifaceted* lawyers. These are times of *mega-firms*, specializations, negotiations and boardrooms. It is a time for lawyers with a business style and for a business advocacy.

The article provided the first data on the size that those *mega-firms* had reached: Garrigues (47 lawyers), Gómez-Acebo & Pombo (38), Cuatrecasas (33), Uría (28), Fabregat & Bermejo (28), Bertran and Musitu (27), Baker & McKenzie (21), Armero (20), Estudio Legal (20), Melchor de las Heras (16), J & B. Cremades (13) and Vega-Penichet (10) (Table 9.3).

Since then, some of the firms mentioned in the article were acquired or merged into other brands. For example, the law firm Armero merged with Uría & Menéndez in 1999. Many others disappeared as such but have been the gem of new firms such as Bruguera, García-Bragado and Miller &Associates, which is the successor to the tradition of Bertran i Musitu

In 1993, leading lawyers described the new landscape in the following way[36]:

- The matters which companies were more concerned about included international tax planning, corporate regulation and compliance of new areas of law such as environmental law.
- Clients started being concerned about cost control and more interested in a closer collaboration with external advisors regarding training of their teams and anticipation of legal risks.

More foreign competitors. When the article about local mega-firms was published, the Spanish firms were not alone. Baker & McKenzie, Clifford Chance and the Big Five already had a presence in the country,

Table 9.3 Number of lawyers in law firms 1987–1997

	Number of lawyers in 1987	*Number of lawyers in 1997*
Garrigues	47	484
Gómez-Acebo & Pombo	39	110
Cuatrecasas		245
Uría	28	115
Baker & McKenzie	21	40

and new and strong competitors were due to arrive before the end of this period. As in other jurisdictions, the international firms that settled in Spain in the 1980s and 1990s followed a similar path. Before arriving, they had usually already been exposed to Spanish clients and transactions. Their teams located in other offices had done those deals and in combination with domestic firms, which in some cases acted as *Spanish Desk* for those. Then, the need to get closer to the decision-makers at large corporations and financial entities in order to obtain the largest and more complex transactions, the opportunities of reaching Latin America from Spain by its links to Europe and the bridge to Latin America, and the advantage of Common Law in relation to financial and capital market operations, encouraged British firms to establish their first local offices. In all cases, the hiring of lawyers with experience and recognition allowed them to compete and offer advice and representation under local law. Kenneth Bonavia, who was the first managing partner of DLA's Madrid office, explained it in an interview "*by definition, an international firm has to become a Spanish firm in order to succeed in the Spanish market*".[37]

In 1980, the Magic Circle member Clifford Chance opened its first office in the country and initiated its activities, but it was not until a decade later when his participation in a ground-breaking operation gave a clear picture on the role Anglo-Saxon law firms were due to play. The innovative perspective and flexibility of common law could definitively contribute to local law and open new fields. The transaction involved the legal design of the securitization of assets from the nuclear moratorium.[38] In 1984, the government of Felipe González negotiated the suspension of investments and the activity of nuclear plants with the Spanish utilities and, in exchange, agreed that the debt assumed by the State—that exceeded the 4000 million Euros—would become callable securities, which would be financed from various taxes. Securitizations began in Britain and spread across the rest of the continent, thanks to investment banks and their advisers of the Magic Circle. The fact that they were drafted under English law, and that only these law firms had the knowledge and trust of the financial institutions, gave them a *monopoly*. In many cases, similar to the Spanish case, as a result of the nuclear moratorium, these lawyers were asked to draft the regulation under which the transaction would be structured. Common law happened to be more flexible and secure, and printed a new rhythm to relationships with clients who found a more sophisticated approach of offering legal services.

By the end of this period, following firms were already in Spain: Loeft Claeys Verbeke (1987), DAC Beachcroft LLP (1989), NautaDutilh (1989), Allen & Overy (1991), Freshfields Bruckhaus Deringer (1991), Stephenson Harwood (1991) and Osborne Clarke (1994).

Local competitors. The 1980s witnessed the foundation of many other domestic firms, which today compete at the highest level. One of those firms is Pérez Llorca Abogados. Jaime García Añoveros and José Pedro Pérez-Llorca founded the firm in Madrid in 1983. Jaime had been Minister of Economy and Revenue during the Suárez's government and José Pedro was Minister of the Presidency and Foreign Affairs, in addition to being one of the Seven Fathers of the Spanish Constitution.[39] Throughout the following decades, the firm's clients—local and international—sought advice on commercial and real estate matters, and it was managed as any other traditional firm. The turning point occurred in 1996 and was, once again, caused by the combination of experience and vision of a lawyer: Pedro, the son of José Pedro who was 28 years old at the time. He graduated in Economics and Business Administration as well as in Law. His first intention was to engage in business but, through his father, he met Rodrigo Uría and joined Uría & Menéndez, where he practiced for three years in the commercial law department. There he learned the type of firm he would like to convert his father's into.

He led a series of changes, from the incorporation of talented professionals, the organization of support functions and the presence of the firm in the international market. The 2003 edition of the prestigious Chambers Global Directory included the firm as one of the seven leading firms in Spain. His rise to the top of the international *league tables* happened in 2006 as advisors to German energy company E.ON in connection with its tender offer for ENDESA, a relevant transaction of the next period.

First destinations. One of the main areas of law of this period is, without doubt, European law. The emergence of this legislation in the Spanish jurisdiction triggered the need for specialized professionals and for contacts with firms who had a solid presence in Brussels. Some firms decided to open an office in the city to ease the management of related deals and advice: Gómez-Acebo & Pombo in 1985, Garrigues in 1986 and Uría Menéndez in 1990.

Moreover, Cuatrecasas' vision prioritized the Iberian expansion, and it was this vision that led him to close a cooperation agreement with the Portuguese firm Gonçalves Pereira, Vinhas, Castelo Branco e Associados in 1994. A year later, Uria signed out a similar agreement with Morais Leitão, J. Galvão Teles & Associados.

Law firms and Media. As indicated above, clients needed more complex legal advice and also sought a preventive counsel. It was clear that executives and lawyers had to go hand in hand, and the economy and businesses should not be understood without each other. Naturally, the business press was interested in law firms.

Since 1986, the leading economic newspaper, Expansion, has been the main source of information of events surrounding the legal sector. Since their foundation, they were aware that they had to inform the legal background of any business movements in a period of excessive regulatory activity. At the beginning, their contacts with lawyers and law firms were sporadic in order to get a clear understanding of a specific regulation before writing about it. Later, journalists got interested in law firms themselves and a specific section was started. This section has its yearly climax, right before the summer break, when the ranking by revenues and numbers of lawyers is published.

The first *attempt to* do the rankings was made in 1992, and journalists Alfonso Lopez-Tello, Rafael Miner and Pilar Viana published it in July.[40] It already mentioned nine law firms[41] with more than 1000 million Pesetas turnover (6 million Euros). The ranking explained this brand new reality because "lawyers are transmuting from playing by themselves in the market to become employees of large organizations".[42]

At the time, it was not easy to gather information for the rankings–neither is it today—and it took months to finish it. One of its authors defined it as "if the mountains were in labor" because of the difficulties they met in obtaining objective data and the complications they came across in assessing its validity and suitability. Until 1995, a second ranking was not published, and it included already 40 law firms. Since 1997, it has been published every year, without interruption. There is no doubt about its importance and value to provide transparency to the sector although some relevant players still refuse to be listed.

From the Golden Years (1996–2008) to the Crisis (2009–2014)

The Golden Years of Big Law began in 1996. The average growth rate during the following 12 years was 3.7%, a superior rate compared to the rest of the European countries. It was mainly driven by the construction, automotive, tourism and services industries. During this period, more than six million jobs were generated. It was an appropriate time for the arrival of foreign investment and generation of a highly competitive business environment ready to go beyond its borders.[43]

The summer of 1996 brought two major events to the legal industry: the process of privatization and the merger of Garrigues and Andersen Legal.

The government of the Popular Party (PP), which was elected a few months earlier, started a series of legal reforms and financial incentives in order to reduce the budget deficit and confront the high unemployment rate, among other objectives. One of the initiatives was to continue with the privatization program, begun under the Socialist Government to reduce state ownership of various industries. Since then, more than 50 companies have gone out of the public sphere and, in many cases, ***they found a national and international market hungry for profitable shares.*** Successful existing companies, many of them leaders in their respective sectors, were partially or completely privatized either through initial public offerings (IPOs), joint sales or auctions. Telecommunications company—Telefonica, oil company—Repsol, the utilities—Endesa, Natural Gas and Red Eléctrica, the airline—Iberia, the financial entity—Argentaria (now, BBVA) and technological company—Indra are some of the privatized companies.

The initial plan of the government was to undertake those processes solely with the help of internal resources:

> We will only appoint external advisors in specific cases, since we believe that our legal team, with 274 State lawyers, should be sufficient to carry out the plan.[44]

But in reality, both Spanish and international law firms were involved. The British firms had an unparalleled experience in similar processes around the world and kept a very special relationship with financial institutions. Other international firms without even having an office in Madrid, received instructions to get involved from best friends in the country. And, finally, the traditional Spanish firms with intense contacts with the government, with the companies themselves and with potential buyers, would play a leading role in the privatization process. In fact, many of the contacts with the companies privatized at that important time would be the origin of the current relationships of trust, which were the pillars of growth and expansion of firms during the following two decades.

The second breaking news was the confirmation of the rumors that Arthur Andersen ALT, the legal branch of Arthur Andersen, the largest in

Spain by revenues (31.8 million Euros) and number of lawyers (230)[45] was in talks to merge with a local firm. In September, the firm was identified as J&A Garrigues.

Other law firms like Roca Junyent and Ecija Abogados, which, ten years later, will be on the list of the 20 largest firms by revenues established at the beginning of this period. They are the visible examples of two types of firms which have the strengths to compete in a market full of brands. The first one based its growth on the political relevance of its founder, one of the seven Fathers of Constitution and the spokesman of the Catalan Group in the Spanish Parliament for 18 years. While the second firm built its success on the specialization of media and technology, an economic sector in full expansion.

Garrigues & Andersen. In January 1997, Andersen LTA—the legal branch of Andersen—announced its merger with J&A Garrigues. The new company had twice as many partners and generated twice the revenues of the second firm in the ranking, Cuatrecasas.

These mergers, once again, caused all sorts of doubts about the independence of lawyers related to auditing companies. Although Garrigues made it clear from the outset that the merger was exclusively with the legal branch, which operated already as an independent company in Spain, the reactions of competitors were immediate and intense[46]:

> Those were difficult times. The content of the rules governing the legal profession, *Estatuto General de la Abogacía*, was under negotiation and there were colleagues who demanded that Garrigues should be left aside. We were even expelled from the Club of the Abogacía, recalled some partners of Garrigues.

Lupicinio Rodríguez, who only a few months later would incorporate his firm to join the Denton International network, declared:

> We are happy with the arrival of competition and delighted to welcome Freshfields or Clifford Chance, but not Andersen. They take advantage of their privileged access to captive clients. In recent years, we have lost about 70% of tax work and 20% of employment law work.

Enric Picañol, a partner in Cuatrecasas, added:

> A company may only access capital markets if it has been audited by one of the Big Six.[47] This is the main issuent. They must stop using accountancy as

a loss-leader to sell other services. The fact that the regulatory authorities have reacted slowly, has granted them a monopoly.

Ernesto Jimenez, a partner of Garrigues & Andersen, said after the merger:

> We now provide an even better legal service. The criticism is not justified; most of it has been about independence. Well, we believe we have independence; the real problem is that we are a strong competitor.

The following years, the issue was discussed, virtually, in every jurisdiction. And in 2002, the Community Court of Justice issued a judgment which declared that the prohibition of association between lawyers and auditors established by Dutch Bar did not cross the standards contained in the EU Treaty concerning protection of free competition. The position in Spain has been to ban auditing firms from providing the same client with legal and audit services, unless different companies provide those services, with different boards of directors.

Once Garrigues & Andersen overcame such crisis, it consolidated itself as the leader of the market and incorporated the best practices from multinational corporations, from human resources to marketing, know-how and technology. On March 16, 2002, managing partners, José María Alonso and Luis Gordillo, made public the decision to separate from Andersen Legal, after the well-known side effects of the Enron scandal. Then, Garrigues went successfully back to practice alone. Other European firms, who had gone through mergers with Andersen, had to join other Big Four firms, as they could not return to practice by themselves.

Massive landing of international firms. More international and interesting manoeuvres followed the merger of Garrigues. In July of the same year, Lupicinio Rodríguez joined the international network Denton International, founded by the English firm Denton Hall. On September 1, the U.S. law firm Squire, Sanders & Dempsey opened an office in Madrid and, in October, the merger of several Spanish firms with a French firm was announced to create Briones-Lefebvre.

This period also witnessed the arrival of: SJ Berwin (1999), which acquired a small firm that had just broken away from B. Cremades; Jones Day (2000) which also integrated with a local firm to position itself within the finance and capital markets industry; a fourth member of the Magic Circle, Linklaters (2000) could not integrate with their best friend Uría Menéndez and launched its own office; the English firms, Simmons &

Simmons (2000) and Ashurst (2001); the American firm, Davis Polk (2001); DLA Piper (2002), which entered Spain after acquiring the Spanish office and team of NautaDutilh, a strategy which would be repeated in 2005 by means of integration of the Spanish business of Squire Sanders; Hammonds (2003), Eversheds (2004), Lovells (2004), Bird & Bird (2005), CMS (2005) which entered Spain through an alliance with Albiñana & Suárez de Lezo and Irwin Mitchell (2005). Finally, when the crisis began to hit the country, two more firms arrived: US firm, Latham & Watkins and the French Salans.

This increase in competition was beneficial for the Spanish market and the chosen formulas varied significantly from the lateral hiring of partners to the acquisition of, usually, small local law firms. It was a breath of fresh air that brought new management practices to the legal profession and tested the real intentions of the Spanish traditional brands to remain independent. The latter development is essential to understand the current legal scenario. Apart from the Garrigues-Andersen deal, no large domestic firm agreed to merge with the strong international brands.

The "sexy" transactions. During this period, large and interesting transactions took place, most of them occupying the front pages of both legal and economic publications. From large IPOs of public companies, to the purchases of the British Bank Abbey National by Banco Santander, BAA, the British airports operator, by Ferrovial or O2 by Telefonica. Other interesting—and profitable—corporate decisions of the time included Sacyr-Vallehermoso acquiring positions in Repsol, while Acciona did the same in Endesa and ACS invested in Union Fenosa and Iberdrola.

This was a very intense period, generating employment for many law firms. We could briefly describe one of the most important operations of this period, which resulted in generation of extensive employment, benefits and an increased presence in the *league tables* of the participating firms. Endesa's[48] sale fight in Spanish and US courts generated interesting takeover bids lasting two years involving Spanish, government-owned Endesa; Spanish companies Iberdrola; Gas Natural and Acciona; German company E.ON; as well as the Italian utility ENEL and their respective financial advisors. Teams from Clifford Chance, Bonelli Erede Pappalardo, Sullivan & Cromwell, Cuatrecasas, Baker & McKenzie, Pérez Llorca, Cravath, Swaine & Moore, Uría Menéndez, Lovells, Wachtell, Lipton, Rosen & Katz, Albiñana & Suárez de Lezo, Jones Day, Freshfields, Allen & Overy, Hengeler Müller, DLA Piper, Cleary Gottlieb Steen & Hamilton, Simpson Thacher & Barlett, Cortés Abogados and Gómez-Acebo & Pombo participated in the deal. The need for such large teams of business lawyers effected major changes in both the relationships inside the firm and outside of it in general. In the first scenario, managing partners and boards of partners were in need of setting up a better internal organization, resulting in the hiring of support staff teams, resolving internal procedures and the quest for talent. In the second circle of relationship, law firms became accustomed to compete for work in more sophisticated ways, in dealing with the legal press and the legal international directories, increasing and expanding their means to reach clients and getting involved with complex beauty parades, forced them to set up their first marketing and business development departments.

New features coming to stay. The need for larger teams to handle larger transactions and the increasing demand for legal services were instrumental in the growth of these structures. This fact brought about the establishment of new firms, which had three main side effects: war for talent, higher turnover and a tough price war.

Graph 9.3 shows the growth of teams of lawyers during this period working at the 20 largest firms in the country in 2013.

The war for talent not only affected the legal industry but also changed the way law firms viewed their relationship with lawyers. The years of crisis had provoked a major drought in the number of professionals with hard and soft skills, and the training and experience needed in order to cope with the next phase of expansion. This led to the migration of lawyers between law firms. It also had other effects.

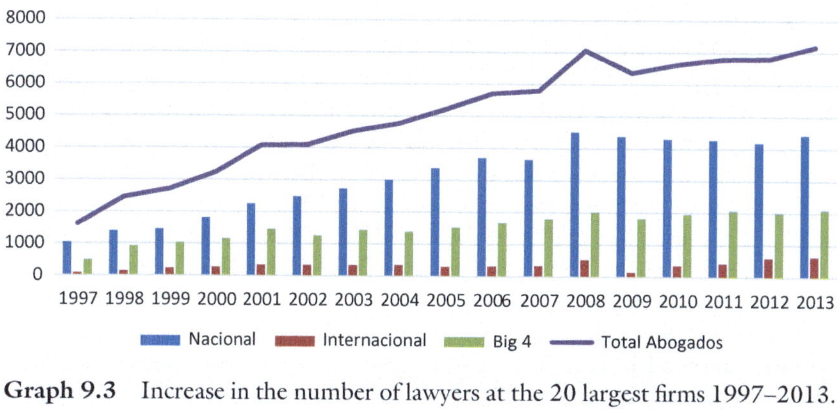

Graph 9.3 Increase in the number of lawyers at the 20 largest firms 1997–2013.

First, the concept "loyalty to firms" becomes "loyalty to individual lawyers or loyalty to work teams". After decades of loyalty to firms, lateral hiring of both partners and associates became the new norm. In addition, there were migrations of teams of lawyers who left their firms and returned a few years later.

Second, the war for talent influenced salary escalations at all levels. The process of *laboralización*, explained later in this chapter, affected salaries as it increased social costs.

Along with this war for talent, the battle for payments followed. Low bids to take over some of the deals and clients even reached media. The 2007 edition of Legal 500 noted that:

> many large domestic firms complain about the existence of a number of law firms that are charging excessively low fees which adds pressure to the rest of law firms to set their prices.[49]

Furthermore, the partner of a medium-sized company, described the situation thus:

> There are four great Spanish law firms, 11 international firms and three American ones. There are more "supply centers" than ever and in a market where the demand does not grow significantly, concentration usually appears. However, in Madrid, we are witnessing decentralization. Increasingly, there are more law firms. Usually, they are launched by lawyers who were in the same "supply center" and have now separated. And that causes huge pressure on prices.[50]

Spanish law firms around the world. The good performances of the Spanish companies allowed them to transcend national boundaries in search of new markets. It is in the mid-1990s when the process of internationalization of Spain's leading banks and companies targeted Latin America due to large privatizations and deregulation of the subcontinent. Then, some lawyers and law firms decided not to lose track of their clients.

This was the case of Uría Menéndez, which had strong ties to corporations and banks. They explored the possibility of expanding their presence in such jurisdictions. Thus, in 1998 and 2001, Uría Menéndez began an expansion policy by opening branches within his b*est friends'* premises in Buenos Aires, Santiago de Chile, Lima, Sao Paulo and Mexico City. This presence allowed Uría to send Spanish lawyers on secondment to coordinate joint assignments.

The expansion into Latin America was accompanied by integrations within Iberia (similar integrations occurred in firms such as Cuatrecasas in 2003, Uría in 2004 and Garrigues in 2005).[51] These integrations with Portuguese firms allowed them to offer full services as an Iberian law firm, which matched the concept of the region already being requested by international firms and clients. In fact, virtually all the Anglo-Saxon firms in the country used the Spanish office as the epicenter of activity for Portuguese-related transactions and advice.

In addition, internationalization was not a concept only related to big brands. For example, Suárez de la Dehesa, the intellectual property niche firm, was one of the first firms to set up an office in Morocco through the hiring of a local lawyer.

An interesting phenomenon during this time was that Spain began to *export* talent to international firms as the consequence of the increasing sophistication of the Spanish market and the challenges that managing partners were facing. It became evident when Spanish lawyers were hired for leading management positions in their firms at a global level. This is evident in the case, among others, of Alberto Sánchez Terol at Andersen and Deloitte, Rafael Jiménez-Gusi at Baker & McKenzie, Ignacio Ojanguren at Clifford Chance, Luis Comas at Landwell-PwC, Juan Picón at DLA Piper, Luis Riesgo at Jones Day or José María Balañá at Hogan Lovells.[52]

The "*Laboralización*". Lawyers, accustomed to advise their clients on their concerns and difficulties, faced major issues between 2005 and 2007. Although the sector had modernized and changed, most of the new professional structures had maintained the traditional labor relationship, and most lawyers were linked to their firms by a commercial contract. Under the new model, professional independence had been replaced by a relationship of complete dependence, and where the work product belonged to partners. The lawsuit that was brought to the Spanish courts by a lawyer working in an international law firm was bound by a commercial contract. This became a common practice in the sector, which could be converted into employment contracts.

Then, the special labor relations of lawyers who rendered their services in individual or collective law firms was regulated by Law 22/2005, on November 18; more changes were made in the Royal Decree 1331/2006 of November 17. As a result of the regulations, thousands of lawyers became employees, and this impacted the business of the firms, essentially an increase of social costs and decisions on how to tackle them: assumption of the same by the "new employees", total assumption by law firms or their distribution between lawyers and law firms.

These regularization of lawyers—which brought an automatic tax control—left the door open for its extension to other groups of professionals. In the words of Esteban Ceca Magán, a labor law specialist "the experiment was run with the group of professionals who were predicted as far more confrontational, and has resulted in no conflict".[53]

Crisis and Challenges

Since 1996, the legal industry *enjoyed* growth rates between 8% and 21%, but the good times would not last long. The economic crisis hit the sector at the end of the fiscal year of 2007, though since 2006, the industry had begun to perceive that "the party is over".

The following table shows total revenues of business law firms from 1997 to 2013. They represent data from the largest law firms (around 50), which provides economic data to the newspaper *Expansion*. In addition, during the last two years, researchers obtained the information directly from the Registry of Companies (Graph 9.4).

During the last months of 2007, the macro-economic situation that the country was facing included the highest inflation rates of the decade, a crisis of confidence in the financial system and in the consumer expectations, serious obstacles to access the credit, growth of financial expenses, a drop in sales, reduction of companies' profits, rise in unemployment and labor costs, and an increase in bad debts. The crisis that began in the real estate sector quickly spread to the rest of the economy.

Inevitably, lawyers were next. On the one hand, law firms noted the increased demand of advice relating to insolvency, litigation and arbitration, restructuring and employment law. On the other hand, they

Graph 9.4 Growth rates of the legal sector 1997–2013

faced difficulties charging and collecting payments. In addition, the rivalry remained the same as in the previous years, and the fight for the available work turned fiercer than ever before. That seriously affected law firms' performance, and law firms reacted by taking measures to meet the crisis by downsizing their structures. But it also became the "perfect storm" for interesting trends such as: the launch of new firms by key partners of Big Law, senior partners and managing partners leaving Big Law to lead the office of a competitor, offerings to clients at almost "zero cost" and the entry of investors in the capital of firms.

The above scenario confirms the fact that the succession issue needs to be addressed by many of the firms in the coming months, the economic situation is slowly heading toward recovery[53] and any adjustments might take a long time. The following paragraphs describe some of the issues plaguing the managing partners at Big Law in the coming months and years.

El Dorado. Latin America is again catching the attention of law firms. The economic contraction in Europe has increased the demands of clients to put their money and resources in more interesting markets such as Brazil, Mexico, Colombia, Chile and Peru, where there is a rapid growth in gross domestic product. The preferred sectors are finance, energy, infrastructure, telecommunications, metallurgy, insurance and services.

Currently, the preferred strategies in the region were Best Friends (Uría Menéndez) and Alliance (such as Garrigues through Affinitas), but the latest events are changing the strategic models; the following results would need further examination in the coming months. We do refer to the recent announcements of Uría Menéndez and Garrigues. The first firm, announced the creation of an alliance with leading firms in Chile and Colombia, which would materialize in a joint venture with a Pacific vision, and that it expected to incorporate firms from Mexico and Peru soon.[54] On a different path, Garrigues has ended its relationship with the Affinitas network and is setting up their branches in Colombia and México, where they will offer advice under local law, and more countries are expected to watch the arrival of the largest continental European firm.

In addition, a Spanish firm, ONTIER—the consequence of the merger between Hermosilla and Gutiérrez de la Roza—is the firm with the largest presence in Latin America. In September 2014, they had ten offices in seven countries under an Alliance strategy with local firms.[55]

Spin-offs. An emerging trend is the launching of new firms, usually boutiques, by partners with relevant legal and managerial experience. They leave their firms to create their own, usually targeting the same type of clients. The last five years in Spain have seen at least 12 partners, who were also head of a department of leading firms, launch their own firms, 11 of these firms being boutiques.[56] The challenge for Big Law is to identify the real reasons behind those decisions and to evaluate the real impact these migrations are having in their numbers and in clients. It is not an isolated trend and other European jurisdictions have reported the same phenomenon. The reduction of set-up costs, the ease of access to promotional tools, and the support of in-house lawyers to those new ventures and initiatives are also behind this trend.

New owners of law firms. In 2007, the Law on Professional Corporations was published. It intended to describe the social reality in which the "*activity of sole practitioners is replaced by a work team that has its origin in the growing complexity of their activities and the advantages that derive from the specialization and division of labor*".[57] Among other measures, the new regulation allowed up to 49% of the share capital to belong to non-professional partners and opened the doors of these societies to external investments.

The measure, which would later emerge in other European jurisdictions, creates an opportunity for those firms interested in accessing external capital to finance acquisitions of other firms or their professionals, to support their international expansion or to make important investments in technology or knowledge management. An example of this trend is seen in the firm Ecija Abogados, which offered a share of the capital to a family office fund in 2013.[58]

In addition, this new Law could be used as a talent retention instrument, since managers (non-lawyers) could be given access to the equity of the firm.

Overcoming the taboo. A major issue on the agenda of most managing partners is dealing with senior partners' exit strategy from the partnership before their retirement age. The situation is not the same in every firm but, generally speaking, the age of managing partners at the top of the pyramid, the benefit-sharing system, the shrinking benefits and the pressure from young lawyers who have seen the number of years lengthened to access capital have brought out glaring issues.

During the golden years, most law firms imported the Of Counsel title as an answer to this problem, since this category would be useful to keep talented professionals in the prelude to the partnership and former partners stepping down the ladder. But that option is no longer available for everyone—due to the downsizing of firms and the decrease of profits. The management of the exits of these partners, who in many cases have also held management responsibilities, cannot be left to improvisation, and new opportunities are arising for those professionals who are happy to extend their professional lives for, at least, another decade.

We foresee firms working toward design and implementation of exit plans that will include not only job profiles such as boards of companies, roles at universities or consultancy roles but also the necessary actions and the time requested for the renewal of their career, which could provide mutual benefits.

Managing the professionals' concerns. Spain, like many other developed countries, has changed socially, and the tendency toward work-life balance and a desire of professionals, regardless of their age and gender, have also changed. This reality makes law firms face a different reality, where they have to deal with the challenge of retaining women and young lawyers—and also confront the fact that many professionals are not interested in partnership.

In relation to the role of *women in the law firms*, the collected data shows a similar situation to other jurisdictions. In 2014,[59] only 13% of partners were women in comparison to 87% of male partners in Big Law. It definitely does not reflect the demographic reality of the law firms, where 46% of lawyers are women and 56% of them are men, and neither does it show the reality at law schools.

The analysis of barriers and invisible ceilings is a major concern in most firms—one of the most frequently taken measures and the implementation of an equality plan in 40% of the major law firms in the country.[60] However, an agreement was signed to increase the presence of women in January 2014 with the Ministry of Health, Social services and Equality counts—only two law firms committed: Broseta and Hogan Lovells.[61] Retaining female lawyers is one of the topics that would require more dialogue and honesty from firms to share best practices, successful actions and failures. A new law and a European regulation likely to be passed in the coming months might also affect larger law firms.

Professionalization. The professionalization of legal firms is a very broad concept that we define here as the appointment of specialized professionals in support areas such as finance, marketing and business development, knowledge management and human resources.

Firms in Spain have come a long way in these decisions since 2000. At the beginning, they were inspired by the Anglo-Saxon model of modern law firm but then, received the benefits of the corporate structure and division of work. Nonetheless, there is still a long way to go to fully incorporate valued professionals into the management of firms. Among the issues to be included in the agendas were the following:

- The need to incorporate valid and realistic metrics to measure the activity of the support departments and to allow the assignment of economic and human resources.
- The need to bring every department and every partner under a unique strategy. It is still very common to find as many strategies as partners and strategies in conflict within one firm.

Define and communicate the strategy of differentiation and positioning. This would help to streamline the work and overcome the "crisis of identity" that many firms are suffering, which facilitates the payment wars and the turnover of professionals.

Social responsibility of the legal profession: beyond pro bono. Social responsibility of the legal profession is at the end of the section, not because it is less important than the previous ones, but because it involves all of those and covers more aspects.

The concept term Social Responsibility of the Legal Profession was born out of the Corporate Social Responsibility. Nevertheless, it also required to be completed and adapted to the important role lawyers are due to play in society: guarantee access to justice and support the rule of law. Though the term is a recent one,[62] its content is not new. It is inherent to the profession; however, there is a trend to reduce it to pro bono work and to restrict the *obligation* to large law firms.

This social responsibility, in broad terms, covers the commitments that lawyers and law firms offer the stakeholders they relate with and to the societies within which they are based and operate. It would go beyond the legal obligations to manage the impact we have on the environment and society in order to make the world a better place. Its inner and outer scope is wide and would cover corporate governance and social action, through those affecting the relationships with the human capital–diversity, life–work balance and professional career. And, of course, it also includes free and disinterested legal advice to groups in a social exclusion situation and non-profit entities working with them: pro bono work.

In Spain, 19 of the firms included in the list of top 20 revenue generators by 2013 have some kind of social responsibility program, as per their public information in their websites. The other firm includes corporate social responsibility (CSR) as one of the services to provide to its clients, so they do advise them. This is still a widespread view among medium-sized and small firms: clients need to comply with social responsibility, not lawyers.

There are two future steps in the CSR in law firms. The first one is working on the internalization of the concept to make it work within the reality of law firms, setting priorities such as transparency, work-life balance or equal access to partnership positions. Second is to identify the areas where lawyers could contribute to regenerate the current toxic atmosphere, which contaminates the rule of law. In Spain, there is already a team of lawyers and public notaries working in this line, through the initiative of the "¿Hay Derecho?" Blog.[63]

The law cannot remain in the background of the social responsibility debate, and professional associations can play a role as promoters and centers for debate. In this sense, we shall highlight the Bar of Madrid, which created the center of Social Responsibility in 2008 and works on various initiatives, including serving as a clearinghouse for pro bono matters.[64] It is not a new discussion. In 1982, in the book "Los abogados y la sociedad industrial", José Juan Toharía made reference to the crisis of confidence in the effectiveness of the judicial organization and the role of the lawyer as social agent. By not performing this function, lawyers could be easily replaced by other professional.[65]

Conclusion

The legal industry in Spain is completely alive. Since its inception in the 1970s, it has never stopped changing for the good. It is a highly competitive ecosystem, with species coming from different habitats—some of them far away—and with simultaneous processes of specialization, which has generated new types of law firms within the country.

The legal environment is far from being stable and calm. Although "lawyers don't like to be scattered" as Professor Friedman says, the increase of data allowed us to put them under the microscope and reach some conclusions in this study. Without any doubt, Spain is a very interesting model for those jurisdictions—like the Latin American ones—which are in the process of receiving international competitors. Some local law firms successfully confronted the strong foreign brands. They have managed to keep their independence and to learn and improve their practices and organizations by importing the right models and best practices from their Anglo-Saxon counterparts.

The current economic and social changes, the technological innovations, and the businesses and clients' pressure have joined to shake up the legal industry again. Now, a new age has begun with new difficulties and a crisis to overcome, which demands a new breed of professionals who may see beyond survival and short-term profitability, and get involved in resolving the crevices of the industry and take the legal industry to a new beginning.

Appendix 1: Total number of lawyers in Spain 1998–2013

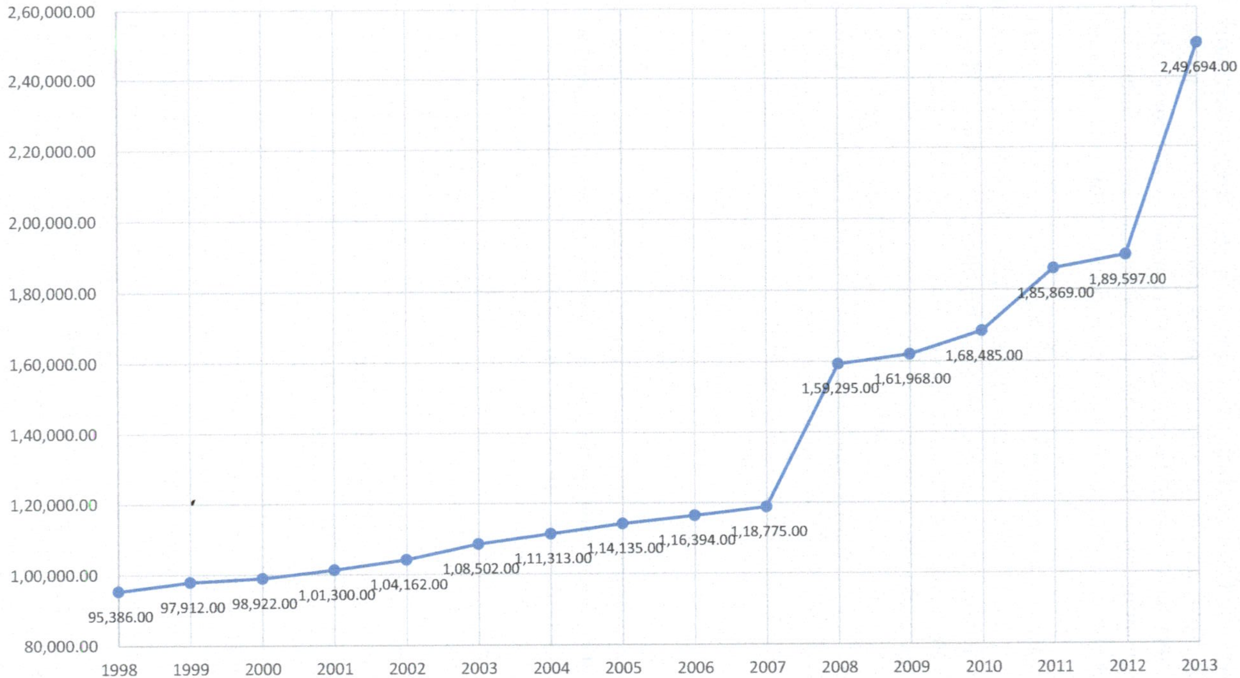

Source: Consejo General de la Abogacía. Annual Review 2008–2013

Appendix 2: Business Generated by the Largest Law Firms in Continental Europe

The following table reflects the earnings generated by the largest law firms in continental Europe, classified by country of origin and the jurisdiction's respective market share:

Country	*Revenue (million Euros)*	*% of Total*
Germany	1,547.60	19
France	964.30	12
Spain	911.86	11
The Netherlands	843.40	10
Norway	589.90	7
Ireland	574.90	7
Italy	547.10	7
Denmark	485.10	6
Switzerland	454.10	6
Sweden	407.70	5
Finland	229.00	3
Luxemburg	174.70	2
Austria	170.10	2
Russia	119.20	1
Portugal	105.70	1
Belgium	86.70	1

Source: European Top 100 2014, The Lawyer

Notes

1. On January 1, 2014, Spain had a total population of 46,507,760. Available at http://www.ine.es. Last visit 30.09.14.
2. Cfr. DIAZ-PICAZO (2006).
3. There are 2.9 lawyers per 1000 people. Data as of December 31, 2013, according to the Consejo General de la Abogacía. Available at http://www.abogacia.es/2013/04/16/censo-numerico-de-abogados/. Last visit September 30, 2014. The data in the US is 3.8 lawyers per 1000 people (1,245,205 lawyers and 322,583,006 population).
4. Cfr. ATIENZA (2014).
5. As far as regulation of the profession, the "Consejo General de la Abogacia Espanola" or General Council of Spanish Lawyers is the entity in charge of overseeing all aspects of the legal industry in Spain. Their role is comparable to that of the American Bar Association in the US. All law universities,

law firms and lawyers must be registered and must comply with the organization in order to be recognized and in good standing.

6. Cfr. ZARAGOZA (1982). Pages 53–55.
7. This refers to the law firms and the legal arms of accounting firms ranked in expansion only. Other law firms and providers of legal services are not included in these calculations.
8. I recommend to read a post by lawyer Emilio Grayer on questions regarding rankings and league tables. Available at http://blogs.cincodias.com/la-cana/2012/07/de-rankings-y-despachos-de-abogados-.html. Last visit October 5, 2014.
9. Jones Day and Dentons have been accounted as American firms as Washington is the headquarters for their managing partners. Nonetheless, both claim to be decentralized firms.
10. "Tres despachos españoles en el 'top ten' de la abogacía europea". Expansión. June 24, 2014. Page 35.
11. "Tres despachos españoles en el 'top ten' de la abogacía europea". Expansión. June 24, 2014. Page 35.
12. The firm is Arriaga Asociados, whose managing partner graduated in law at the age of 50 and in just three years has entered the Top 30. More information on "Arriaga, el letrado de los preferentistas". Expansión. February 18, 2014. Page 27.
13. The "Big Four" refers to PriceWaterhouse Coopers, KPMG, Deloitte, and Ernst & Young. The names of the legal arms in Spain are the following: PwC Tax & Legal Services, KPMG Abogados, Deloitte Abogados y Asesores Tributarios and EY Abogados.
14. UK and Continental Europe Universities have been taken into account.
15. In 2013, the Big Four posted an average revenue growth of 6.75%, while the four leading Spanish law firms had a negative growth of 0.8%. The growths were the following: Garrigues (–2.8%), Cuatrecasas Gonçalves Pereira (0.4%), Uría Menéndez (3.3%), Gómez-Acebo & Pombo (–4.1%), PwC Tax & Legal Services (8.8%), KMPG Abogados (3.3%), Deloitte Abogados y Asesores Tributarios (6.1%) and EY Abogados (8.8%). See Expansión Ranking 2013 published July 2, 2014.
16. Esteban, María Jose and Wilkins, David B. Page 97.
17. On the one hand, there is an increasing importance of in-house counsels within the bar associations. On the other hand, there are very active associations such as the In-House Club of Iberian Lawyer. More information at http://www.iberianlawyer.com/index.php/in-house/in-house-club.
18. This matter is explained in-depth in the chapter "Los abogados de empresa" of the book "Deontología y práctica de la abogacía del siglo XXI". The author is Roger Mariona, Secretary General of ONO.
19. More information at http://www.boe.es/diario_boe/txt.php?id=BOE-A-2012-4132.

20. ESADE (2011).
21. The IBEX 35 is the official index of the Spanish Continuous Market. It is comprises the 35 most liquid stocks traded on the Continuous market. It includes companies such as Banco Santander, Telefónica, Iberdrola, BBVA and Repsol YPF, which are not only responsible for about 90% of the usual business of the Spanish stock exchange, they also have high interests in Latin America, a high weight in two large sectors of the Spanish economy: energy and banking, and they are big employers and, therefore, need a continuous flow of multidisciplinary legal advice.
22. The tables have been created giving priority to the data published in Expansion in its Ranking on July 1, 2014, and when that data was missing, the source of information has been Chambers Europe and/or Legal 500.
23. Refers to inception date for domestic firms and date of entrance into Spanish market for international firms.
24. Every international firm in Spain has Spanish lawyers and provides advice under Spanish law, with the exception of the American firm, Davis Polk & Wardwell which, since the opening of its office in Madrid in 2001, has been limited to US law.
25. This well-known case has been analyzed in various publications, being the latest in Gil Pecharromán (2013), pp. 77–103.
26. "Antonio Garrigues Díaz-Cañabate, abogado, diplomático y ex ministro". El País. February 25, 2004. Available athttp://elpais.com/diario/2004/02/25/agenda/1077663610_850215.html.
27. "Antonio Garrigues Díaz-Cañabate, abogado, diplomático y ex ministro". El País. February 25, 2004. Available athttp://elpais.com/diario/2004/02/25/agenda/1077663610_850215.html.
28. The White Book is still kept in the law firm. Cfr. Gil Pecharromán (2013). Pages 185 y 186.
29. It is recognized as the principal organ of expression of Spanish corporate lawyers.
30. "Los despachos que no cedan el poder a sus socios morirán". Expansión. August 14, 2013. Page 17.
31. Ibid.
32. An inflation rate between 13% and 15%, an unemployment rate of 16% of the active population and a weak productive activity were some of the indicators of the economic situation.
33. The 1980s are also sadly famous for an entrepreneurial culture linked to short-term profitable operations linked to corruption which affected politicians. As a consequence, the courts were the ones to resolve political problems in a process named the "'judicialization' of politics and the politicization of the judiciary". Cfr. GARCÍA CORTAZAR y GARCÍA DE CORTAZAR (2012).

34. In a conference, Emilio Cuatrecasas revealed an anecdote from 1983 about the incorporation of the up-to-then-head of Arthur Andersen's legal services, Rafael Fontana: "During a meeting, Rafael told us that the first thing we need to do was getting rid of every single pen and quill and starting using pencils, rubbers and an adhesive tape". There should be not a crossing-out in our drafts[...].This speeded up the drafting process and ensured greater reliability. [...] He brought order to the law firm. Then there were only 10 or 11 of us". "Ayer y hoy de los despachos profesionales" February 8, 2007. Available at http://canalasesor.wke.es/ver_detalleArt.asp?idArt=67409. Last visit August 22, 2014.
35. ZARATE, José Ramón. "Los ilustres árbitros del juego empresarial", Actualidad Económica, n° 1517, July 13–19, 1987.
36. "Suspensiones de pagos, temas laborales y preocupación por el medioambiente, en el candelero". Expansión. December 21, 1993. Page 28.
37. "25 years of English law firms in Spain". Iberian Lawyer. Available at http://www.iberianlawyer.com/index.php/styles-2/table-designs.
38. Clifford Chance, Garrigues and Uría & Menéndez were the main advisors.
39. The so-called Fathers of the Constitution is a term which refers to the seven members of the constituent legislature responsible for the discussion and signature of the draft of the Constitution of 1978: Gabriel Cisneros Laborada (por UCD), Manuel Fraga Iribarne (AP), Miguel Herrero Rodríguez de Miñón (UCD), Jordi Solé Turá (PSUC), Jose Pedro Pérez-Llorca Rodrigo (UCD), Miquel Roca i Junyent (Pacte Democràtic per Catalunya), founder of Roca Junyent and Gregorio Peces-Barba (PSOE).
40. "Ranking de las firmas españolas de abogados". Expansión. July 21, 1992. Page 36.
41. It refers to the Garrigues, Cuatrecasas, Uría & Menéndez and Gómez-Acebo & Pombo and the five legal branches of the main audit companies.
42. Words of Rodrigo Uría at Amado (2005). Page 12.
43. "Una agenda de crecimiento para España". FEDEA y McKinsey. Available at http://www.crisis09.es/agenda/20101201_Agenda.pdf.
44. "Grandes bufetes y consultoras intentan ganarse al Gobierno en las privatizaciones". Expansión. September 6, 1996. Page 36.
45. "Arthur Andersen casts a net for prestige Spanish merger" The Lawyer. Available at http://www.thelawyer.com/arthur-andersen-casts-a-net-for-prestige-spanish-merger/85555.article. Last visit August 10, 2014.
46. From IE case study "Transformation of multidisciplinary firms".
47. The Big Six was the name given before the merger of Price Waterhouse and Coopers & Lybrand.
48. Information from: "Los bufetes se enchufan" in Expansión, February 28, 2006, "Guía para no perderse en el lío judicial de las opas sobre Endesa"

in Expansión, January 21, 2006, "Crónica jurídica de una OPA" in Expansión, April 2, 2007, and Chambers Europe 2006 and 2007 editions.
49. "El sector jurídico en España se queja de la fuerte competencia en los precios". Expansión. May 1, 2007.
50. Pedro Pérez-Llorca in conference titled "Strategy and management of an emerging law firm: Pérez-Llorca's experience". Recoletos Conferencias. January 27, 2004.
51. Uría Menéndez merged with Vasconcelos, F. Sá Carneiro, Fontes y Asociados and remained as Uría Menéndez. Cuatrecas integrated with Gonçalves Pereira, Castelo Branco & Asociaddos and changed its name to Cuatrecasas Gonçalves Pereira. Garrigues merged with Leónidas, Matos & Asociados.
52. Cfr. "Los abogados españoles llegan a lo más alto". Expansión. June 19, 2010. Page 30.
53. Different sources such as IMF, OECD have expressed that Spain is on the road to recovery as the increase in GDP in 2013 and 2014, mainly due to an increase in exports. But the high unemployment rate remains an issue, and there is a high risk of deflation.
54. "Uría Menéndez toma participación en la primera gran firma de abogados latinoamericana". 09.09.2014 Available at its website: http://www.uria.com/es/actualidad/Noticias.html?id=944.
55. More information in "La pugna de los grandes bufetes españoles por Latinoamérica", Expansión, September 17, 2014, page 41 and "Ontier se sitúa como la firma con mayor presencia en Latinoamérica, Expansión, December 9, 2014, page 37.
56. "Refugiados de los estudios de abogados". La Revista Legal. December 2014. Pages 36 and 37.
57. See Explanatory Memorandum of Ley 2/2007, de Sociedades Profesionales.
58. More information at "Ecija, la primera firma española que da entrada a un fondo". Expansión, March 13, 2013. Page 32.
59. Data obtained by Expansión. See "Sólo el 13% de los socios de bufetes en España son mujeres". March 25, 2014. Page 28.
60. The adoption of equality plans are compulsory in companies with more than 250 employees.
61. A total of 31 companies signed out this agreement which set commitments such as approval of effective measures on organization and flexibility at work for both men and women, and set the progress towards a more balanced participation when vacancies in trainee and management positions occur. More information at https://www.msssi.gob.es/ssi/igualdadOportunidades/iEmpleo/promocionprofesionalfoto.htm.

62. The term was coined by José María de Areilza in 2008 and a quick search in Google (June 2014) identified more than 22,000 pages in which the term is used.
63. More information at http://www.hayderecho.com.
64. More information at http://crsa.icam.es.
65. Zaragoza (1982), pp. 15 y 21.

References

Books, Articles and Papers

Amado, Jordi. 2005. *La asesoría y el despacho profesional del siglo XXI*. Planificación Jurídica.

Amado, Jordi, and Luis M. Huete. 1999. *Asesorías del siglo XXI. CISS.*

Atienza Becerril, Soledad. 2014. *Enseñar Derecho ¿Puede servirnos la experiencia de Estados Unidos?* Thomson Reuters Aranzadi.

Barranco Avilés, María del Carmen, Rafael de Asis Roig, and Alberto Iglesias Garzón. 2014. *Estudio sobre el Pro Bono en la Comunidad de Madrid*. Ilustre Colegio de Abogados de Madrid.

Carrasco, Sansón. 2014. *¿Hay Derecho?*. Ediciones Península.

Cortázar, Fernando, and José Manuel González Vesga. 2012. *Breve Historia de España*. Alianza Editorial. Sexta edición.

Diez-Picazo, Luis María. 2006. *El oficio de jurista*. Siglo XXI.

Empson, Laura, ed. 2007. *Managing the Modern Law Firm*. Oxford: Oxford University Press.

Esteban, María José, and David B. Wilkins. *Regreso al futuro: la reactivación de las divisiones jurídicas de las Big 4 en Europa y el futuro de la abogacía de los negocios. Revista Española de Relaciones Internacionales* 5: 92–106. Available at http://reri.difusionjuridica.es/index.php/RERI/article/view/64.

Friedman, Lawrence M., and Rogelio Pérez Perdomo. 2003. *Legal Cultures in the Age of Globalization/Latin America and Latin Europe*. Stanford

García-León, Carlos, and Borja Martínez-Echevarría. 2014. *Antonio Garrigues Walker: Testigo clave de medio siglo de nuestra historia*. Ediciones Península.

GilPecharromán, Xavier. 2013. *Abogados del Poder.* La Esfera de los Libros.

González, Carmen, Marisa Méndez, and Almudena Rodríguez. 2005. *El libro rojo del marketing en las firmas de abogados*. Ediciones Experiencia.

Mañas, Elena. 2011. *Impacto de la abogacía en la economía. 2011*. Editorial Civitas.

Marcos, Francisco. 2001. La eficiencia de los bufetes de abogados. Instituto de Empresa. Available at http://profesores.ie.edu/fmarcos/Publicaciones_archivos/Eficiencia%20Spanish%20Law%20Firms.pdf

Menéndez, Adolfo, and Juan José Torres-Fernández Nieto, eds. 2008. *Deontología y práctica de la abogacía del siglo XXI*. Aranzadi.
Zaragoza, Ángel. 1982. *Los abogados y la sociedad industrial*. Ediciones Península.

Case Studies

Areilza, Jose María. 2006. *Pioneer International Lawyers in Spain: The Case of Jose Mario Armero*. IE Law School.
Atienza, Soledad, and Méndez Marisa. 2009. *The Recruitment Challenge at Perez Llorca*. IE Law School.
Eccles, Robert G., and Partha Bose. 2008. *Uría Menéndez*. Harvard Business School.
Méndez, Marisa. 2006. *Transformation of multidisciplinary firms*. IE Law School.
———. 2007. *Declaring independence*. IE Law School.

Other References

Chambers Europe. Editions 2007–2014.
Chambers Global. 2002 to 2006 editions.
Estudio del Sector Legal de los Negocios. 2011. Sandra Enzler and Eugenia Navarro. Diario La Ley N° 7596, 03/2011, p. 1–19.
Estudio del Sector Legal de los Negocios. 2011. Sandra Enzler and Eugenia Navarro. ESADE 2014.
Expansión Jurídico. 1992–2014.
Méndez, Marisa. *La jungla legal*. Expansión 2007–2008.
Iberian Lawyer. 2008–2014.
The Legal 500. Editions 2005 to 2013.

Marisa Méndez Sordo is an Adjunct Professor in Management and Legal Trends Issues at the IE Law School in Madrid (Spain). Professor Méndez is the author of important publications on the Spanish corporate legal sector, the evolution of law firms and the legal profession.

CHAPTER 10

Big Law in Venezuela: From Globalization to Revolution

Manuel Gómez and Rogelio Pérez-Perdomo

Lawyering, Oil and Politics in Contemporary Venezuela

This chapter focuses on Venezuelan corporate lawyers during the period 1994–2014, a time in which the country experienced abrupt changes in its political orientation and economic policies. In 1989, as a response to a crisis partially credited by a failure of the model of import substitutions and national industrialization, Venezuela opened its economy to the world, allowing foreign investment, freeing export-import trade and eliminating currency exchange controls. In particular, in 1994, following a policy of economic openness touted as "oil opening" (*apertura petrolera*) Venezuela allowed the entry of foreign investors in the oil business—an activity that had been reserved to the state since 1974—and conversely, Venezuela acquired important refineries and expanded its business presence into foreign countries. Even though the oil opening policy was short lived, it had a profound impact on the transformation of Venezuelan business law firms and the legal profession at large. Starting in the early 2000s,

M. Gómez (✉) • R. Pérez-Perdomo
Florida International University, Miami, FL, USA

Universidad Metropolitana, Caracas, Venezuela

M. Gómez, R. Pérez-Perdomo (eds.), *Big Law in Latin America and Spain*, https://doi.org/10.1007/978-3-319-65403-4_10

Venezuela's political, social and economic landscape changed drastically, which affected all segments of society, including the business sector, and the lawyers that serve it.

Most of the recent changes are associated with former President Hugo Chavez, who led a radical change in the political system reflected in a brand new constitution approved in 1999, which limited the power of the legislative branch, dwindled the importance of political parties, and increased the power of the executive branch. The Supreme Court and the Attorney General also became more powerful. Under the appearance of a more direct democracy, the country became progressively more authoritarian. President Chavez referred to his movement as the Bolivarian Revolution and later on as socialism of the twenty-first century. President Chavez succumbed to a long battle with cancer in March of 2013, while he was still in office. Soon thereafter, his vice-president Nicolas Maduro became elected President by a very slim margin in a controversial election. Maduro vowed to continue down the same political path set by Chavez during the last decade. The adjectives "Bolivarian" and "Socialist" have been contested and the trend today is to point out the key role of Chavez and to declare themselves "Chavistas" as a way to honor the memory of the undisputed father of the regime.

The Chavista regime curtailed foreign investments and many domestic and foreign enterprises fell under the grip of the government, mostly as a result of a wave of expropriations and confiscations, which in turn provoked a flurry of legal claims filed by foreign investors before international tribunals. The oil prices reached a historic high between 2004 and 2014, thus allowing the government to implement its unconventional agenda comprised of unorthodox economic policies. The windfall of petrodollars also allowed the government to strengthen its clientelistic network, which has in turn helped the Chavista governments in consolidating their political power. Notwithstanding, during the last quarter of 2014, oil prices fell abruptly, which plunged Venezuela into a deep economic and political crisis that the country was still suffering from when this chapter was written.

One of the most evident signs of authoritarianism in Venezuela during the last decade has been the political manipulation and tight control exercised by the central government over judges, prosecutors and state agencies. Unsurprisingly, this has had an impact on the legal profession and business lawyers are not exempt from this political interference. The impact of such volatile environment on the legal profession is precisely what we are set to explore in this chapter. Our main interest is to study business lawyers and, more importantly, their firms. These are organizations mainly devoted to provide legal services to corporate clients, government agencies and individual businesspeople. In terms of size, the selected firms range between 10 and 82 lawyers. Almost all the firms that comprise our research population promote themselves as multiservice legal service providers.

For our study, we were able to obtain interview data from representatives of almost every business law firm with ten or more members that operate in Venezuela. To further define our target population, we looked into the ranking and classification prepared by the leading international directories of lawyers such as Martindale-Hubbell, Chambers & Partners, and Latin Lawyer. In order to ensure a comprehensive coverage of the Venezuelan legal market, we also considered other professional publications and periodicals that routinely cover Latin American corporate lawyers, in house counsel and the corporate legal sector in general.

Our personal knowledge of the Venezuelan legal market and our own previous scholarly work involving the legal sector in Venezuela (Pérez-Perdomo 1981, 2001, 2006; Gómez 2003, 2007, 2010, 2011, 2013) also proved valuable, because it helped us interpret the data, and also triangulate it with other sources in order to confirm its accuracy.

We interviewed at least one representative per firm. Our interviewees were comprised of mostly partners, many of who currently hold or have held one or more leadership positions in their respective law firms, as managing partner, board member, director and/or founder. Many interviewees were selected from among our own personal contacts and the rest by following a snowball sampling technique.

Although most of our interviewees were based in Venezuela when the interviews took place, we also interviewed lawyers who practice or live in other jurisdictions such as Miami, but who routinely serve Venezuelan-based clients, or who have had a significant impact on the organization and development of corporate law firms in Venezuela. By interviewing lawyers located abroad, we were also able to obtain a more ample and certainly different view of the Venezuelan market. In total, we conducted about 35 interviews.

For the sake of maintaining consistency across interviews and to ensure a thorough exploration, we followed a general interview protocol. The average interview lasted about two hours, and in some cases we had more than one conversation or a follow-up interview in person or via email. In order to facilitate openness and to promote candor, all interviews were also conducted under a promise of confidentiality. Hence, all the references to real names that appear in this chapter were obtained from publicly available information, and not from our interviews.

From the 1950s to 1978, Venezuela had a very dynamic economy mostly based on a policy of industrialization by import substitution. The country became a magnet for immigrants, first from Western Europe, and later on from other Latin American countries. The country also experienced a cultural flourishing that included the promotion of higher education, scientific research, music, theater, and so on. During the 1960s and 1970s, the national universities had ambitious programs to prepare their professors in the top scholarly centers of the world, and the leading law schools benefited greatly from this. Private universities—and law schools—were created, and a number of scientific journals, including law reviews, appeared in the scene.

Most of this momentum was lost toward the mid-1980s in part due to a mounting economic crisis. The crisis helped set the stage for the advent of a radically different government led by Hugo Chavez, a retired Lieutenant colonel who had been recently released from prison after a frustrated coup-attempt carried out in 1992.

Chavez's electoral success in 1998 was undoubtedly facilitated by the widespread popular discontent prevailing in Venezuela at the time. The precarious economic situation coupled with a series of corruption scandals, and the rampant crime rates were among the factors that contributed to the loss of credibility of the traditional political leaders and their parties. This crisis did not affect the growth of the Venezuelan legal profession, as it is shown in Table 10.1.

Another contributing factor to the growth in the number of legal professionals was the establishment of new law schools. In 1950, there were only four law schools in the country, all of them in public universities. Over the next decades, private universities multiplied and in the last two decades a small number of them have become the main feeders of the corporate law firms.

Even more important than the strength of a particular law school is their perceived value as environments that facilitate social connections and life-long friendships among the students, professors and alumni. Law schools are the breeding ground for the social networks that have traditionally permeated the Venezuelan business sector and the legal professionals that serve them (Gómez 2003).

Table 10.1 Law graduates in Venezuela from 1950 to 2015

Year	*Law graduates*	*Law graduates per 100,000 inhabitants*
1950	2,067	41
1981	16,045	111
1990	31,350	160
2000	66,383	282
2010	122,636	423
2015	181,367	585

Source: Pérez-Perdomo 1981, 2006, and estimate from Inpreabogado registry. As the previous table shows, the population of lawyers increased very quickly in Venezuela from 1950 onward. A partial explanation for such growth could be that the universities became increasingly accessible to more people. Women were first enrolled in law schools during the 1930s, and in the 1970s became the majority among law students. The 1960s also witnessed an influx of university students of lower socio-economic strata. Another plausible factor could rest on the prospect of employment in the different sectors of the social and political system for those holding a law diploma.

The stratification of the profession also became visible, especially during the last 40 years, which also coincided with a period of demographic expansion of lawyers and with the multiplication and growth of law firms. Lawyers dealing with important business matters are usually placed at the highest echelon of the profession. They have professional prestige and high income, and are often affiliated with the elite law firms. If we look at their size, most Venezuelan corporate law firms would not even qualify as mid-sized level firms by United States standards. Notwithstanding, the Venezuelan firms that we are considering here are well organized and routinely have the infrastructure to serve the needs of big corporate clients, government agencies and individual business people, in a similar way how "Big Law" does it in the United States. Some are also part of big international law firms.

With some variations that will be explained later, the client management strategies, internal structure and governance, and level of expertise and professional services offered by these Venezuelan corporate law firms resembles their multinational counterparts. Thus, the expression Big Law will be used throughout this chapter to suggest the provision of complex legal services usually in the context of business transactions, by organizations incorporated as law firms, to high-end business clients, regardless of the size of the provider.

Law firms are certainly not alone in the top stratum and are not the only ones serving business clients. In-house counsels are important as well and have been gaining more salience since at least the mid-twentieth century. Small and specialized law firms ("boutiques") are also present. Finally, there are the well-known superstar lawyers or "grand advocates" (Galanter and Robinson 2013), who offer highly specialized legal advice to corporate clients. These lawyers routinely work as solo practitioners or in relatively small offices, and have almost no infrastructure aside from a minimum support staff. The strength of these grand advocates is not in their capacity to handle high volumes of legal work, but instead to lend their sophisticated knowledge to handle a single or few matters usually of very high profile and complexity. As a result, these grand advocates are only brought into the cases for specific and very important tasks, such as filing an extraordinary petition before the highest court, presenting oral arguments, or leading high stakes negotiations. In other words, they do not to handle every aspect of a case but only the parts that require specialized or highly skilled intervention.

Regardless of the organizational structure adopted by the lawyers who serve the business sector in Venezuela,—be it a large firm, in-house or boutique firm—they share at least two seemingly incongruous traits. On the one hand, most Venezuelan business lawyers view themselves as members of a lucrative trade or profession where hourly fees and other financial incentives are common. On the other hand, Venezuelan business lawyers also strive to maintain their image as intellectuals and scholars, and commonly boast their connections with academia. Moreover, it is a common trait among the most prominent Venezuelan law firms to brandish the academic accolades of their partners, including publications, membership in academies and learned societies, tenured professorships, and other university affiliations. The prestige of the firm seems to be enhanced by the intellectual prestige of its members, and not only by their professional skills.

Venezuelan business lawyers have been attuned with the internationalization of law practice from early times. The arrival of several American and European lawyers in Caracas from early twentieth century helped in the creation of firms like Travieso Evans and Benson Perez-Matos. The appearance of Baker & McKenzie as the first foreign law firm to open a Venezuelan outpost in the mid-1950s had an important effect. In great part, due to the foreign influence, local Venezuelan "bufetes de abogados" redefined their internal structures and became law firms with a management structure and created departments by areas of practice.

Baker & McKenzie was the first foreign outpost of this firm, but also the first foreign law office formally established in Venezuela. The Caracas office of Baker & McKenzie grew steadily to eventually become the largest law firm in the country. At the same time, Ramón Díaz became the first foreigner to become partner of the fast-growing Chicago law firm.

A few years later, Díaz left the firm to establish Díaz Egaña Hung & Aveledo. This firm developed a close connection with Curtis Mallet-Prevost & Mosle, a New York law firm with strong ties throughout Latin America since the late 1800s. This is another trend: Curtis Mallet-Prevost and other international law firms never opened an office in Venezuela, but they have developed a longstanding relationship with prominent Venezuelan lawyers throughout the twentieth century, and thus maintained some indirect presence there. A more recent and discreet case is Foley Hoag, a Boston-based firm with growing experience in Latin America. Like Curtis Mallet-Prevost, more recently, Foley Hoag does not appear to have a local representative.

The 1970s were a decade of optimism, economic and social change in Venezuela. A fast-growing economy and a stable democracy attracted hundreds of thousands migrants from other Latin American countries. By 1979, there were eight law firms with ten or more lawyers. This list included the four original business law firms founded in the late nineteenth and early twentieth century, to wit, Mendoza Palacios Páez-Pumar, Tinoco Travieso, Rodriguez & Mendoza, and Travieso Evans. The list also included Baker & McKenzie, which was still the only international firm with a formal presence in Venezuela and Lares Martinez, established in 1967. In terms of size, the average number of lawyers among the top five firms was 15, which might have seemed small for United States standards, but was large considering the local market.

In addition to the strengthening and expansion of the domestic elite law firms, the decade of the 1970s also witnessed the emergence of several other law firms that would eventually become heavy-duty competitors in the market for high-end corporate legal services. Torres Plaz & Araujo[1] founded in 1972, D'Empaire Reyna also founded in 1972, and Rodner Martínez & Asociados founded in 1978. Since its inception, Torres Plaz & Araujo positioned itself as a specialized law firm in tax and corporate law, and in which only one other firm, Octavio & Asociados, specialized at the time.

Another trend during those years was the growing number of Venezuelan lawyers who sought to obtain graduate degrees from foreign universities. LL.M. programs from the United States became a popular choice particularly among lawyers working at elite business law firms, and almost a necessity for those aspiring to become partners in the larger ones.

During the 1980s, pursuing graduate studies abroad was expensive, and the number of scholarships was limited but many young lawyers decided to make a financial sacrifice and join the ranks of foreign-trained Venezuelan lawyers. After all, an LL.M. diploma from a well-known American law school such as Harvard, Yale or Columbia was an important status symbol among Venezuelan elite business lawyers (Interviewee 3). In general terms, a foreign LL.M. degree coupled with a membership to a foreign Bar Association was, and still is perceived as a symbol of competency in a foreign legal system, or at the very least, proficiency in a foreign language (Interviewee 4). What is really interesting nonetheless is that the aspiration of the Venezuelan lawyers who became members of the New York Bar was not necessarily to work permanently in New York, to represent clients in that jurisdiction, or to work in cases where New York law applied. Instead, the New York-admitted Venezuelan lawyers saw this credential as part of their symbolic capital as transnational lawyers.

The opportunity to study law in the United States also gave many Venezuelan lawyers the chance to work as foreign associates during the year of optional practical training allowed to foreign graduates in that country. Being part of an American law firm, albeit during a relatively short period of time, was important to the young Venezuelan lawyers because it allowed them to witness first-hand the operation of an American law office, and gave a glimpse of the ins and outs of practicing law in the United States.

Unsurprisingly, upon returning to Venezuela and rejoining the local firms, some of these lawyers led the efforts to modernize the local legal market and to adapt some of the features of American law firms into their own organizations, including the adoption of the hourly billing system, client management techniques and some aspects of their internal administrative structure. It was also during this period that Venezuelan law firms began investing in marketing and promotion, and appeared more routinely in international lawyer directories such as Martindale-Hubbell.

As visitors to the offices of an average Venezuelan elite lawyer, we can attest to the display of an American Bar membership certificate alongside an LL.M. diploma are routinely brandished as a sign of prestige and professional reputation. Moreover, the law firms' brochures and websites often highlight the credentials obtained in foreign jurisdictions, among the most important accolades of their members.

The following session will analyze the impact of opening the market to foreign investors, particularly the oil opening of the nineties. The section "Big Law During the Chavista Revolution" will analyze the impact of the Chavist revolution on business and business lawyers. In the last section, we will place the Venezuelan events in the large panorama of change generally called globalization and the response of lawyers to this brave new world.

The Impact of the Oil Opening on Venezuelan Business Lawyers

There appears to be a general agreement among our interviewees that the last two decades in Venezuela have felt like a roller coaster ride (interviewees 6, 1, 14). This may also be the general opinion of most Venezuelan citizens regardless of their political affiliation; but those in the business sector claim to have felt the ups and downs particularly strongly, and the lawyers that serve the corporate world feel the same way. The ride upward for the business lawyers occurred between 1990 and 2000, when two government policies dubbed the Big Turnaround (*Gran Viraje*) and the Oil Opening (*Apertura Petrolera*) were launched. The ride downwards, started in the early 2000s, and has generally continued to this day.

Big Law and the Political Maneuvering of the Venezuelan Oil Sector

Since its incorporation in 1975, the Venezuelan national oil company (PDVSA) became a regional role model in terms of managerial independence, efficiency and profitability; three qualities rarely seen in Latin American state-owned entities. PDVSA's creation was part of the strategy to nationalize the oil industry led by the first Pérez administration (1973–1978), which helped the state gain control over its natural resources, and also made Venezuela a major player in the global energy market. The then newly formed company took advantage of the know-how and talent of many Venezuelan oil executives that had previously worked for the oil multinationals that operated in the country since the early 1900s. PDVSA used this talent to build a world-class competitive enterprise where professional merits not politics were the driving factor. Lawyers were present in this meritocracy (Pérez-Perdomo 2001).

The oil industry was too important to the government, so the political leaders decided not to risk it, or as one of our interviewees eloquently pointed out, "the government of the time did not want to kill the goose that laid the golden eggs, so it let PDVSA be managed as a real company instead of another bureaucratic government agency" (Interviewee 15).

Similar to how any major multinational company functions, PDVSA armed itself with the best talent in the industry, and hired the best lawyers it could get. For major international contracts, complex cross-border transactions, project finance and high-stake international litigation and arbitration, PDVSA routinely retained the services of prominent foreign law firms such as Cleary Gottlieb Steen & Hamilton, Shearman & Sterling and other Wall Street outlets. For most other matters, PDVSA relied on its own legal department, which in its heyday reached the astonishing number of 140 lawyers, thus making it the largest legal service provider that has ever existed in Venezuela (Pérez-Perdomo 2001).

By the 1980s and 1990s, PDVSA was also sending work to some of the elite local law firms, with whom it forged a mutually beneficial business relationship that saw its peak during the oil opening years of the mid-1990s, and lasted until the oil strike of 2003. This period was clearly different from the revolutionary times that ensued (Interviewees 3 and 14).

Rafael Caldera was the president during the oil opening. His second term in office (1994–1999) was very tense and difficult. His own party, the Christian Democratic Party (COPEI), which he had helped found in 1946, did not support him. He ran instead supported by an unlikely coalition of small groups under the umbrella of a new party called National Convergence (Convergencia), which included leaders from across the ideological spectrum from right to left. He received power in the mid of a financial crisis. Early in his tenure, the number of financial institutions under special government oversight reached 17, which represented 53 percent of the national banking system, and the recovery cost to the government was estimated between 18 and 31 percent of the GDP (Krivoy 2000). Another major setback for the Venezuelan economy was a decline in the price of oil to 11 dollars per barrel, a 30 percent drop in the rate of foreign investment, and a decrease in the nation's foreign reserves by 17 percent (Brooke 1994).

The intervention of so many banks created panic among the major Venezuelan law firms, which had them among their most prominent clients. To some corporate lawyers, the crisis not only harmed their business portfolio. Many lawyers that held positions at distressed financial institutions were indicted and prosecuted for financial crimes regardless of whether those positions were real or nominal (Interviewee 8). Some fled the country, while others were imprisoned for the duration of the trials steered by fierce prosecutors who sought to make an example of them.

While the firms where some of the indicted lawyers worked were fighting to defend their members and preserve their clientele, others had been warming up their engines and preparing themselves for an imminent announcement by the government that would shake the corporate legal sector one more time.

In April of 1994, President Caldera announced that that the oil sector would "be opened without limitations to private enterprise, national or foreign" (Brooke 1994). This policy, which continued the reversal of the oil nationalization strategy of the 1970s, aspired to make the Venezuelan oil sector more competitive in the global arena. Moreover, the Caldera administration sought to attract the necessary foreign capital and technical expertise to explore the vast reserves of crude located in the Orinoco Belt, one of the largest deposits of petroleum in the world. At the same time, Caldera announced a similar policy geared to open the steel and aluminum sector to foreign investment.

The effort toward the internationalization of PDVSA and to attract foreign capital via strategic associations with multinational oil companies had begun in 1991 with Pérez, but it was not until Caldera that the effort crystallized, obtained full-fledged political support and a legal framework to make it happen (Tejera 2012).

Aside from spearheading the amendment of the tax and hydrocarbons legislations as a way to attract foreign investors, and to allow their participation in the oil business, the Venezuelan government ratified a series of international arbitration-related conventions. The negotiations were successful, and the multinational companies were enticed to participate in the Oil Opening, which brought a group of heavyweight foreign investors to the country, including ConocoPhillips, Total, Mitsubishi, Itochu, Shell, Chevron and ExxonMobil.

Although some of these companies, or their predecessors, had operated oil concessions in Venezuela prior to the 1975 nationalization policy, none of them had kept an operational presence in the country. Some foreign companies, however, had maintained connections with their former Venezuelan counsel, which facilitated their comeback and gave them a lead. Their lawyers also viewed themselves to be in a dominant position.

As one of our interviewees said, "some of us already had a foot in the door because some oil multinationals were already our clients, or we had worked for them in the past, and therefore had an advantage vis-à-vis our competitors" (Interviewee 10). Local law firms had begun preparing for the oil opening as early as 1991 when the internationalization of Venezuela's hydrocarbons sector was foreseeable.

Among the first work that Venezuelan lawyers did, were hundreds of legal opinions that discussed the feasibility of the proposed associations between PDVSA and the foreign companies, draft legislation, financial and legal planning, project finance, incorporation of subsidiaries, and lobbying with government officials. Some of the work did not come directly from the clients but instead from American law firms that had been retained to lead the legal strategy, and sought to subcontract Venezuelan lawyers to assist them (Interviewee 10).

Although this meant that local counsel got a small slice of the pie and did not "own" the client, such arrangement did not bother the Venezuelan law firms whose aspirations, "at least, during this first stage was simply to get a foot at the door, and a share in the proceeds regardless of how small that was" (Interviewee 30).

After the first operating agreements between PDVSA and the foreign partners were underway, the leading Venezuelan corporate law firms began to compete with each other more fiercely for the fast-growing business. In order to cope with the increased demand for specialized legal advice, the local firms focused on expanding their operations through launching new departments or practice groups dedicated to oil, gas, labor, tax, project finance and administrative law, just to name the most salient areas.

This, in turn required the hiring of new lawyers, supporting staff and legal consultants. Lawyers with foreign language skills, and an American LL.M. were in high demand, and the firms fought to hire some of them. Although the number of Venezuelan law graduates had been on the rise for a number of years, the population of highly competent bilingual attorneys sought by the growing firms remained relatively small. However, in general terms, "it was a buyer's market for law firms [like ours], which meant that we could really pick and choose the cream of the crop, which we mostly did", explained the former hiring partner of one of the largest law firms operating in the country at the time (Interviewee 5).

Whereas the more visible growth occurred in the larger law firms, the leading boutique law firms did not stay behind. "There was enough business for everyone" one lawyer pointed out, and then added "even the smaller shops (referring to small law firms) had a chance to partake in the feast, so everybody sought to expand their offerings in order to attract new clients" (Interviewee 21).

The oil opening offered a sigh of relief to an embattled corporate legal sector that was still trying to recover from the recent banking crisis. The oil opening also revitalized the political networks that operated between the private sector and the government, and the business lawyers were at the epicenter of it. The influx of influential foreign players also helped break down the traditional walls that divided the traditional elite law firms from the rest, and enabled new players to attain a prominent role relatively quickly.

The following table shows ups and downs of Caracas law firms with longer history or major size between 1990 and 2015.

In 1979, there were just 7 law firms with 10 or more lawyers in Venezuela. The largest one had only 16 members, and the average number of lawyers among the top 5 was 15 (Pérez-Perdomo 1981). All these law firms still exist, with various degrees of prominence, and 3 of them continue to be among the largest in the country.

By 1990, the law firms with 10 or more members rose to 14, and the average number of lawyers working in the top 5 largest firms was 30, a large increase. The largest law firm in the country was Baker & McKenzie with 46 members. The data for 1990 reflects the expansion of the market occurred during the 1980s. As Table 10.2 shows a real upsurge in the number of lawyers per firm, but not necessarily in the overall population of law firms, took place during the 1990s. The exponential increase in the number of lawyers, which for some law firms such as Baker & McKenzie, Tinoco Travieso, Rodriguez & Mendoza, D'Empaire Reyna, Benson Pérez-Matos and others, was twice as much as in the previous decade; is a direct consequence of the rise in the demand for legal work stemming from the oil opening and other business opportunities.

The Arrival of the Foreign Competitors, and the "Americanization" of the Local Law Firms

Another interesting occurrence during the 1990s was the arrival of two North American law firms, Macleod Dixon from Canada, and Steel Hector & Davis from the United States. A third firm, Clyde & Co. from the United Kingdom, also opened a small office during those years, but it has remained small and is not considered a big player.[24] Macleod Dixon was an

Table 10.2 Ups and downs of Venezuelan law firms (1990–2015)

Name	*1990*	*1999*	*2009*	*2014*
Alvarez Gamus & Padrón (1975)[2]				(5) 12
Antequera Parilli & Rodriguez (2001)[3]	–	–	(4) 14	(4) 10
Aveledo Kempler Rivas (1973)	(13) 14			(4) 16
Araque Reyna Sosa & Viso (1986)[4]		(13) 25	(14) 35	(17) 30
Baker & McKenzie (1955)[5]	(16) 46	(20) 76	(35) 84	(40) 82
Baumeister & Brewer (1983)	10	(10) 24	–	–
Benson Pérez-Matos Antakly Watts (1953)[6]	12	(20) 22	(10) 24	(10) 19
Bentata Abogados (1954)[7]	(5) 11	(15) 24	(3) 23	(4) 13
D'Empaire Reyna (1972)[8]	21	(13) 35	(15) 38	(17) 53
De Sola, Pate & Brown (1944)	(4) 10	(4) 14		
DLA Interjuris (2010)[9]	–	–	–	(11) 21
Hoet Peláez Castillo & Duque (formerly, Bentata Hoet & Asociados) (1942)	25 (27)	59	11 (48)	13 (43)
Hogan Lovells (2004)[10]	–			(3) 11
Lares Martínez & Asociados (1967)[11]	(16) 18			(4) 8
Littler Mendelson (2011)[12]	–	–	–	(4) 27
Mendoza Palacios Acedo Borjas (1945)[13]	(12) 30	(15) 40	(13) 34	(16) 31
Norton Rose Fullbright (Macleod Dixon) (1997)[14]	–	(4)[15] 12	(13)[16] 48	(18)[17] 47
Rodner Martínez & Asociados (1978)[18]	–	(7) 11	(6) 10	(6) 10
Rodríguez & Mendoza (1910)[19]	(9) 23	(13) 44	(10) 35	(10) 41
Tinoco Travieso Planchart & Nuñez (1914)[20]	(7) 15	(16) 34	(13) 42	(14) 32
Torres Plaz & Araujo (1972)[21]	(5) 10	(20) 33	(12) 28	(11) 25
Travieso Evans Arria Rengel & Paz (1920)[22]	(12) 24	(15) 45	(19) 43	(11) 52
WDA Legal (formerly, Squire Sanders & Dempsey, and Steel Hector & Davis) (1997)[23]	–		(6) 24	(3) 12

Sources: For 1990: Martindale Hubbell; for 2009 and 2015: Latin Lawyer, and firms' web pages

Remarks: The numbers in parenthesis next to the firm's name show the year when each firm was founded or, in the case of international firms, the year of opening their office in Venezuela. The numbers in parenthesis in the other columns indicate the partners, and the other numbers reflect the total amount of lawyers per firm

energy industry focused law firm originally founded in Calgary in 1912. Its Caracas operation started with less than ten lawyers was the first office of the firm in South America. A few years later, they opened an outlet in Río de Janeiro, and in 2011 arrived in Bogotá. What came as a surprise, however, was how fast the Caracas office of Macleod Dixon grew, and how it became a dominant player in the energy sector in just a few years. In less than a decade, the firm quadrupled in size, amassed an enviable portfolio of international clients, and, according to some of our interviewees, "also incited important changes in the local culture of corporate law firms in Venezuela" (Interviewee 23).

Macleod Dixon's drew its original crop from law firms such as Clyde & Co., Baker & McKenzie, Rodriguez & Mendoza, and others. Given their high volume of foreign clients, many of which were Fortune 500 companies, Macleod Dixon hired almost exclusively bilingual lawyers, many of whom had also pursued graduate studies in the United States or Europe. They also offered their associates an overall compensation package that was well above market value, which made their hiring very competitive. Different from most traditional firms, Macleod Dixon focused almost exclusively on the oil and gas industry, and built its team around it. This gave them a competitive advantage vis-à-vis other players in the market who in the best cases had only one or two people who really understood the industry, as opposed to a practice group or an entire firm.

Another distinctive feature of Macleod Dixon was their large number of women lawyers that it hired, and particularly holding leadership positions at the firm. This is largely credited to Elisabeth Eljuri, one of the firm's founding members, a top-ranked individual by Chambers Latin America, and "Latin America's only serving female leader of an established law firm", according to Latin Lawyer.

Miami-based Steel Hector & Davis was the other foreign law firm that entered the Venezuelan market in 1997. The firm considered Venezuela a strategic jurisdiction to begin their expansion toward Latin America. The high volume of foreign investments in Venezuela fueled by the oil opening, and the longstanding business ties between Miami and Caracas, were sufficient reasons for the American law firm to make the move. Miguel Zaldivar, Jr., a Venezuelan lawyer who was also trained in the United States, led the opening of Steel Hector & Davis' Caracas office, and was also instrumental in the expansion of the firm toward other Latin American jurisdictions including Brazil and the Dominican Republic.[25] Before relocating to Miami and pursuing a Juris Doctor degree in an American law school, Zaldivar, Jr. worked at Baker & McKenzie in Caracas, which gave him an insider's perspective on the internal culture of Big Law in Venezuela, and also helped him understand the market.

When Steel Hector & Davis opened its doors in Venezuela, it only recruited lawyers that fit the following three criteria: have graduated at the top of their law school class, have obtained an LL.M from a reputable foreign school, and have previous work experience at a global law firm (interviewee 25). This, they believed, would enable the firm to hit the ground running; and it certainly did. Soon after opening its doors in Venezuela, Steel Hector & Davis was able to secure a US$ 2.3 billion petrochemical joint venture between state-owned Pequiven, and a major United States energy company.

The firm also assisted PDVSA in expanding its operations in to Brazil, and provided legal advice in connection to the construction of a US$ 260 million disposal plant for a consortium between Venezuela-owned Bauxilum and Pechinet. In an interview given in 2001, Zaldivar, Jr. credited his firm's rapid success to the fact that they were "a U.S. firm that is able to staff projects in Latin American with Latin American lawyers".[26]

The role of the Caracas-based lawyers of Steel Hector & Davis, Macleod Dixon and other firms went beyond the Venezuelan borders. Soon enough, they were assisting their American and Venezuelan clients on transactions throughout the entire Latin American and Caribbean region.

During this period, several firms branched out to other cities where their clients had established some presence, and opened satellite offices as a way to keep the work in-house and avoid referring it to other lawyers. Among the law firms that established offices outside of Caracas during those years were Travieso Evans, Mendoza Palacios and Tinoco Travieso. Baker & McKenzie, which already had offices in the industrial city of Valencia, followed the trend with new branches in Puerto Ordaz, Puerto La Cruz and Maturín. As we learned during our interviews, the idea to expand geographically sometimes came from the American clients, while in other cases it originated within the local firms themselves in an attempt to become more "Americanized."

The firms that chose not to expand ended up forging cooperating agreements with local practitioners or simply flew their lawyers out as often as they were needed in other cities. Interestingly, none of the foreign firms except for Baker & McKenzie opened branches outside Caracas.

The firm's lawyers based in Caracas, usually performed the work that required extensive research and high-level expertise such as legal opinions and court briefs, and billed those accordingly at a higher rate. It was also during the 1990s, that the Venezuelan law firms began projecting themselves internationally, and investing more resources in promoting their image. Glossy brochures and other publicity materials, both in English and Spanish, became common among the larger firms, and with the popularization of the internet, most firms also began launching their own websites.

The décor of the offices was also an important symbol of success; so most elite law firms spent incredible amounts of money in computers and high-end office equipment, expensive furniture, and sumptuous lobbies that displayed famous works of art. The most traditional firms were also keen in displaying their heritage through antique portraits of their founding members, and covered the walls with vast collections of old books, treatises and academic publications that conveyed the intellectual pedigree of the firm's members.

In terms of international exposure, more and more Venezuelan law firms began advertising their presence in professional directories such as Martindale Hubbell, Latin Lawyer and more recently Chambers and Partners. The editors of Latin Lawyer recognized this fact in their 1999 edition: "For a country of its size—and one that is so completely dominated by the oil sector—Venezuela has a broad representation in this publication" (Latin Lawyer 1999:107).

The information about how much money each law firm made during those years is not available to the public but judging from the rapid expansion of law firms, the upsurge in their international work and other signs, it is reasonable to infer that the 1990s were a very good decade for the Venezuelan business lawyers. Although the traditional firms maintained a dominant position in the market, unprecedented opportunities opened up to new players including boutique-sized law firms and the foreign law firms mentioned earlier. The excitement among elite business lawyers was such that one of our interviewees eloquently described it "as if instead of oil, the multinational companies had struck holy water, and the lawyers were carrying buckets of it", and then added, "there was plenty for everyone, as long as you knew how to play" (Interviewee 30). Unbeknown to most, the tides would turn again during the following decade, thus posing incredible challenges to the corporate legal services market, and forcing the local players to adapt, and in some cases to reinvent themselves.

Big Law During the Chavista Revolution

The Chavista years have been a period of continuous social unrest and extreme political polarization. Market-oriented practices have been rejected and demonized, and the government has supplanted them with openly paternalistic and interventionist economic policies heralded as being part of Chavez's vision of a twenty-first-century socialism. Such ideas were initially well received by a broad sector of the Venezuelan population, and even gained the sympathy of political leaders and activists from around the world. The overhaul proposed by Chavez included a sweeping constitutional reform, and a purge of the public sector, both of which were accomplished within the first three years of his first term.

While the Chavism was dismantling the old clientelistic networks, it was also nurturing the emergence of other groups with equal or even more power than the ones that Chavez had criticized so fiercely. Under such state of affairs, even the most trivial interaction with a public official or a government agency is conditioned on the political affiliation of the parties involved. Furthermore, those who oppose the Chavista movement or who show any sympathy for the opposition are routinely mistreated or at the very least put at a disadvantage vis-à-vis those who appear to be openly pro-government.

To anyone in the corporate sector, being placed on the wrong political side might entail losing valuable business opportunities, or even their entire company due to a politically motivated expropriation or confiscation of assets. In the particular case of law firms, our interviewees described how those firms that aligned themselves with the anti-Chavez opposition became victims of a political vendetta. This caused the affected law firms to lose all business with the government, including providing advice to any private contractors in their dealings with government controlled agencies; and also to become blacklisted and therefore deprived from an important share of the market for high-end corporate legal services, much of which stemmed from oil-related activities.

Since his early days in power, Chavez adopted an anti-American anti-business rhetoric, and announced his intention to reverse Caldera's oil opening policies. After a strike that paralyzed the country and shook the government, the Chavez administration dismissed almost 19,000 workers that represented 40 percent of PDVSA's workforce, and brought criminal charges against the protest leaders. After such drastic action and oil prices rapidly on the rise, the Chavista administration was ready to wage war against the multinationals. The lawyers were not spared.

Although the prosecution of business leaders was widely advertised, the animosity toward their lawyers was instead handled *sotto voce*. According to our interviewees, the lawyers or law firms who represented anyone whom the government deemed anti-Chavez were placed on a blacklist. Depending on how close these lawyers were to the opposition movement, they were also regarded as acceptable or unacceptable to the government.

Some of our interviewees revealed that government officials used the code phrase "radioactivity level" to convey whether a particular law firm or lawyer were acceptable, and often suggested their counterparts to "limit themselves to use lawyers with zero radioactivity" (Interviewees 22 and 28). As one of our interviewees said: "any lawyers deemed radioactive were not only denied business with the government; they were also prevented from accessing the PDVSA premises and from participating in any meetings involving high government officials, even if those meetings were held in a private office" (Interviewee 10). And another lawyer added, "it really felt as if we were pariah or lepers; to some of us lawyers who had engaged in extensive government dealings for years, such cold treatment was tantamount to a commercial death" (Interviewee 12). Given the prominence of PDVSA and the law-related business it generated domestically, and the importance of the hydrocarbons industry to many service providers including the leading law firms, this situation was a major blow to Venezuelan corporate lawyers and their portfolios.

In the following months, hundreds of people were prosecuted and indicted for allegedly conspiring to overthrow the government, including some prominent lawyers who were accused of providing legal advice to the conspirators or for participating in the de facto government that was formed briefly. Several elite business lawyers fell during this first wave, including prominent law firms such as Baumeister & Brewer.

After Brewer's departure from Venezuela, his law firm became a small one and some of his former associates and partners set up their own firms. Perhaps the most prominent of the spin off firms that stemmed from Baumeister & Brewer is Ayala Dillon Fernández Linares & Chavero, an eleven-lawyer office that has distinguished itself for their experience and expertise in constitutional and human rights law, international law, and environmental litigation, among others. Ayala Dillon maintains a similar profile to its predecessor firm, as most of the named partners are also law professors.

The demise of administrative law as a profitable area of practice in Venezuela could be mainly attributed to the dismantling of the traditional state bureaucracy by the Chavista administrations. Most interactions with the government have become highly dependent on politics, and much less on a formal set of rules. As a result, the filing of petitions before government agencies and administrative litigation has increasingly become a fruitless effort (Canova 2009; Canova et al. 2014).

Notwithstanding the grim fate of administrative law in Venezuela, the field of human rights litigation experienced an upsurge. As a result, a handful of law firms became very active in filing cases on behalf of victims of alleged human rights violations, both in domestic and international courts. Gómez (2010) has shown that the recent wave of human rights-related cases in Venezuela have gone beyond the protection of the traditional disenfranchised client. Some of the rising human rights litigation boutiques represent high-profile clients.

"Radioactive" Lawyers and the Boom of the New Players

The veto instituted by the Chavista administration in 2003 had a much more harmful effect on the corporate law firms than any previous threat. The firms that had brandished PDVSA among their most important clients were suddenly left without a significant source of revenue, and even worse, they were denied any possibility of working on any present or future oil-related matters in Venezuela. This sanction even affected their relationship with their private clients who were also deterred from working with any banned lawyers as long as the government had any interest in the matter. Nonetheless, some law firms continued doing government-related work in the shadows or through intermediaries, but it obviously diminished their capacity, and made them much less competitive.

As no blacklist was ever made public by the government, there are conflicting versions as to how many law firms or lawyers were effectively vetoed by the Chavista administration, although the most extreme cases seem to be public knowledge in the community of corporate lawyers. There is also disagreement regarding the extension of the sanctions, even among those who admit having been vetoed. What seems to be clear from our interviews, however, is that most of the business law firms that were active at the time in Venezuela suffered from some form of discrimination or were shunned in one way or another, thus preventing them from partaking in the still very profitable energy law practice and other areas of government work.

Such state of affairs presented an incredible opportunity to a few firms whose members managed to stay completely outside of the political realm, or had some powerful connections within the government, and therefore were not perceived as a threat. Interestingly, despite the anti-American anti-imperialistic discourse of the Chavista administration, foreign firms such as Steel Hector & Davis, were left alone and continued operating normally although their billing might have diminished as a result of the difficult situation in the country. Independently from what was occurring in Venezuela at the time, Steel Hector & Davis underwent an internal crisis that led to its demise and was subsequently acquired in 2005, by Squire Sanders & Dempsey (Now, Squire Patton Boggs), a Cleveland-based law firm. The Caracas office was obviously part of this package, so in the eyes of the local legal community it was just a change of brand. Hogan Lovells was another American law firm that had laid eyes on Venezuela as an entry point to the Latin American market.

The Caracas office of Hogan Lovells, which has always had no more than 10 or 11 lawyers, quickly became a very profitable operation with an enviable portfolio of clients that included Citgo, PDVSA and Pequiven. Although they operate in the same market as all the other Venezuelan law firms, the fact that Hogan was never vetoed by PDVSA put them in an advantageous position vis-à-vis those who had. In recent years, Hogan Lovells' Caracas has continued to thrive. With a team assembled from lawyers previously affiliated to other leading firms such as Anzola Bóveda Rafalli & Rodriguez, and Hoet Peláez Castillo & Duque, Hogan Lovells became a robust operation with the capacity to intervene in complex cross border transactions, including serving as a hub between the parent American firm and the Latin American region.

Squire Sanders & Dempsey underwent important changes in 2010, which resulted in the transformation of the Caracas office into a 12-lawyer independent non-exclusive affiliate firm called WDA Legal.[27] Since the days of Steel Hector & Davis, the firm has been able to remain involved in the oil sector, which in addition to allowing it to do work for PDVSA, it was able to acquire representation of foreign companies such as the Russian conglomerate Rosneft on a project based in the Orinoco belt.[28]

While the government began disfavoring and even excluding most American corporations from operating in Venezuela, it also started courting investors from countries with whom Chavez was interested in forging political alliances. As a result, an influx of businesspeople from China, Russia, Iran, India, Vietnam, Belarus, Brazil and Argentina started to arrive, prompting many local law firms to embark on a quest to gain access to these new players.

The law firms that finally managed to obtain some of these new clients were obviously pleased, but also had to adjust to the culture of their new clients, who in some cases treated them very differently from the American or western European companies that they had usually served in the past.

In some instances, the lawyers were asked to engage in political lobbying instead of just performing professional legal work or giving expert advice to their clients. In other cases, the clients were the ones doing the political legwork, and only used the lawyers to dress the transactions with a shroud of contractual formality expressed in legalese. Some firms also had to modify the billing system in order to accommodate to this new reality, because their new clients were not used to the Anglo-American style of client management and demanded to pay fixed fees.

The Rise of International Arbitration and Labor Law

Another interesting development driven by the restructuring of the oil business under Chavez, and more specifically by the abrupt termination of the oil contracts signed between PDVSA and the multinationals during the 1990s, was the rise of international arbitration. Many of the agreements negotiated during the oil opening provided for international arbitration as the sole method for handling any legal claims that could arise from those contracts. In the wake of a mounting pressure by the Chavista administration to renegotiate the terms of their agreements with PDVSA or forgo their investment, many multinational companies chose not to capitulate and instructed their lawyers to pursue legal claims in international fora instead. The local bar had developed expertise in the field of domestic commercial arbitration, but had no meaningful experience in handling large and complex investment cases.

In just a few years, Venezuela became the second country in the world with the largest number of investor-state arbitration cases filed against it before tribunals acting under the rules of the International Centre for Settlement of Investment Disputes (ICSID); a total of 36 by the end of 2012.[29] In addition to the investment treaty claims, Venezuela and its agencies also faced the filing of several commercial arbitration claims in different jurisdictions around the world, in connection with contracts of commercial nature that were allegedly breached by the government and/or PDVSA.

In most cases, the grieved companies sought the assistance of global law firms with vast experience and a reputable name in the international arbitration field, but this also created an opportunity for several Venezuelan law firms such as D'Empaire Reyna, Norton Rose, Travieso Evans, DLA Interjuris and WDA to obtain a slice of the pie. Sometimes, they acted in a supporting capacity as local counsel; but in other cases as lead counsel in charge of defining the strategy, filing the briefs or representing the client directly during the international proceedings. To some Venezuelan law firms, the arrival of these international arbitration cases was a blessing in the financial sense, as they brought along a sizable revenue, and also revived the relationship between the Venezuelan law firms and their foreign counterparts, thus reopening the doors to new collaborations and the referral of cases.

On the other hand, the Venezuelan government did not stay behind and retained global powerhouses such as Shearman & Sterling,[30] as well as other American firms such as Boston-based Foley Hoag[31] and New York-based Curtis Mallet-Prevost, to fight the claims. More recently, Venezuela has also relied on Hogan Lovells, and the Argentine boutique firm Guglielmino & Asociados[32] for matters that have arisen lately.

A few years later, when the investment arbitration claims were filed against Venezuela by some disgruntled investors, PDVSA turned to Curtis. The firm did not share the reputation of the international arbitration powerhouses. Curtis, however, had successfully represented Libya, which was one of Chavez's closest allies, in a number of default judgments issued against the Arab nation in the late 1970s, and also in some arbitrations.

Curtis's work on behalf of PDVSA has expanded beyond their involvement in the pending arbitrations, as the firm has also advised the Venezuelan government in several multimillion dollar financing transactions related to oil projects. Despite the vast amount of work generated by PDVSA, Curtis does not have a representative office in Venezuela or even an affiliated local law firm or individual lawyer to rely on. The same can be said about Foley Hoag, the other American law firm that the Venezuelan government has hired to handle some of its international arbitration matters, and the related US-based litigation. The traditional Venezuelan law firms appear to have been left out completely from this, which did not surprise any of our interviewees. A local lawyer familiar with the oil and gas industry, explained it in the following terms:

> PDVSA's foreign law firms must be dealing directly with the Attorney General's Office, and perhaps with one or two individual lawyers chosen by the Ministry of Energy; so they really have no need to seek assistance from any of the local firms. Moreover, they must also be thinking that the only way to keep an airtight strategy and to ensure that the client remains exclusively theirs is to avoid interaction here, and to keep their contact with local people at a minimum. None of it surprises me at all. (Interviewee 7)

Aside from oil, gas, natural resources law and international arbitration, the recent years have witnessed an upsurge in other areas such as labor and employment law, particularly after the 2012 amendment of the Organic Labor Act.[33] This is revealed by the fact that law firms such as Norton Rose Fulbright, Baker & McKenzie, and Travieso Evans, have invested important resources in strengthening their presence in this practice area, and have built robust teams of labor and employment lawyers. Furthermore, Venezuela was the first jurisdiction chosen by the San Francisco-based law firm Littler Mendelson to begin their international expansion.[34] A branch in the city of Valencia followed the opening of the Caracas office. After Venezuela, Littler continued expanding into Latin America.

Labor and employment law is one of the few areas that remain profitable in the Venezuelan legal market. The competition in this field became very aggressive. At the time of writing, Littler Mendelson had 25 lawyers in Caracas, and 5 more in Valencia, and it is the only specialized firm exclusively dedicated to the labor and employment field in the country. The firm's managing partner in Venezuela is Juan Carlos Varela, who was also responsible for opening the office, and for Littler's expansion throughout the region.

Other firms have solid labor and employment law departments including the acquisition of specialized boutique firms by the larger multiservice firms. As example, Araque Reyna acquired the boutique law firm Aguirre & Moschiano in 2012. In 2013, Hoet Peláez acquired the nine-lawyer labor and employment law boutique Mangieri Benavente.[35] As a result of this move, Hoet Peláez's labor department doubled from 6 to 13 lawyers. These acquisitions are not only a testament of the growth of labor and employment law practice in Venezuela, but are also an example of changes in the culture of corporate legal practice in that country.

The Globalization of Venezuelan Lawyers

Split-ups, Mergers and Hiring Practices

Split-ups among corporate law firms throughout the years were a common occurrence, but mergers are a recent one. In the history of the law firms, almost every single new firm has been the result of a split-up of a larger one, but split-ups and mergers have intensified lately. An interviewee pointed out the fact that "the competition for clients and for lawyer participation in a larger share of the profits under the current circumstances has led to unbelievable in-firm fights, some of which have prompted some partners to leave, take their clients, and set their tent apart" (Interviewee 10).

Some of our interviewees attributed this phenomenon to the confluence of several factors, including the globalization or "Americanization" of the market for corporate legal services (Interviewees 8 and 10). Another factor noted is the current size of the Venezuelan market. As one lawyer said, "there are today enough large law firms in Venezuela with the capacity to absorb an entire small firm or a practice group, and not just one or two lawyers" (Interviewee 9).

Another explanation is the increased view of law practice as a revenue generating activity, instead of just being an intellectual enterprise. Or as one of our interviewees put it: "Nowadays, Venezuelan law firms operate more as corporations or for profit enterprises than as family-owned intellectual clusters like in the past . . . the intellectual pedigree and the personal connections are still important to us business lawyers, but the capacity to generate revenue and attract a robust clientele seems to trump that old-fashion vision more and more" (Interviewee 20).

Regarding the weight given to the personal/social versus the professional qualities of a candidate in the hiring practices of Venezuelan law firms, another lawyer pointed out that when he started practicing several decades ago, "most of the respectable Caracas law firms, perhaps with the exception of Baker & McKenzie, would not look seriously at a candidate unless he or she had some pedigree, social or family connection with any of the firm's partners" (Interviewee 12). He added:

> Being hired by certain law firms was almost the same as being admitted as a member into the Caracas Country Club. People would ask around about you in their social circles, and seemed to be more interested in your background than in your professional competence; although in all fairness, unless you were the son of one of the firm's name partner or married to his daughter, there was also an expectation that you had to have good law school grades and a graduate degree from a reputable university. (Interviewee 13)

The importance given by some law firms to the social stature and personal connections of its members should not be trivialized, though. Personal relations were very important for attaining success in the legal profession (Gómez 2007, 2010, 2011), and business was intertwined with social networks. As we learned during some of our interviews:

> The most important conglomerates and hence the most desirable clients were in the hands of families or lifelong friends and associates who shared

> many traits in common, so it should come as no surprise that the law firms followed the same model, and only hired known people. (Interviewee 15)

The change in hiring practices that put much more emphasis on the professional qualifications, experience and skills of the potential candidates, than on their social connections is visible. As one interviewee explained:

> That used to be the criteria to get hired at Baker & McKenzie. The professional qualifications trumped everything else. Almost no one else was like that before, or at least until the arrival of Macleod Dixon, Steel Hector & Davis, and the other foreign firms. Because of their purchasing power, those firms were able to snatch the talent from other places, which created a bit of turmoil at the beginning. Also, during the *apertura petrolera*, our foreign clients increasingly demanded that we got the best possible people for our team, and did not care at all about social connections, or simply did not understand them . . . so we began looking at those objective factors more seriously. One could say that with regard to our hiring practices, we have become 'Americanized', and that may also explain why some firms began opening offices in different cities thus emulating the long-standing practice of American lawyers to follow their client. (Interviewee 26)

Another aspect that conveyed the Americanization of Venezuelan law firms was the adoption of hourly fees, which became popular during the 1980s and 1990s among the lawyers representing foreign clients, who then extended this practice to some of their local clients. Such system has become increasingly difficult in recent times. One reason is the pressure exerted by the clients who refuse to be billed, and to pay for every single interaction with their lawyers regardless of whether they obtain favorable results or useful advice. "The clients are being more discerning, and some have even forced us to reconsider the hourly billing system and to charge them a fixed amount or to at least give them an estimate beforehand" (Interviewee 1), said the managing partner of one firm that became of one the first local adopters of the hourly billing system decades ago.

Subsidiaries, Networks, "Best Friends" and Lawyers Without Borders

The fierce competition for foreign clients has also motivated several Venezuelan corporate law firms to seek a permanent affiliation, a strategic alliance with a foreign law firm, or to turn their attention to the various regional and international referral networks[36]. An example of the former can be found in the strategic alliance forged in 2000, between Tinoco Travieso Planchart & Nuñez and the Florida-headquartered law firm Holland & Knight.[37]

A more stable arrangement is the one reached in 2011 between the global firm DLA Piper and Caracas-based Interjuris, which resulted in the renaming of the latter as DLA Interjuris. This firm has 21 members, of which 10 are partners, and the 3 founders form the executive committee.[38] Although the firm's main office is based in Caracas, under their agreement with DLA Piper several executive committee members joined DLA Piper's Miami office as foreign legal consultants.[39]

DLA Interjuris concentrates their practice in serving clients from the BRICS countries. Until recently, they also worked closely with a Venezuelan-trained expert in oil and gas law residing in Myanmar, who was formerly a partner a Macleod Dixon, and supported them remotely for certain complex matters. On a separate note, and similarly to Norton Rose, DLA Interjuris has helped close the gender gap in the Venezuelan corporate legal sector, by including women in prominent leadership positions, and maintaining an equal gender distribution overall.

The regional and international networks provide a somewhat less formal arrangement that facilitates the relationship between firms across jurisdictions. These are basically organizations of independent law firms, which main objective is to support their members, to advertise their services regionally and internationally, to facilitate referrals, and to foster opportunities for exchanging information that may help increase the competitiveness of small and mid-size firms in the global arena. The law firm networks, which became fashionable in the nineties, might have been inspired by the similar structures set up by accounting firms several decades ago.

According to a recent list compiled by the international legal directory Chambers & Partners (2011) there are about 135 international and regional lawyer networks in the world. Although most of them have American and Canadian firms among their members, there are some networks that boast affiliates from other parts of the world such as Europe, Asia, Africa, and obviously Latin America. With regard to Venezuela, we can affirm that the distinction between national and international firms have practically disappeared. Venezuelan law firms are branches of international firms or part of international networks like Interlaw, Lex Mundi,

Terra Lex, Mackrell International, Multilaw, TAGlaw, Club de Abogados Iberoamérica and others. Some law firms have entered into "best friends" agreements with select foreign counterparts, which basically consist of a system for the mutual referral of cases, although not in exclusivity. In addition, Venezuelan law firms have become increasingly interested in being considered for rankings by the leading international law directories. In fact, some of our interviewees boasted their accolades endorsed by Chambers & Partners, as a measure of success and notoriety. When asked about the importance of these rankings to their firms, the response was generally in the affirmative. As one lawyer said:

> Given the economic situation in Venezuela and the scarcity of foreign currency, a membership to Chambers, Latin Lawyer, or Martindale Hubbell looks very expensive and some people could argue that is not an essential service, but we see it as an investment … Latin Lawyer and Chambers are our windows to the region, and to the rest of the world. Besides, our competitors are advertising there as well so we cannot afford to stay behind. We think that foreign clients care about the directories and rankings, and lawyers from other jurisdictions do too … we cannot risk not to have all our bases covered, so we'll continue subscribing to the international directories as long as we can. (Interviewee 6)

The landscape of the corporate legal sector described in the previous sections is undoubtedly very complex, and the current state of affairs in Venezuela has posed grueling challenges to the law firms and their members. Many Venezuelan lawyers are now working in international law firms outside Venezuela. The problem now is to keep the lawyers in the firm.

One way how some Caracas-based law firms are outwitting the potential departure of talented partners, and possibly turning it to their advantage, is by looking to expand their operations into the legal markets of neighboring countries such as Colombia, Panama, Costa Rica and even Miami. This is what we have observed in the case of some Caracas-based foreign law firms that have recently supported the migration of selected Venezuelan partners to other jurisdictions, and have advertised it as part of a broader strategy to penetrate new markets. Whereas the Venezuelan firms might be able to capitalize on the potential interest of some of their partners to relocate elsewhere, the situation with the associates is different. They generally lack the reputation and experience needed to attract and maintain clients, and may not have a vested interest or long-term commitment that partners do.

Regarding this issue, another interviewee said, "there is obviously a lot of anxiety among our associates, and people talk about leaving all the time, but. However, many get cold feet when they find out that starting over is not easy in the United States. Our younger members are smart and know that it is better to have job security; we also try to make them feel valued so they decide to stay with us" (Interviewee 22).

In order to keep their associates content, some local firms offer them very competitive compensation packages considering the local market; but more importantly, also give them realistic expectations about becoming partners. The low associate-partner ratio of most Venezuelan law firms, with the highest being approximately 4:1, ensures that most associates work closely with the partners. Such low leverage also increases the chance of the associates to work directly with the firm's clients, thus making them feel as valuable members of the organization in a relatively short period of time.

Finally, the small number of associates per partner also has the potential of helping dilute the sense of an internal hierarchy within the firm, and of facilitating a closer personal relationship between associates and partners. Interestingly, despite the fact that, as we discussed earlier, Venezuelan firms appear to have moved away from relying on non-strictly professional considerations to hire new members, such as social status and family connections; the social and personal relationships that develop within the firm over time are precisely what might end up keeping them together, preventing the departure of their lawyers, and ensuring their viability during times of turmoil.

Conclusion

The mounting interest of foreign law firms to establish themselves in Venezuela might seem counterintuitive to an outsider who is distracted by the constant news reports that depict the country as a lawless run-down society ruled by a government that has destroyed all forms of private initiative. The Venezuelan society has undoubtedly deteriorated in the last two decades, and its main institutions have succumbed to political manipulation. But even the most manipulative regimes nowadays are forced to coexist and compete with other players at the international level, mostly if their economic survival depends on it, as is the case of the oil industry in Venezuela.

In Venezuela, the most important competitors of the state are other foreign governments, and powerful multinational corporations equipped with armies of lawyers and other highly qualified advisers. The Chavista regime seems to have understood that, and has therefore resorted to the same tools as its competitors. This has, perhaps unintentionally, placed business lawyers in a prominent position, which they have come to realize very well, and have certainly reaped the benefits associated with it.

The centrality of the oil industry to the Venezuelan economy, and its importance to the survival of the government has also meant higher stakes, and obviously high risks, which became exacerbated by the political volatility of recent times. Although the current situation is somewhat unique and different from any past experience in Venezuela or perhaps in any neighboring country, the political volatility and rapid changes are not new to the Venezuelan business lawyers.

During the last century, the country has lived through several ups and downs conditioned by the rise, development and growth of the energy sector. As a result, a great capacity to improvise, to adapt to new challenges and also the skills to interact with a politically unstable situation, have accompanied Venezuelan business lawyers since the opening of the first law firms in the nineteenth century. Their successors are just putting into practice their seemingly inherited adaptability and skills to navigate in choppy waters, but have also evolved and undergone important transformations influenced by their interaction with foreign lawyers, multinational clients and the overall impact of globalization.

The recent arrival of foreign law firms has had an influence on the evolution and modernization of Venezuelan law firms, and has also raised their awareness about certain issues, such as the gender gap, partner/associate relationships, compensation schemes and client management policies; all of which have been preoccupying the high-end corporate legal services industry for several years now. As a result, Venezuelan law firms have adapted, and even adopted some features typically present in global law firms, but at the same time have also managed to keep their own identity. One example is the value given to interpersonal connections, whose role has diminished in certain aspects such as hiring practices, but has conversely become paramount in keeping the firms alive. Our study, which has only looked at these issues from the standpoint of the business lawyers, has done much more than simply scratch the surface, and has uncovered a host of interesting problems that call for a more comprehensive investigation that considers the clients, and the other providers that operate in the complex ecosystem of Big Law.

Notes

1. The firm was originally known as Gil, Vargas & Torres.
2. http://abogadosagp.com.
3. http://www.antequera.com.ve.
4. http://www.araquereyna.com/.
5. http://www.bakermckenzie.com/Venezuela/Caracas/.
6. http://www.bpmaw.com/.
7. http://www.bentata.com.
8. http://www.dra.com.ve/.
9. http://www.dlainterjuris.com.
10. http://www.hoganlovells.com/caracas/.
11. http://lma.com.ve.
12. http://www.littler.com/locations/caracas.
13. http://www.menpa.com.
14. http://www.nortonrosefulbright.com/latin-america/offices/caracas/.
15. All four partners were international, which means that they have participation in the revenues of all offices of the firm.
16. Includes eight international partners, and five local partners.
17. Includes 11 international partners, and 7 local partners.
18. http://www.rodnermartinez.com.
19. http://www.romen.com/.
20. http://www.ttpn.com.ve.
21. http://www.tpa.com.ve/.
22. http://www.traviesoevans.com.
23. http://www.wdalegal.com/.
24. http://www.clydeco.com/offices/caracas/.
25. http://articles.sun-sentinel.com/1999-01-22/business/9901220235_1_growth-strategies-brazil-hector-davis.
26. http://www.thefreelibrary.com/Steel+Hector+%26+Davis.-a071710667.
27. http://www.wdalegal.com/index.php.
28. http://www.chambersandpartners.com/229/354/editorial/9/1.
29. Argentina topped the list as a result of the multiple of claims filed against it by disgruntled investors affected by the economic collapse of 2001.
30. http://www.shearman.com.
31. http://www.foleyhoag.com/.
32. http://www.quepasa.cl/articulo/ojos-de-la-llave/2012/03/17-7924-9-chavez-cambia-estrategia-contra-chilenos-en-ciadi.shtml.

33. http://linkis.com/www.lawgazette.co.uk/iz5kG.
34. http://www.littler.com/.
35. http://www.iflr1000.com/newsandanalysis/hoet-pelaez-incorporates-legal-boutique/index/291
36. http://www.chambersandpartners.com/15649/2357/editorial/2/4.
37. http://www.thelawyer.com/turnover-and-pep-up-at-holland-and-knight/1011405.article.
38. http://www.dlainterjuris.com/en/team/?pg=1.
39. http://www.dlainterjuris.com/en/about-us/.

References

Brooke, James. 1994. Venezuela Proposes Opening Oil Industry to Private Investment. *The New York Times*, April 28.

Canova, Antonio. 2009. La realidad del Contencioso Administrativo Venezolano (Fundación Estudios de Derecho Administrativo).

Canova, González, Herrera Orellana, Rodríguez Ortega, and Graterol Stefanelli. 2014. *El TSJ al servicio de la revolución*. Galipán: Caracas.

Galanter, Marc, and Nick Robinson. 2013. India's Grand Advocates: A Legal Elite Flourishing in the Era of Globalization. *International Journal of the Legal Profession* 20 (3): 241.

Gómez, Manuel A. 2003. Los abogados de negocios en Venezuela. *Revista de la Facultad de Derecho de la Universidad Central de Venezuela* 125: 23–51.

———. 2007. *All in the Family: The Influence of Social Networks on Dispute Processing*. Doctoral Dissertation Submitted to Stanford University (On File with Author).

———. 2010. *Political Activism and the Practice of Law in Venezuela*. In *Cultures of Legality: Judicialization and Political Activism in Latin America*, ed. J. Couso, A. Huneeus, and R. Sieder. Cambridge: Cambridge University Press.

———. 2011. *Greasing the Squeaky Wheel of Justice: Lawyers, Social Networks and Dispute Processing*. In *Lawyers and the Rule of Law in an Era of Globalization*, ed. Yves Dezalay and Bryant Garth. New York: Routledge.

———. 2013. *Malleable Law: The (mis)Use of Legal Tools in the Pursuit of a Political Agenda. ILSA Journal of International & Comparative Law* 19: 509–554.

Krivoy, Ruth de. 2000. *Collapse: The Venezuelan Banking Crisis of 1994*. Group of Thirty.

Pérez-Perdomo, Rogelio. 1981. *Los abogados en Venezuela*. Caracas: Monteávila.

———. 2001. Oil Lawyers and the Globalization of Venezuelan Oil Industry. In *Rules and Networks: The Legal Culture of Global Legal Transactions*, ed. R. Appelbaum, W. Felstiner, and V. Gessner. Oxford: Hart.

———. 2006. La educación jurídica en Venezuela 1960–2005: expansión y diferenciación. In *La educación jurídica en América Latina. Tensiones e innovaciones en tiempos de globalización*, ed. R. Pérez Perdomo and J. Rodríguez Torres. Bogotá: Universidad Externado de Colombia.

Tejera Pérez, Victorino J. 2012. *Arbitraje de Inversiones en Venezuela*. Colección Estudios Jurídicos No. 97, Editorial Jurídica Venezolana, Caracas.

Manuel Gómez is Associate Professor of Law and Associate Dean of International & Graduate Studies at Florida International University College of Law, USA. Gomez' research and teaching focuses on comparative civil procedure, dispute resolution, the globalization of the legal profession and legal education, and private systems of governance.

Rogelio Pérez-Perdomo is Professor of Law, and Dean Emeritus of the Universidad Metropolitana Law School (Caracas, Venezuela), frequent Visiting Professor at Stanford Law School, former Scientific Director of the Institute for the Sociology of Law (Oñati), and member of the National Academy of History in Venezuela. Perez-Perdomo's research and teaching focuses on the legal profession, law and society, and legal history.

PART III

The Bigger Picture

CHAPTER 11

Reconstructing Big Law: The Big Picture

Deborah R. Hensler

The larger project that instigated the research for this book began at least six years ago, funded by a significant gift to Stanford Law School by a prominent Big Law firm to try to get behind the hype: to find out what was (and is) going on in Big Law in the aftermath of the great recession and in the shadow of the collapse of Dewey & LeBoeuf LLP. At that time, the business press, the legal press and even the general press like the *New York Times* were awash in these stories about the death of Big Law. There was a spread in the *New Republic* titled The Last Days of Big Law (Scheiber 2013), Jordan Weismann (2012) wrote an article for *The Atlantic* magazine, which title was "The Death Spiral of America's Big Law Firms".

Similarly, Richard Susskind (2010), the well-known English analyst of what is going on in the legal profession was talking about the death of law and law firms, as we know them. These works were receiving the kind of attention that Anthony T. Kronman's book *The Lost Lawyers: The Failing Ideals of the Legal Profession* had received little more than a decade earlier. Kronman (1995) attributed the "decline in the prestige of prudence and public-spiritedness within the legal profession" to a number of forces including "the explosive growth of the country's leading law firms".

D.R. Hensler (✉)
Graduate Studies, Stanford Law School, Stanford, CA, USA

M. Gómez, R. Pérez-Perdomo (eds.), *Big Law in Latin America and Spain*, https://doi.org/10.1007/978-3-319-65403-4_11

Whereas Kronman and his contemporaries were bemoaning the death of professional ideals, the new doomsayers were heralding the death of the business of law: declining revenues, lawyer layoffs and law firm bankruptcies. Scholars of the legal profession—Yves Dezalay & Bryant Garth, Robert Nelson, Robert Gordon and others—were well aware that the death of Big Law had been pronounced many times over the previous decades but the media hype this time around seemed to be rattling not just law firms but also law school deans. Arguably, this has been one of the factors in contributing to what has been a significant decline in the number of law school applications in the United States, which of course has other ripple effects.

Before we could begin, we had to start out with answering the question: What is Big Law? Or, at least what definition we would adopt in our research? In recent years, Big Law has come to mean "big" in the material sense: law firms with large numbers of lawyers—perhaps huge numbers of lawyers—and large amounts of revenue. The image of Big Law in the media and academic was the large general purpose commercial law firm, organized as a pyramid, with a relative few partners at the top whose income was generated by remarkable returns on labor of large numbers of junior lawyers (associates) at the bottom: the "tournament" firm of Galanter and Palay's (1991) book. But if one reviews stories about Big Law over the course of the twentieth century what one sees is that while Big Law always connoted the larger law firms in town, more importantly the "big law firms" were the elite law firms that served the biggest corporations (e.g. the trusts, the railroads, the insurance companies) or biggest companies in town and the most affluent families, the firms where the "best [white] men"—always men—went after they graduated from the "best" law schools—Harvard and Columbia if you were talking about Boston and New York. Interestingly, these were also the firms whose partners rotated in and out of government. In other words, Big Law comprised the firms that served the powerful and by reflection were powerful themselves.

So, Big Law in a more sociolegal way is the practice of elite law by elites in an elite organization for large powerful institutions. The definition of Big Law that we adopted for our study draws on both the "scale" dimension of the image of big law and the status and power dimension: the focus of our research, what we term Big Law, is the nexus of large elite law firms that serve large multinational (and powerful) corporations, the new incarnation of the old trusts and the new affluent class. As shorthand, we call this the "high end" of the corporate legal sector, comprising both the buyers of law—the corporate customers—and the sellers—traditional large corporate law firms and an increasing variety of other providers (and this is part of the story we tell).

The research methodology that we have employed is a combination of analysis of long-term quantitative trend data, so we are not somehow caught up in what happened in the last three years and may get a better sense of the trajectory, and qualitative intervew-based research, which included interview with to general counsel, principals at different legal service providers, managing partners and senior members of law firms.

One of the most striking aspects of many previous discussions of the legal profession is the apparent sense among the legal profession's leaders that legal practice is sui generis—that because law is a professional practice and not "just a business", it is somehow set apart from—perhaps even impervious to—perhaps even supposed to be impervious to—what is going on in the environment around it. Of course, this was never true: lawyers and law firms like all organizations operate within, are shaped by and in turn shape their environment.

Perhaps the most important change in corporate law practice is the decline if not the total elimination of this belief: the lawyers we have interviewed for our project were focused on what was going on in the legal market and hungry for more information and analysis of trends and factors driving those trends. We did not hear many bemoaning the "death of the profession" and we talked to a good many who seemed to relish trying to figure out what the future holds and how to respond to it. Much of our research, including the research presented in this book and the related US centric project (Hensler et al. forthcoming), is aimed at understanding how the changes in the environment of these large corporate law firms are impacting the profession, what the most important changes are, and how law firms are responding to them.

We began the US centric project by analyzing trends in the corporate legal services market, using publicly available quantitative data. But our research relied mainly on interviews: with general counsel and other staff of corporate legal departments of mainly Fortune 100 corporations, with managing partners and other senior partners of ALM 100 law firms, and with principals of other legal service providers, all mainly in the United States. Our strategy was first to attempt to identify key aspects of the corporate legal services market (based on quantitative and qualitative data and on the extensive contemporary literature on this market) and then to investigate how Big Law firms are attempting to respond to these changes.

The market for corporate legal services has never been static: as the economy expanded and diversified, the demand for legal services changed and law firms changed in response. Whether change is now more dramatic, intense or rapid is impossible to say with great confidence given the absence of long-term systematic and comprehensive research on the market (as contrasted to studies of individual firms and specific legal markets). However, legal journalism and legal scholarship and our interviews with corporate and outside counsel reflect a shared perception that the corporate legal market is in a period of significant change that poses challenges for established firms and opportunities for legal entrepreneurs.

Among the changes, a few seem most important. First, there is clearly increased competition among these firms at least in the United States. What used to be very tight social bonds between corporate counsel at the corporations (the customers) and the senior people at the law firms (the providers), which produced a steady book of business for the latter, have broken down and law firms are operating in a very competitive environment. They need to justify more than ever what value they add to their clients. On a related note, law firms are also facing competition from their own clients, some of which results from increased pressure on the general counsel to reduce legal expenses as the need for legal assistance expands, itself a result of new compliance standards, increased regulation and increased cost of litigation. General counsel and other corporate legal managers are increasingly able themselves to analyze the corporation's needs, using corporate databases and analytic software, and appointing "legal operations" directors to manage in-house employees and procurement. General counsels' perception is that they hold the reins in the relationship between the corporation and their outside legal service providers, including the big law firms that have traditionally served their organizations.

A second change is the very substantial ongoing effect of technology. It would be odd to think that what really has been a revolution in technology would somehow not affect law firms, or lawyers in general. Law firms took very long to realize is that you can actually use software to manage the practice of law, and lawyers don't need to keep folders with sticky notes for calendar management and other issues. During some of our interviews, when we have asked lawyers about technology, instead of discussing document review or electronic discovery they told us about new software for managing budgets and expenses and calendars, which is really the most obvious and elementary thing.

Perhaps because law is so text based and because not just litigation but transactional practice is so document oriented, the advent of really effective search software has had a big effect, since in the past document review generated much work for law firms who gave their associates the task of doing that. A dramatic increase in the sophistication of search algorithms, enabling e-discovery and electronic review for "due diligence" operations that significantly reduced the need for human document handling and analysis, leading to reduced need for entry-level lawyers (associates) and permitted substitution of lesser skilled/trained contract attorneys for more expensive associates. Contract creation software has also eliminated the need for "bespoke" contracts for a significant fraction of corporate business.

The big changes that are yet to come might be related to big data analytics increasingly substituting for lawyers' judgment and helping with routine processes (e.g. Lex Machina), but we do not really know how far that is going to go, the same way how we do not know when and if robots are going to substitute doctors and doctor's offices. What seems true, though, is that lawyers will be affected by that very much like any other element of the economy.

A third change, which is also related to technology, is the diversification of legal service providers and the rise of other kinds of organizations, for profit firms that are not traditional law firms and that are not owned by lawyers but are taking up some of the space by providing cheaper and more efficient legal services. These providers include not just outsourcers that permit labor arbitrage but more importantly legal process engineers and legal technology solutions.

This brings me to the research carried out by the authors of this book regarding the growth of capacity in legal markets outside the United States. If we look at trend data over the past several decades, we can see the steady rise of international or foreign offices of US-based firms. We know that the same thing has been also happening to UK firms. There has really been a surge of what I call the internationalization of law firms. I think in the most recent period there were some Big law firms that saw expanding their markets overseas as a way they were going to at least make up for the contraction in demand for their services inside the United States because of these other competitive forces including from technology based schemes. During our interviews with managing partners of US law firms, we noticed that they talked a lot about globalization. But it seemed to us that the obvious question to ask was why did they think that an American firm could just march into another country that had opened up its market and start an office as if no one else had occupied the space. It was clear to us from these interviews, and from what others have written on this topic—including obviously my colleagues who are the authors of this book—that this was a faulty impression. So, we decided to take a closer look at the development of high-end corporate law practice or what we call Big Law, in other parts of the world. Latin America was the obvious place to start given the incredible resources that we had access to through the scholars featured in this book, and the systematic work and coordinating efforts of Professors Gómez and Pérez-Perdomo. The Latin American dimension therefore became a stand-alone project and the result is this book, which features a unique look at this phenomenon in 15 Latin American countries and Spain.

References

Galanter, Marc, and Thomas Palay. 1991. *Tournament of Lawyers: The Transformation of the Big Law Firm.* Chicago: University of Chicago Press.

Hensler, Deborah R., et al. forthcoming. *Reconstructing Big Law: How Corporate Legal Services Are Responding to Globalization, the Information Technology Revolution and Economic Change.* Cheltenham: Elgar Publishing.

Kronman, Anthony T. 1995. *The Lost Lawyers: The Failing Ideals of the Legal Profession.* Cambridge, MA: Harvard University Press.

Scheiber, Noam. 2013. The Last Days of Big Law. *The New Republic.* https://newrepublic.com/article/113941/big-law-firms-trouble-when-money-dries

Susskind, Richard. 2010. *The End of Lawyers? Rethinking the Nature of Legal Services.* Oxford: Oxford University Press.

Weismann, Jordan. 2012. The Death Spiral of America's Big Law Firms. *The Atlantic.*https://www.theatlantic.com/business/archive/2012/04/the-death-spiral-of-americas-big-law-firms/256124/

Deborah R. Hensler is the Judge John W. Ford Professor of Dispute Resolution and Associate Dean for Graduate Studies at Stanford Law School (United States), and holds a personal chair in Empirical Studies on Mass Claims Resolution at Tilburg University (The Netherlands). Hensler's research and teaching focuses on complex litigation, including mass torts and class actions. Prior to joining Stanford, she was the director of the RAND Institute for Civil Justice.

CHAPTER 12

Big Law Today and Tomorrow

Lawrence M. Friedman

The title of this book uses the phrase Big Law; the phrase refers to the large and very large law firms that deal primarily with "high-end corporate legal services." These firms are a striking feature of the modern legal profession. They evolved gradually, notably in the United States; but now Big Law has migrated into other parts of the world. Fifty years ago, a firm with 100 lawyers was considered a giant in the United States. In the late 1950s, only 38 law firms in the United States, mostly in New York, had more than 50 lawyers. In 1985, there were 500 firms of this size. By 1995, Baker & McKenzie had 1,754 lawyers on its staff. The biggest firms today are leviathans; or perhaps brontosauruses would be a better term. They have thousands of lawyers, and they have branches in city after city. Baker & McKenzie, incidentally, was, as Gómez and Pérez-Perdomo point out, the first of the mega-firms to invade Latin America. Its first office in that part of the world was in Caracas (Gómez and Pérez-Perdomo, Big Law in Venezuela, in this book). Today this firm has hundreds of lawyers in Spain and Latin America, in various cities.

Big Law of the indigenous sort was slow to arrive in Latin America. Big Law hardly existed in, say, Mexico or Brazil, as recently as a few decades ago. The situation has changed, dramatically. The Latin American firms are much smaller than the international giants; but they are larger than

L.M. Friedman (✉)
Stanford Law School, Stanford, CA, USA

M. Gómez, R. Pérez-Perdomo (eds.), *Big Law in Latin America and Spain*, https://doi.org/10.1007/978-3-319-65403-4_12

anything in the past, and they seem to be growing. There are firms with more than 100 lawyers in Mexico, Argentina, Chile, Colombia, and Brazil. If we could bring back to life a Brazilian or a Mexican lawyer who died in, say, 1950, that lawyer would find all sorts of things in our world that might astonish him: smart phones, computers, email, and self-driving cars. Our lawyer would be amazed, too, at Big Law, at mammoth firms, with tentacles in country after country. His own firm, perhaps, has also grown, from a cozy dozen, say, to 100, or 200, or more.

We have to remember, of course, that Big Law, in the sense of Big Law firms, rests on, and presupposes, dramatic changes in technology—and the economics of high technology. The things that astonished our reborn lawyer—computers, say—are global products. They are part of a complex trade and business world on which the brontosaurus feeds. Big Law, in the sense of the big firms, depends on the new world of technology; the products that never existed before, the products that support these products; and the activities that support the support. And Big Law firms depend on another kind of Big Law. That is, the equally astonishing increase in the sheer *volume* of law: the cases, statutes, decrees, ordinances, rules, and regulations, in every modern society. These pour out of legislatures, executive offices, local governments, administrative bodies, in ever greater amounts.

Modern law, in every developed country, in every semi-developed country, and even in underdeveloped countries, is absolutely ubiquitous. Of course, globalization is an important part of the story—the story of the Big Law firms, but also the story of Big Law in the broader sense. But it is not the whole story, or, maybe, not even the most important part of the story. Modern life *creates* Big Law. Or, at least, it creates the conditions that underlie Big Law—the facts that put pressure on society to make bigger and bigger law. Many of these are technological facts. Every country has an international airport. Jets land in Bolivia, in New Zealand, in the Chad Republic: everywhere. And this means rules about air traffic control, about baggage claims, about security, passports, visas, and much more. The automobile has virtually created traffic law, which hardly existed before. Radio and television created the need for communications law. Patent and trademark law feed on new technology, new products. And so it goes. Some libertarians dream about ending the reign of Big Law. It is hard to see how this is possible. Even privatization comes about through law. Marginal changes are possible. But big Law is here to stay.

Big Law is, to a great extent, what Big Law firms do, what they contend with. Of course, the giant law firms only concern themselves with some aspects of Big Law: corporate affairs, government regulation of business, and so on. The giant firms have nothing to do with traffic law, for example, or with motorcycle accidents; or with divorces. The business of Big Law is business. But this is more than enough to keep them healthy and rich, to give them fuel to fire their engines. As modern research—including the chapters in this book—makes clear, the size of the legal profession has been increasing by leaps and bounds and in almost every country. Big growth is certainly true of Latin America: dramatic numbers, dramatic growth. There are now over 800,000 lawyers in Brazil, up from about 150,000 in 1990; in Chile, the profession increased more than 400% in this period. And of course, there is the United States: a cool million lawyers (or more). And, more and more, these hordes of lawyers are tending, as we said, the legal affairs of business, small, medium, and large; from pizza parlors and rooming-houses, to giant corporations who sell or buy or act all over the world. And this is true in Latin America as well: the subtitle of this book refers to "high-end corporate legal services."

To be sure, most businesses in Latin America (as elsewhere) are not particularly international. Neither are their lawyers. The study of lawyers in the city of Chicago found that the *percentage* of lawyers who work on issues of individuals (rather than companies) has been shrinking (Heinz et al. 2005). These are the lawyers who help people get a divorce, or make out a will, or buy a house, or copyright a novel, or sue some careless driver who rear-ends their car. But although the *percentage* may be shrinking, the sheer numbers are not shrinking. There are more of these lawyers, but their ranks are not growing as fast as the ranks of the army of business lawyers. This is undoubtedly true elsewhere as well.

I want to suggest even a third meaning of Big Law. The first meaning referred to big firms; the second, to the rules, regulations and laws piling up inexorably, a tower of law that seems to reach up to the moon. But law is also "big" in the sense that it touches the lives of more and more people; perhaps everybody in society. Of course, most people, in developed countries, and elsewhere, never set foot in a courtroom, never sue anybody, and never get sued. The ordinary citizen in Brazil or Mexico does not have a lawyer, and has never consulted a lawyer. Yet the law affects them, touches them, influences them—every day, and in countless ways. Law is almost like the air we breathe. We hardly notice it, but there it is. And it is completely indispensable. In a real sense, law is totally intertwined with everyday life. The two are, as it were, like Siamese twins. If we talk about marriage and divorce, husband and wife, buyer and seller, crime and punishment, landlord and tenant, worker and boss, we use words, language, and ideas which, on the one hand, are normal, common, popular, but which on the other hand are also *legal* terms, concepts and relationships defined and bound by law. Crossing the street or driving a car, we take traffic law for granted. Nonetheless, it is there, and it determines the very way in which we cross the street or drive our car. Labor law, contract law, and property law are with us every day also. Any trip to the supermarket to buy a can of soup or a loaf of bread is a legal journey as well. And a thick blanket of regulation—housing codes, building codes, securities law, air traffic control, intellectual property law, welfare law, pensions and unemployment rules, health care rules, safety measures—impinges on every business, envelopes every shop, every house, every household; and, in short, affects every human being in society.

Big Law in sense two and sense three has a long history; they may be, in a way, centuries old. But Big Law two and Big Law three have exploded in the modern period. The explosion of city life is an important reason why this is true. Rural people, at one time, grew their own food, made their own clothes, built their own shacks. People in small, traditional villages all know each other. Kinfolk and neighbors: that was their social world. Social life was a web of interdependence; but the people on which someone depended was a relative, a neighbor, a friend.

City life is profoundly different. Human beings are social animals; and life in the city is, for most people, as social as village life—although, to be sure, in cities there are more isolated people, homeless people, people cast adrift and lost in an ocean of strangers. But everybody in the city, no matter how tight their network, is in a new situation: a situation of utter dependence on utter strangers. This is associated, mainly, with city life. Meanwhile, in our times, the rural population shrivels; the cities burst with new arrivals. Today, Mexico City is a megacity; the population of Mexico City is about 9 million; the metropolitan area has more than 20,000,000. São Paulo, Buenos Aires, Rio de Janeiro: these are also huge conglomerates. In fact, every country has its capital or metropolis. Of the 4.5 million people in Costa Rica, about 40% live in and around San Jose. Montevideo dominates Uruguay; the metropolitan area of Santiago contains a third of the population of Chile.

This is, of course, not simply an aspect of life in Latin America. Megacities are all over the world: London, Moscow, Seoul, Tokyo,

Nairobi, Shanghai, Mumbai, Cairo, and many others. All of these cities have sucked in millions of people from the countryside. The rural people, who come to the city, find there a different way of life. One of the most salient of these is one we mentioned before: dependence on *strangers*, on people they do not know, people they cannot control. Even crossing the street, you are safe only when other people follow the rules: bus drivers, taxi drivers, ordinary people driving cars. Or consider passengers on airplanes. The pilot, behind the locked door of the cockpit, is the master of their fate. How can we be sure he/she is competent, is not dead drunk, and knows what he/she is doing? Only if there are rules and regulations that guarantee this; and which also guarantee that the plane is in good mechanical order, has enough fuel, and will fly only when the weather permits. The passengers, of course, have no control over any of this. They depend on the work of total strangers—and they depend, also, on law.

A family from a distant village moves to the big city, and takes up life in some slum apartment. They look for work. Perhaps the wife gets a job, cleaning floors and emptying wastebaskets, high up in a tall building. Perhaps these are the offices of one of the Big Law firms. With her mop and broom and pail, she rides the elevator to the twentieth floor. Her safety depends on the men and women who built, serviced, and inspected the high-speed elevator. Other rules and regulations will prevent, one hopes, fires or collapsing masonry in the building. The woman has some influence on her children, her kinfolk, her neighbors. But for health, for safety, for life itself, she relies on rules and regulations, on the law itself. As she empties the wastebaskets in the offices of Big Law, what the attorneys do in those offices seems incredibly remote from this woman's life, her problems, her hopes and dreams. But what those lawyers work on, every day, has a close connection to Big Law two; and Big Law two, in turn, directly touches the woman, her life, and the life of her family—touches, in short, Big Law three.

And in other senses, too, the three layers of Big Law are interconnected. Big Law in the broad sense is an important rationing system. It rations goods and services; and it rations space. It allocates, for example, television and radio channels. Without some agency of government, we would hear nothing but static, a jumble of voices, all trying to get heard. The screen would not show us a telenovela, or a football game, but something more like a Jackson Pollock painting. Traffic lights—and, sometimes, traffic cops—monitor the flow of cars and pedestrians on the streets;

they prevent (or try to prevent) gridlock. Big Law firms no doubt handle the affairs of the giant companies who run the television stations—and the companies that advertise on the programs. Ultimately, mass entertainment, mass culture, depends on the rationing function of Big Law; and even the very fact that movement flows on the streets. And, of course, Big Law, in a society made up of different groups, types, occupations, ways of life, has the job of settling disputes, in ways village elders and Khadi justices sitting under a tree could never cope with. Big Law firms handle disputes among the giants, the leviathans; for little people, there may be other ways and means, formal and informal.

The trends this book chronicles—the explosive growth of Big Law firms in Latin America—may *seem* a far-off fact, of no concern to the peasant who has moved to Mexico City; or to his wife, who scrubs the floors in the offices of these firms. And, of course, the partners in the firm pay no attention to this man and his family; the cleaning woman is essentially invisible to them; their clients are the big companies, the high-end companies, the international companies, not the little people, the workers in the anthills of great cities. But what the firm does, how it does it, depends on the modern fabric of law in society; the dense jungle of rules and regulations; the national and international tangle of laws, customs, and arrangements that govern commerce and trade; and all of this leaves an indelible mark on everyone in the city, indeed, everyone in the country—including the woman who cleans, her husband, who digs ditches, their children, their neighbors, their friends and relatives. And, in less obvious ways, it even affects the people left behind in their village. Globalization, in fact, touches everybody. It transforms everybody's life. The T-shirt the workers wear, the flip-flops on their feet, the mops and brooms and soap; the canned food and the bottled soda, which the family buys, the equipment on construction sites; the cars, buses and taxis on the street; the ubiquitous cell-phones; the television sets in the home; the medicines the doctors prescribe: these products are the end-stage of long, sinuous supply chains, chains that snake across borders; chains that tie the whole globe together. The big multinational companies control and move these chains; they battle each other for position; they compete for market share. These multinationals are, of course, clients of Big Law firms, international firms. Big Law feeds on them; services them in their struggles for power.

Of course, what they do also depends, in the end, on ultimate consumers. Workers in the city—and more and more, the people in the villages—drink the Coca-Cola, and wear the T-shirts made in China. The bus the workers ride to their job-sites was either made elsewhere, or had imported components. The movies they watch were made in America; the telenovelas they see were filmed in studios in various cities of Latin America. The cleaning ladies and the ditch-diggers have no direct contact with Big Law firms; these firms work for big manufacturers, big banks, big suppliers of goods and services; but what the firms do, what they handle every day, impacts the lives of all the pawns in the giant global chess game of modern times.

The world is economically interdependent; and getting more so. This is not just a matter of elites, jet setters, big lawyers, and big business people. As we have seen, an international economy also affects the mass of the population. People talk about a global village. The phrase strikes me as somewhat off the mark. The modern world is not like a village at all. Global city would be closer to the truth: the world is more like a swollen, bloated metropolis, more like a Mexico City or a Tokyo, than like a small village, asleep in the countryside.

Economic interdependence is obvious; but cultural interdependence is also an overwhelming fact of modern life. Big Law and the Big Economy manufacture culture, entertainment, fun, as well as cars, clothing, medicine and other concrete products. Most people, even those who are very traditional in other ways, get drawn inexorably into global mass culture. Millions, maybe billions, use social media. Millions, maybe billions, own cell phones. Millions, maybe billions, watch movies and television dramas; and listen to rock and roll music. There is, in short, a kind of global convergence, culturally speaking. In Asuncion, the capital of Paraguay, one of the poorest Latin American countries, there is a branch of the Hard Rock Café. The cafe advertises food with "authentic American flavors" and it is located inside "one of the city's most renowned buildings, the iconic Hotel Guarani"—a hotel whose name refers to a language and a people who lived and died long before Columbus ever set foot in the Western hemisphere. Three layers of culture converge in the Hard Rock Café in Asuncion: and none of the layers would be possible without Big Law. A multinational company owns Hard Rock Café itself. The chain of cafes began in London; but is now a feature in city after city, all over the world. Big Law is surely in charge of its corporate affairs.

In the megacities, the Nairobis and Mumbais, and, yes, in Mexico City and Caracas and Rio de Janeiro, life can be grim for millions of poor people; their home is some teeming urban slum, their lives are lives of hard work and deprivation. But still the millions flock to the cities. In our times, the cities are like giant magnets, pulling people in. Immigration scholars in fact talk about pull and push. Push is what drives people out of their homes; pull refers to forces that attract them to new places. An exploding population is one of the push factors. The countryside can no longer feed all of the hungry mouths. Sometimes, too, wars and destruction drive people out—falling bombs, drug gangs, and murderous violence.

The pull factor has, of course, an economic core. The city offers jobs and (people hope) a chance at a better life, if not for them, then for their kids. Some people go to join relatives, who are already in the city, and offer them welcome, and a bed, and maybe a job. If danger pushes people out, safety in the city pulls them in. People run to countries where they can sleep at night. There is also a strong *cultural* pull. Over time, this has made all the difference. Truly traditional people never leave home. Life outside the village is unthinkable. A member of a tribe in the Brazilian jungle, suddenly dropped down in Rio de Janeiro or Sao Paulo, could hardly survive; could not speak the language; could not get a job; could not cope with modern technology; would be as lost as an alien from outer space. *Cultural* globalization is what makes emigration possible. The very idea that emigration is possible. Some familiarity with life in big cities, gotten from television, perhaps. New people, to be sure, find adjustment in a different culture very hard. A Somali refugee, in Stockholm or Berlin, has to cope with a brand new world, a frightening world; the winter is appalling; the people often hostile; religion, habits, attitudes, and ways of life, fit in badly in the new country; the differences are crude and stark. But the newcomers already have come halfway, culturally speaking. They have adopted at least some minimum of cultural modernity. They already know about T-shirts and cell phones; they are familiar with cars and television sets; with clocks and the rhythm of big cities; with stoplights and buses; with doctors and hospitals and vaccinations. Adjustment may be slow—for the first generation, certainly—but it almost always happens. The typical newcomer will have no contact to speak of with Big Law firms. These firms are one of the most alien parts of an alien world. But their shadow inevitably falls across their paths.

To sum up: Big Law (in the sense of Big Law firms) implies two other senses of Big Law: one refers to the explosive growth of law, in the broadest sense, in modern societies; the expansion of codes; the inexorable spread of the welfare-regulatory state. The third sense, closely related, refers to the way Big Law (in sense two) insinuates itself into the life of the mass of the public—into everybody, big and small. What binds these three senses together is, of course, the process of globalization. And globalization, in turn, consists of two interlinked phenomena: economic convergence, and cultural convergence.

The chapters in this volume tell us how Big Law (in sense one) has developed over the years; what its dimensions are, and how it operates. We might ask, though, what lies ahead for these Big Law firms? Recent years have been years of mad, mushroom growth. The legal profession has swollen, almost to the point of bursting. The firms get larger and larger, year-by-year. Is this trend going to continue? If some Latin American city now has a firm with hundreds of lawyers, and two or three branches in other cities, can we expect thousands of lawyers in the future, and dozens of branches—if not because of internal growth, then because of mergers. Will giant international firms swallow up the Latin American firms?

Of course, we have no answer; the future is and always will be unknown country. But nothing ever stays the same. Big Law firms, after all, are businesses. They exist to make money. They depend on clients. Without clients, they shrivel and die. In our times, no type of business seems truly secure. New technology kills and displaces, ruthlessly. The automobile doomed the carriage business, and destroyed the demand for horses, stables, and associated paraphernalia. The computer killed the typewriter industry. This kind of destruction gets even stronger with the passage of time. On-line retailers have basically put an end to book stores; and threaten to destroy even large department stores. Huge commercial enterprises, the dinosaurs of our day, are staring extinction in the face. The gig economy may, in time, disrupt the auto industry, the hotel industry, perhaps even the restaurant industry. Wind and solar power might doom the giant oil companies. Is there something comparable, just over the horizon, that might disrupt or destroy Big Law and its world? Some sort of technological fix that would replace the firms; that would make their work, or at least some of it, obsolete?

Nobody can rule this possibility out. Essays on law firms, 20, 30, 50 years from now, might sound themes entirely different from the themes of the chapters in this book. Our times might be some sort of climax, followed by slow or fast decline. The firms might be fossils in another century. Or the opposite, of course, might happen: greater and greater growth. For Big Law in sense two and three, it is harder to imagine a possibility of this kind of decline and fall. But even here, it is hard to be sure. The Roman Empire, at one point, must have seemed eternal to its citizens.

Reference

Heinz, J., R. Nelson, R. Sandefur, and E. Laumann. 2005. *Urban Lawyers: The New Social Structure of the Bar*. Chicago, IL: University of Chicago Press.

Lawrence M. Friedman is the Marion Rice Kirkwood Professor of Law at Stanford Law School (United States), Professor (by courtesy) of History and Professor (by courtesy) of Political Science at Stanford University. Friedman is a leading expositor of the history of American law to a global audience of lawyers and lay people alike—and a leading figure in the law and society movement. He is a prolific author on crime and punishment, and law and society, and his numerous books have been translated into multiple languages. He is the recipient of six honorary law degrees and is a fellow in the American Academy of Arts and Sciences.

PART IV

Looking Ahead

CHAPTER 13

Conclusion

Manuel Gómez and Rogelio Pérez-Perdomo

In addition to having an obvious impact on the regulatory and policy fields of international trade, finance, labor relations, and other aspects of commerce, globalization has also had an important influence on legal professionals. The most visible case is that of corporate lawyers. The complexity of today's business world, where a seemingly simple commercial transaction may have implications beyond the domain of the national legal system, has forced contemporary lawyers to become versed on the transnational dimension of the relevant legal fields, in addition to having the expertise to function domestically. Such legal diglossia (Friedman 2001) is what enables Latin American and Spanish business lawyers to understand both the local and the transnational dimensions of law simultaneously, and to be able to navigate back and forth between one and the other.

Since time immemorial, lawyers have learned such competences directly from the workplace, learning-by-doing, so to speak. For example, if the client is a bank, then the lawyers usually learn banking terms as well as the ins and outs of financial transactions, also by working in

M. Gómez (✉)
Florida International University, Miami, FL, USA

R. Pérez-Perdomo
Universidad Metropolitana, Caracas, Venezuela

M. Gómez, R. Pérez-Perdomo (eds.), *Big Law in Latin America and Spain*, https://doi.org/10.1007/978-3-319-65403-4_13

tandem with bankers or alongside other lawyers experienced in the field. When the client is a foreign company or deals with foreign firms, then the lawyers tend to learn foreign languages and also become well-versed in foreign legal terms and institutions. If we consider that foreign and multinational companies have had an active presence in Latin America and Spain for more than a century, then the internationalization of the local lawyers who represent them is not new, like we saw in the cases of the different countries represented in this book. The existence of lawyers able to navigate across legal systems is not new. What is new, however, is that those transnational skills are not exclusive to a handful of lawyers anymore but are rather being disseminated widely across the different strata of legal professionals.

With the exception of one or two legal fields that are invariably domestic in nature, most of today's national legal systems include a patchwork of interrelated global/domestic components. From family law related issues like adoption, to labor and employment disputes, lawyers from one country are increasingly familiar with foreign legal standards, principles, and practices of another country. The recent introduction of the jury system in most Latin American criminal justice systems, offers a good example. It is because of these reforms that the criminal defense bar and public prosecutors of, say, Chile have become familiarized with the legal system and institutions of the United States. Some judicial rulings and new legislation in areas like consumer protection also reflect an increased awareness regarding foreign legal institutions, and their transplantation into the national contexts of Latin America and Spain. The examples are numerous and more common every day.

Despite the pervasive penetration of globalization throughout almost every corner of the Latin American and Spanish legal systems, the business sector remains the most visible recipient of such influence, and the lawyers and other legal professionals that operate in the so-called Big Law world are obviously an important part of the equation. As we were able to see throughout this book, the growing complexity of most legal matters pertaining to business clients have pressured the lawyers to adapt and respond to their demands efficiently. Very much like the multinational, or large and mid-size clients that they serve, most Latin American and Spanish business lawyers have acquired new professional sets of skills and knowledge, and have created organizational arrangements that are also multiservice and have the capacity to operate in a multinational environment, too.

As the different chapters of this book have shown, the modern infrastructure, visibility and corporate image, organizational arrangement, the profile of their members, and client management strategies employed by the Latin American and Spanish law firms studied here resemble the so-called Big Law of the United States. As it has been explained throughout the different chapters, Big Law is a term traditionally used to convey the professional partnerships of lawyers who are routinely hired by multinationals, large domestic corporations, and other business clients to perform sophisticated, complex, and generally costly legal work. The size of these organizations tends to be in the hundreds or even thousands of legal professionals distributed across offices in different cities or countries. As we mentioned in the introductory chapter, the largest global firm (Dentons) has more than 7,000 lawyers, and the runner up (Baker & McKenzie) has about 4,245. Baker is also the largest foreign firm with presence in Latin America with 15 offices across seven countries, which is explained in part by its historical ties with the region spanning more than 60 years (Gómez and Perdomo, Chapter 10, in this book; Bauman 1999).

As we also saw, globalization does not necessarily entail an absence of barriers to practice law across countries. In Brazil, for instance,foreign law firms are prevented from establishing a direct presence, and are thus impaired from competing with local firms. As a result, the way in which they have entered the region is usually through local representatives, so-called best friend alliances, mutual referral arrangements with local lawyers, and professional networks like Lex Mundi and Affinitas. In the wake of this global competition, the local corporate law firms of most Latin American countries have been forced to evolve from the traditional and small family-owned practice to large and strong organizations with multiple offices, hundreds of lawyers, and the capacity to compete with the largest global players both locally and abroad. Pinheiro Neto and Mattos Filho from Brazil, Allende & Brea from Argentina, Ferrere from Uruguay, Brigard & Urrutia and Posse Herrera Ruiz (now allied with Spain's Cuatrecasas) from Colombia, and D'Empaire Reyna & Bermúdez from Venezuela are some examples. The Spanish legal sector has experienced a similar growth vis-a-vis the rest of Europe, although the scale and barriers are somewhat different from what occurs in Latin America.

Not all the law firms that have become prominent players in the Latin American landscape are big or have multiple offices. An important number of them are small but highly specialized, which is why they are called boutique firms. This designation denotes the sophistication of their services, their ability to offer personalized attention to their clients, and the commensurate high price charged by their professionals. Many boutique firms have resulted from the spin-off of a practice group or specialized department at large multiservice law firms. Another organizational form that appears to be on the rise is the legal department or in-house counsel's office typical of medium size to large companies, state agencies, and non-governmental organizations. The typical legal department consists of one or several lawyers, and occasionally other professionals such as accountants, economists, and engineers; whose main role is to advise an entity in its daily legal matters. They are single-client lawyers, so to speak (Van Houtte 1999), and tend to also be tasked with overseeing the hiring of outside-counsel, and working in tandem with them.Another category of important —yet controversial— players are the big accounting firms that in certain countries are allowed to provide legal services and compete with the traditional law firms. We saw how their presence in Spain and Central America has been important in the development of the corporate legal sector.

The emergence of the above-mentioned legal services providers, and the expansion of the corporate legal sector in Latin America and Spain is certainly correlated to the consolidation of democracy, changes in the pattern of foreign and domestic investment and other economic incentives, government policies, upward social mobility, and other external factors. Recent studies have shown that the variations in the rate of investments in particular countries have also affected the emergence of business law firms, and obviously the landscape of legal professionals. Taking Argentina as an example (Bergoglio, Chapter 2, in this book)—which is one of the most important economies of the region—by 1999, the number of local corporate law firms rivaled those in Brazil in terms of average size: 85.4 lawyers for Argentina, and 87.3 lawyers for Brazil. In 2009, Argentina felt slightly far behind Brazil, but by 2015, the gap between the two countries was much wider (114.6 for Argentina and 372.8 for Brazil).

This latter period coincided with a decrease in the Argentine economy and an expansion of the Brazilian economy (Conti Craveiro and Gómez, Chapter 3, in this book). A similar situation occurred in Chile (De la Maza et al., Chapter 4, in this book) and Colombia (Lamprea and Díaz Chalela, Chapter 6, in this book), where the average size of business law firms almost tripled between 1999 and 2015—also a period of economic expansion. In the case of Peru, the growth during the same period is 376%. Conversely, Venezuela (Gómez and Pérez-Perdomo, Chapter 10, in this book) has experienced stagnation with just a slight negative variation, which should come as no surprise, given the deep crisis that has affected the country during the entire period.

At the time of writing, Brazil is undergoing a deep political crisis, which led to the impeachment of President Dilma Roussef amidst a series of corruption allegations and other scandals, which also involve her predecessor, Luis Inácio Lula da Silva, who had just then been sentenced to nearly ten years for corruption. The region is also marred by corruption scandals stemming from dealings involving Petrobras, Odebrecht and other powerful corporate actors. The Odebrecht affair is said to have spread to more than twenty countries including many in Latin America. Although the most visible suspects are politicians and businesspeople, some prominent corporate lawyers have been mentioned. Similarly, a recent scandal related to a leak of documents pertaining a vast amount of off shore transactions involving corporations, individuals and several law firms sent shockwaves from Panama to the rest of the world, and revived the debate about lawyers' ethics. Conversely, there seems to have been an improvement in Argentina's economic forecast, with the recent arrival of what is perceived as a pro-business government led by President Mauricio Macri. These events may tilt the scale differently and reverse the previous trends of these two countries, but it is too early to see any results.

Economic, social, and political crises tend to stimulate the migration of lawyers and other professionals to other countries, thus affecting not only the landscape of law firms, but also the legal profession in general. Perhaps the most dramatic example these days, is the case of Venezuelan business lawyers, many of whom—given the dire economic and political situation of their country—have sought to relocate to neighboring countries such as Colombia, Panama, Costa Rica, and the United States (Gómez and Pérez Perdomo, Chapter 1, in this book). There are no statistics regarding the total number of Venezuelan lawyers who have migrated in the last decade, but the perception is that it may be in the thousands, and on the rise.

Until now, most of the Venezuelan lawyer émigrés seem to have left their country for economic reasons, although many also cite safety concerns or political persecution. Similarly to the generation of Cuban lawyers who left their country during the early 1960s amidst the revolution, and before them the Spanish and German jurists who fled during the Spanish

Civil war and World War II, respectively; the most recent generations of migrant lawyers are often forced to reinvent themselves and adapt to a new professional environment with a great deal of uncertainty. The obstacles that they face may be difficult, but their ability to acclimatize to their new conditions has eased, thanks to the effect of globalization.

Big Law operates in a changing landscape. As Friedman says (Chapter 12, in this book), it not only has to do with the number of lawyers in a law firm, or the number of branches or representative offices that it has around the world. More importantly, the concept of Big Law also refers to the sheer amount of legislation, and the breadth and widespread impact of law—business and otherwise—to every facet of human life. Such is the reality that legal professionals face today, and will continue to face for years to come.

References

Bauman, John. 1999. *Pioneering a Global Vision: The Story of Baker & McKenzie.* Chicago: Hartcourt Professional Education Group.

Friedman, Lawrence M. 2001. Erewhon: The Coming Global Legal Order. *Stanford Journal of International Law* 37: 347.

Van Houtte, Jean. 1999. Law in the World of Business: Lawyers in Large Industrial Enterprises. *International Journal of the Legal Profession* 6 (1): 7–25.

Manuel Gómez is Associate Professor of Law and Associate Dean of International and Graduate Studies at Florida International University College of Law (United States). Gomez's research and teaching focus on comparative civil procedure, dispute resolution, the globalization of the legal profession and legal education, and private systems of governance.

Rogelio Pérez Perdomo is Professor of Law and Dean Emeritus of the Universidad Metropolitana Law School (Caracas, Venezuela), frequent Visiting Professor at Stanford Law School, former Scientific Director of the Institute for the Sociology of Law (Oñati), and Member of the National Academy of History in Venezuela. Perez Perdomo's research and teaching focus on the legal profession, law and society, and legal history.

Index[1]

[1]Note: Page number followed by 'n' refer to notes.

M. Gómez, R. Pérez-Perdomo (eds.), *Big Law in Latin America and Spain*, https://doi.org/10.1007/978-3-319-65403-4

The manufacturer's authorised representative in the EU is Springer Nature Customer Service Centre GmbH, Europaplatz 3, 69115 Heidelberg, Germany. If you have any concerns regarding our products, please contact ProductSafety@springernature.com

Printed and bound by CPI Group (UK) Ltd, Croydon, CR0 4YY
25/09/2026
02222859-0008